MOON

BLUE RIDGE
& SMOKY
MOUNTAINS

JASON FRYE

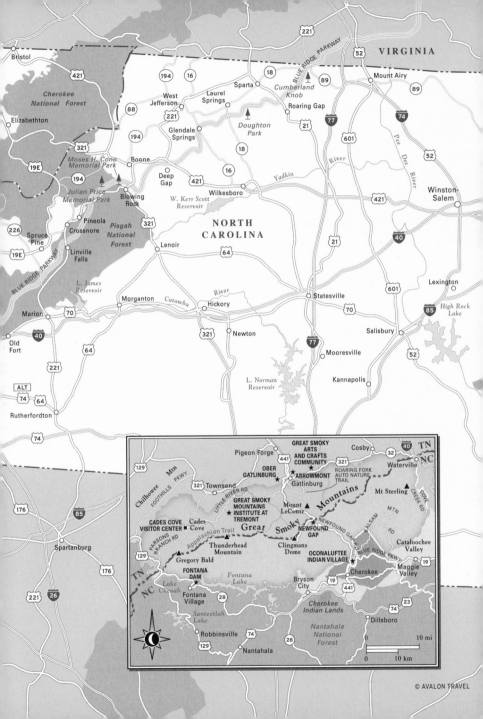

Contents

DISCOVER

Blue Ridge & Smoky Mountains

The mountains here are aptly named. In the Smokies, mist rises in the morning and evening, resembling the smoke from cook fires and chimneys, and it lifts to reveal coves and hidden hollows. Along the Blue Ridge, from the tallest peak to the lowest gap, the mountains appear to grow blue with distance. Wildflowers blanket high mountain meadows, and rhododendron, mountain laurel, and flame azalea compose wild, fragrant thickets along roadsides and trails.

The Blue Ridge Parkway traces a path along the ridges of this storied Appalachian range, offering visitors a glimpse of the scenery. Stop the car to stretch your legs on a trail or admire the view and you'll find yourself drawn into the landscape. Talk to someone who lives here and you'll find yourself immersed in the place.

The music of the mountains is everywhere: spring peepers, cicadas, birds, streams and waterfalls, and the bugling call of elk make up the natural soundscape. Though the front-porch jam session is long gone from all but a few places here, those high harmonies—the twang of a banjo string, the strum of a guitar—are still heard in concert halls and on street corners throughout the region.

Clockwise from top left: Blowing Rock; the Western North Carolina Pottery Festival; Linn Cove Viaduct; Blue Ridge Parkway overlook; lambs on the Biltmore Estate; winding road through the Smoky Mountains.

There's a photo in my home (a tintype actually) of my parents and me in the Smoky Mountains. It's from my first trip, one I can only remember because of this tintype. In it, we are dressed in old-timey garb, as if we'd stepped out of the mountains 150 years ago. I like to think that, aside from cars and smartphones, not much has changed since those times. The mountains remain lush and wild; the people friendly and open; the culture strong. And when you find yourself surrounded by forest, the mist rising from some far-off cove, the mountains blue in the distance, you'll be changed.

Clockwise from top left: Cades Cove; Hickory Nut Falls in Chimney Rock State Park; old cabin on Roaring Fork Motor Nature Trail; downtown Asheville.

Planning Your Trip

Where to Go

North Carolina High Country

The North Carolina High Country is all about the mountains. The peaks here are snowy and skiable in winter, rife with hiking trails and rock-climbing routes in spring and summer, and positively stunning in fall. The peak of **Grandfather Mountain** looms high over the **Blue Ridge Parkway,** and places like **Blowing Rock,** a stunning outcrop where snow falls upside down, add to the magic of the region. The spectacular **Linn Cove Viaduct,** which seems to float above the mountainside, is part of the commute, and countless **waterfalls** are just a short hike away. Friendly foothills towns like **Mount Airy** and **Wilkesboro** are rich with mountain music, while nearby college town **Boone** is progressive and eclectic.

Asheville Area

Located between the Blue Ridge and Smokies, with easy access to the mountains, Asheville is home to the lauded **Biltmore Estate** and some of the best **restaurants** in the South. Filled with **galleries, boutiques,** and the general weirdness you expect from bigger cities, Asheville boasts artistic wealth and deep creative passions.

Southern Blue Ridge and Foothills

Between Asheville and Cherokee is the **highest and most crooked part of the Parkway.** Here, the mountains are tall and steep, making for **dramatic views** from hikes and overlooks. Small, appealing towns like **Dillsboro, Waynesville,** and **Sylva** are rich with history and culture.

the Biltmore Estate

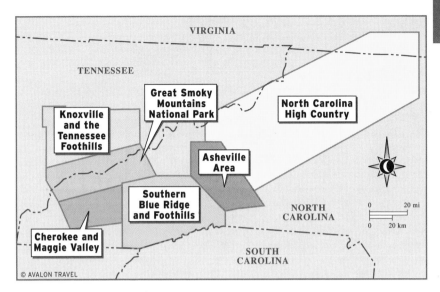

Cherokee and Maggie Valley

Cherokee, where **the Blue Ridge Parkway ends,** is the ancestral home of the **Eastern Band of the Cherokee Nation,** who celebrate their history and culture, past and present, on the **Qualla Boundary.** Visit the **Oconaluftee Indian Village** to immerse yourself in the daily life of a Cherokee village. In the small towns throughout this region, you'll find the **Great Smoky Mountain Railroad,** outdoor recreation from hiking to **fly-fishing,** and charming small towns that may just have you rethinking city life.

Great Smoky Mountains National Park

Straddling North Carolina's border with Tennessee, Great Smoky Mountains National Park is the **most-visited national park** in the country. The scenery and **wildlife** are incredible:

rounded peaks and jagged mountaintops, crystal-clear trout streams and white-water rivers, elk and bear, and morning mist and evening **firefly shows** all delight millions of visitors every year. Crisscrossed by more than **800 miles of trails** and studded with waterfalls, this is a hiker's paradise.

Knoxville and the Tennessee Foothills

Knoxville, a big-time college town and one of Tennessee's music cities, offers a taste of city living at the edge of the Smokies. Nearby **Pigeon Forge** is home to **Dollywood,** the mountain-themed amusement park from country music legend Dolly Parton, while **Gatlinburg** is the western **gateway to the Smokies.** All three towns are tourist draws in their own right, and their blend of Southern hospitality, humor, and **mountain culture** makes quite the impression.

Tree buds welcome spring in the mountains.

When to Go

Autumn

Autumn is the obvious season to visit the mountains. With leaves showing their last—and brightest—bit of **fall color** from the end of **September** through **October,** you can have as long a season of leaf peeping as you want. Most days are warm and sunny in the daytime, chilly in the evening, and even cold at the highest elevations. You'll be fine in long sleeves and a vest or light jacket most of the time, but you'll want something a little heavier if you're visiting late in the season.

Winter

Winter in this region varies by elevation. At the highest points, the temperatures drop—plummet, even—and the chance of snow or ice is real; at the lowest elevations, it's a little warmer, but make no mistake, it's still winter. **Expect snow** several times a season, with a few significant snowfalls, and expect the **Blue Ridge Parkway to close** for most of winter: The high-elevation route is

unmaintained, meaning once ice and snow take hold, they're in place until spring. The Blue Ridge Parkway maintains a live link of road closures online (www.nps.gov/maps/blri/road-closures). No matter where you visit in winter, you'll want some warm layers, a hat, and maybe gloves.

Spring

Spring rains bring **wildflowers** and **waterfalls** back to life and though trails can be muddy, it's a fabulous time to visit, especially for **wildlife viewing.** In the Smokies—particularly **Cades Cove** and **Cataloochee**—you'll see bear cubs, deer fawns, and elk calves trailing their mothers at the forest's edge. Spring temperatures are similar to those in fall, with warm days and cooler or even cold evenings, so pack accordingly—and remember to throw in a rain jacket.

Summer

Summer draws a **big number of visitors**

seeking to escape the heat at these cooler high elevations and spend their vacation days in a beautiful part of the world. **Dollywood** is booming, with throngs of people here for the rides and a taste of mountain charm. You'll want to plan for warm weather in summer—meaning shorts and light tops—and remember to pack a bathing suit. Who knows when you'll go for a dip, wade, or float on the river?

Before You Go

The Blue Ridge Parkway and Great Smoky Mountains National Park are free to visit and use. **Reservations** are recommended at **campgrounds** in the national park and along the Blue Ridge Parkway, especially during the peak seasons of summer and fall. Reservations for **hotels and B&Bs** along the route are recommended during peak times as well.

Transportation

Several roads lead to the Blue Ridge and Smoky Mountains, and depending on how you want to drive (slowly on the Blue Ridge Parkway or quickly on the interstate), your trip can vary in duration, distance, and scenery.

BLUE RIDGE PARKWAY

The Blue Ridge Parkway officially begins in Waynesville, Virginia, and follows the mountains southwest to **Cherokee**, North Carolina, at the edge of Great Smoky Mountains National Park. The North Carolina state line is roughly the midpoint of the Parkway; **Fancy Gap, Virginia**, provides the best starting point for the Parkway through North Carolina.

Passing through **West Jefferson, Blowing Rock, Boone, Asheville,** and **Cherokee,** the Parkway brushes past **Morganton, Brevard, Waynesville, Dillsboro,** and **Sylva.** Speeds are slow and traffic can be heavy, but take your time and enjoy it.

GREAT SMOKY MOUNTAINS NATIONAL PARK

At the southern end of the Blue Ridge Parkway, near **Cherokee,** North Carolina, **Newfound Gap Road** stretches north into Great Smoky Mountains National Park and up to **Gatlinburg, Tennessee.**

Interstate 40 cuts an east-west line across North Carolina and into Tennessee. From **Asheville,** I-40 goes through the heart of the region, skirting Great Smoky Mountains National Park to roll into **Knoxville, Tennessee.** From Knoxville, the **western entrance** to the Smokies is 35 miles south in **Gatlinburg.**

Best of the Blue Ridge and Smoky Mountains

In seven days you can get a good dose of North Carolina's Blue Ridge and Smoky Mountains, including the Blue Ridge Parkway and Great Smoky Mountains National Park, before wrapping up in Tennessee. It's a trip of about 320 miles, but you'll be taking your time to soak it all in, see the sights, and immerse yourself in the culture.

Day 1
ARRIVE IN NORTH CAROLINA'S HIGH COUNTRY

Arrive in **Blowing Rock** in time for lunch at **Bistro Roca,** then make your way to the town's namesake, a windy escarpment of stone forever tied to a story of love, longing, and an Indian princess. Whether the legend is true or not, the view from **the Blowing Rock** is more than worth the price of admission. Head to nearby

Boone for a predinner pint at **Appalachian Mountain Brewery,** then it's off to Valle Crucis for dinner at **Over Yonder.**

Day 2
BOONE TO ASHEVILLE

Get an early start and take breakfast at the **Dan'l Boone Inn,** where they serve a family-style country feast, and then head south on the Blue Ridge Parkway. Soon **Grandfather Mountain** will loom large overhead and the **Linn Cove Viaduct,** a curving bit of roadway clinging to the mountainside, will carry you through its shadow. Take the time to drive to the top of Grandfather Mountain and cross the **Mile High Swinging Bridge.**

Continue south toward Asheville with a stop at **Linville Falls** for a leg-stretching waterfall hike. Or take a break at **Mount Mitchell,** where

Blowing Rock

Best Hikes

This is a beautiful country to tour by car, but you're not doing the landscape justice if you only experience it through your windshield. Here are some fantastic chances to get out and be surrounded by nature.

BLUE RIDGE PARKWAY

- **Beacon Heights Trail (MP 305.2):** This trail gives you an awesome look at Grandfather Mountain; after a short, at times steep hike to a rocky bluff, you'll get big views to the southeast.

- **Linville Falls (MP 316.3):** On the mile-long Erwin's View Trail, you'll pass a pair of overlooks, but for the real prize continue to the top for a picture-postcard look at both cascades of this roaring falls.

- **Mount Mitchell Summit Trail (MP 355.3):** In Mount Mitchell State Park, take this short, paved path to the summit where you'll see the Blue Ridge and Smokies from the top of the highest peak in the mountain chain.

- **Devil's Courthouse Trail (MP 422.4):** A hike of less than one mile round-trip takes you up and down a steep trail to a gnarly rock outcropping and some awesome panoramic views.

- **Richland Balsam Trail (MP 431.4):** This 1.4-mile loop at the Parkway's highest point is dotted with benches that provide a place to rest and take in the sights.

GREAT SMOKY MOUNTAINS NATIONAL PARK

- **Andrews Bald Trail:** At Clingmans Dome, a few miles off Newfound Gap Road, this 3.5-mile

hiking the trail to Linville Falls

round-trip trail is one of the loveliest and most rewarding hikes you'll find.

- **Hen Wallow Falls Trail:** In Cosby, a few miles northeast of Gatlinburg, this 4.4-mile trail leads to a delicate waterfall some 90 feet high.

- **Grotto Falls Trail:** This popular hike to a picture-perfect waterfall off the Roaring Fork Motor Nature Trail is only 2.6 miles round-trip.

- **Rich Mountain Loop:** This 8.5-mile loop in Cades Cove is one of the most fabulous hikes in the park.

---

a short walk will take you to the observation deck at the top of the highest peak east of the Mississippi River. Once in Asheville, check into the **Sourwood Inn,** just outside of town, or at the **ASIA Bed and Breakfast Spa,** a few blocks from downtown. Make dinner as adventurous or as affordable as you like; your options for food and drink are nearly endless here.

Day 3
A DAY IN ASHEVILLE, A NIGHT IN BREVARD

After breakfast at **Early Girl Eatery**, it's time for a tour of the **Biltmore Estate** where the house and gardens—both of storybook proportion—will impress with their opulence and beauty. Take lunch on the estate and spend the afternoon tasting at the **winery,** strolling the gardens, or doing both. Afterward, hop on the Parkway and go south to **Brevard** in time to check in to the **Sunset Motel,** a retro motel in this cool town. Dine at **The Square Root** before checking out the taproom at **Oskar Blues.**

Day 4
BLUE RIDGE PARKWAY TO CHEROKEE

It's not far to Cherokee, but once you get on the Parkway you'll find plenty of stops. Admire **Looking Glass Rock,** take a short hike to **Devil's Courthouse,** and stop to photograph **Cold Mountain.** There's a longer hike waiting at **Richland Balsam,** the highest point on the Parkway, or you could hike to the peak of **Waterrock Knob** where a huge, four-state panoramic view awaits. In Cherokee, stay at **Harrah's Cherokee Casino Resort** and dine on-site, but not before checking out the traditional artwork at the **Qualla Arts and Crafts Mutual.**

Day 5
CHEROKEE TO GATLINBURG

On your way out of Cherokee, spend time getting steeped in the culture with a visit first to the **Museum of the Cherokee Indian,** and then the **Oconaluftee Indian Village.** At the entrance to Great Smoky Mountains National Park, ask the rangers at the **Oconaluftee Visitors Center** about elk sightings, wildflower reports, and other park info. As you drive **Newfound Gap Road** north across the park, stop at the overlooks for long views of the Smoky Mountains before driving over the crest of the range and into the heart of the park. Should you want a stroll, short roadside hikes dot the route; or you could save your energy for a long hike in **Cades Cove** on the Tennessee side of the park. Check into your

hotel in Gatlinburg and stroll the main drag of this tourist haven, stopping to taste some moonshine at **Sugarlands Distilling Company** and grabbing a pizza at **Big Daddy's Pizzeria** or a steak at **Alamo Steakhouse.**

Day 6
GREAT SMOKY MOUNTAINS

It's your choice today: ride wild roller coasters at **Dollywood** or explore the wilderness of **Great Smoky Mountains National Park.** If Dollywood's your call, head to nearby **Pigeon Forge** to Dolly Parton's amusement park; you'll find coasters and rides, concerts and craftspeople, every one of which speaks to the culture and history of the area. For national park explorers, head to the **Roaring Fork Motor Nature Trail** where you'll have your choice of waterfall hikes like **Rainbow, Grotto,** and **Baskins Falls,** and a lovely drive to boot. No matter your choice, it's back to town for dinner at **Smoky Mountain Trout House** in Gatlinburg, or for a burger, fries, and a shake at **Mel's Diner** in Pigeon Forge.

Day 7
KNOXVILLE

Enjoy breakfast at Tennessee's first pancake house, **Pancake Pantry** in Gatlinburg, and then head to **Knoxville.** Go for a walk in **World's Fair Park** and head to the top of the **Sunsphere,** a Knoxville icon that offers the best views of the city. The **Knoxville Museum of Art** and the **East Tennessee History Center** give visitors a well-rounded look at this city's past and future. Dine at any of the restaurants on **Market Square** downtown and enjoy the people-watching and free evening concerts; the music may be from buskers or it may be from a band on stage, but whatever it is, it'll be good.

Best of Great Smoky Mountains National Park

Many visitors are puzzled by what to do in Great Smoky Mountains National Park. Most of the park is wild, and hiking trails rather than roads lead into every holler, corner, and cove. Here's an idea on how to spend three days here, and to spend them well.

Day 1
NEWFOUND GAP ROAD

Begin in **Cherokee**, North Carolina, and drive **Newfound Gap Road** north through the park. As you come to the crest of the mountains, take the time to visit **Clingmans Dome**, the highest peak in the park. From the viewing platform at the top (an easy walk), you'll have an unparalleled view of the surrounding country. There's a lovely hike to **Andrews Bald** nearby, an easy three-hour trek to a high mountain meadow that's often ablaze with wildflowers.

Back on Newfound Gap Road, hit the challenging trail to **Chimney Tops**, a steep and strenuous four-mile hike that rewards you with a view many visitors never see. If you prefer to keep driving, do the **Cades Cove Loop** and take in the historic structures and wildlife in this early Smoky Mountain community.

In **Gatlinburg**, you'll have all manner of entertainment temptations easily at hand. Try combining dinner with a show at the **Dixie Stampede,** a sort of Southern feast combined with a live-action play with horses, gunfire, and all sorts of excitement. Afterward, hit **Sugarlands Distilling** for a little moonshine to calm your nerves.

Day 2
ROARING FORK

Get in the car and head for the **Roaring Fork Motor Nature Trail** for today's hike. Depending on how adventurous you feel, this can be a

Motorcyclists use Cherokee as a base to cruise the Blue Ridge Parkway.

Views from the Top

summit view from Waterrock Knob

Along the Blue Ridge Parkway are a number of overlooks and roadside attractions. In every instance below, it's worth pulling over for an eyeful:

- **Beacon Heights (MP 305.2):** Whether you stay at the car and admire the view of Grandfather Mountain or take the short hike to a rocky bluff with massive views, you won't be disappointed.

- **Richland Balsam Overlook (MP 431.4):** From the highest point on the Blue Ridge Parkway you'll have great views of several mountain ranges.

- **Waterrock Knob Visitor Center (MP 451.2):** This visitors center parking lot is the perfect vantage point for taking in the sunset and star-filled sky.

half-day exploration of a waterfall or two, or a strenuous 14-mile trek to Mount LeConte and back. Either way, start off by hiking to **Rainbow Falls,** an 80-foot waterfall on LeConte Creek. For a short hike, turn around and hoof it back to the trailhead. To reach the summit of Mount LeConte, continue on the trail but be ready for a long, hard day of it. **Baskins Falls** is a smaller waterfall—only 30 feet—but few people make the tough hike in to see it, so it's a bit of a hidden gem.

Since you've earned your supper, go for some traditional, stick-to-your-ribs country cooking at **Mama's Farmhouse** in Pigeon Forge.

Day 3
CATALOOCHEE

From Gatlinburg, head east to **Cataloochee,** a mountain community that has a story similar to that of Cades Cove. Check out historic structures like the **Palmer House, Beech Grove School,** and **Palmer Chapel and Cemetery.** In Cataloochee you'll find the largest concentration of **elk** in the park. The elk and other wildlife are most active around dawn and dusk, so watch for them in the tree line as the day wanes. There's a lovely **campground** here if you want to turn it into an overnighter. If you can, stay for full dark and gaze at the stars overhead—it's dizzying.

Music, Mountains, and Moonshine

Mountain culture extends beyond arts and crafts, and two of the most recognizable—and most lampooned—cultural exports are music and moonshine. The music comes in several flavors: bluegrass, old-time, gospel, and country most notably, and to the untrained ear it sounds pretty much the same. But believe me, that is not the case. Moonshine started with one variety: clear, white-hot lightning, the best of which tastes faintly of sweet corn, and the worst of which tastes like paint thinner. Following are the best places to experience both.

Asheville

Asheville's a music-loving town if ever there was one. And the music scene revolves around the lauded, almost legendary, **Orange Peel Social Aid and Pleasure Club** (page 91). Everyone who's anyone in rock and improvisational music has played or will play here. The cool downtown venue offers shows just about every night of the week, including local and regional acts in addition to major players and the "next big thing" bands. The **Grey Eagle Tavern and Music Hall** (page 91) is another of Asheville's long-running spots to catch a show.

One of the biggest annual shows in Asheville is the **Warren Haynes Christmas Jam** (page 92), an all-star concert fund-raiser featuring a lineup of some of the top rock musicians playing with their bands, with one another, and in any mix imaginable.

In North Carolina there are several brands of moonshine available, some from famous folks like NASCAR legend Junior Johnson, others from less recognizable names. Troy Ball from **Troy & Sons** (page 90) is one of the latter. She

The Old Mill in Pigeon Forge

uses an heirloom recipe to make her much-talked-about moonshine.

Gatlinburg and Pigeon Forge

If there is an epicenter of traditional Appalachian music, it may just be Gatlinburg and Pigeon Forge. Traditional music has been played here since the first European settlers arrived. As tourism increased and the towns grew into that "aw-shucks, we're hillbillies" character, traditional music also played a role. Today, you can hear everything from very strict traditional music to bluegrass covers of modern pop songs being played and sung on the streets and in any number of small theaters and shows. There's no marquee venue; the closest thing is **Dollywood** (page 229), which draws a big crowd and will do a lot to get a musician or band's name out there.

Anywhere you go in the mountains you'll find both music and moonshine (it seems they've been a good way to pass the time for quite a while), but the commercial 'shine operations tend to be centered on the western Smokies in Gatlinburg. **Sugarlands Distilling Company** (page 221)

and **Doc Collier** (page 221) are the best, with tasting rooms and folks steeped in the lore and production methods ready to chat with curious imbibers. You'll find all sorts of flavors—butterscotch, apple pie spices, cinnamon, lemon—but moonshine aficionados will turn up their nose at these and go for the straight, unadulterated, XXX-on-the-bottle moonshine. (Legend has it that each X means once through the distillery, growing purer with each passing). At Sugarlands, you can taste several flavors and even combine your drink with a concert if someone's playing on the Back Porch, their in-house concert venue.

Knoxville

Knoxville has a busy college music scene; major musical acts roll through town, but smaller, no-less-talented bands come through as well. Traditional music is heard throughout the city; musicians from novices to virtuosos saw on fiddles, pluck banjo strings, and slap out bass rhythms on the street, in bars, and in concert halls like the **Tennessee Theatre** (page 238) and **Bijou Theatre** (page 241).

North Carolina High Country

Look for ★ to find recommended
sights, activities, dining, and lodging.

Highlights

★ **Andy Griffith Sights:** Stay in Andy Griffith's childhood home and see some Mayberry-inspired sights (page 27).

★ *The Merry-Go-Round* **Show:** Mount Airy has a rich musical tradition and a great small-town radio station, WPAQ. The weekly *Merry-Go-Round* show is broadcast in front of a live audience from the old movie theater downtown (page 28).

★ **MerleFest:** For one long weekend in April, many of the best artists in American roots music are in North Wilkesboro, along with thousands of their fans (page 45).

★ **Brown Mountain Lights:** The mysterious lights that hover over Brown Mountain have been seen by Carolinians since at least 1833. Whether they're vapors, reflections, or a supernatural phenomenon has never been settled. If

you're in the right place at the right time, you may see them for yourself (page 66).

★ **Grandfather Mountain:** Grandfather Mountain is smaller than Mount Mitchell but still fully a mile high and no less beautiful (page 68).

★ **Penland School of Crafts:** One of the venerable centers of art in the mountains, Penland offers residential classes in dozens of media. The innovative studio creations of many of the artists are exhibited and sold in the elegant gallery (page 72).

★ **Mount Mitchell:** You'd have to travel west until you hit the Black Hills of South Dakota before you could find a higher mountain. The East's tallest peak was the subject of a scholarly feud in the mid-1800s, and one of the feuders, Mitchell himself, is buried at the summit (page 75).

There was a time when this region of rolling mountains and foothills was the Wild West of colonial America, enticing the brave and foolhardy to carve out a place among the hollows and hills.

In 1752 one of the first written impressions of the area was recorded by Bishop Augustus Spangenberg, who was traveling from Pennsylvania on the Great Wagon Road (which followed a long, essentially continuous valley from Philadelphia to Alabama) in search of a suitable tract of land for his Moravian church and community. He eventually found a welcoming spot, but his first sight of the Blue Ridge filled him with dread. Cresting a ridge, Spangenberg, who had crossed the Atlantic and braved thousands of miles of the frontier, wrote, "We have reached here after a hard journey over very high, terrible mountains and cliffs.... When we reached the top we saw mountains to the right, to the left, before and behind us, rising like great waves in a storm."

This corner of the state wasn't just the frontier in Spangenberg's time; until the 20th century the farthest northwestern counties of North Carolina were known as the "Lost Provinces" because they were so remote and difficult to reach. As automobiles and improved roads, including the Blue Ridge Parkway, found their way to this area, so too did the flatlanders. Since then the region has evolved into a popular year-round vacation destination. The mountains around Boone—a town named for the famed frontiersman and his kin—feel subtly different from the ranges closer to Asheville and the Smokies farther south and west; they're more spread out and softened. The northern Blue Ridge is no less beautiful, and the valleys become even wider and the peaks less craggy.

Although the wilderness is a little less wild now, the region is still isolated. Stands of virgin forest, or at least forest that hasn't been logged in more than a century, still stand in remote coves, and spots like Linville Gorge challenge the most intrepid outdoor enthusiasts. Getting lost in the tangle of winding mountain roads is easy, especially as you move

Previous: Mile High Swinging Bridge on Grandfather Mountain; the Linn Cove Viaduct. **Above:** hand-carved Appalachian art.

North Carolina High Country

TENNESSEE

NORTH CAROLINA

VIRGINIA

To Asheville

Swannanoa

Black Mountain

Old Fort

MOUNT MITCHELL

Mt Mitchell State Park

Pisgah National Forest

Burnsville

Penland

PENLAND SCHOOL OF CRAFTS

Erwin

Marion

Silver Fork Winery

Lake James

Little Switzerland

BLUE RIDGE

ORCHARD AT ALTAPASS

Spruce Pine

Linville Gorge

Crossnore

PARKWAY

LINVILLE FALLS

LINVILLE GOLF CLUB

GRANDFATHER MOUNTAIN

Beech Mountain

Valle Crucis

BEECH MOUNTAIN

Elk Knob State Park

BOONE

Cherokee National Forest

Watauga Lake

Bristol

Morganton

South Mountains State Park

Lake Rhodhiss

BROWN MOUNTAIN LIGHTS

Pisgah National Forest

Lenoir

Blowing Rock

TRADITIONS POTTERY

FORT DEFIANCE

West Jefferson

Mt Jefferson State Park

New River State Natural Area

Blue Ridge Parkway

Cumberland Knob Recreation Area

Hickory

Lake Hickory

Wilkesboro

MERLEFEST

North Wilkesboro

Blue Ridge Mountains

Stone Mountain State Park

Conover

Lake Norman

Statesville

Doughton Park

Elkin

To Charlotte

To Winston-Salem

ANDY GRIFFITH SIGHTS

THE MERRY GO-ROUND SHOW

Mount Airy

Divine Llama Vineyards

© AVALON TRAVEL

0   0
10 km
10 mi

closer to the Tennessee state line, where the mountains get taller and the valleys narrower. Here you'll find back roads and hollows (pronounced "hollers" in much of these parts) where only the noonday sun reaches the valley floor, and in winter some are lucky to see a few hours of true daylight. The trees are gnarled and mossy and cling to the edge of windy ridges and cliffs. You'll find waterfalls and wide rivers perfect for wading, floating, or fishing.

Much of the Appalachian folklore collected and popularized in the last 100 to 150 years has come out of this section of North Carolina. It was here that the young Confederate army veteran known as Tom Dooley—who was a real person and whose actual identity is still debated around these parts—killed his girlfriend, Laurie Foster, a ghastly crime immortalized in legend and song. In Wilkesboro you can see the jail cell where he waited to go to the gallows in Statesville. Another crime immortalized in legend is the 1831 murder of Charlie Silver, apparently in self-defense, by his young wife, Frankie. She too was carried down the mountain to hang, and was executed in Morganton. It's not all ghost stories, though. Many of the "Jack Tales," which became a sort of signature of Appalachian storytelling, were recorded around Beech Mountain and have been told by families here for generations. Head into Mount Airy or any other mountain town on any weekend and you'll find old-time musicians singing traditional songs the way their daddy (and their daddy's daddy) taught them, or old-timers telling Jack Tales old and new on some front porch or park bench.

When you visit, leave room in your luggage for some cheese: Ashe County is known for it, along with homemade jam or preserves. Take home a piece by one of the area's potters or weavers, eat dinner at a barbecue joint and get a feel for western North Carolina style 'cue, and visit a winery and carry a bottle back with you. Go skiing, rafting, caving, and gallery hopping—just remember to leave time to explore the back roads at your own pace, windows down, soaking it all in.

PLANNING YOUR TIME

Three days will give you a general overview of the area and let you experience parts of what these mountain towns have to offer, but **five days** will provide ample time to explore by car, on foot, and by raft. If you're planning on spending most of your time in the deep mountains near Tennessee or around Mount Mitchell and Grandfather Mountain, Linville Gorge, Banner Elk, or Beech Mountain, **Boone** offers the convenience of bigger-town amenities (a wider selection of restaurants and shopping for day-trip supplies), but **Blowing Rock** offers picturesque mountain-town digs. Both towns are not far from the Blue Ridge Parkway, and most destinations are 30-60 minutes' drive from either one. Mount Airy and Wilkesboro are both at the edge of the mountains and easily accessible to the junction of I-77 and U.S. 421, a jumping-off point for most foothills locations.

When to Go

Be aware of the weather when traveling in the region. Thick mountain fog in spring and fall, even in summer, can form out of nowhere, making driving on twisting, unfamiliar roads dangerous. Pop-up thunderstorms in **summer** can put a damper on hiking, especially in high or exposed places, and can slow your drive to a crawl as your windshield wipers struggle to keep up. Snow squalls and even black ice in **winter** and cold days in **spring** and **fall** will slow you down too. When unexpected weather descends, slow to a comfortable, safe pace or find a good spot to pull over and wait it out; most of the time, you won't be there long. With a little foresight, seasonal planning, and weather updates, you'll have no trouble discovering the beauty of this part of North Carolina. Know too that the mountain roads can be confusing, so bring a good paper map, gazetteer, or road atlas with you.

The state Department of Transportation operates a real-time **Road Conditions**

Map (http://apps.dot.state.nc.us/tims). For current conditions along the Blue Ridge Parkway, you can check the recorded message at 828/298-0398. Hospitals are located in most of the major towns in this region, but in case of an emergency, help might be delayed by weather, road conditions, or distance. In many areas—not just deep in the woods, but in populated areas as well—there may be no cell phone signal.

Mount Airy and Vicinity

SIGHTS

In downtown Mount Airy you'll notice 1960s police squad cars, business names that may seem oddly familiar, and cardboard cutouts of Barney Fife peering out from shop windows. Mount Airy is the hometown of Andy Griffith and a mecca for fans of *The Andy Griffith Show*. People who grew up in small towns in the Carolinas and elsewhere recognize their families and neighbors in the fictional residents of Mayberry; the show's inspired writing and acting are a deep well of nostalgia, and its fans are legion. **TAGSRWC** (www.imayberry.com) is an intentionally obtuse acronym for *The Andy Griffith Show* Rerun Watchers Club, the show's international fan club whose hundreds of chapters have names that reference the series, such as "Her First Husband

Got Runned Over by a Team of Hogs" (Texas) and "Anxiety Magnifies Fearsome Objects" (Alabama). The Surry Arts Council hosts the citywide **Mayberry Days** (www.mayberrydays.org), an annual fall festival entering its second decade in which TAGSRWC members, other fans, some of the remaining cast members, and impersonators of Mayberry characters come to town and have a big-eyed time getting haircuts at Floyd's barbershop, riding in squad cars, and arresting each other.

One roadside oddity in Mount Airy makes for an interesting sight. It now advertises Pet Milk, but the **Giant Milk Carton** (594 N. Andy Griffith Pkwy./US-52), a 12-foot-tall metal sculpture, has advertised for Coble Dairy and Flavo-Rich Milk since its creation in the 1940s.

Mount Airy, also known as Mayberry on *The Andy Griffith Show*

Mount Airy

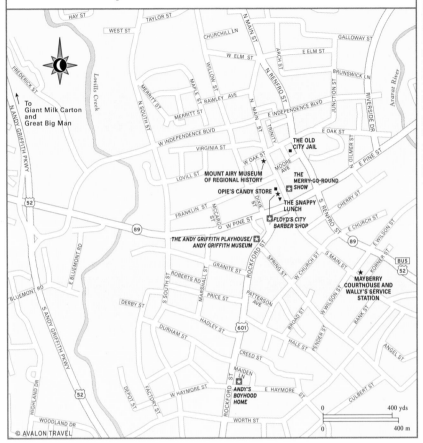

★ Andy Griffith Sights

You can't leave Mount Airy without paying a visit to the sites that honor favorite son Andy Griffith. It isn't open for tours, but you can rent **Andy's boyhood home** (711 E. Haymore St., 336/789-5999, $175/night) if you care to spend the night. The **Andy Griffith Museum** (218 Rockford St., 336/786-1604, www.andygriffithmuseum.com, 9am-5pm Mon.-Fri., 11am-4pm Sat., 1:30pm-4:30pm Sun., $6, audio guide $2) features hundreds of pieces of memorabilia from Griffith's long career in television, movies, and music, including scripts and props from his still-running eponymous TV show. Outside the museum and the attached **Andy Griffith Playhouse** (336/786-7998, www.surryarts. org, showtimes and ticket prices vary) stands a lifelike statue of Andy and Opie with fishing poles in tow that looks like it was grabbed right out of *The Andy Griffith Show*'s opening credits.

If you can't get enough of Andy and Barney, hop into a Mayberry squad car to tour all the major sights in town. **Mayberry Squad Car Tours** (625 S. Main St., 336/789-6743,

Welcome to Mayberry R.F.D.

"People started saying that Mayberry was based on Mount Airy. It sure sounds like it, doesn't it?"

Andy Griffith

Surely the bucolic town of Mount Airy was the inspiration for Mayberry. Comedian and actor Andy Griffith grew up here, drawing inspiration for his stand-up comedy, hit television show, and just about every character he ever played during his long career from its landscape and people. Like its fictional counterpart, Mount Airy is filled with friendly folks, and something in the air here just feels like yesteryear. It's calmer, easier, slower.

Griffith got his break in 1953 when a recording of one of his stand-up routines, a story called "What it was, was Football," sold more than 800,000 copies and landed him a spot on *The Ed Sullivan Show* the next year. The premise is pretty simple: a country preacher, naïve to all but his little world, happens upon a college football game. Having never heard of nor seen football, he's a bit confused. Griffith describes the game and field ("a purty little green cow pasture") like this: "somebody had took and drawed white lines all over it and drove posts in it and I don't know what all. And I looked down there and I seen five or six convicts a-runnin up and down and a-blowing whistles…I looked down and I seen 30 or 40 men come a-running out of one end of a great big outhouse down there. And everybody where I was a-sittin got up and hollered." The quote only does it so much justice and you owe it to yourself to hear Griffith deliver it in his charming drawl.

www.tourmayberry.com) leave from "Wally's Service Station" and cost "$35 for a carload." And if that's not enough, stop by **Floyd's City Barber Shop** (129 N. Main St., 336/786-2346, 7am-5pm Mon.-Wed. and Fri., 7am-3pm Sat.) for a haircut. You won't find Floyd the barber in there, but you will find some friendly folks in an old-fashioned barbershop. If you're in the mood for a trim, you may just sit in the same seat as Andy Griffith, who received many a haircut here during his Mount Airy days.

★ *The Merry-Go-Round* Show

In partnership with WPAQ 740 AM, the Surry Arts Council hosts *The Merry-Go-Round* (Earle Theater, 142 N. Main St., Mount Airy, 336/786-2222 or 336/786-7998, www.surryarts.org, shows 11am-1:30pm Sat., $6), the country's third-longest-running live bluegrass and old-time music radio show. Come to the Earle Theater for the show, or show up as early as 9am toting an instrument if you'd like to join in the preshow jam session. It's one of the state's great small-town treats.

ENTERTAINMENT AND EVENTS

When you're in the area, tune in to **WPAQ** (740 AM, www.wpaq740.com), which has provided a venue for live local talent to perform old-time, bluegrass, and gospel music for more than 60 years. To get a really good idea of this community's life, tune in for the live Saturday-morning *The Merry-Go-Round* Show (11am-1:30pm Sat.), or any other day of the week when you'll hear local call-in shows, old-style country preaching, and more music.

Festivals and Events

A local institution that has a great deal to do with the vitality of Mount Airy's musical traditions is the **Bluegrass and Old-Time Fiddlers Convention** (631 W. Lebanon St., Mount Airy, 336/345-7388, www.mountairy-fiddlersconvention.com), held for almost 40 years during the first full weekend in June at Veterans Memorial Park. Thousands of people come to the festival from around the world to play old-time and bluegrass music with their friends and compete in what is a very prestigious competition in this genre.

The heart of the action takes place at the hundreds of individual campsites that spring up all over the park in informal jam sessions among old and new friends. It's some of the best old-time music to be heard anywhere.

The Surry Arts Council is a hub of artistic activity in the Mount Airy-Surry County area. They sponsor and host many events throughout the year that showcase local talent in drama, visual arts, and especially music. Local and regional old-time and bluegrass bands perform in the **Voice of the Blue Ridge Series** (7:30pm on the third Sat. of the month, $7 adults, free under age 6) at the Earle Theater (142 N. Main St., Mount Airy, 336/786-2222).

SPORTS AND RECREATION
Golf

A rare golf course among the pastures and hayfields is the beautiful **Cross Creek Country Club** (1129 Greenhill Rd., Mount Airy, 336/789-5131, www.crosscreekcc.com, 18 holes, par 72, greens fees $40 for 18 holes, $20 for 9 holes, includes cart). Course conditions are always fantastic, and the course presents quandaries to golfers of all levels.

If you want a fun little par-3 course, head to **Hardy's Custom Golf** (2003 W. Pine St., Mount Airy, 336/789-7888, www.hardrockgolf.net, 18 holes, par 54, greens fees $8, with cart $10, 9 holes $5, with cart $8). The course is lighted for play day or night. If the weather isn't cooperating, try the golf simulator (18 holes $25, 9 holes $15), where you can play 40 different world-famous courses, including St. Andrews and Pinehurst.

ACCOMMODATIONS AND FOOD

In Mount Airy, **Quality Inn** (2136 Rockford St., 336/789-2000, www.qualityinnmountairy.com, from $90), **Holiday Inn Express** (1320 Ems Dr., 336/719-1731, www.igh.com, from $100), and **Hampton Inn** (2029 Rockford St., 336/789-5999, www.hamptoninn.com, from $110) are good options.

While you're in Mount Airy, you have to eat at ★ **The Snappy Lunch** (125 N. Main St., 336/786-4931, 5:45am-1:45pm Mon., Wed., and Fri., 5:45am-1:15pm Tues., Thurs., and Sat., $1-5), a diner whose claims to fame include mentions on *The Andy Griffith Show* and a "World Famous Pork Chop Sandwich," which is notoriously sloppy, delicious, and cheap. Eating here is like stepping back in time. The Snappy Lunch has been in the community since 1923.

There's only one source for good strong coffee in Mount Airy: the **Good Life Café** (Main-Oak Emporium, 248 N. Main St., 336/789-2404, www.mainoakemporium.com, 10am-5:30pm Mon.-Sat., 1pm-5pm Sun.), which makes a surprisingly good cappuccino. **The Copper Pot Restaurant** (123 Scenic Outlet Lane, Ste. 4, 336/352-4108, www.copperpotrestaurant.com, 6am-8pm Mon.-Thurs., 6am-9pm Fri.-Sat., around $10) is a down-home restaurant specializing in dishes of the "meat and two" or "meat and three" variety. It's country cooking all the way, so prepare for fried okra, pinto beans, and inexpensive food.

TRANSPORTATION AND SERVICES

You can reach Mount Airy from the Blue Ridge Parkway by turning south on US-52 at Fancy Gap (MP 199.5), a 14-mile journey; by taking I-77/74 south to NC-89 west, a trip of 24 mostly interstate miles; or by taking a curvy back road that will let you catch a glimpse of life on the slopes of the Blue Ridge Mountains. To take the back road, VA-679/NC-1717, turn onto Orchard Gap Road at Milepost 194, then stay straight on Wards Gap Road, which will lead you into town over the course of a 14-mile, 30-minute journey.

Find out more of what Mount Airy has to offer by stopping by the **Mount Airy Visitors Center** (200 N. Main St., 800/948-0949 or 336/786-6116, www.visitmayberry.com, 8:30am-5:30pm Mon.-Fri., 10am-5pm Sat., 1pm-4pm Sun.).

There is a hospital in town, **Northern Hospital of Surry County** (830 Rockford St., 336/719-7000, www.northernhospital.com). If you require the police, contact the **Mount Airy Police Department** (150 Rockford St., 336/786-3535, www.mountairy.org).

PILOT MOUNTAIN STATE PARK

Pilot Mountain State Park (1792 Pilot Knob Park Rd., Pinnacle, 336/325-2355, http://ncparks.gov, 8am-6pm daily Dec.-Feb., 7am-9pm daily Mar.-Apr. and Oct., 7am-10pm daily May-Sept., 7am-8pm daily Nov.) is a beautiful place for hiking, swimming, rock climbing, rappelling (in designated areas), canoeing on the Yadkin River, and camping. There are a dozen trails here, ranging in length from 0.1 mile (from parking lot to overlook) to 4.3 miles (circling the mountain) to 6.6 miles (connecting the two sections of the park). Pilot Mountain, the park's namesake, is a 1,400-foot-tall rocky protrusion—a startling sight that reminds some of a UHF knob on an old television set (the kind you may have used to watch *The Andy Griffith Show*). Pilot Mountain is so named because it's a prominent and obvious landmark; it appears in *The Andy Griffith Show* as Mount Pilot.

Accommodations and Camping

Pilot Knob Inn Bed and Breakfast (361 New Pilot Knob Lane, Pinnacle, 336/325-2502, www.pilotknobinn.com, $129-249) is an unusual B&B in that guests can stay in suites in the main lodge or in one of several restored century-old tobacco barns on the property. Each one-bedroom barn-turned-cabin is well equipped with modern conveniences, including two-person hot tubs and stone wood-burning fireplaces. Children and pets are not allowed, but horses can occupy a stall on the property for an additional $50 per night.

Pilot Mountain State Park (1792 Pilot Knob Park Rd., Pinnacle, 877/722-6762 or http://northcarolinastateparks.reserveamerica.com for reservations, Mar. 15-Nov. 30, $10-17) contains three distinct camping areas, each catering to a different type of camper. On the lower slopes of the mountain there are 49 sites for tents and trailers in the **Family Camping Area**, which has tent pads, tables, and grills, as well as drinking water and washhouses with hot showers. On the north side of the Yadkin River is a camping area for youth groups or other large organized groups. To get there, you have to drive across a trio of shallow streams, so these sites are unavailable when the water is too high. Campers also have to pack in their water and firewood; the campsite has only picnic tables, a fire circle, and primitive vault toilets. Finally, there are two **canoe campsites** on the south bank of the Yadkin River, available by permit only. These are totally primitive, meaning no water and you pack in/pack out all waste and trash. Advance reservations are required.

HORNE CREEK LIVING HISTORICAL FARM

At **Horne Creek Living Historical Farm** (308 Horne Creek Farm Rd., Pinnacle, 336/325-2298, www.nchistoricsites.org, 9am-5pm Tues.-Sat., free), the farm life of the Hauser family—an ancient clan in this area—is recreated as Thomas and Charlotte Hauser, and their lone daughter and 11 sons, would have experienced it around 1900. Costumed interpreters demonstrate the old ways of farmwork while livestock of historic breeds go about their own work, probably not realizing that they're museum docents. The Hausers had an orchard, of which only a single superannuated pear tree remains, but today a new orchard has taken its place. The Southern Heritage Apple Orchard preserves old Southern heirloom species, trees grown from seeds that have been passed down within families for generations.

HANGING ROCK STATE PARK

The 400-foot rock faces that extend for two miles are the most striking feature of **Hanging Rock State Park** (1790 Hanging

grapes on the vine in the Yadkin Valley

Rock Park Rd., Danbury, 336/593-8480, http://ncparks.gov, 7am-7pm daily Dec.-Feb., 7am-9pm daily Mar.-Apr. and Oct., 7am-10pm daily May-Sept., 7am-8pm daily Nov., free), about 40 minutes outside Mount Airy. If you've exhausted the routes on Pilot Mountain (doubtful), this is a great place for rock climbing and rappelling (a permit and registration with park staff are required; climbers must also finish their route and exit the park by closing time). You can also hike to waterfalls and beautiful overlooks, and swim (11am-5:45pm Mon., 10am-5:45pm Tues.-Sun., $5 ages 13 and up, $4 ages 3-12) in a nearby lake.

The **campground** (1790 Hanging Rock Park Rd., Danbury, 336/593-8480, http://ncparks.gov) has 73 tent and trailer campsites ($10-17), one of which is wheelchair-accessible. Each site has a tent pad, a picnic table, a grill, access to drinking water, and access to a washhouse (mid-Mar.-Nov.) with hot showers and laundry sinks. There are also two-bedroom, four-bed vacation **cabins** (around $470

weekly in summer, $88 daily off-season) for rent. Reserve campsites or cabins at least one month in advance at the park office.

YADKIN VALLEY
Wineries

The Yadkin Valley stretches from the Virginia state line down past Winston-Salem and includes stretches of both the Blue Ridge foothills and the Piedmont. The terrain, climates, and microclimates are remarkably similar to those of France's Burgundy and Italy's Piedmont, two areas where viticulture has thrived for centuries. Winemakers discovered that North Carolina's soil was ideal for a number of familiar varietals, including the sweeter native muscadine and scuppernong grapes. There are three dozen vineyards in this 1.4-million-acre American Viticultural Area, most within an easy drive of Elkin, Mount Airy, and Winston-Salem.

Raffaldini Vineyards and Winery (450 Groce Rd., Ronda, 336/835-9463, www.raffaldini.com, tours 1pm and 4pm Mon. and Wed.-Sun., tasting room 11am-5pm Mon. and Wed.-Sat., noon-5pm Sun.) has a stunning Tuscan villa-style tasting room that overlooks 27 acres of vines. There are 10 wines to sample and purchase in the tasting room. The Vermentino Riserva 2011 is particularly good, as is their Montepulciano, which sells out quickly. After a tasting and tour, grab your favorite bottle and a bite to eat—they have a nice selection of antipasti on hand—and enjoy it on the terrace overlooking the vines and the valley.

McRitchie Winery and Ciderworks (315 Thurmond Post Office Rd., Thurmond, 336/874-3003, www.mcritchiewine.com, 10am-5pm Wed.-Sat., 1pm-5pm Sun.) has nine wines, including one blackberry wine that's sweet but interesting, and a pair of ciders. Their wines are fair, but their cider, which comes in semisweet and dry, is intriguing because it's sparkling, and they use heirloom apples that have been grown in the area for many years. The vineyard and kitchen garden are operated as sustainably as possible

Yadkin Valley

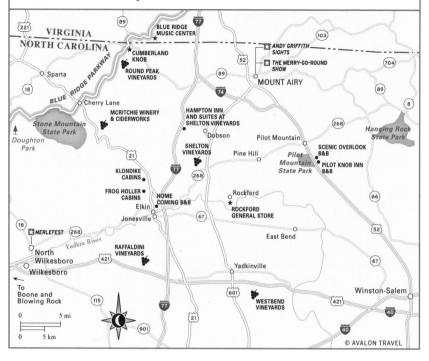

© AVALON TRAVEL

using low-impact methods that other wineries have yet to adopt.

Shelton Vineyards (286 Cabernet Lane, Dobson, 336/366-4724, www.sheltonvineyards.com, tasting room 10am-6pm Mon.-Sat., noon-6pm Sun. Mar.-Oct., 10am-5pm Mon.-Sat., noon-5pm Sun. Nov.-Feb.) is a perennial North Carolina favorite, available at most grocery stores across the state. They offer tours and tastings ($5 pp) on the half hour, or you can elevate your tasting to the Reserve Tasting (11:30am, 1:30pm, and 3:30pm Fri., 1:30pm and 3:30pm Sat., 3:30pm Sun., $25), which includes a tasting of Shelton's Reserve wines and a souvenir crystal wine glass, or even go for the Gazebo Tasting (3:30pm Fri.-Sun., $160/four tasters). Be sure to try their dry riesling and port; they're one of the only vineyards that makes port.

While you're at Shelton Vineyards, grab

a meal, not just a snack, at **Harvest Grill** (336/366-3590, 11am-9pm Mon.-Thurs., 11am-10pm Fri.-Sat. year-round, 11am-6pm Sun. Mar.-Oct., 11am-5pm Sun. Nov.-Feb., $14-35). This bistro serves what the chef calls "sophisticated comfort food," featuring many North Carolina ingredients. Try the cornmeal-dusted rainbow trout, the crispy corn bread crab cakes with Texas Pete tartar sauce, or the grilled North Carolina black grouper. They serve a number of vegetarian and gluten-free options.

One of the most fun wineries to visit is **Divine Llama Vineyards** (5349 Macedonia Rd., East Bend, 336/699-2525, www.divinellamavineyards.com, noon-5pm Fri.-Sat., 1pm-5pm Sun., noon-9:30pm Fri. in July, Sat.-Sun. only Jan.-Feb.). Divine Llama has five acres of grapes and 20 acres of pasture for miniature horses and regular-size llamas. The cabernet franc is tasty, and they have several wines named for their llamas. Throughout the year they host concerts at the vineyard. You can arrange for a creekside picnic and have the llamas pack your chairs, food, and wine in for you; call in advance to set up your llama picnic (starting at $50/person).

Cellar 4201 (4201 Apperson Rd., East Bend, 336/699-6030, www.cellar4201.com, noon-6pm Fri.-Sun.) produces a number of red and white blends and varietal wines. Try their stainless chardonnay or, if they have it, their sangiovese. You might be surprised by their Rose Frizzante, which has a little sparkle and fizz, but still pairs well with a dish like barbecue, which is great because you are in North Carolina and if there's one thing we have a lot of, it's barbecue joints.

Round Peak Vineyards (765 Round Peak Church Rd., Mount Airy, 336/352-5595, www.roundpeak.com, noon-5pm Sun.-Thurs., noon-8pm Fri., 11am-6pm Sat., 11am-sunset Sat. June-Aug., open Sat.-Sun. only Jan. 15-Mar. 15) has 13 acres of vineyards producing 10 French and Italian varietals. Unlike some of the larger vineyards in the Yadkin Valley, Round Peak makes wine using only grapes grown in its own vineyards. On Saturday during summer there are concerts and tastings, lawn games, and a number of special events. Round Peak is dog-friendly, and they have an area set aside for your four-legged traveling companion to stretch out and play while you taste wine.

Sports and Recreation

It's an 18-mile trip south from Mount Airy, but sometimes you have to take a little drive if you want to ride in a hot-air balloon. Balloon pilots Tony and Claire Colburn lead tours of the Yadkin Valley by hot-air balloon any time of year, weather permitting. Their **Yadkin Valley Hot Air Balloon Adventures** (Rockford Rd., Booneville, 336/922-7207, www.balloonadventure.net) requires advance reservations, but it's an amazing way to see the Carolina foothills. While you're near Rockford, you might as well make a day of it by renting a kayak from Yadkin River Adventures.

Yadkin River Adventures (104 Old Rockford Rd., Rockford, 336/374-5318, www.yadkinriveradventures.com, canoe trips: 2 hours $65, 4 hours $75, 6 hours $85; kayak trips: 2 hours $40, 4 hours $50, 6 hours $60) offers rentals of canoes, kayaks, and sit-ontops, along with shuttle service for full- and half-day paddling adventures. The Class I Yadkin River is great for paddlers of all ages and experience levels, and it has beautiful views of Pilot Mountain.

Accommodations and Food

To really tour the wine country, you'll need to spend a night or two. **The Rockford Bed and Breakfast** (4872 Rockford Rd., Dobson, 800/561-6652, www.rockfordbedandbreakfast.com, $119-139) is a beautiful mid-19th-century farmhouse south of Mount Airy in Dobson, convenient to many of the Yadkin Valley wineries.

At **Frog Holler Cabins** (564 E. Walker Rd., Elkin, 336/526-2661, www.frogholler-cabins.com, $125-135) you can stay in a well-appointed cabin with a fireplace and a hot tub overlooking Big Elkin Creek. Three cabins—The Cottage, Hawks Nest, and Mill House—are around 400 square feet and suitable for a couple; Deer Run is a bit bigger and sleeps four. There's plenty of peace and quiet, and they're within 30 minutes of more than two dozen vineyards and wineries. On the property are miles of hiking trails and a fishing pond, but one of the big draws is the fact that you can park and take a tour ($60) of wineries and let Frog Holler be your guide so that everyone can enjoy tasting.

222 Public House (222 E. Main St., Elkin, 336/526-0067, www.222publichouse.com, 5pm-midnight Thurs., 11:30am-midnight Fri.-Mon., $7-15) serves wood-fired pizzas, wings, salads, and chicken sandwiches, with a very good selection of microbrews in a sports bar atmosphere. Don't let the sports bar vibe fool you though—the food's good.

Blue Ridge Foothills

The foothills of the Blue Ridge are among the most beautiful stretches of countryside in North Carolina. The land is incredibly rich: Just as the mountain streams bring nutrient-laden water to the valley floors, the valley fosters what we think of today as "mountain music." Several major festivals are held here in the spring and summer, most famously North Wilkesboro's annual MerleFest, which has become one of the country's most important music festivals, drawing major bluegrass, country, old-time, and Americana artists for a weekend of outdoor performances. Since the 1920s, old-time and bluegrass musicians from the countryside between Mount Airy and Galax, Virginia (which has an incredible festival of its own, the Old Fiddlers Convention), have been known as some of the greatest string-band artists. Aficionados of the genre who can recognize the cadences of string-band and bluegrass music can pick out a fiddler or banjo player from this region almost immediately, and the best can tell you which side of the Blue Ridge—Virginia or North Carolina—they're from. From Mount Airy west to Wilkesboro, north to Galax, Virginia, and east to Floyd, Virginia, you'll find that 20-something old-time and bluegrass musicians number almost as many as musicians in their 70s. In the world of folk and traditional music, this is something of an anomaly, but it speaks to the genre's deep and strong roots.

BLUE RIDGE MUSIC CENTER (MP 213)

Just across the Virginia state line at Blue Ridge Parkway Milepost 213 is the **Blue Ridge Music Center** (700 Foothills Rd., Galax, VA, 276/236-5309, www.blueridgemusiccenter.org, museum 10am-5pm daily May-Oct., free, concerts $10, daily midday music free), a museum dedicated to the roots music of the hills in this part of North Carolina and Virginia. Midday Mountain Music concerts

(noon-4pm daily, free) give area musicians opportunities to play for a crowd, while regular evening concerts by more established acts draw crowds from all over.

CUMBERLAND KNOB (MP 217.5)

The section of the Blue Ridge Parkway between the Virginia state line and Boone is stunning in any season. There are a number of trails and sights in addition to numerous scenic overlooks with panoramic views of the valleys and mountains.

Cumberland Knob (Milepost 217.5) is where construction began on the Blue Ridge Parkway on September 11, 1935. The 1,000-acre recreation area is a great place to stop and have a picnic. The **Cumberland Knob Trail** is an easy 0.5-mile hike that's the perfect way to stretch your legs after a couple of hours in the car. Also at Milepost 217.5, the 2-mile Gully Creek Trail leads across a stream to a small, picturesque waterfall.

STONE MOUNTAIN STATE PARK (MP 229)

You can't see the namesake Stone Mountain upon entering **Stone Mountain State Park** (3042 Frank Pkwy., Roaring Gap, 336/957-8185, www.ncparks.gov, 7am-6pm daily Nov.-Feb., 7am-8pm daily Mar.-Apr. and Sept.-Oct., 7am-9pm daily May-Aug., closed Christmas Day), but when you do, you'll remember it. Just a few miles south of the Blue Ridge Parkway along US-21, this 14,000-acre park's most prominent feature is the 600-foot granite dome that is Stone Mountain. The 25-square-mile pluton (an upthrust of igneous rock) is fun to hike, but difficult to see from the park. For the best views, get back on the Blue Ridge Parkway and head to the **Stone Mountain Overlook** (MP 232.5).

Stone Mountain State Park was established in 1969 and named a National Natural

Blue Ridge Foothills

TENNESSEE

NORTH CAROLINA

Roan Mtn
Roan Mtn

Appalachian Trail

Elk Park

To Little Switzerland, Crabtree Falls, Mount Mitchell, and Asheville

LINVILLE CAVERNS

Linville Falls Recreation Area

BLUE

Banner Elk

GRANDFATHER MOUNTAIN

Linville

HAWKSNEST SNOW TUBING

BEECH MOUNTAIN

SUGAR MOUNTAIN

Valle Crucis

FLAT ROCK

LINN COVE VIADUCT

BEACON HEIGHTS

Foscoe

BOONE

Elk Knob State Park

West Jefferson

Jefferson

New River State Natural Area

NEW RIVER OUTFITTERS

River

BROWN MOUNTAIN LIGHTS

Memorial Park

Julian Price Memorial Park

RIDGE

Moses H. Cone Memorial Park

Blowing Rock

To Hickory

Happy Valley

LENOIR

FORT DEFIANCE

E.B. Jeffress Park

THE LUMP

Mt Jefferson State Park

Glendale Springs

Laurel Springs

PARKWAY

Blue Ridge Parkway

North Wilkesboro

Wilkesboro

Doughton Park

Stone Mountain State Park

To Elkin

Cumberland Knob and Roanoke

0   10 km
0   10 mi

To Statesville

To Winston-Salem

© AVALON TRAVEL

Driving the Blue Ridge Parkway

The Blue Ridge Parkway rides the crest of the mountains as it follows its course from Waynesboro, Virginia, to Cherokee, North Carolina. Known as America's Byway, this 469-mile, two-lane road traverses some of the most rugged and most picturesque mountains in the East. It's the most-visited unit of the National Park Service: Somewhere around 15 million visitors will drive some (or all) of the Parkway in a given year.

It's easy to get on the Parkway in North Carolina's High Country. Pick up the Blue Ridge Parkway in Virginia, just eight miles from the North Carolina state line at a town called Fancy Gap, and then follow it south to Boone, Asheville, or even Cherokee. You can also get on the Parkway near Stone Mountain State Park and US-21; near Boone and Blowing Rock, US-421 and US-321 meet the Parkway. A number of other roads—US-221, NC-80, NC-181, and I-26—intersect the Blue Ridge Parkway between Blowing Rock and Asheville.

Along this section of the Parkway you'll encounter twice as many awe-inspiring vistas as there are overlooks (and there are a lot of overlooks), and you'll pass a number of sights that are as close to mandatory as you'll find along any route. If you stopped to take in the landscape at every view, or paused to investigate every sight of note, it would take four days to drive from Boone to Asheville. To save you some time, here's a list of a few places (measured in mileposts) where you should stop and smell the mountain laurel.

· **MP 238.5:** Brinegar Cabin in Doughton Park is a typical mountain cabin dating to the 1870s, with great short trails nearby.

· **MP 294:** Moses Cone Manor, the home of the Southern Highland Craft Guild Shop, has a lovely walk around a bass-filled lake and some challenging trails.

· **MP 304.4:** The Linn Cove Viaduct is one of the most-photographed sections of the Parkway; this elevated section of road seems to float in space.

· **MP 305:** Grandfather Mountain is an impressive peak. Visit one of the sub-peaks and cross the Mile High Swinging Bridge to a pinnacle where you'll have one of the best views along the whole of the Parkway.

· **MP 316:** Linville Falls are in Linville Gorge, a spot often called the Grand Canyon of the East. They're impressive, especially in autumn.

· **MP 355:** The highest peak east of the Mississippi, Mount Mitchell has an observation deck that gives you unobstructed views in every direction.

· **MP 364:** Rocky crags, rhododendron thickets, and piles of mountain laurel give Craggy Gardens an eerie beauty.

Landmark in 1975. In the years before it was a park, the lands around were settled by the typical mix of Europeans who make up much of the Appalachian ancestry—English, Irish, Scots-Irish, and German, with a few French families thrown in for good measure. They shaped churches, farms, log homes, and all they needed to create a community out of these woods, and three sites around the park show different aspects of life for the area's early European inhabitants. The **Mountain Culture Exhibit** in the park office provides some historical context to these bold families who settled here. The **Hutchison Homestead** was built in the mid-1800s and is representative of a typical homestead for the region; it includes a log cabin, barn, outbuildings, and even a blacksmith shop. Finally, the **Garden Creek Baptist Church,** built in 1897, is one of the few historic churches in the county that stand in nearly original form, having undergone no remodeling or major repairs during its long life.

Hiking

There are a number of hiking trails in the park, ranging from easy forest strolls to the challenging Stone Mountain Loop Trail that takes you to the top of the impressive granite dome.

STONE MOUNTAIN LOOP TRAIL

Distance: 4.5-mile loop
Duration: 3-3.5 hours
Elevation gain: 500 feet
Difficulty: strenuous
Trailhead: Upper Trailhead parking lot
Directions: Exit the Parkway at MP 229 and follow US-21 south and turn onto Oklahoma Road/Old Gap Road/Stone Mountain Road. Once in the park, follow the road to the trailhead across from the Stone Mountain State Park campground.

This hike is a killer, especially during late summer when the granite gets so hot that you feel like you're baking as you cross the wide stone face. Fall (specifically, mid-October) is when the views are best and the weather is ideal for this hike.

Start on a short spur trail that leads to a sign marking the trail. Follow the trail to the left and head to Stone Mountain Falls, a 200-foot waterfall. A set of nearly 300 very steep stairs leads to the bottom of the falls.

Continue on the trail to a pair of side trails leading to Lower and Middle Falls Trails. Unless you are a big waterfall fan, you can skip these (save your energy for the uphill portion of the hike, as the spur trail is about 0.5 miles). About 1.7 miles into the hike, you'll notice the trees start to thin and Stone Mountain begins to show a little granite. Just down the trail from here is the Hutchison Homestead, which is a good spot to catch your breath. The parking area for the lower trailhead is nearby. That trail is a more direct approach to the summit, but you should go for the loop because the whole hike is worthwhile, not just the main attraction.

Soon after you leave the homestead, the trail gets steep enough that there are a few cables along the way to help you climb. Don't stray far from the trail—it's marked with orange dots—because the granite can be slick. From the summit you'll have a good view of the mountains. Look to the northwest and west; you may see the Blue Ridge Parkway cutting across the opposite hills. To complete the trail, simply follow the markings off the summit, back into the trees, and back to the spur trail that leads to the trailhead.

CEDAR ROCK TRAIL

Distance: 1 mile out and back
Duration: 30 minutes
Elevation gain: 250 feet
Difficulty: moderate
Trailhead: Lower Trailhead parking lot near the Hutchison Homestead

Some say this hike is easy, others say moderate, but it's relatively easy except for a couple of short, steep spots that may make you winded on the way up and give your quads a workout on the way back. Depart from the Lower Trailhead parking area (where you'll also find the Wolf Rock and Black Jack Ridge Trailheads). Follow the sign and the round red blazes. From the trailhead, you'll take the Stone Mountain Loop past the homestead and then turn right. When the trail forks, Cedar Rock stays to the right and you'll ascend to the small summit. Along the way, and especially at the top, you'll have some good views of Stone Mountain.

Accommodations and Camping

At Milepost 229 on the Parkway, the **Glade Valley Bed and Breakfast** (330 Shaw Lane, Glade Valley, 336/657-8811 or 800/538-3508, www.gladevalley.com, $120-170) has six bedrooms and a private cabin built to look like a classic frontier cabin. This bed-and-breakfast sits on 29 acres of mountainside with miles of walking trails and tremendous views, making it a relaxing place to rest for a night or two. In addition to breakfast, they provide guests with complimentary bottled water, making the hikes a little easier.

The 94 campsites in **Stone Mountain State Park** (3042 Frank Pkwy., Roaring Gap,

336/957-8185, www.ncparks.gov) are divided into three types: non-electric sites ($17), sites with electricity ($22), and group campsites ($45). They have a two-night minimum stay on holiday weekends, and they lock the gates when the park closes, so if you have to leave, it had better be an emergency because you'll be dialing 911 in order to get out. If you're a backpacker, they do have six backpack camping sites along Widow's Creek; these sites are available by permit only, with no more than six campers per permit/site.

DOUGHTON PARK (MP 238.5)

Just off the Parkway at Milepost 238.5 stands the **Brinegar Cabin,** one of the relics of human habitation along the ridgetops of the Blue Ridge Mountains. Originally part of a 125-acre farm purchased in 1876 (for the princely sum of $200), this cabin was the home of the bachelor Martin Brinegar for two years until he took for his wife the 16-year-old Carolina. On this farm they raised four children and the crops of food needed to sustain them through the year. Martin made shoes and acted as a justice of the peace and a notary public. When he died in 1925, Carolina became sole owner of the farm. In 1935, when

the Blue Ridge Parkway made plans to come through their farm, she sold it to the state of North Carolina for inclusion in Parkway lands. As was common at the time, the Park Service granted her lifetime rights to the cabin, which would have allowed her to live on the property for as long as she wanted (with a few restrictions on hunting, wood gathering, and the like). Shortly after the park was established, she left the farm, saying the traffic had made her mountaintop home too "noisy" a place to live.

Today, you can peek in the windows of the small cabin, learn about farming techniques that the Brinegars would've used at the garden maintained by the Park Service, and check out their springhouse (where the spring still flows). On weekends in peak seasons, a park ranger gives presentations about the garden and about other aspects of daily life here.

Hiking

Thirty miles of trails crisscross Doughton Park, and hiking is what lures many visitors out of their cars here. A number of trails lead through the park, the shortest of which is **Wildcat Rocks Overlook,** a five-minute, 0.1-mile, leg-stretching loop that will take you from the defunct Bluffs Lodge to an overlook

hiking in Doughton Park

where you can see the miniscule **Caudill Cabin** and the expanse of Basin Creek Cove. In this tiny, one-room cabin, Martin and Jamie Caudill raised 14 children, a tremendous family until you consider that Martin's father, who lived just down the hill (his cabin is no longer standing), had 22 children.

Of the other hikes in Doughton Park, the one-mile **Fodder Stack Trail** is short and sweet, while others grow longer and more strenuous as you climb the peaks and explore waterfalls.

FODDER STACK TRAIL

Distance: 1 mile out and back
Duration: 45 minutes
Elevation gain: 40 feet
Difficulty: easy to moderate
Trailhead: far end of the Bluffs Lodge upper parking area (MP 241.1) on the southeast side of the Parkway

Unobstructed views to the east make this hike popular for early risers staying at the campgrounds in Doughton Park. From the Bluffs Lodge upper parking area, follow the marked trail down a short, steep section, then along an easy path to the end, where the stone outcropping known as Fodder Stack stands. Along the way, you'll see a range of wildflowers depending on the time of year.

BLUFF MOUNTAIN TRAIL

Distance: 15 miles out and back
Duration: 8-9 hours
Elevation gain: 400 feet
Difficulty: moderate
Trailhead: Brinegar Cabin Overlook parking area, MP 238.9

The toughest thing about this hike is the distance, which is especially tough to handle when it's hot. Most of the trail is pretty easy, and some folks call this "the best walking" on the Parkway.

Start at the trail sign at the end of the Brinegar Cabin parking area and ascend. A quarter mile in, you'll reach an intersection with the Cedar Ridge Trail (to the left); keep to the right and continue on Bluff Mountain Trail. The path widens and you'll enter a field

shortly after the trail intersection; then, a mile in, you'll walk through the RV portion of the campground. At 1.3 miles you'll cross the Parkway and come to the main part of the campground and a trail map poster. Keep going and head into the hardwood forest and rhododendron tunnels.

Two miles into the hike you'll come to another field, followed by another crossing of the Parkway. At 2.7 miles you'll reach the (unfortunately) closed Doughton Park Coffee Shop at Milepost 241.1. Keep going up the steps at the far end of the parking lot to cross the Parkway again and head into the woods.

A little over four miles in, you'll intersect with Bluff Ridge Trail (to the left); stay right to reach Bluff Mountain. Immediately after the intersection are a cliff and a set of switchbacks. Here is one of the best views of the Parkway.

For the next mile or so, you'll parallel the Blue Ridge Parkway. At mile 4.7, you'll reach the Alligator Back Overlook (MP 242.4), followed by the Bluff Mountain Overlook (MP 243.4) at 5.8 miles. There's an old road at mile 6.3; don't follow it. Stay left for the pathway below the roadbed. You'll soon cross Grassy Gap Fire Road and another large meadow. From here it's an easy walk to the end of the trail. Flat Rock Ridge Trail intersects your trail at mile 7.4. At mile 7.5, you're at the end.

CEDAR RIDGE TRAIL

Distance: 9 miles out and back
Duration: 5-6 hours
Elevation gain: 2,100 feet
Difficulty: moderate to strenuous
Trailhead: Brinegar Cabin Overlook parking area, MP 238.9

Starting from the Brinegar Cabin Overlook parking lot, you'll ascend the Bluff Mountain Trail for a quarter mile, then turn left through the fence stile to continue along Cedar Ridge Trail. Soon after you split off from the Bluff Mountain Trail, you'll enter a rhododendron tunnel and a series of switchbacks. The trail will narrow and ascend a little over the next mile, until you begin to walk along a ridgeline.

A set of switchbacks at 1.8 miles will take you up, then down a steeper section. At 2.3 miles, you'll be descending again.

The mountain laurel becomes abundant at 3.5 miles. Continue along this trail until you reach Grassy Gap Fire Road. From here, you can turn around or head up Basin Creek Trail to see a few waterfalls and Caudill Cabin.

BASIN CREEK TRAIL

Distance: 5.6 miles out and back
Duration: 3-3.5 hours
Elevation gain: 1,200 feet
Difficulty: moderate to strenuous
Trailhead: Cedar Ridge Trail and Grassy Gap Fire Road
Directions: From the Brinegar Cabin Overlook parking area, hike the 4.5-mile Cedar Ridge Trail to the Basin Creek Trailhead.

As you ascend alongside Basin Creek, keep in mind that the prolific Caudill family called this cove home. Along the way, you'll spy a few signs of their existence, and you'll end the hike at Caudill Cabin (which you can see from Wildcat Rocks Overlook).

Begin the trail at the intersection of Cedar Ridge Trail and Grassy Gap Fire Road. Walk a quarter mile up the fire road to Basin Creek Trail to your right. The trail is lined with rhododendron, and there are a number of deep pools in the creek. Anglers love to visit this area because the streams are rife with trout. As you continue up the trail, you'll pass several more pools, some of which may just be the perfect place to cool off in warmer weather.

At 0.6 miles and 1.9 miles, you'll pass the remnants of old chimneys. You'll find some pretty cascades and small waterfalls around a mile in. At 1.3 miles is one of two 30-foot waterfalls that's quite nice. Cross the stream several times as you climb on through pastures and then through steeper grazing lands. At 2.4 miles, you'll cross Basin Creek and see the second 30-foot falls. Soon you'll arrive at the Caudill Cabin, where you'll take a breather and retrace your steps back to Grassy Gap Fire Road, then back along Cedar Ridge Trail to the trailhead at Brinegar Cabin.

Camping

At Milepost 241 there is a **campground** (336/372-8877, www.recreation.gov for reservations, all sites $19/night) with 110 campsites, 25 trailer/RV sites, four restrooms, and a fire circle where many folks like to gather. Campsites are well maintained and pleasant. (Note that maps on the National Park Service website incorrectly show a coffee shop and small gas station here. The coffee shop has closed.)

SALLY MAE'S ON THE PARKWAY (MP 259)

Formerly the Northwest Trading Post, **Sally Mae's on the Parkway** (414 Trading Post Rd., Glendale Springs, 336/982-2543, 9:30am-5:30pm daily Apr. 15-Nov. 15) is a great version of the "old country store" right on the Parkway. It's worth a stop to stretch your legs and grab a sandwich (around $7), as this is one of the few places along the Parkway where you can get something more than a snack. Take a long look at the handcrafted art, jewelry, and food items they carry.

There is a great little hike just down the road from here. At Milepost 260.3, you'll find the **Jumpinoff Rocks** parking area and small picnic area. From there, you have a relatively flat one-mile hike to a rock observation deck with expansive views. Given that most folks will drive right by, it's a great place to take some fall foliage shots.

WEST JEFFERSON AND VICINITY (MP 261)

The charming small town of West Jefferson is a good jumping-off point to explore this corner of the North Carolina High Country. **West Jefferson, Jefferson,** and **Todd** are in Ashe County, which is where the North and South Forks of the New River join to create the second-oldest river in the world, the New. The New flows through North Carolina, Virginia, and West Virginia, where it joins other rivers on the way to the Ohio. In West Virginia, the New River is known for white-water rafting and an impressive single-span arch bridge.

Here, though, the river is wide, gentle, and slow, and you're more likely to wade in it while casting a fly rod or float it in an inner tube than brave rapids in a raft or kayak.

Ashe County is also the center of two of North Carolina's more interesting industries: Christmas trees (Fraser firs, mostly) and cheese. North Carolina is the second-largest producer of Christmas trees in the United States; the industry brings in more than $100 million annually. The cheese here is also quite good.

West Jefferson is a surprisingly artsy town. There are 15 (at my last count) murals adorning buildings downtown, creating a lovely walking tour that gives you a look at how local artists have interpreted their history and surroundings. You'll also spot these strange concrete squares, once utilitarian (they were the bases of long-gone streetlights), now painted in whimsical forest scenes.

NC-194, which runs through West Jefferson and is connected to Jefferson by US-221, roughly parallels the Parkway. It's a beautiful drive in and of itself, leading by red barns and countless tree farms with orderly rows of Fraser firs. Many of these barns are decorated with vivid color-block paintings that resemble old-fashioned quilts. They're part of the **Quilt Trails of Western North Carolina** (www.quilttrailswnc.org), an ongoing art project. There are two dozen in the vicinity of West Jefferson, and even more in other parts of North Carolina.

Festivals and Events

The center of the arts community is the **Ashe County Arts Council** (303 School Ave., 336/846-2787, www.ashecountyarts.org, 9am-5pm Mon.-Fri., 10am-4pm Sat. Apr.-Dec.). They have a gallery showing a rotating series of exhibitions by local artists and art collectives working in any medium imaginable, and they help put on musical events and plays in the community. The Arts Council is also heavily involved in the **West Jefferson Arts District Gallery Crawl** (second Fri. of the month, June-Oct.), with a final **Christmas Crawl** taking place in early December.

There are plenty of goings-on in West Jefferson. The **Backstreet Park Concert Series** (5:30pm-7pm on the third, fourth, and fifth Fri. May-Aug., free) brings in family-friendly musical entertainment in the form of traditional, old-time, and bluegrass musicians. Every July 3 and 4 they have the **Christmas in July Festival** (www.christmasinjuly.info), with music, a street fair, a farmers market, Civil War reenactors, activities for kids, and a pretty sizable crowd. September brings the **On The Same Page Literary Festival** (www.onthesamepagefestival.org), the **Old Time Antiques Fair** (336/846-1231), and **Art on the Mountain** (www.ashecountyarts.org).

Shopping

Broomfields Gallery (414 E. 2nd St., 336/846-4141, www.broomfieldsgallery.com, 11am-5pm Mon. and Wed.-Sat.) is chock-full of a diverse selection of fine art, crafts, and antiques. The proprietors have been collecting for more than half a century, and they're selective in what they bring in to the store. **Originals Only Gallery** (3-B N. Jefferson Ave., 336/846-1636, www.originalsonlygallery.com, 10am-5pm Tues.-Sat.) has works by only a few Ashe County artists, but the pieces they carry—paintings, pottery, and furniture—are excellent.

Recreation

There are two undeniable natural features in West Jefferson that beg to be explored: Mount Jefferson (visible from the Mount Jefferson Overlook at Parkway MP 267) and the New River.

MOUNT JEFFERSON STATE NATURAL AREA

Just outside of town is the **Mount Jefferson State Natural Area** (1481 Mt. Jefferson State Park Rd., 336/246-9653, www.ncparks.gov, park 8am-sunset daily, office 8am-5pm Mon.-Fri., closed Christmas Day). The two main activities here are picnicking and hiking. A winding road dotted with scenic overlooks takes you close to the summit of the 4,683-foot Mount Jefferson, and from there you can reach the summit after a short 0.3-mile hike. From the **Summit Trail,** you can join up with the strenuous **Rhododendron Trail** (1.1 miles), which circles the summit ridge and passes through innumerable rhododendron thickets. From Rhododendron Trail you can hike out to Luther Rock, an odd, exposed piece of the black volcanic rock that makes up this massif. There's also **Lost Province Trail,** a 0.75-mile loop off Rhododendron Trail that passes through a lovely hardwood forest. These trails are accessible from the Summit Trail trailhead in the parking lot and are well marked, making it quite easy to doing a little hiking. If you do anything, though, be sure to hit the summit; from here you can see a number of Christmas tree farms and the New River (on a clear day).

NEW RIVER STATE PARK

New River State Park (358 New River State Park Rd., Laurel Springs, 12 miles from West Jefferson, 336/982-2587, www.ncparks.gov, 7am-7pm daily Dec.-Feb., 7am-9pm daily Mar.-Apr. and Oct., 7am-10pm daily May-Sept., 7am-8pm daily Nov., closed Christmas Day) is 2,200 acres of hills, meadows, and river just northeast of West Jefferson. This is a great park for **canoeing** and **kayaking** (there are no rentals available in the park, so bring your own or contact the park office for a current list of outfitters). Bass **fishing** is quite good on the North and South Forks of the New River, while trout fishing is best along the feeder streams and smaller, faster tributaries. You'll need a North Carolina fishing license (available at the Walmart in West Jefferson or online at www.ncwildlife.org/licensing, $20-36) and heed fishing regulations as established by the North Carolina Wildlife Resources Commission (www.ncwildlife.org/fishing). There are also six miles of trails spread throughout the park. The best hikes are accessible only by canoe, so be sure to hop

in a boat and head to the Alleghany Access for the **Farm House Loop Trail** and **Riverview Trail;** they're both filled with beautiful views of the river and park environs.

ELK KNOB STATE PARK

The small and scenic New River town of Todd is a slow, winding 12 miles north of Boone. **Elk Knob State Park** (5564 Meat Camp Rd., Todd, 828/297-7261, http://ncparks.gov, office 8am-5pm Mon.-Fri., 7am-6pm Nov.-Feb., 7am-8pm Mar.-May and Sept.-Oct., 7am-9pm June-Aug.) is one of the newest parks in the North Carolina state park system, and some areas are still under development. Elk Knob is the second-highest peak in Watauga County at 5,520 feet; a 1.9-mile hike takes you to the summit. Photographers love it here because wildflowers carpet the forest floor in spring and summer, providing breathtaking photo opportunities. Backcountry campers love it too, as a handful of primitive campsites, including a nice backcountry spot, accommodate only a few campers ($10-13/night, reservations required at improved campsite). The sites are reached by a short hike; the closest is about one mile from the trailhead and the farthest about two miles.

OUTFITTERS

RiverGirl Outfitters (4041 Todd Railroad Grade Rd., Todd, 336/877-3099, www.rivergirlfishing.com, 9am-5pm daily, closed seasonally, call for availability, $35 and up) offers fishing lessons, fly-fishing guided trips, kayak and canoe rentals, and tubing trips on the New River. Kelly, the RiverGirl herself, changed careers from being a fisheries biologist to a river guide and angler, and has ingrained herself into the community of Todd, drawing in thousands of visitors every year for fishing, tubing, and other river activities. Before you leave, take your picture with Petunia, a huge potbellied pig.

New River Outfitters (10725 US-221 N, Jefferson, 800/982-9109, www.canoethenew.com, 8:30am-6pm daily, call for offseason availability, from $15) gets you on the water for a short, 3.5-mile paddle or an overnight adventure. They also have tubing trips, which is a popular way to pass an afternoon here. Located just nine miles north of Jefferson, they're close enough to the Parkway for an impulse tubing session.

GOLF

At **Jefferson Landing** (148 E. Landing Dr., Jefferson, 336/982-7767, www.visitjefferson-landing.com, 18 holes, par 72, greens fees $59 Mon.-Thurs., $69 Fri.-Sun. mid-Oct.-mid-May, $39 Mon.-Thurs., $49 Fri.-Sun. mid-May-mid-Oct.) you'll find a course designed to challenge golfers. Deceptively easy holes, like Number 16, can coax you into hitting your tee shot too long or too short and put you in a bad position for your second shot. The possibility of year-round play (when the weather cooperates) makes this course appealing in shoulder seasons.

Mountain Aire (1396 Fairway Ridge Dr., West Jefferson, 336/877-4716, www.moun-tainaire.com, 18 holes, par 72, greens fees $33-37 Apr.-May 19, $34-49 May 20-Oct., $27-30 Nov.-Dec.) uses the natural terrain to create a course that plays longer than it measures (5,900 yards, give or take). The course opens with a par 3, but Number 2 takes you straight uphill. You'll fight your way uphill on Number 4, a long par 5 that plays even longer. On Number 5, you get a little break, so take in the mountain views.

Accommodations

There are a few B&Bs and cabin rentals in and around West Jefferson, as well as options for camping.

There aren't a whole lot of choices in the area north of Boone, but a solid option is **Doughton-Hall Bed and Breakfast** (12668 Hwy. 18, Laurel Springs, 336/359-2468, http://doughtonhall.webs.com), named in part for an important but often forgotten member of the U.S. House of Representatives, Robert Doughton. He was responsible for ensuring the Blue Ridge Parkway ran through North Carolina rather than an alternate route

through Tennessee. The Queen Anne-style home dates to the 1890s, and it has been a B&B since the early 1990s. Guest rooms are filled with antiques, but don't be afraid to make use of what you find.

Buffalo Tavern Bed and Breakfast (958 W. Buffalo Rd., 877/615-9678, www.buffalo-tavern.com, $80-160) is a four-bedroom B&B built in 1872. This beautiful home is situated just outside of West Jefferson, surrounded by Bluff, Buck, and Three Top Mountains. Though it was a tavern in its early days, now it's a tastefully decorated, comfortable spot to rest your head for a night or two.

★ **River House Country Inn and Restaurant** (1896 Old Field Creek Rd., Grassy Creek, 336/982-2109, www.riverhousenc.com, $99-225) has close to a dozen rooms and cabins spread out across a farm along the banks of the North Fork of the New River. The property and rooms are stunning. Whether you go for a cozy room in The Caretaker's Cottage, The Chicken House (which is much more romantic than it sounds), or the Carriage House, your accommodations will be outstanding. They also have a great restaurant on-site, serving prix-fixe ($45) and à la carte menus ($20-36) filled with fine-dining delights. If you're looking for a luxurious stopover in this area, River House is it.

In Deep Creek, south of West Jefferson, is **Fall Creek Cabins** (176 Surber Rd., Fleetwood, 336/877-3131, www.fallcreek-cabins.com, $200-225), a 78-acre private retreat with eight two-story cabins and a trout stream running right through the property. It's beautiful and private, and close to the Parkway. Exit at Milepost 276 and you're just a few minutes away.

Camping

The best camping in the area is at **New River State Park** (358 New River State Park Rd., Laurel Springs, 12 miles from West Jefferson, 336/982-2587, www.ncparks.gov), where you'll find campsites accessible only by canoe ($13/day), two dozen canoe-in/walk-in sites ($20/day, $15/day 62 and up), a pair of improved group campsites ($48/day, maximum of 35 people), a primitive group site ($2/person per day, $13 minimum), and 20 drive-to campsites for tents and RVs ($25/day, $19/day 62 and older). The improved campsites, especially the tent/RV sites, are very nice, with water, restroom, and shower facilities available and picnic tables and grills at each site.

Food

Breakfast at **Hillbilly Grill** (601 S. Jefferson Ave., 336/846-4745, 7am-2pm daily, around $6) is of the down-home variety, and you can fill up on a stack of pancakes for just a few bucks. They have fun with those pancakes too, offering up bunny, snowman, and heart-shaped flapjacks on the appropriate holiday, and even writing your name (ok, your kid's name, but if you ask nicely, you never know) in pancake batter for a birthday treat. Their burgers are handmade and dripping with greasy-spoon goodness.

Over the last few years, North Carolina has experienced a brewery boom, but West Jefferson only has one brewpub—**Boondocks Brewing Tap Room & Restaurant** (108 S. Jefferson Ave., 336/246-5222, www.boondocks-brewing.com, 11am-9pm Sun.-Thurs., 11am-11:30pm Fri.-Sat., $6-27). Boondocks serves their own beer—they have a Kolsch, IPAs, a stout, a saison, and other seasonal creations—and a number of North Carolina brews, in addition to a handful of domestics and imports. The menu includes steaks, quiche, flatbread pizza, burgers, and other expected pub fare.

Black Jack's Pub & Grill (18 N. Jefferson Ave., 336/246-3295, www.blackjackspubandgrill.com, 11am-late daily, $6-10) is known for two things: fantastic burgers and wings galore (seriously, you can get an order of 30). If you're not in the mood for either of those, try the Philly Jack, a tasty take on the Philly cheesesteak. But if you are in the mood, especially for a burger, try the Black Jack's Hamburger Challenge, a timed race to eat a three-pound burger and giant order of fries. This is a sports bar, so expect larger crowds on game days and fight nights.

For a sit-down meal, try **The Hotel Tavern** (6 W. Main St., 336/846-2121, www.thehoteltavern.com, 11:30am-9pm Tues.-Thurs., 11:30am-10pm Fri.-Sat., 11:30am-2pm Sun., closed Mon., $9-24), where you'll find a mix of higher-end entrées like short ribs, steaks, and seafood, as well as pizza, burgers, and bar noshes. When the weather is good, you'll often find a band playing on the outdoor patio. Sunday brunch has been popular here of late.

Though it's not a restaurant, **Ashe County Cheese** (106 E. Main St., 800/445-1378, www.ashecountycheese.com, 8:30am-5:30pm Mon.-Sat.) is worth a visit. They've been making cheese here since 1930, and you can watch the process or just pick up some cheese, butter, fudge, or other homespun food goods in their store. You can pick up any number of styles of cheese, all made here in North Carolina's Blue Ridge Mountains, at specialty shops and grocers at stops all along the Parkway.

The **Todd General Store** (3866 Todd Railroad Grade Rd., Todd, 336/877-1067, www.toddgeneralstore.com, 10am-5pm Mon.-Thurs., 10am-9:15pm Fri., 10am-4:30pm Sat., 11:30am-4pm Sun., closed Jan.-mid-Mar.) has a deli and ice cream counter in addition to assorted snacks, homemade foodstuffs, collectibles, and gift items. Every Tuesday evening they have storytelling, a mountain tradition, and live bluegrass music on Friday nights 6:30pm-9:30pm.

The other option in Todd is the **Todd Mercantile** (3899 Todd Railroad Grade Rd., Todd, 336/877-5401, www.toddmercantile.com, 10am-4pm Mon., 9:30am-5pm Wed.-Sat., 9:30am-4pm Sun., closed Tues.). They have a bakery here, so don't come looking for a full meal. The cinnamon rolls are legendary, however, so grab a couple for the road.

Transportation and Services

West Jefferson is located just 11 miles from the Blue Ridge Parkway at Milepost 261 on NC-163. From here, New River State Park is only

12 miles away and the quaint little community of Todd is only 16 miles to the southwest.

More information on West Jefferson and its goings-on is available online (www.ashechamber.com or www.visitwestjefferson.org). If you need a hospital, the nearest is **Ashe Memorial Hospital** (200 Hospital Ave., Jefferson, 336/846-7101, www.ashememorial.org).

THE LUMP (MP 264.4)

The Lump, despite its lackluster name, is a must stop. The name is well earned: a tall, grassy knoll rises oddly from the hillside, forming a sort of lump of earth that you can wander at your leisure. A sign telling an abbreviated version of the story of Tom Dula (pronounced *Dooley*—yes, the Tom Dooley of folk-song infamy) stands at the foot of the Lump. A short trail up the side of the small, round, treeless Lump leads to some spectacular views of the Yadkin Valley and the transition from the Blue Ridge Mountains to North Carolina's Piedmont region.

E. B. JEFFRESS PARK (MP 272)

When the creators of the Blue Ridge Parkway were first discussing the project, the idea of it being a toll road came up. One of the men who led the fight for keeping it free of charge was E. B. Jeffress, onetime chairman of the North Carolina State Highway and Public Works Commission. At **E. B. Jeffress Park**, named in his honor, you'll find some picnic tables, restrooms, and a great little hike to **Cascade Falls** (one mile).

Hiking
CASCADE FALLS TRAIL
Distance: 1-mile loop
Duration: 30 minutes
Elevation gain: 175 feet
Difficulty: moderate
Trailhead: E. B. Jeffress Park, opposite the picnic area

Thanks to some signage installed by the Park Service, this trail gives you a good idea of the ecological diversity you'll find all along the Parkway. Twenty plaques tell about the environment here, and on a trail this short, they pack in a lot of information.

Keep right where the trail splits, just a few dozen paces into the hike, and descend through some lovely wildflowers. At 0.1 miles in, there's a bench. Then at 0.3 miles you'll cross Falls Creek. Bear right here and you'll quickly find yourself at the upper viewing platform at the cascades' top. The lower viewing platform is nearby and gives you a closer look at the falls. Once you've seen your fill, retrace your steps to the trail junction and bear right again. Ascend the trail and take one more right turn and you're back at the start of the trail. The falls are best in the spring, after a rain, or in the late fall and early winter, when they're bearded with ice.

TOMKINS KNOB TRAIL
Distance: 1.2 miles out and back
Duration: 1 hour
Elevation gain: negligible
Difficulty: easy
Trailhead: E. B. Jeffress Park, at the back of the picnic area

Starting from the picnic area at E. B. Jeffress Park, follow the trailhead into the woods, where you'll soon enter a stand of pine trees. You'll climb a little through sassafras trees and wildflowers until you reach the Cool Spring Baptist Church. It's not what you'd expect—steeple and white clapboard—but a rather rustic structure. This is because the congregation usually only met inside during inclement weather; the rest of the time they met outside, surrounded by the glory of nature. Soon after the church is Jesse Brown's Cabin, and almost immediately the Tomkins Knob parking lot at Milepost 272.5. Reverse course and head back to the start.

WILKESBORO AND VICINITY
★ **MerleFest**

It began as a small folk festival more than 20 years ago, but **MerleFest** (www.merlefest.org, late Apr., $40 per day, multiday packages

The Real Tom Dooley

Probably North Carolina's most famous murder case, the 1867 murder of a young Wilkes County woman named Laura Foster by her lover, Tom Dula, is known around the world because of a 1950s recording by the Kingston Trio of "The Ballad of Tom Dooley," as it has come to be known. The song was sung in the North Carolina mountains long before its emergence as a folk-revival standard; most notably, the Watauga County banjo player and balladeer Frank Profitt kept the story alive through song. Even today, almost 150 years later, the intricacies of the Dula case are debated in this area by descendants of the principal players and by neighbors who have grown up with the legend.

The story is sordid. Tom Dula was 18 years old when he enlisted in the Confederate Army, and by that time he had already been involved for several years in a romantic relationship with a woman named Ann Melton. Following the Civil War, much of which he spent as a prisoner at the notoriously ghastly Point Lookout prison in Maryland, Dula came home to Wilkes County, older but

Tom Dula, of the folk song "Tom Dooley," hailed from these parts.

apparently no wiser. He picked up where he left off with Ann Melton, by then married to another man, and at the same time started living with another local woman, Laura Foster. In one version of the story, he was seeing yet a third woman, another Melton.

The subtleties of the motives and means that led to Laura Foster's death are still subjects of hot debate, but the facts are that on May 25, 1866, Laura Foster set off from home riding her father's horse. The next day, the horse returned without her. After searchers had combed the woods and riverbanks for nearly a month, Laura Foster's body was finally discovered; she had been stabbed to death and buried in a shallow grave. When news got out that the body had been found, Dula disappeared.

Dula was caught a few weeks later in Tennessee. Back in Wilkes County, Tom Dula and Ann Melton were indicted for murder. Officials moved the trial down the mountain to nearby Iredell County, where a jury found Dula guilty; Ann Melton was acquitted. After a series of appeals and the eventual overturning of the verdict by the state supreme court, a new trial was convened, and Dula was again convicted. He was hanged on May 1, 1868, in Statesville. Historians write that even before the hanging, people in the area were singing a song with the verse, "Hang your head, Tom Dula / Hang your head and cry / You killed poor Laura Foster / And now you're bound to die."

$135-260) has grown into one of the premier roots-music events in the country. It was founded in honor of Merle Watson, the son of legendary guitarist Doc Watson. Merle, also a guitarist, died unexpectedly in 1985 in a tractor accident, cutting short an influential career. Doc Watson, who grew up in the nearby community of Deep Gap, was the festival's ceremonial host until his death in 2012, and though his absence is deeply felt by musicians and fans alike, MerleFest is as strong and successful as ever, speaking to his lasting legacy in bluegrass, roots, and Appalachian music. MerleFest draws thousands of visitors every year for many of the top-name performers in folk, country, and bluegrass music. Recent headliners have included Steep Canyon Rangers, Chatham County Line, Sam Bush, Jim Avett, The Avett Brothers (Jim's sons), and Tift Merritt. With multiple stages and dozens of artists, there's a great deal of musical variety to sample.

Springtime in the mountains can be change-ful; some years it's boiling hot and sunny at MerleFest, other times as damp and raw as winter, and sometimes it's both by turns. If you're traveling through the northern mountains during MerleFest, keep in mind that all the motels within an hour's drive of North Wilkesboro, and probably farther, will be booked solid, so be sure to reserve a room well in advance. Tenting and RV camping are available on the festival grounds. Before you pack a cooler full of adult refreshments that may be common at other music festivals, note that tobacco, alcohol, and pets are not allowed at MerleFest.

Food
North Wilkesboro's **Brushy Mountain Smokehouse and Creamery** (201 Wilkesboro Blvd., 336/667-9464, www.brushymtnsmokehouse.com, 11am-9pm Mon.-Sat., $12) is famous for its pulled pork barbecue and country sides (biscuits, fried okra, baked apples), but it's also a great ice cream shop. The ice cream is made here, and they bake their own waffle cones, so it's as fresh as it can be. Fried apple pie, cobbler, and ice cream pie are all available by the slice.

Transportation
Wilkesboro is on US-421, 30 miles east of Boone.

Union Grove
Follow Highway 901 southeast out of Wilkesboro to the little town of Union Grove, home of two great local music institutions, one a year-round venue and one an annual festival. The **Cook Shack** (Hwy. 901, 2 miles west of I-77, Union Grove, 704/539-4353, 7am-late Sat.) is a little country store and grill that has been hosting live bluegrass, old-time, and country music for more than 40 years. Owners Myles and Pal Ireland open the Cook Shack early Saturday morning for a community jam session that begins at 8am—and for musicians to get up that early on a Saturday, you know this place has to be special. There are also concerts throughout the year, including evenings midweek, so this is a great place to catch touring bands between stops in Asheville and the Triangle. Come to listen or to play, and have a burger or a livermush sandwich between tunes.

Union Grove is also one of the most important festival sites on both the old-time and bluegrass summer festival circuit. The **Fiddler's Grove Ole Time Fiddlers and Bluegrass Convention** (late May, Fiddlers Grove Campground, Union Grove, 828/478-3735, www.fiddlersgrove.com, $25 festival pass or $10 Fri., $15 Sat., $5 Sun., camping $7-15) has taken place every year on Memorial Day Weekend since 1924. Hundreds of musicians and fans come every year, camping at the festival or staying nearby, to jam with friends and hear some of the best old-time and bluegrass music you'll find anywhere.

Boone

Boone is the quintessential western North Carolina city, a blend of old and new, where proponents of homesteading and holistic living find a congenial habitat in the culture of rural Appalachia. It's also a college town, home to Appalachian State University and some 18,000 students, lending the city an invigorating youthful verve. Boone continues to grow as more people discover how amenable this part of the state is for year-round living. In recent years, the town has received a number of accolades, including being named one of the 10 Best Places to Retire by *U.S. News.*

Daniel Boone and his family inspired the name for the town. Local legend, and historical evidence, says Boone camped here several times on trips to explore the region and blaze his trail west into Tennessee and Kentucky.

Boone

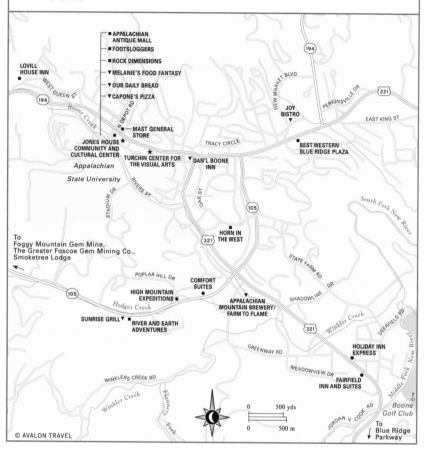

APPALACHIAN ANTIQUE MALL
FOOTSLOGGERS
ROCK DIMENSIONS
MELANIE'S FOOD FANTASY
OUR DAILY BREAD
CAPONE'S PIZZA
LOVILL HOUSE INN
WEST QUEEN ST
194
Boone Creek
N DEPOT RD
MAST GENERAL STORE
JONES HOUSE COMMUNITY AND CULTURAL CENTER
Appalachian State University
TURCHIN CENTER FOR THE VISUAL ARTS
DAN'L BOONE INN
TRACY CIRCLE
NEW MARKET BLVD
194
PERKINSVILLE DR
221
JOY BISTRO
EAST KING ST
BEST WESTERN BLUE RIDGE PLAZA
STADIUM DR
RIVERS ST
OAK ST
105
South Fork New River
To Foggy Mountain Gem Mine, The Greater Foscoe Gem Mining Co., Smoketree Lodge
321
HORN IN THE WEST
STATE FARM RD
POPLAR HILL DR
COMFORT SUITES
105
HIGH MOUNTAIN EXPEDITIONS
Hodges Creek
SHADOWLINE DR
APPALACHIAN MOUNTAIN BREWERY/ FARM TO FLAME
Winkler Creek
DEERFIELD RD
SUNRISE GRILL
RIVER AND EARTH ADVENTURES
321
GREENWAY RD
HOLIDAY INN EXPRESS
WINKLERS CREEK RD
MEADOWVIEW DR
FAIRFIELD INN AND SUITES
Middle Fork New River
Winkler Creek
Flannery Fork
0   500 yds
0   500 m
JORDAN V COOK RD
Boone Golf Club
To Blue Ridge Parkway
© AVALON TRAVEL

His nephews, Jesse and Jonathan Boone, were founders of the first church in town, Three Forks Baptist, which still stands today. *Horn in the West*, an outdoor drama running since 1952, tells the story of Daniel Boone and an interesting slice of the region's history.

SIGHTS
Turchin Center for the Visual Arts

The mountains of North Carolina are loaded with artists and art lovers. At Appalachian State University, the **Turchin Center for the Visual Arts** (432 W. King St., 828/262-3017, www.tcva.org, 10am-6pm Tues.-Thurs. and Sat., noon-8pm Fri., free) provides access to the arts for the community and visitors of Boone. The Kay Borowski Sculpture Garden displays contemporary sculpture outdoors, while six indoor galleries exhibit the Turchin's permanent collection as well as traveling exhibitions. Throughout the year, photography and drawing competitions grace gallery walls.

Jones House Community and Cultural Center

In the heart of downtown Boone, the **Jones House Community and Cultural Center**

(604 W. King St., 828/268-6280, www.joneshousecommunitycenter.org, noon-5pm Tues.-Fri., concert and event prices vary), a beautiful home built in 1908, serves as a gallery for community artists, a meeting place for area groups, and a center for Independence Day and Christmas celebrations. Outdoor summer concerts and indoor fall concerts bring in string bands, bluegrass and roots country musicians, and other mountain music acts.

ENTERTAINMENT

Appalachian Mountain Brewery (163 Boone Creek Dr., 828/263-1111, www.appalachianmountainbrewery.com, 4pm-10pm Mon., 4pm-11pm Tues.-Thurs., 3pm-11pm Fri., 1pm-11pm Sat., 1pm-10pm Sun.) is a microbrewery that's become popular with beer connoisseurs and the college crowd. They brew about three dozen beers (and a cider), some of which are seasonals. Though many love their IPAs, their dark beers—Belgian dark strong, oatmeal stout, porter, imperial stout, schwarzbier, and the like—are quite good. On any given night, some college band will set up in the corner of the main room and play for the evening. Outside there's a giant set of Jenga blocks to play with. And if you're hungry, the brewery also owns the **Farm to Flame** food truck (www.f2flame.com, at the brewery 5pm-10pm Mon.-Fri., 3pm-10pm Sat., $8-12). There's a sizable wood-fired pizza oven onboard, and it takes about 90 seconds to them to cook a pie.

Horn in the West

Boone's outdoor drama, *Horn in the West* (591 Horn in the West Dr., 828/264-2120, www.horninthewest.com, $24 adults, $16 students, $12 ages 3-12) runs every summer and is the nation's oldest Revolutionary War drama. It tells the story of early settlers and patriots in these mountains, using Daniel Boone as both character and narrator. The amphitheater is adjacent to the **Hickory Ridge Living History Museum** (828/264-2120, www.hickoryridgemuseum.com, $3, call for hours), a collection of cabins and structures that reveal life here in the late 1700s.

SHOPPING

Several antiques shops in Boone make the downtown a great place for browsing. **Appalachian Antique Mall** (631 W. King St., 828/268-9988, www.appalachianantiquemall.com, 10am-6pm Mon.-Sat. and 11am-6pm Sun. summer, 10am-5pm Mon.-Sat., noon-5pm Sun. winter) is one of the best and biggest in the area. You'll find everything from farm implements to paintings and furniture. For outdoor enthusiasts, **Footsloggers** (139 S. Depot St., 828/262-5111, www.footsloggers. com, 9:30am-5:30pm Mon.-Thurs., 9:30am-8pm Fri.-Sat., noon-5pm Sun.) has been selling gear for climbing, hiking, and camping for 40 years. They have a 40-foot climbing tower that simulates many conditions you might find while climbing the region's rock faces.

There are several branches of the **Mast General Store** (630 W. King St., 828/262-0000, www.mastgeneralstore.com, 10am-6pm Mon.-Thurs., 10am-8pm Fri.-Sat., 11am-6pm Sun.) in the Carolina High Country, but the original is in Valle Crucis (Hwy. 194, 828/963-6511, www.mastgeneralstore.com, 7am-6:30pm Mon.-Sat., noon-6pm Sun. summer, hours vary in winter), about 20 minutes west of Boone. It has been a visitor attraction for about 30 years, but its history as a community institution goes back before the 1880s. When the Mast family owned it the store had the reputation of carrying everything "from cradles to caskets," and today it still has a varied inventory, with specialties in outdoor wear (Carhartt, Columbia, Mountain Hardwear, Patagonia, Teva), camping gear, and more penny candy than a modern-day store should have.

SPORTS AND RECREATION
Rock Climbing

Rock Dimensions (139 Depot St., 828/265-3544, www.rockdimensions.com, from $65) is a guide service that leads rock climbs at gorgeous locations throughout western North Carolina and parts of Tennessee and Virginia. Guides teach proper multi-pitch, top-rope anchoring, and rappelling techniques, and they lead caving expeditions ($330 for 4 people). There's a Discovery Course (around $75), a series of towers that make up a sort of vertical playground. Think balance beams, tightrope walks, and cargo nets to traverse high above the ground. It's fun, safe, and an interesting challenge.

If you're an experienced climber, take a look at the **Boone Adventure Guide** (http://advguides.com/boone), a website that will lead you to some nice pitches and help you find places for other outdoor activities such as fly-fishing, hiking, and dog-friendly adventures.

Winter Sports

Between Boone and Blowing Rock is one of the best places to learn to ski, **Appalachian Ski Mtn.** (940 Ski Mountain Rd., Blowing Rock, 800/322-2373, www.appskimtn.com, lift tickets $28-59, rentals $11-37). Home of the French-Swiss Ski College, they've been teaching since 1969 and designing ski instructional programs (for the Special Olympics and for elite military units) ever since, so they know how to get you on your feet and on the slopes. Unlike some other mountains, at Appalachian the slopes are very beginner-friendly for both skiers and snowboarders.

Hawksnest Snow Tubing (2058 Skyland Dr., Seven Devils, 828/963-6561, www.hawksnesttubing.com, 1.5 hours $25-30, zip-lining $80-90) is on a 4,800-foot mountain in Seven Devils. It has 12 slopes dedicated to the family-friendly art of tubing, making it one of the largest snow-tubing parks on the East Coast. Throughout the year you can experience the thrill of zip-lining on more than four miles of zip lines, including two longer than 2,000 feet, at speeds up to 50 mph.

Rafting

High Mountain Expeditions (1380 Hwy. 105 S., Boone, 800/266-7238, www.highmountainexpeditions.com, $65-199) leads rafting trips on the Watauga River (Class I-III) and the much more challenging Nolichucky River (Class III-IV). They also lead caving expeditions ($75) for adults and children, for which no experience is necessary, and guided hikes ($50 adults, $40 kids) up to 10 miles long.

Gem Mining

Many people don't know that North Carolina is rich in gems and gold. Around Boone and the more heavily visited places in the mountains you'll find businesses that offer gem "mining." You don't need a pick and a shovel, just a keen eye and a few bucks. To "mine," you buy a bucket of material, graded and priced according to the likelihood of it having a valuable gem in it, and then sort, sift, and pan it yourself. You get to keep what you find, and you really can come across some beautiful specimens, some even worthy of jewelry.

River and Earth Adventures (1655 Hwy. 105, 866/411-7238, www.raftcavehike.com) offers gem mining ($15-100), while at **Foggy Mountain Gem Mine** (4416 Hwy. 105, 828/263-4367, www.foggymountaingems.com, $15-325) you can get gemstones cut and polished in-house.

Golf

Around Boone are a number of private golf courses; among the few public courses is **Boone Golf Club** (433 Fairway Dr., 828/264-8760, www.boonegolfclub.com, 18 holes, par 71, Apr.-Nov., greens fees $41-57), which has wide, forgiving fairways that are playable for all skill levels and from any tee set. Designed by Ellis Maples in the late 1950s, the course is picturesque and enjoyable to play.

ACCOMMODATIONS

The **Lovill House Inn** (404 Old Bristol Rd., 828/264-4204, www.lovillhouseinn.com, $139-209) is close to the Appalachian State University campus, and it was in the parlor of this 1875 farmhouse that the papers were drawn up that led to the founding of the university. The inn sits on 11 evergreen-shaded acres and is a lovely place to relax and read. **Carolina Mountain Lodge** (467 Whispering Hill Rd., 831/601-7820, www.carolinamountainlodge.com, $85-165) has five rooms, beds from twin to queen, and an on-call massage therapist.

The **Yonahlossee Resort** (Shulls Mill Rd., Boone, 828/963-2393, www.yonahlossee.com, $99-1,200), between Boone and Blowing Rock, is a former girls camp built in the 1920s. The resort has a big stone inn and studio cottages, a fitness center and sauna, tennis courts with a pro shop, and a 75-foot indoor heated pool. **Parkway Cabins** (599 Bamboo Heights, 828/262-3560 or 866/679-3002, www.parkwaycabins.com, $140-200) is just 5 minutes from downtown Boone and 10 minutes from Blowing Rock; it sits at 4,000 feet in elevation, providing a panoramic view of Grandfather Mountain, Beech Mountain, Seven Devils, and other peaks. Most of the cabins sleep four or more, making them perfect for mountain excursions with a group.

Among area chain motels, some good bets are **Fairfield Inn and Suites** (2060 Blowing Rock Rd., 828/268-0677, www.marriott.com, from $109), **Comfort Suites** (1184 Hwy. 105, 828/268-0099, www.choicehotels.com, from $149), and **Holiday Inn Express** (1943 Blowing Rock Rd./Hwy. 321 S., 828/264-2451, www.igh.com, from $140).

FOOD

Boone is a college town and has dining that suits both students and their visiting parents. That means three things must be done well: pizza, breakfast, and moderately priced bistro or steakhouse fare. This town delivers on all counts.

★ **Sunrise Grill** (1675 Hwy. 105, 828/262-5400, 6:30am-2pm Mon.-Fri., 7am-3pm Sat.-Sun., around $8) is widely considered the best breakfast joint in Boone. It's a regular bacon-and-eggs sort of place with some interesting omelets, tasty grits, hot coffee, and excellent specials. Those specials range from red velvet pancakes to corned beef hash to the Lonestar Benedict, which uses biscuits and gravy in lieu of English muffins and hollandaise.

The menu at **Our Daily Bread** (627 W. King St., 828-0173, www.ourdailybreadboone.com, 11am-8pm Mon.-Thurs., 11am-10pm Fri.-Sat., noon-6pm Sun., about $10) includes no fewer than 30 specialty sandwiches, from their best-selling Jamaican Turkey Sub to the Fruity Chicken Sammy—chicken salad with shredded apples, red grapes, and walnuts on a fresh croissant. Try their tempeh Reuben, a daring mixture of flavors that features marinated tempeh, sauerkraut, swiss cheese, and mustard on rye. It sounds outrageous but it works. Our Daily Bread also makes a variety of fresh soups and meat and veggie chilies every day.

Melanie's Food Fantasy (664 W. King St., 828/263-0300, www.melaniesfoodfantasy.com, 8am-2pm Mon.-Sat., 8:30am-2pm Sun.) is worth a special trip to Boone. The breakfast menu is nothing short of spectacular, with a variety of whole-grain waffles, pancakes, and French toast ($6-9); all sorts of fancy omelets (try the spinach, garlic, provolone, and swiss, $7); and enough options to keep both carnivores and vegetarians full. Lunch at Melanie's is every bit as good.

The **Dan'l Boone Inn** (130 Hardin St., 828/264-8657, http://danlbooneinn.com, hours vary, dinner $18 adults, $11 ages 9-11, $9 ages 6-8, $7 ages 4-5, free under age 4, breakfast $11 adults, $8 ages 9-11, $7 ages 6-8, $6 ages 4-5, free under age 4) serves old-time country food family style. Despite the complicated pricing system, the food is straight-up good. At breakfast you can feast on country ham and red-eye gravy, stewed apples, and grits; at dinner, there's fried chicken, country-style steak, ham biscuits, and lots of vegetable sides.

For good college-town pizza, **Capone's Pizza** (454 W. King St., 828/265-1886, http://caponesboone.com, 11am-10:30pm Mon.-Thurs., 11am-11pm Fri.-Sat., noon-10:30pm Sun., $8-22) hits the spot. The staff is funny, friendly, and they make a good pie. You can go with the standard pepperoni and cheese or go off the rails with some odd topping combinations. Try Big Joe's Buffalo Pizza, with spicy sauce, blue cheese, buffalo chicken, crumbled bacon, and red onion; it's different and delicious.

The ★ **Gamekeeper Restaurant and Bar** (3005 Shull's Mill Rd., 828/963-7400, www.gamekeeper-nc.com, bar from 5pm daily, dinner from 6pm Wed.-Sun., $24-49) is tucked away between Boone and Blowing Rock at the Yonahlossee Resort. Since opening, this restaurant has built and maintained a reputation for high-quality meals using exotic meats. It's common to see ostrich, venison, bison, boar, and the like on the frequently changing menu. Don't miss the bourbon bread pudding and white Russian cheesecake—or the seemingly endless wine list ($20-215 per bottle).

★ **Joy Bistro** (115 New Market Centre, 828/265-0500, www.joybistroboone.com, lunch 11:30am-2pm Wed.-Fri. and Sun., dinner from 5:30pm Tues.-Sun., lunch $9-14, dinner $12-35) is Southern-French cuisine—not from the south of France but rather a fusion of French techniques and Southern flavors. You'll find a lot of ingredients from local and regional food producers, such as in the baby beet salad, which uses beets from a local farmer, and the ravioli, made fresh by a local pasta maker. Standards like the filet mignon (served with Boursin cheese mashed potatoes and roasted garlic and chive compound butter) are fantastic, and dishes like the scallops au poivre or lamb loin chop deliver big flavor.

CoBo Sushi Bistro & Bar (161 Howard St., 828/386-1201, www.cobosushi.com, 5pm-10pm Mon.-Thurs., 5pm-midnight Fri., 5pm-2am Sat., $4-20) showed up in Boone to much fanfare. A hip spot for drinks and some excellent sushi, the place has been crowded since it opened. They're closed on Sundays, and to eliminate waste, they run a late-night special on Saturday starting at 11pm that uses up every available bit of fish in half-price rolls. It's a tasty bargain and smart for both the restaurant and for sushi lovers.

At ★ **Lost Province Brewing Company** (130 N. Depot St., 828/265-3506, www.lostprovince.com, 11am-10pm Mon.-Wed.,

11am-11pm Thurs.-Sat., noon-10pm Sun., $8-18) expect some fine wood-fired pizza and wood-fired everything else, for that matter. Mac and cheese, veggies, and pretzels all spend time in the giant, copper-topped, wood-fired oven. The pizzas range from expected pies to ones topped with eggs, so they're both creative and accessible. Don't forget to order a tasting flight, as their brewery is excellent. The brewer, a former toxicologist for the state of North Carolina, and the chef are twins.

TRANSPORTATION AND SERVICES

Boone sits at the junction of Highways 421 and 321. Charlotte is 2 hours south (via Hwy. 421 and I-77) and Asheville is 2 hours west (via Hwy. 321 and I-40). Blowing Rock is only 15 minutes away (south on Hwy. 321), and the Blue Ridge Parkway is a few miles closer.

AppalCart (828/297-1300, www.appalcart.com) operates a dozen free bus routes in Boone, with maps and schedules available online.

You can find all sorts of visitor information at the official site of the **Watauga County Tourism Development Authority** (www.exploreboonearea.com). You can also stop by the **High Country Host Visitor Center** (1700 Blowing Rock Rd./US-321, 828/264-1299, 9am-5pm Mon.-Sat., 9am-3pm Sun.). The **Blue Ridge National Heritage Area** (www.blueridgeheritage.com) has a great deal of traveler resources available online, covering not just Boone and the High Country, but the entirety of North Carolina's Blue Ridge Mountains.

Radio stations include **WASU** (90.5 FM) and **WQUT** (101.5 FM).

Watauga Medical Center (336 Deerfield Rd., 828/262-4100, www.apprhs.org) is a 117-bed complex with primary and specialty care.

VALLE CRUCIS

Valle Crucis traces its first recorded land sale back to the 1700s, and it doesn't appear that much has changed since then. There's a two-lane blacktop road winding through the valley now, but the shape of the hills and the sweet mountain air is much the same. This small community is known far and wide for four things: the stunning beauty of the place; The Mast Farm Inn and its restaurant, Simplicity; and the Original Mast General Store.

Valle Crucis lies about nine miles west of Boone along NC-105.

Sights

The Original Mast General Store (Hwy. 194, 828/963-6511, www.mastgeneralstore. com, 7am-6:30pm Mon.-Sat., noon-6pm Sun.) is the mother to the other iterations of this fine country store and community gathering place. Though the locations in Asheville, Boone, and several other mountain towns don't lack for charm, the original has a certain something that's hard to pin down. The building dates back to 1883; the floor has a rich patina that speaks of hundreds of thousands of boots and shoes crossing its surface; you'll find marks from axes, adzes, and saws on the floor and wallboards; and you'll see more than a few crooked door frames. It's dim in parts of the store, and it feels like a time machine slowly catching up to the present. Still, it's a working country store that's every bit as part of the community as it was when it opened. You can get work boots and some sturdy overalls, a hat and a pocketknife, and various sundries and foodstuffs that will hold you over for a couple of days until you decide to make the arduous (read: 15-minute) trek to a full-fledged grocery store. You can also pick up your mail here, grab a cup of coffee, and jaw with the clerk, the shopkeeper, or any other mail-getter or shopper who'll listen. All this, in addition to a selection of outdoor gear, toys, candy, and a few bits of tourist tchotchke.

Recreation

Down the road from the Mast General Store, **River and Earth Adventures** (1655 Hwy. 105, 866/411-7238, www.raftcavehike.com) leads all sorts of exciting trips on the water, in the woods, and in the area's deep caves. Rafting expeditions ($45-85 adults, $45-75

children) ride the French Broad River (Class III-IV) and Watauga River (Class II-III), or, for big white water, try the Watuga Gorge Ex-Stream Whitewater trip ($125, three-person minimum), which gives you more than five miles of Class III, IV, and V rapids. This trip runs spring through fall, using rafts during high water and inflatable kayaks during low water. Participants must be at least age 18. Cave trips (daily year-round, $75) meet at their Elizabethton, Tennessee, outpost, about an hour away, for a day's spelunking in Worley's Cave. Guided hiking trips are available that include all-day kids-only hikes with adult guides to free up parents who'd like a day on their own. If you're looking to hike or go rock climbing or bouldering, they offer guide services; inquire about routes and rates.

Accommodations and Food

Just across the street from the General Store is ★ **Over Yonder** (3608 Hwy. 194, 828/963-6301, www.overyondernc.com, 11am-8pm Wed.-Sat. and 11am-3pm Sun. Jan.-Mar., 11am-8pm Mon. and Wed.-Sun. Apr.-Dec. $7-17), a restaurant in the "Hard" Taylor house, a home built in 1861 with lumber milled and bricks fired on-site. Over Yonder was opened by the folks who run The Mast Farm Inn down the road, and it serves a menu of updated Appalachian cuisine that "Hard" Taylor himself would find familiar, comforting, and delicious. Menus are seasonal, so the tomato pie and tomato cobbler are strictly for summer (unless they lay aside a few cans of tomatoes), but dishes like mountain trout and pork chops are ever present.

The Mast Farm Inn (2543 Broadstone Rd., 828/963-5857, www.themastfarminn. com, $99-419) is perfectly at home in Valle Crucis. The inn has seven guest rooms, each with tastefully rustic decorations and big, comfortable beds. There are also eight cabins on the property, several of which date to the mid-1790s to 1820s. Everything here is warm wood, antiques and rustic contemporary pieces, and luxe country comfort. Mast Farm Inn has received a number of awards and nominations as a historic hotel—it's in the National Register of Historic Places—and for its restaurant, **Simplicity at the Mast Farm Inn** (828/963-5857, 5:30pm-9pm Fri.-Sat., call for seasonal specifics, á la carte around $30, four-course prix fixe $43-53). Simplicity always has a vegetarian option on the menu, and it's often hearty enough to turn the heads of carnivorous diners. They also serve dishes like crispy duck breast with fig and balsamic gastrique; smoked trout; pheasant; and a steak or chop. These bold flavors are brought to you by a husband-and-wife duo: Chef Andrew Long oversees the kitchen, while his wife, Megan, runs the farm.

BANNER ELK

Located eight miles west of Valle Crucis along NC-194 (and less than 20 miles west of Boone), Banner Elk (www.townofbannerelk. org) is one of the highest towns in the eastern United States, and as such, summers here are blissfully cool, with only the rarest of days creeping into the 80s. This mountain-top town is small, tightly knit, and, thanks to the weather and the popular ski destination of Sugar Mountain, a town on the map of more than just a few folks. Small and beautiful, it's worth the visit in any season.

If you want to do something unusual in Banner Elk, visit the town on the third weekend in October for the **Woolly Worm Festival** (www.woollyworm.com, $5 adults, $3 kids). For those of you who don't know, the woolly worm is a black-and-brown fuzzy caterpillar whose stripes foretell the winter weather with *Farmer's Almanac*-like accuracy. Festivalgoers dress as woolly worms, they check the weather against several woolly worms, have woolly worm races, and generally make merry at this street fair that attracts close to 20,000 every year.

Recreation

Sugar Mountain (1009 Sugar Mountain Dr., Banner Elk, 828/898-4521, www.skisugar. com, lift tickets $43-72 adults, $34-49 children, rentals $23-41 adults, $15-41 children) is North Carolina's largest winter resort, with 115 acres of ski slopes and 20 trails. In addition to skiing, activities on the 5,300-foot-high mountain include snow tubing, skating, and snowshoeing; in summer, the slopes are open to hikers, chairlift riders, and mountain bikers. The best bikers will go from summit to base in five exhilarating minutes. They offer lessons in skiing and snowboarding for adults and children.

snowshoeing at Sugar Mountain Resort

High Mountain Expeditions (3149 Tynecastle Hwy., Banner Elk, 828/898-9786, www.highmountainexpeditions.com) has an outpost here and one in Boone. They guide white-water trips ($65-199), caving ($75), and hiking ($50 adults, $40 kids), as well as river tubing trips on the New River ($20).

The **Greater Foscoe Gem Mining Co.** (8998 Hwy. 105, Banner Elk, 828/963-5928, www.foscoeminingco.com, $16-212) is where 24 kinds of gemstones can be found. The owner, a master goldsmith and stonecutter, will cut and polish the larger gems you find.

Accommodations and Food

Banner Elk Winery & Villa (60 Deer Run Ln., 828/898-9090, www.bannerelkwinery. com, noon-6pm daily Apr.-Dec., open until 8pm Fri. June-Aug., noon-6pm Wed.-Sun. Jan.-Mar.) was the first winery built in Avery and Watuga Counties, and they've won a few awards for their wines. Tastings ($10) are held year-round, but tours (2:30pm and 4:30pm Fri.-Sun., $12) are only from May to October. Their wines include a seyval blanc, an ice wine, and a very fruity blueberry wine. You can stay here at their **Villa** (828/260-1790, from $230), where eight rooms, each with awesome mountain views and private Jacuzzis, book up fast.

Quaint **Little Main Street Inn & Suites** (607 Main St., 828/898-6109, www.littlemainstreet.com, $70-200) has one- and two-bedroom condo-style rooms that are an excellent place to return after a day on the slopes. The **Smoketree Lodge** (11914 Hwy. 105 S., 800/422-1880, www.smoketree-lodge.com, from $75 summer, from $55 off-season) is another good choice; it's a large hotel with basic but comfortable guest rooms and efficiencies, a spacious, rustic lobby, a nice indoor pool, and saunas.

For dinner, make a reservation at **Artisanal** (1290 Dobbins Rd., 828/898-5395, www.artisanalnc.com, 5:30pm-10pm Tues.-Sun. May-Oct., prix fixe $60). It's a chic spot where reservations are recommended and business attire is acceptable, but a jacket is preferred. The menu is killer, though. Charred octopus, tuna sashimi, crab beignets, Korean-style lamb belly, and braised beef cheeks are among the seasonal offerings.

There's also **Jackalope's View** (2489 Beech Mountain Pkwy., 828/898-9004, www. archersinn.com, 5pm-10pm Fri.-Mon., $22-30), which, despite the silly name, serves some good food. Try any preparation of the trout, and ask for a recommendation of wine to accompany dinner—they have a nice bottle list and a big by-the-glass list.

BEECH MOUNTAIN

Holding the distinction of being the highest town in the eastern United States, Beech Mountain (www.beechmtn.com) stands at 5,506 feet (that's 226 feet higher than Denver if you're counting). Thanks to that elevation, fall comes early here, and some years the leaves begin to change in mid-September. The elevation also means Ski Beech Mountain Resort can get snow on the slopes early and keep it later in the season.

The town of Beech Mountain lies about seven twisty miles north of Banner Elk along NC-184.

Recreation

Ski Beech Mountain Resort (1007 Beech Mountain Pkwy., Beech Mountain, 800/438-2093, www.skibeech.com, lift tickets $50-77 adults and $40-57 ages 5-12, rentals $10-39) peaks 300 feet higher than Sugar Mountain and has 15 slopes and 10 lifts, as well as skating and snowboarding areas. In summer they shift focus to mountain bikes and disc golf, with a beautiful disc course as well as challenging downhill biking trails that range from beginner-friendly to expert. Don't miss the 5,506-foot Sky Bar, a snack and beverage spot with killer views at the summit. They also have a brewery on-site: **Beech Mountain Brewing Company** (noon-7pm Thurs.-Fri., 10am-7pm Sat., noon-6pm Sun.), in the ski village, makes a half-dozen beers in-house and serves them in their taproom.

The beers are quite good, especially after a day on the slopes.

Most folks come here for skiing, but Beech Mountain Resort offers more than just snowy fun. In summer, the green slopes are home to some outstanding mountain biking through **Magic Cycles** (828/265-2211, lift tickets $10 one trip or $35 all day; mountain bike lessons from $90, tours $30, rentals $80-120; helmet and armor $20-40). There are bike runs for beginners and expert downhill bombers, so don't be shy when it comes to riding—just know your abilities and limits and stay safe.

Emerald Outback at Beech Mountain (www.emeraldoutback.com) is a town park with more than eight miles of single- and double-track trails and gravel paths that traverse the mountain. The Oz Forest Run is an easy one-mile trail that will give you a sense of the place.

The Oz Forest Run Trail is so named because of a nearby amusement park that's only open once a year: **The Land of Oz** (1007 Beech Mountain Rd., 828/387-2000, www.landofoznc.com). The first weekend in October, they open the door for **Autumn at Oz**, where you can walk the Yellow Brick Road (made with 44,000 yellow bricks), interact with characters, explore the Munchkin Village, and even rent Dorothy's House ($555-610 with three-night minimum, $950 per week). The house sleeps four and it's a really weird place to stay—not because it isn't comfy, but because it's surrounded by a half-abandoned amusement park, giving it a creepy, Ray Bradbury-esque vibe (which also makes it incredibly fun).

Accommodations and Food

Rooms at **The Pinnacle Inn** (301 Pinnacle Inn Rd., 828/387-2231, www.thepinnacleinn. com, $65-165) are popular with skiers and mountain bikers. Located on a peak opposite the ski resort, reaching the inn requires a short drive or shuttle ride, but the rooms are nice (and affordable) and they have an indoor pool, a sauna and steam room, and a free weekend shuttle to Ski Beech.

Mile High Tavern (1003 Beech Mountain Pkwy., 828/387-4171, www.milehightavern. com, 5pm-10pm Mon.-Thurs., 11am-close Fri.-Sat., 11am-10pm Sun., $8-18) has 18 North Carolina beers on draft and an even bigger selection of bottles. Throw in pizzas, wings, burgers, and sandwiches, and you've got a winner. In winter, grab a drink and have it outside by the fire bar or stay inside for the band, the game, or the grub.

Fred's General Mercantile (501 Beech Mountain Pkwy., 828/387-4838, www.fredsgeneral.com, 7:30am-10pm daily, deli 7:30am-3pm daily) has all sorts of food, snacks, and outdoor gear (think gloves and hats, not parkas), but, most importantly, serves breakfast. **Fred's Backside Deli** (breakfast $2-7, lunch $4-10) dishes up a hot, cheap, hearty plateful. Their biscuits are awesome and will fill you up for a day of skiing.

Blowing Rock

Blowing Rock, named for a nearby geological oddity, is an old resort town filled with beautiful homes that once belonged to wealthy early-20th-century industrialists. It's a small town, but the surprising array of restaurants, cafés, and galleries make it pleasant to stroll, window-shop, and sit to enjoy an ice cream.

Aside from the Blowing Rock itself, the best thing to see in Blowing Rock is downtown. Main Street is lined with shops, galleries, and restaurants, and it's a good spot for people-watching most of the year (winter excluded). The vibe here is very relaxed, so you won't find much by way of active entertainment; for that you'll need to venture out onto the Parkway or into Boone.

SIGHTS
Blowing Rock (MP 291.9)

Many of western North Carolina's best-known attractions are geological: Chimney Rock, Linville Caverns, Mount Mitchell, and stately Grandfather Mountain. The Blowing Rock (US-321 S., 828/295-7111, www.theblowing-rock.com, hours vary, $6 adults, $1 ages 4-11, free under age 4) is a strange rock outcropping purported by *Ripley's Believe It or Not* to be the only place in the world where snow falls upward. Indeed, light objects (think handkerchiefs, leaves, hats) thrown off Blowing Rock—not allowed, by the way, to prevent the valley from filling with litter—do tend to come floating back up.

Adding to its otherworldly draw, there's a Native American legend associated with Blowing Rock. The story goes that a Chickasaw chieftain, fearful of the admiration his beautiful daughter was receiving, journeyed far to Blowing Rock, where he hoped to hide her away in the woods and keep her safe and pure. One day, the maiden spied a Cherokee warrior wandering in the valley below. Smitten by his looks, she shot an arrow in his direction, hoping he would seek her out. Soon he appeared at her home, courting her with songs of his land. They became lovers, and one day, a strange reddening sky brought the pair to the Blowing Rock. He took it as a sign that he was to return to his people in their coming time of trouble; to her it spelled the end of their love. She begged him not to go, and he was torn between staying loyal to his duties and following his heart; in his desperation he leapt from their perch into the gorge below. The young maiden prayed for him to be spared death, but it didn't work. She remained at the site, and one day the sky reddened and the now-famous winds of the John's River Gorge shifted, blowing her lover back into her arms. Since that day, a perpetual wind has blown up onto the rock from the valley below.

Moses Cone Manor (MP 294)

The Moses Cone Manor (828/295-7938, 9am-5pm daily Mar. 15-Nov., free), more commonly called Flat Top Manor, is a wonderfully crafted house, a huge and ornate mountain palace built in 1901 that was the country home of North Carolina textile baron Moses Cone. He became a leading philanthropist, and as you drive around the state, especially in the northern Piedmont, you'll notice his name on quite a few institutions. Today, the manor is the centerpiece of the Moses H. Cone Memorial Park. Appropriately, it is home to one of the Southern Highland Craft Guild (828/295-7938, www.southern-highlandguild.org, 9am-5pm daily mid-Mar.-Nov.) stores, a place to buy beautiful textiles, pottery, jewelry, furniture, and dolls handmade by some of the best craftspeople of the Appalachian Mountains.

The 3,500-acre Moses H. Cone Memorial Park is one of the Parkway's largest developed areas set up for public recreation. There are 25 miles of trails for hiking and horseback riding, a 16-acre lake stocked with trout, and

Blowing Rock

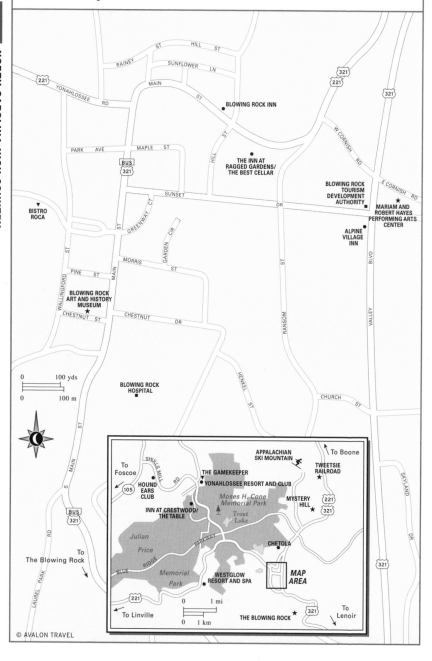

© AVALON TRAVEL

a 22-acre bass lake on the property. You can pick up a map of the trails at the manor house or the Bass Lake Entrance (on US-221). The trails here are largely old carriage roads, so they're wide, well maintained, and pretty gentle.

Julian Price Memorial Park (MP 297.1)

Julian Price Memorial Park (828/936-5911, www.recreation.gov) abuts Moses H. Cone Memorial Park, but unlike Cone, which was a family home and estate, Price was set aside as a retreat for the employees of Julian Price's insurance company. Price's death in 1946 put those plans on hold and the land was deeded to his company. His company, with the approval of his family, turned the land over to the National Park Service for inclusion in the Blue Ridge Parkway—so, in a roundabout way, Price's wish that this beautiful mountain land be used and enjoyed by his employees came to be. The park contains a 47-acre pond that was created by the damming of Boone Fork, as well as a large amphitheater, more than 100 picnic sites, **camping,** and the 13.5-mile **Tanawha Trail,** which parallels the Parkway and skirts the lower edges of Grandfather Mountain.

Blowing Rock Art and History Museum

The **Blowing Rock Art and History Museum** (159 Chestnut St., 828/295-9099, www.blowingrockmuseum.org, 10am-5pm Tues.-Wed., 10am-7pm Thurs., 10am-5pm Fri.-Sat., 1pm-5pm Sun., $8 adults, $5 over age 5, students, and military) opened in October 2011 after more than a decade of work. In addition to rotating exhibits of fine art from private collections, gallery shows by local and regional artists, and traveling exhibitions, BRAHM also has galleries with rotating exhibits displaying artifacts of historical value to the area. It's small, but the art displayed is carefully curated and of excellent quality. It's easy to spend a couple of hours here admiring the collections.

Tweetsie Railroad

Between Blowing Rock and Boone, **Tweetsie Railroad** (300 Tweetsie Railroad Rd., 828/264-9061, http://tweetsie.com, 9am-6pm Fri.-Sun. mid-Apr.-late May, 9am-6pm daily late May-mid-Aug., 9am-6pm Fri.-Sun. late Aug.-Nov., Ghost Train 7:30pm Fri. late Sept.-early Nov., $37 over age 12, $23 ages 3-12, free under age 3) is a veritable gold mine for kids who are into trains. In the park's themed

Moses Cone Manor, as seen from Bass Lake

areas, visitors can pan for gold and gems, ride midway rides, or visit a saloon, a blacksmith, and an antique photo parlor. And, of course, there's the train: The Tweetsie Railroad's steam engines, *Tweetsie* and *Yukon Queen*, circle the amusement park on a narrow-gauge track as part of a Wild West show featuring a frontier outpost and Indian attacks. The railroad isn't all fun and games—it's also partly a history lesson, as the *Tweetsie* was an actual working train in the early part of the 20th century until washed-out tracks and the advent of reliable automobiles and roads rendered it obsolete.

Mystery Hill

One little oddity in Blowing Rock is Mystery Hill (129 Mystery Hill Lane, 828/264-2794, www.mysteryhill-nc.com, 9am-8pm daily June-Aug., 9am-5pm daily Sept.-May, adults $9, seniors $8, children 5-12 $7, 4 and under free). Like Mystery Hills in other states featuring some gravitational anomaly (really, just optical illusions where rooms are built to certain scales and pitches, designed to make you think a ball rolls uphill), this one is fun, but only to a point for grown-ups. It's best for kids, which is fine, because it's fun to watch them try to figure out the mystery of Mystery Hill.

Doc's Rocks Gem Mines

Adjacent to Mystery Hill is Doc's Rocks Gem Mines (129 Mystery Hill Lane, 828/264-4499, www.docksrocks.net, 9:30am-5pm Mon.-Thurs., 9:30am-6pm Fri.-Sun.). Like other gem mines, here you'll buy a bucket of ore that they source from a variety of mines across the Blue Ridge, and then you pan and sift through it for gems and fossils. As you make your way through your bucket (buckets are $12-55), they will help you identify the stones you find. You can find all sorts of things, from a variety of fossils to gems like rubies and emeralds.

FESTIVALS AND EVENTS

Blowing Rock may be a small town, but you won't want for things to do. You won't find a free concert or wine tasting every night of the week, but the events and activities that go on here are put on well and are well attended.

The biggest event to hit Blowing Rock kicks off in spring and brings thousands of foodies to town. The Blue Ridge Wine & Food Festival (various locations, 828/295-7851, www.blueridgewinefestival.com) takes place during the second week of April. The tastings, classes, dinners, and events are held at hotels, inns, bars, and restaurants all around town. The Grand Tasting Tent is home to Taste!, a tasting event featuring some of the top restaurants and wineries in the area, and the Grand Wine Tasting. Generally running from Thursday through Sunday, it's four days of great food and drink, and many of the locals and visitors at the festival are ready to cut loose and celebrate the passing of winter and arrival of spring.

From May through mid-October, the Blowing Rock Farmers Market (4pm-6pm Thurs.) takes over Park Avenue, bringing all sorts of baked goods, artisanal cheeses, and the usual bounty of fruits and veggies. The Music on the Lawn (5:30pm-8:30pm Fri. May-Oct.) series has made The Inn at Ragged Gardens (203 Sunset Dr., 828/295-9703, www.ragged-gardens.com) a hot spot every Friday night. They have a cash bar and serve a limited menu, so get there early, find a place for your blanket, and order a bite to eat.

SHOPPING

Morning Star Gallery (1151 S. Main St., 828/295-6991, www.morningstargalleryusa.com, 10am-5pm Mon., Wed., and Fri., 11am-5pm Tues., Thurs., and Sat.) showcases fine arts and crafts by contemporary American artists, including a good number of local and regional artists. Works include blown glass, pottery and ceramics, paintings, prints, photography, and fiber arts.

At **Bolick & Traditions Pottery** (1155 Main St., 828/295-6128, www.traditionspottery.com, 10am-6pm Sun.-Thurs., 9am-7pm Fri.-Sat.) fifth- and sixth-generation potters have their own works and wares on display alongside pottery and ceramics from other local artists.

There's more than a fair share of antique stores, boutiques, and gift shops on Main Street. If you're in the market for antiques, it's hard to beat **Windwood Antiques** (1157 Main St., 828/295-9260) and **Carriage Trade Antiques** (1079 Main St., 828/295-3110), both on Main Street. **Blowing Rock Estate Jewelry & Antiques** (167 Sunset Dr., 828/295-4500) has a large and constantly changing selection of fine estate jewelry; with an eye for precious gems and heirloom pieces, this is the spot to look for a piece of stunning jewelry from past ages. **Possum Hollow Antiques** (247 Possum Hollow Rd., 828/295-3502, www.possumhollowantiques.com), just a few minutes out of downtown, specializes in antique furniture, and you can find some truly marvelous specimens.

At **Gaines Kiker Silversmith** (132 Morris St., 828/295-3992, www.gaineskikersilversmith.com, 11am-5pm Tues.-Sat.) the silver jewelry is exquisite. Gaines Kiker finds inspiration for the shapes and curves of his jewelry in the mountains around him, and his work displays a simplicity and elegance that's difficult to master.

Celeste's (1132 Main St. #1, 828/295-3481, www.celestesinteriors.com, 10am-5pm Sun.-Thurs., 10am-6pm Fri.-Sat.), a boutique offering a range of lifestyle, fashion, and home goods, was named one of *Southern Living* magazine's "Favorite Stores," and for good reason. Their selections range from whimsical to funky, but all with a touch of Southern class.

If it's a souvenir T-shirt you're looking for, try **Sunset Tee's & Hattery** (1117 Main St., 828/295-9326). They have loads of gift items from tacky to fridge-worthy, and the selection

of hats is huge. In the back of the store, everything from poker visors to baseball caps to leather stovepipe hats to bowlers and derbys are available for purchase.

RECREATION

Sky Valley Zip Tours (634 Sky Ranch Rd., Blowing Rock, 855/475-9947, www.skyvalleyziptours.com, $79) operates one of the best zip lines I've been on. Their signature zip, Big Mamma, is massive—more than 1,600 feet long and nearly 300 feet high—but one of the wildest parts of this zip line tour is the "Leap of Faith" between lines five and six, where you hook into a self-belay device and step off the edge of a 40-foot cliff. It's fun and the staff knows how to make zipping comfortable for novices and exciting for veterans.

VX3 Trail Rides (828/963-0260, www.vx-3trailrides.com, rides depart at 10am and 2pm daily, $100) offers horseback-riding outings with Tim Vines, a trail guide with decades in the saddle. Groups are small, typically a maximum of four riders (unless it's one family or group), and you need reservations at least a day in advance.

ACCOMMODATIONS AND CAMPING

The lavish 1916 Greek revival mansion of painter Elliot Daingerfield is now home to the ★ **Westglow Resort and Spa** (224 Westglow Crescent, 828/295-4463 or 800/562-0807, www.westglow.com, B&B $275-795, all-inclusive $440-725 per person/per night). In addition to the cushy guest rooms, many of which have whirlpool tubs, private decks, and views of Grandfather Mountain, the menu of spa treatments and health services befits the elegance of the surroundings. All kinds of massage and body therapy are available, as well as fitness classes, cooking and makeup lessons, and a variety of seminars in emotional well-being. Taking advantage of the spa's wonderful location, visitors can also sign up for hiking, cycling, snowshoeing, and camping trips. All guests have use of the spa facilities.

★ **Blowing Rock Inn** (788 Main St., 828/295-7921, www.blowingrockinn.com, open seasonally Apr.-early Dec., rooms $80-130, villas $129-169) has the feel of an old motor court, with rooms wrapped around a lawn and parking area, but it's been upgraded to modern standards. Just a short walk or even shorter drive to downtown, Blowing Rock Inn is both quiet and conveniently located. The inn provides free Wi-Fi, and you can add all sorts of packages to your room or villa, including a wine basket, cake, and flowers.

The **Inn at Ragged Gardens** (203 Sunset Dr., 828/295-9703, www.ragged-gardens.com, from $175) is a stone-walled and chestnut-paneled manor, a handsome and stylish turn-of-the-20th-century vacation home. The plush guest rooms feature goose-down bedding, fireplaces, and, in most rooms, balconies and whirlpool tubs. A sister property to the Inn at Ragged Gardens, the **Blowing Rock Ale House and Inn** (152 Sunset Dr., 828/414-9254, www.blowingrockalehouseandinn.com, $125-175) is a seven-room bed-and-breakfast and full-service pub. It has been in operation as a B&B since the late 1940s, once heralded as a fancy place to stay because most guest rooms had private baths. The addition of the restaurant and tavern, **Blowing Rock Brewing Co.** (828/414-9600, http://blowingrockbrewing.com, 11am-6pm daily, $14), has helped keep this long-running institution going in a new era.

Alpine Village Inn (297 Sunset Dr., 828/295-7206, www.alpine-village-inn.com, from $70), in downtown Blowing Rock, has comfortable accommodations at good rates. The guest rooms are located in the main inn and in a motel-style wing. It's a convenient location for checking out the shops and restaurants in town. Another good value is the **Cliff Dwellers Inn** (116 Lakeview Trail, 828/414-9596, www.cliffdwellers.com, from $159-215), with clean, simple guest rooms and a beautiful lakefront view.

Julian Price Memorial Park (828/936-5911, www.recreation.gov) abuts Moses H. Cone Memorial Park and has 197 **campsites** with spaces for tents and RVs. Campers can enjoy canoeing on the lake.

FOOD

★ **The Chestnut Grille** (9239 Valley Blvd., 828/414-9230, www.greenparkinn.com, from 6pm Tues.-Sun., $13-26) is in the Green Park Inn on the edge of town. The food draws inspiration from across the globe: Cuban spice-rubbed scallops, seared tuna with wasabi and soy-ginger sauce, rigatoni with chicken, lamb, steaks, pulled pork, and even tempeh grace the menu. The **Divide Tavern** (9239 Valley Blvd., 828/414-9230, www.greenparkinn.com, from 5pm daily, $8-11), also in the Green Park Inn, serves a smaller menu of pub food such as wings and other handhelds.

Storie Street Grille (1167 Main St., 828/295-7075, www.storiestreetgrille.com, 11am-3pm and 5pm-9pm daily Apr.-Dec., Wed.-Sat. Dec.-Mar., lunch $5-13, dinner $10-30) has a long lunch menu of sandwiches and main-course salads. Try the ever-elusive Monte Cristo, the salmon cake, or the bacon, brie, and apple panini. For dinner they serve a few Italian choices, grilled steak, and seafood. The vegetarian sauté, a mix of mushrooms, spinach, roasted garlic, almonds, and shallots served with smoky adobo sauce and fingerling potatoes, will satisfy even a hungry carnivore.

★ **Bistro Roca and Antlers Bar** (143 Wonderland Trail, 828/295-4008, http://bistroroca.com, 11:30am-3pm and 5pm-10pm daily, bar 11am-midnight daily, $10-30) serves hearty and creative dishes like lobster mac-and-cheese, their take on coq au vin (made with riesling instead of red wine), and a pork rib eye with goat cheese "butter" and a peach *gastrique*. An interesting note is that the Antlers Bar has been open since 1932, making it the oldest continuously serving bar in the state.

Twigs (7956 Valley Blvd., 828/295-5050, http://twigsbr.com, 5:30pm-9:30pm Tues.-Thurs. and Sun., 5:30pm-10pm Fri.-Sat., bar until 11pm Sun. and Tues.-Thurs., until 1:30am Fri.-Sat., $10-35) is popular with locals and visitors alike. It has both a casual bar and a fancier dining room, and serves popular regional dishes like shrimp and grits and mountain trout alongside more unusual fare like venison. They have about 18 wines available by the glass and another 200 by the bottle, featuring a wide selection of California wines as well as Australian, European, and Argentine choices.

Foggy Rock Eatery & Pub (8180 Valley Blvd., 828/295-7262, www.bobcatalley.com/foggyrock, 11:30am-9:30pm daily, around $15) is a sports bar with upgraded food. Seafood graces their menu, with dishes like Appalachian Fish 'n' Chips (fried catfish and waffle fries) and Trout Trout Trout (a trio of trout), and they have a good selection of sandwiches, burgers, and Philly cheesesteaks. The Notorious P.I.G.—with house-smoked pork, pulled ham, diced bacon, pepper jack cheese, and Sriracha aioli—is a fine and filling sandwich.

Roots Restaurant (7179 Valley Blvd., 828/414-9508, www.roots-restaurant.com, dinner from 5:30pm Tues.-Sun., $13-35) has a great menu filled with rich and creative takes on some classic dishes. Everything they serve has some sort of tie back to simple country food, but it's all prepared with a bent toward fine dining.

In downtown Blowing Rock, there's not much going on after 10pm, so if you're looking to grab a beer and a bite to eat a little later in the evening, your options are limited. At the north end of Main Street you'll find **The Town Tavern** (1182 Main St., 828/295-7500, www.towntavernbr.com, 11am-2am Mon.-Sat., 11am-midnight Sun., around $10). This is a sports bar, with all the wings, fried appetizers, burgers, and nachos you'd expect to find. With more than 30 bottled beers and about a dozen local brews on draft, they have a good beer selection too.

TRANSPORTATION AND SERVICES

Blowing Rock is eight miles south of Boone via US-321. You can also access Blowing Rock from US-221 and the Blue Ridge Parkway at Milepost 291.9.

You'll find all the information you need about Blowing Rock at the **visitors center** inside of the Blowing Rock Art and History Museum (159 Chestnut St., 828/295-4636, www.blowingrock.com).

The nearest hospital is the **Watauga Medical Center** (336 Deerfield Rd., Boone, 828/262-4100, www.apprhs.org).

SOUTH ALONG US-321

Pretty US-321 winds south from Blowing Rock through Happy Valley to Lenoir (in 20 miles) and Hickory (in 37 miles).

Lenoir

The seat of Caldwell County, Lenoir (pronounced "luh-NORE"), was named for General William Lenoir, a Revolutionary War hero and chronicler of the Battle of Kings Mountain. **Fort Defiance** (1792 Fort Defiance Dr./Hwy. 268, Happy Valley, 828/758-1671, www.fortdefiancenc.org, 10am-5pm Thurs.-Sat., 1pm-5pm Sun. Apr.-Oct., 10am-5pm Sat., 1pm-5pm Sun. and by appointment Nov.-Mar., $6 adults, $4 under 14), his 1792 plantation house in Happy Valley, is beautifully restored and open to visitors. Among its unusual charms are a 200-year-old oriental chestnut tree, an English boxwood garden of the same vintage, and the largest beech tree in the state.

Traditions Pottery (4443 Bolick Rd., 3 miles south of Blowing Rock, Lenoir, 828/295-5099, www.traditionspottery.com, 10am-6pm Mon.-Fri., 9am-7pm Sat., 12:30pm-6pm Sun.) is a hotbed of Piedmont and Appalachian folk traditions. The Owen-Bolick-Calhoun families trace their roots as potters back through six generations in the Sandhills community of Seagrove and here in Caldwell County. They have also become renowned old-time musicians and storytellers. In addition to ceramics with an impeccable folk pedigree, Traditions Pottery is the location of numerous music jams and kiln openings throughout the year as well as the

Jack Tales Festival in August; Glenn Bolick learned storytelling from the great Ray Hicks of Beech Mountain, a National Heritage Award winner.

Every year on Labor Day weekend in early September, Caldwell County is home to the **Historic Happy Valley Old-Time Fiddlers Convention** (828/758-9448, 3590 NC-268, Lenoir, http://happyvalleyfiddlers.org), a laid-back event in a gorgeous location, the Jones Farm. The festival includes music competitions and concerts, drawing some great traditional artists from all over the hills. Other events include a rubber duck race, demonstrations by instrument makers, tours of Fort Defiance, and visits to the grave of Laura Foster, the 1867 victim of North Carolina's most famous murderer, Tom Dooley, who happened to be a fiddler. The crime is a common theme in bluegrass and roots music death ballads. Participants and visitors can camp ($10) along the Yadkin River on the Jones Farm during the festival. No alcohol is allowed; pets are permitted as long as they're leashed.

FOOD

If you're traveling between Lenoir and Hickory on a weekend, take a detour to the little community of Dudley Shoals, where you'll find **Sims Country BBQ** (6160 Petra Mill Rd., Granite Falls, 828/396-5811, www.simscountrybbq.com, 5pm-close Fri.-Sat., all-you-can-eat buffet $12). Sims is known not only for its all-you-can-eat Texas-style barbecue, which they pit-cook all day, but for live bluegrass music and clogging (starts at 7pm). It also hosts the annual Molasses Festival on the second Saturday in October, with bluegrass, dancing, and harvest-time activities.

Hickory

The **Hickory Museum of Art** (243 3rd Ave. NE, Hickory, 828/327-8576, www.hickory-museumofart.org, 10am-4pm Tues.-Sat., 1pm-4pm Sun., free) was established in the early 1950s and was the first major museum of American art in the Southeast. Its early partnership with the National Academy of Design in New York gained it the nickname the "Southern Outpost of the National Academy." The museum has an impressive permanent collection, with special emphases on American painting, outsider and folk art, North Carolina folk pottery, and American studio pottery and glass.

One-part spectacle, one-part shopping experience, one-part North Carolina heritage, the **Hickory Furniture Mart** (2220 US-70 SE, Hickory, 828/322-3510 or 800/462-6278, www.hickoryfurniture.com, 9am-6pm Mon.-Sat.) houses more than 100 factory outlets, stores, and galleries representing more than 1,000 furniture and home accessories manufacturers. It's a draw for designers, shop owners, and those looking for a serious redecoration project; the spectacle of the four-level showroom is amazing.

The Catawba Valley is an important place for North Carolina folk pottery, with a tradition all its own dating back to the early-19th-century potter Daniel Seagle and exemplified in modern times by the late Burlon Craig, one of the giants of Southern folk art, and contemporary master Kim Ellington. Hickory's annual **Catawba Valley Pottery and Antiques Festival** (Hickory Convention Center, 828/324-7294, www.catawbavalley-potteryfestival.org, late Mar., $6 adults, $2 children) brings together more than 100 potters and dealers in pottery and antiques. It's a great introduction to Southern folk pottery, and the covetable wares are dangerous if you're on a budget.

The **Hickory Crawdads** (828/322-3000, www.hickorycrawdads.com) baseball team is a Class A affiliate of the Texas Rangers. They were the 2015 South Atlantic League champions, and they play at the modern Frans Stadium (2500 Clement Blvd. NW, Hickory), where you may meet the mascot, Conrad the Crawdad.

Golfers may want to stop at **Hampton Heights Golf Course** (1700 5th St. NE, Hickory, 828/328-5010, 18 holes, par 72, greens fees 18 holes, weekdays $21 with cart or $15 to walk, weekends $27 with cart or $18 to walk, 9 holes weekdays $15 with cart or $10 to walk, $15 walk or ride weekends) for a round. The fairways aren't judiciously wide, but they are forgiving enough to help you keep a shanked shot or two in play. The greens can vary from hole to hole, so judging putting speed can be difficult at times.

FOOD

★ **Highland Avenue** (883 Highland Ave. SE, Hickory, 828/267-9800, www.highlandavenuerestaurant.com, dinner 5pm Mon.-Sat. $12-23) serves the best food in Hickory. The philosophy of the restaurant revolves around using the freshest ingredients available from local sources. The menu does change, but the staples—shrimp and grits, pork shoulder, and the burger—are consistently delicious. Chef Kyle McKnight does an amazing job making his own charcuterie, so a plate of cured meats is a must. Since it opened, Highland Avenue has garnered a stack of accolades, including being named to a list of must-dine restaurants by *Our State Magazine* and being called one of "The South's Best Restaurants 2015" by *Southern Living*.

Highland Avenue is in an old hosiery mill, a relic from Hickory's recent past, and downstairs is a brewpub, **American Honor Ale House & Brewing** (883 Highland Ave. SE, Hickory, 828/855-9999, www.americanhonoralehouse.com, 11am-close daily, $8-14). The menu, designed by Chef McKnight, consists of burgers and sandwiches (try the flounder sandwich), as well as wings, pretzels, and other pub bites. The brewery is tied to Blowing Rock Brewery in Blowing Rock; they make 19 different brews, though some of the best are seasonal.

MORGANTON

Morganton, a charming but often overlooked town on I-40, is actually a vibrant little community with an active arts scene, a handful of good restaurants, and a budding wine industry.

Sights

The **Hamilton Williams Gallery** (403 E. Union St., 828/438-1595, www.hamiltonwilliams.com, 10am-6pm Mon.-Fri., 10am-5pm Sat.) started as a studio and gallery for potter Hamilton Williams, but he realized the space he was renovating—a 100-year old warehouse and storefront—had enough room for a big gallery where he could sell his work and display works by dozens of other artists. You'll find pottery, jewelry, sculpture, and textiles in this bright, inviting gallery. **Signature Studio and Gallery** (106 W. Union St., 828/437-6095, 10am-4pm Tues.-Sat.) is an active art studio and gallery dedicated to serving the creative-expression needs of and providing learning opportunities for adults with intellectual and developmental disabilities. The work is incredible, and many of the resident artists have shown nationally and internationally.

Along a 30-mile stretch of I-40 east and west of Morganton is the **Catawba Valley Wine Trail** (www.catawbavalleywinetrail.com). A recent and growing addition to North Carolina's vineyard and winery population, there are five wineries to visit, each making wine in different styles and geared toward different palates. I found **Silver Fork Winery** (5000 Patton Rd., off I-40 exit 94, 828/391-8783, www.silverforkwinery.com, noon-7pm Wed.-Fri., noon-6pm Sat.-Sun.) to have a beautiful tasting room. The cabernet sauvignon is especially nice, as is their rosé. Taste a few and pick your favorite bottle, then enjoy it on their shaded patio or stick around for a movie or some live music in the summer months.

Morganton's **Fonta Flora Brewery** (317 N. Green St., 828/475-0153, www.fontaflora.com, 5pm-10pm Mon. and Thurs.-Fri., 5pm-9pm Wed., 3pm-10pm Sat., noon-7pm Sun., closed Tues.) creates some outstanding beers from their little brewery in downtown Morganton. Fonta Flora brews a number of saisons and they get pretty creative with the ingredients they use; don't be surprised if you find miso, beets, pine needles, or rye giving your pint a flavor boost. IPA fans will want to try their Hop Beard Mountain Man IPA, while porter lovers should try whatever iteration is on tap.

★ BROWN MOUNTAIN LIGHTS

One of North Carolina's most enduring mysteries are the **Brown Mountain Lights.** These mysterious orbs are seen floating in the air on some evenings around Brown Mountain, along the Burke County-Caldwell County line. A number of official agencies have studied the phenomenon, and the U.S. Geological Survey determined the orbs may be the reflection of the headlights of cars and trains in the valley below, completely ignoring the fact that the lights have been seen since at least 1833. The Brown Mountain Lights are believed by many to be supernatural. One legend, related in the song "Brown Mountain Lights," says the lights are the lanterns of a hunter lost in these woods and the dutiful slave who lost his life searching for his master.

I'd heard about the lights for years and I'd had several conversations with the director of Burke County Tourism about them; on one visit to Morganton, he and I headed up to the overlook. After 45 minutes of conversation, we saw a light. At first we dismissed it, thinking we didn't really see anything, but then it appeared again and we watched first one light and then two traverse the mountain for the next 30 minutes. Neither of us are sure what we saw, except to say we saw the Brown Mountain Lights. If you want to look for them, try a clear evening in the summer, right around dusk.

Ghost fanciers will be delighted to know that the Brown Mountain Lights can be observed by visitors from the Lost Cove overlook on the southeast side of the Blue Ridge Parkway (near Milepost 310), but an even better place to see them is at a **marked turnout along NC-181,** about 20 miles north of Morganton. The parking area gives you plenty of space to set up a chair and a tripod for your camera so you can get comfy while you wait for the lights to make an appearance.

Recreation

Quaker Meadows (826 N. Green St., 828/437-2677, www.qmgolf.com, 18 holes, par 71, greens fees $21-33, includes cart) has been challenging golfers with numerous water hazards and sloping greens since the 1960s. It is a pretty course, and its history is quite interesting: The "Over Mountain Boys" met here in

Take in the view from the Brown Mountain overlook.

1780 before marching to Kings Mountain, a key battle in the Revolutionary War.

At **The Beanstalk Journey Zip Line** (701 Sanford Ave., 828/430-3440, www. thebeanstalkjourney.com, 10am-4pm Tues.-Sun.) you can go zip-lining ($40-65), challenge the climbing tower ($19 one hour), and test your nerves on the Quickjump ($17). Beanstalk is located inside Catawba Meadows Park, where you'll find a disc golf course, picnic shelters, baseball fields, sand volleyball courts, playgrounds, and several miles of the 4.8-mile Catawba River Greenway Trail.

SOUTH MOUNTAINS STATE PARK

Between Hickory and Morganton, outside the town of Connelly Springs, is one of the state's most rugged recreational areas, **South Mountains State Park** (3001 South Mountain Park Ave., Connelly Springs, 828/433-4772, http://ncparks.gov, office 8am-5pm daily, park 7am-7pm Dec.-Feb., 7am-9pm Mar.-Apr. and Oct., 7am-10pm May-Sept., 7am-8pm Nov.), rising to elevations of 3,000 feet. One trail follows the Jacob Fork River to the top of 80-foot-tall High Shoals Falls. Another 0.75-mile trail travels along the lower reaches of Jacob Fork and is wheelchair-accessible. There are 17 miles of strenuous mountain-biking trails. Hike-in **campsites** ($10-22) are located in various spots throughout the park 0.5-5.5 miles from the Jacob Fork parking area. Pit toilets are located near campsites, but all supplies and water must be packed in.

Food

For such a small town, dining in Morganton is surprisingly good. **Wisteria Southern Gastropub** (108 E. Meeting St., 828/475-6200, http://wisteriagastropub.com, dinner 5pm-10pm Tues.-Sun., brunch 11:30am-3pm Sat.-Sun., pub opens at 5pm Tues.-Sun., dinner $9-24, brunch $6-10, pub $5-12) has been making waves with their seasonal menus and quality preparations. It's a cozy place, serving familiar dishes that have been turned up a notch. The trout cakes and deviled eggs three ways are twists on classics, as are the scotch eggs and the chicken and waffles.

★ **Root and Vine** (139 W. Union St., 828/433-1540, http://rootandvinerestaurant. com, lunch 11am-2:30pm Tues.-Sat., dinner 5pm-9:30pm Mon.-Sat., lunch $8-10, dinner $17-30) is a hip, slightly more upscale place than other venues in Morganton. The menu changes with some frequency, but entrées are grilled on a wood fire and draw on all sorts of culinary inspiration: vindaloo curry with shrimp, scallops, mussels, or organic tofu; grilled North Carolina mountain trout served with tasso ham gravy and collard greens; and the seared duck breast with pork belly and an orange-raspberry coulis. The cocktails are good, and their wine list is well done for a restaurant this size. When the weather is mild, take your dinner on the patio and dine alfresco.

Along the Blue Ridge Parkway

The **Blue Ridge Parkway** (828/298-0398, www.blueridgeparkway.org) is a stunning bit of roadway, especially south of Boone. There are a number of sights on and near this stretch of the Parkway, including plenty of places to pull off for pictures or exploration, and marked trails meander up and down the mountain and into thick woods, rocky coves, and waterfalls. Stop at the wide spots in the road to photograph a tree in a field, a herd of cows grazing, a trail wandering into the shadows of the trees, or the mountains marching off into the distance.

LINN COVE VIADUCT (MP 304.4)

One of the most iconic spots along the Blue Ridge Parkway, the **Linn Cove Viaduct**

(Blue Ridge Parkway MP 304.4) is a bridge-like structure hanging from the side of the mountain in a dizzying S-curve. At nearly 1,300 feet long, this amazing feat of engineering makes you feel like you might just fly off into space if you lose focus. A pair of viewing areas about 0.25 miles from either end of the viaduct give you the chance to stretch your legs and snap a few pictures of this amazing part of the road.

Grandfather Mountain looming above offers great photo opportunities, as does the road itself when it ducks back into one deep cove and emerges on the side of the mountain opposite, snaking away into the trees. The sight of this lifelike concrete and asphalt peeking out from the trees and following the contours of the mountains is enough to take your breath away.

Linn Cove Viaduct Visitors Center

The story of the viaduct is a long one, but one well told at the **Linn Cove Viaduct Visitors Center** (828/733-1354, 9am-5pm daily May-Oct.). It was the last piece of the Parkway to be completed, and upon its completion on September 11, 1987, 52 years after construction began on this jewel of a road,

the route from the Shenandoah Valley to the Great Smoky Mountains was whole. What caused the delay? One reason was the route. Hugh Morton, the owner of Grandfather Mountain, wasn't fond of the proposed site of the Parkway, which would have climbed much higher up the side of Grandfather Mountain. After the Parkway route was settled at a lower elevation, Morton donated land to the National Park Service, and all that was left was the engineering.

★ GRANDFATHER MOUNTAIN (MP 305)

Grandfather Mountain (US-221, 2 miles north of Linville, 828/733-4337, www.grandfather.com, 8am-7pm daily summer, 9am-6pm daily spring and fall, 9am-5pm daily winter, weather permitting, $20 adults, $18 over age 60, $9 ages 4-12, free under age 5), at a lofty 5,964 feet, is not the highest mountain in North Carolina, but it is one of the most beautiful. The highest peak in the Blue Ridge Mountains (the only peak higher, Mount Mitchell, is in the Black Mountains), Grandfather is a United Nations-designated biosphere reserve. Privately owned for decades though open to the public, Grandfather Mountain has remained a great expanse of

Mile High Swinging Bridge at Grandfather Mountain

deep forests containing abundant wildlife and many hiking trails.

Sights

The main attraction is the summit and the Mile High Swinging Bridge. It is indeed a mile high, and it swings a little in the breeze, but it should be called the "Singing Bridge" because of the somewhat unnerving sound of the constant wind through the steel cables holding it in place. The view from Grandfather Mountain is stunning, and the peak is easily accessible via the scenic road that traces the skyward mile. From the parking lot just below the summit, you can access a number of trails (open during park hours only) that lead to nearby peaks, under the crest of Grandfather, and along nearby ridgelines.

The Mile High Swinging Bridge seems a lot scarier than it really is, despite its fearsome name—the bridge, while it is a mile above sea level, isn't really that high. Connecting a pair of sub-peaks of the mountain, it's at best 60 feet high. That said, with the giant views all around and the dizzying distance to the valley floor below, some visitors find themselves more than a little nervous when it comes time to cross the bridge. If you find that the bridge is a little much for you, don't sweat it, just take in the impressive view from the parking lot and spend some time at the other attractions on Grandfather Mountain. The Wildlife Habitats are always popular. Here, large enclosures provide a place for white-tailed deer, eagles, river otters, black bear, and cougars to live. Daily feedings draw the animals out of their secret places in each enclosure and bring them into view.

Hiking

Aside from the view, many come to Grandfather Mountain for the hiking. There are a few short hikes along the drive to the top, and more hikes that will test your stamina and mettle as your climb to the true summit of Grandfather Mountain. At the Grandfather Mountain Picnic Area, the 0.4-mile Woods Walk trail leads you

on an easy walk through the forest on the lower flanks of the mountain; it's gentle on the youngest and oldest visitors. Near the Swinging Bridge, park in the Trails parking area and hike the Bridge Trail, another 0.4-mile winding trail that takes you under the Swinging Bridge.

BEACON HEIGHTS (MP 305.2)

Beacon Heights (Blue Ridge Parkway MP 305.2) sits on the edge of Grandfather Mountain, affording you a fabulous view of the slope and one of the peaks of Grandfather as the Parkway sweeps around the massif. The Grandfather Mountain view is from the parking area, but a spectacular view of the lands south of the Parkway can be had at the actual Beacon Heights—a rocky escarpment reached by a short, strenuous, trail that departs from the parking lot.

Hiking

BEACON HEIGHTS TRAIL

Distance: 0.2 miles out and back
Duration: 30 minutes
Elevation gain: 300 feet
Difficulty: moderate
Trailhead: Beacon Heights parking area at MP 305.2
This trail is short and often in a state of disrepair, making for some rocky footing nearly the whole way. The reward, though, are the excellent views sweeping from the southeast to the northeast as the trail emerges onto a rocky bluff.

LINVILLE AND VICINITY

Linville's Eseeola Lodge (175 Linville Ave., 800/742-6717, www.eseeola.com, from $289) has been in the business of luxury mountain vacations for more than 100 years. The first lodge was built in the 1890s; after the original lodge burned down, it was replaced by the present lodge. Today, Eseeola Lodge offers a complex but splendid array of lodging packages, with breakfast and dinner at the lodge's restaurant included, and depending on your predilections, tee times at the on-site Linville Golf Club, spa services, and even croquet lessons.

In 1924, Donald Ross was engaged to build the championship golf course now known as the **Linville Golf Club** (18 holes, par 72, greens fees $125, same-day replay $63). The greens here are small and difficult, requiring excellent approach play and patience. *Golfweek* magazine called the par-4 number 3 one of the "Greatest 100 Holes in Golf," and named Linville one of the best courses you can play in North Carolina.

Linville is located less than two miles north of the Parkway, off Roseboro Road.

Crossnore Weaving Room

Since the early 1920s, the master weavers of the **Crossnore Weaving Room** (Crossnore School, 100 DAR Dr., Crossnore, 828/733-4660, www.crossnoreweavers.org, 9am-5pm Mon.-Sat.) have produced beautiful textiles—afghans, rugs and runners, baby blankets, and scarves—that they've sold to benefit the Crossnore School. Founded in the 1910s for orphaned and disadvantaged children, the Crossnore School is today a children's home for western North Carolina kids who have no guardians, and for some local children who live with their families but whose educational needs are best served by the structure that the school offers. The fame of the weaving room is much more than a fund-raising program. The skills of the Crossnore Weavers are highly regarded, and the sales gallery is an essential stop for anyone interested in North Carolina's fine crafts.

From Linville, follow US-221 south for six miles to the town of Crossnore.

LINVILLE FALLS (MP 316)

Linville Falls (Blue Ridge Parkway MP 316) is one of the most-photographed places in North Carolina—a spectacular series of cataracts that fall crashing into the gorge. It can be seen from several short trails that depart from the **Linville Falls Visitors Center** (Blue Ridge Parkway MP 316, 828/765-1045, 9am-5pm daily Apr. 25-Nov. 2).

Linville Gorge

The deepest gorge in the United States, **Linville Gorge** is located near Blue Ridge Parkway Milepost 316 in a 12,000-acre federally designated Wilderness Area. It's genuine wilderness, and some of the hollers in this preserve are so remote that they still shelter virgin forests—a rarity even in these wild mountains. Linville Gorge has some great climbing spots, including Table Rock, parts of which are popular with beginning climbers and other parts of which should only be attempted by experts. Other extremely strenuous options are the Hawksbill cliff face and Sitting Bear rock pillar. Speak to the folks at the visitors center or at **Fox Mountain Guides** (3228 Asheville Hwy., Pisgah Forest, 888/284-8433, www.foxmountainguides.com), a Hendersonville-area service that leads climbs in the gorge, to determine which of Linville Gorge's many climbing faces would be best suited to your skill level.

Linville Caverns

A complete visit to the Blue Ridge Mountains includes more than looking at their outsides: **Linville Caverns** (US-221, between Linville and Marion, 3 miles south of MP 317, 800/419-0540, www.linvillecaverns.com, 9am-4:30pm daily Mar. and Nov., 9am-5pm daily Apr.-May and Sept.-Oct., 9am-6pm daily June-Aug., 9am-4:30pm Sat.-Sun. Dec.-Feb., $7.50 adults, $6.50 over age 61, $5.50 ages 5-12) is one of the venerable underground attractions of the Southern mountains. The natural limestone caverns feature all sorts of strange rock formations, underground trout streams, and, of course, a gift shop. Don't worry if you're mildly claustrophobic; the caverns are much bigger than you might think.

Hiking
LINVILLE FALLS TRAIL

Distance: 2 miles out and back
Duration: 1-1.5 hours
Elevation gain: 300 feet
Difficulty: easy to moderate
Trailhead: Linville Falls Visitors Center

There are three overlooks providing the best views of Linville Falls and the Linville Gorge from the west side. This trail will lead you to all three. For the most part, this trail is easy, though if you're speed hiking it, the steep parts can be a little challenging, and there is a section of the trail that's often wet; for those reasons, it's a moderate rather than easy hike.

From the Visitors Center, cross the bridge over the Linville River and along a parallel path. A little less than 0.5 miles in, you'll come to an intersection with a sign directing you to turn left for Upper Falls and right for the other views. Turn left and take the short spur trail to an overlook at the falls. Here, the drop is small—only 15 feet—but the pool below is huge, and you can feel the power of the water rushing toward the bigger drop just downstream.

Rejoin the main trail and follow it for another 0.1 miles, then turn left again to descend some steep, often wet, steps to Chimney View, where you'll have a great look at the whole falls. Many people find this to be their "picture postcard" view, and it's good, but I prefer the vista at **Erwin's View.** To get there, head back up the steps and climb into the piney woods. The trail dead-ends at Erwin's View, where a set of steps and platforms leads to views of the gorge from several spots and then a massive view of the gorge, river, and falls that truly shows the size of this place. When you're done, head back.

Golf

Linville Falls Golf Club (210 Blue Ridge Dr., off US-221, 6 miles south of Linville Falls, www.linvillefallsgolfclub.com, 828/756-4653, 18 holes, par 71, greens fees $35 Mon.-Thurs., $39 Fri.-Sun.) features a few water hazards, but none like its namesake waterfall. Golf legend Lee Trevino designed this course, which opened for play in 1995, to have firm, fast fairways that make the course play shorter than it actually is, a rarity for mountain courses. The placement of water hazards on some holes make aggressive play

both risky and very rewarding if your ball placement is extremely accurate.

Camping and Food

The National Park Service operates the **Linville Falls Campground** (Blue Ridge Parkway MP 316.3, 828/765-2681, www.linevillefalls.com, $20) near the falls. Tent and RV sites are interspersed, and water and flush toilets are available May-October.

Famous Louise's Rockhouse Restaurant (23175 Rockhouse Lane, Linville Falls, near Blue Ridge Parkway MP 321, 828/765-2702, 6am-8pm daily), built in 1936 with stones taken from the Linville River, is not a large restaurant, but the dining room is spread out over three counties: The lines of Burke, McDowell, and Avery Counties meet on this exact spot, and customers, for reasons of loyalty or legality, often have preferences about where to take their repast. Famous Louise's is owned by a mother and daughter, and Louise, the mom, is a cook of some renown. The fare is traditional and homemade—the pimento cheese is mixed here, the corn bread and biscuits are whipped up from scratch, and the pot roast stewed at a leisurely simmer. On your way out, pick up a jar or two of Louise's homemade berry jams, probably the best $3 souvenirs to be found in the mountains. You'll find them in the Avery County part of the restaurant.

ORCHARD AT ALTAPASS (MP 328)

At Milepost 328 on the Blue Ridge Parkway, the **Orchard at Altapass** (1025 Orchard Rd., Spruce Pine, 888/765-9531, www.altapassorchard.org, 10am-6pm daily Sept. 13-Nov. 1, 10am-5:30pm Mon. and Wed.-Sat. and noon-5:30 Sun. May-Sept. 12) is much more than an orchard, although it does produce apples in abundance. The land on which the orchard grows has been settled since the 1790s, when Charlie "Cove" McKinney and his large family lived here. McKinney had four wives—at the same time—who bore him 30 sons and a dozen daughters. An early chronicler of local history wrote that the four wives "never had no words bout his havin so many womin. If it ware these times thar would be har pulled." Many of the McKinneys are buried on the mountain. Around the turn of the 20th century, the land became an orchard, and in its best years produced 125,000 bushels of apples. To get a sense of how many apples that would have been, consider that today's standard for a bushel of apples is 48 pounds.

Today, the Orchard at Altapass continues to turn out wonderful apples. It is also a favorite music venue in this region. Country, bluegrass, old-time, and gospel musicians as well as artists in a variety of other styles perform at the orchard on the weekend. There is a staggering amount of musical talent in these mountains, and the Orchard at Altapass is a showcase of local treasures.

MUSEUM OF NORTH CAROLINA MINERALS (MP 331)

The mountains around here are absolutely packed with minerals and gems; in fact, they're some of the richest in the nation. The Museum of North Carolina Minerals (214 Parkway Maintenance Rd., Spruce Pine, at MP 331 and NC-226, 828/765-2761, 9am-5pm daily year-round, free) displays more than 300 types of minerals and gems found in the vicinity. You can also view interactive displays on mining and exhibits outlining the geological processes that put rubies, emeralds, and other precious and semiprecious gems in the ground here.

★ PENLAND SCHOOL OF CRAFTS

In the 1920s, Lucy Morgan, a teacher at a local Episcopal school, and her brother embarked on a mission to help the women of the North Carolina mountains gain some hand in their own economic well-being. Equipping several households in the Penland area with looms, they touched off a local cottage industry in weaving, which quickly centralized and grew into the Penland School, a center for craft instruction and production. Several "folk schools" sprouted in the southern Appalachians in that era, most of them the projects of idealistic Northerners wanting to aid the benighted mountaineers. The Penland School, however, has the distinction of being one of the few such institutions that was truly homegrown, as Miss Lucy was herself a child of the rural Carolina highlands.

Today, the Penland School of Crafts (off Blue Ridge Parkway MP 331, 67 Doras Trail, Bakersville, 828/765-2359, www.penland.org) is an arts instruction center of international renown. More than 1,000 people, from beginners to professionals, enroll in Penland's one-, two-, and eight-week courses every year to learn about crafts in many different media. Tours of the campus (Tues. and Thurs. Apr.-Dec., reservations required) are available, and the school operates a beautiful shop, the Penland Gallery (Conley Ridge Rd., 828/765-6211, www.penland.org, 10am-5pm Tues.-Sat., noon-5pm Sun.), where the work of many of the school's instructors and students can be purchased.

LITTLE SWITZERLAND (MP 334)

Little Switzerland earned its name thanks to the views of the surrounding mountains and deep valleys, which are reminiscent, many say, of the foothills of the Swiss Alps. The mountains around here have been mined for years— millennia, if some archaeological findings are correct. Mica, that shiny stone, is found here in abundance, and there's evidence to suggest that Native Americans mined for it here some 2,000 years ago. Hernando de Soto is thought to have visited the area around 1540, searching for gold and silver but finding mica instead. Mica was mined here during the Civil War and Reconstruction. In 1895, emerald mining began. Soon Tiffany's and the American Gem & Pearl Company had a large mine here. That mine is abandoned today, but gem hunters and rock hounds still find their way inside to see what they can find. And for good reason:

One of the emerald mines at Emerald Village.

In addition to mica and emeralds, mines nearby have produced aquamarine, beryl, garnet, kyanite, and smoky quartz.

History

Little Switzerland was founded in 1910 by Heriot Clarkson, a North Carolina Supreme Court justice and powerful member of the state's Democratic Party. Clarkson held some despicable beliefs that informed the creation of this town, which he saw as a "whites only" village. Thankfully the town has shed this ugly part of its past, but the powerful personality of Clarkson influenced the development of both the town and the Blue Ridge Parkway. Proposed routes had the Parkway detouring to Tennessee near Linville, though some continued along the present-day route. After the route through North Carolina was settled, Clarkson, one of the largest landholders in town, was appalled at the acreage that the National Park Service was seeking. He hired several lawyers and fought for a higher price for his land, getting $575 per acre, nearly 10 times the average paid for land elsewhere. His demands also included an interchange at the Switzerland Inn and a very narrow right-of-way. Luckily, Little Switzerland has shaken off the avarice and ill-informed biases of its founders and embraces both the Blue Ridge Parkway and anyone who chooses to travel any part of its length.

Sights

Emerald Village (331 McKinney Mine Rd., Spruce Pine, 800/765-6463, www.emerald-village.com, 10am-4pm daily Apr., 9am-5pm daily May and Sept.-Oct., 9am-6pm daily Memorial Day-Labor Day, free), a can't-miss collection of gem mines and historical attractions, tells the story of Little Switzerland's long mining history. Emerald Village has seven mines to explore, the **North Carolina Mining Museum** (a self-guided underground mine tour, $7 adults, $6 seniors, $5 students), and gem mining, gold panning, and dig-your-own emeralds. The very unusual Black Light Mine Tour ($10-15) is held on select Saturday evenings. This tour is wild, as the minerals shine with otherworldly glow when viewed under the black light.

Hiking

An easy hike leads to the pretty **Grassy Creek Waterfall** (trailhead on Grassy Creek Falls Rd., off Chestnut Grove Church Rd. after it passes under the Parkway). Park before the "No Parking Beyond This Point" sign and follow the road about 0.6 miles, then turn at the sign and go another 0.3 miles to the 30-foot falls. It's mossy and lush, and when there's been rain, the thin sheets of water flowing over the falls are quite lovely.

Accommodations and Food

The ★ **Switzerland Inn** (86 High Ridge Rd., Little Switzerland, 800/654-4026, www.switzerlandinn.com, $69-230) opened in 1910 and still serves travelers with accommodations ranging from The Diamondback Motorcycle Lodge (a collection of eight rooms and a central living area catering to motorcyclists) to the luxurious Heidi and Alpine Suites. There are two restaurants on site, the **Fowl Play Pub** (hours vary by season, entrées around $12) and the **Chalet Restaurant** (serving breakfast, lunch, and dinner year-round, hours vary by season, breakfast and lunch under $15, dinner around $18), that dish up some tasty food from pub grub to more refined fine-dining dishes. This inn is simply stunning, so if you want to stay at a place with fabulous views, make reservations early.

Big Lynn Lodge (10860 NC-226A, Little Switzerland, 828/654-5232, www.biglynn-lodge.com, $105-169) is another fixture in the Little Switzerland lodging community. It started 75 years ago with a collection of cabins on a dahlia farm and has grown into a 42-room lodge. Rooms include breakfast and dinner, and it really is a charming little spot to stay.

The **Switzerland Café** (Blue Ridge Parkway MP 334, 9440 NC-226A, Little Switzerland, 828/765-5289, www.switzerlandcafe.com, 11am-4pm daily mid-Apr.-Oct., under $12) is a combination restaurant and general store, so you can pick up everything from a barbecue sandwich to a souvenir T-shirt. Most of their food is smokehouse inspired, and their trout is surprisingly good.

In nearby Spruce Pine is ★ **knife & fork** (61 Locust St., Spruce Pine, 828/765-1511, www.knifeandforknc.com, lunch 11:30am-3pm Tues.-Fri., dinner 5:30pm-9pm Tues.-Fri. and 5pm-9pm Sat., brunch 10:30am-3pm Sun., lunch $4-18, dinner $4-28, brunch $6-16), one of the best restaurants in North Carolina. This is New Appalachian Cuisine at its best. Chef Nate Allen forages for and grows forgotten ingredients like morels, ramps, tuber rose, day lily, chicory, wild grapes, and more. The Trout Marrow is a dish that's incredibly flavorful and shows a mastery of technique and creative flair you don't find often. This spot is decidedly upscale but totally accessible, and it takes a look at the past of Appalachian food while bringing it into the present.

CRABTREE FALLS (MP 339.5)

Crabtree Meadows Recreation Area is a small recreation area—only 253 acres—but it's quite scenic. One of the best waterfalls on the Parkway is here, the 70-foot **Crabtree Falls,** easily accessible via a 2.5-mile trail.

Hiking

CRABTREE FALLS TRAIL

Distance: 2.5-mile loop
Duration: 1.5-2 hours
Elevation gain: 480 feet
Difficulty: moderate
Trailhead: Crabtree Meadows Campground at MP 339.5

At the parking area is a trailhead sign and a short spur trail leading to the loop. Once at the loop, turn right and wind your way into a shady cove and down some steep stone steps. You'll cross a bridge that's dry most of the time, but can be wet and slick if the falls are raging or if it's rained recently. When you cross the bridge, you'll find that the trail has become a bit rougher and you can hear the falls not far off.

The trail goes through several switchbacks, rock steps, and damp areas before you reach the falls. At the base of the 70-foot falls there's a bridge with benches, a great spot to sit and look. These falls are particularly photogenic, thanks in no small part to the strange little "island" below the falls. Take shots from the left or right for foolproof angles.

Continuing on the loop, just beyond the falls is the hardest part of the hike—a 200-foot elevation gain in less than a quarter mile. Climb up and catch your breath at the bench on top before heading out. The next section is a long set of stairs that lead to the ridge above.

Follow the ridge for a little ways until you arrive at a rocky outcrop with a handrail. You can see the falls from here, barely, but to do so, you have to lean out past the rail, so don't bother. Continue along the trail and begin to descend, crossing a couple of streams as you do. Soon you'll see a trail and sign at an intersection. This leads to the campground, so continue on down the trail and you'll soon find the place where the trail from the parking area meets the loop.

Camping

Crabtree Falls is home to a great **campground** (877/444-6777, www.recreation.gov, $19/night), with close to 100 tent and RV sites.

★ MOUNT MITCHELL STATE PARK (MP 355.3)

At 6,684 feet, **Mount Mitchell** (accessible from Blue Ridge Parkway MP 355.3, near Burnsville, 828/675-4611, http://ncparks.gov) is the highest mountain east of South Dakota. It is the pinnacle of the Black Mountain range, a 15-mile-long J-shaped ridge that was formerly considered one mountain. Now that the various peaks are designated as separate mountains, six of them are among the ten highest in the eastern United States. Elisha Mitchell, for whom the mountain is named, is buried at the summit. He was one of North Carolina's first great scholars, a geologist and botanist who taught at the University of North Carolina in Chapel Hill. His skill as a scientist is demonstrated by his 1830s calculation

of the height of the peak that now bears his name; amazingly, he estimated the height within 12 feet of today's measurement. In the 1850s, he became embroiled in a controversy when Senator Thomas Clingman, one of his former students, disputed the calculation. On a return trip to re-measure Mount Mitchell, Elisha Mitchell fell from the top of a waterfall (now Mitchell Falls) and drowned in the water below. The rivalry recalls the climactic moment when Sherlock Holmes and his nemesis, Dr. Moriarty, fall to their deaths from the top of a waterfall—although in this case, Senator Clingman went on to live another 40 years. He also has a mountain named for him, Clingmans Dome, a mere 41 feet shorter, which glares up at Mount Mitchell from the Tennessee state line.

From the Blue Ridge Parkway, the best view of the mountain is at Milepost 350.

Hiking
MT. MITCHELL SUMMIT TRAIL

Distance: 0.3 miles out and back
Duration: 20 minutes
Elevation gain: 40 feet
Difficulty: easy
Trailhead: upper parking lot just below the summit

You can take NC-128 right to the top of Mt.

the viewing platform at the summit of Mount Mitchell

Mitchell, some 6,684-feet above sea level, and this hike puts you in the parking lot and leaves you with a very short hike to the observation tower. Park in the parking lot, then walk up the ramp. It's that easy. If you're able, the better option is to spend the day hiking all the way to the top on the strenuous **Mt. Mitchell Trail** (12 miles, 6-7 hours). Whichever way you decide to get here, the views are fantastic from the highest peak east of the Mississippi.

Camping and Food

Mitchell State Park (Blue Ridge Parkway MP 355.3, 2388 NC-128, 828/675-4611, http://ncparks.gov) is not only a place to get an amazing panoramic view—up to 85 miles in clear weather—it also has an education center, a gift shop, and nine **campsites** (877/722-6762, late Apr.-late Oct., $20, $15 seniors, off-season $12). There is also a **restaurant** (828/675-1024, 10am-8pm daily May-Aug., 10am-7pm daily Sept.-Oct., around $15), which is unremarkable to all but hungry hikers.

CRAGGY GARDENS (MP 364.6)

Craggy Gardens is one of the most appropriately named spots on the Parkway. The principal features here are the rocky crags studded with rhododendrons, mountain ash, wildflowers, and other rare plants. As with much of Appalachia, this area was settled by Scots and Scots-Irish, and the rugged rocks along the peak reminded them of the craggy mountains back home.

The **Craggy Gardens Visitor Center** (Blue Ridge Parkway MP 364.6, 10am-5pm daily Memorial Day-Oct.) has information on the flora and fauna of this part of the park, and the folks there can answer just about any question you throw at them.

Asheville Area

Look for ★ to find recommended
sights, activities, dining, and lodging.

Highlights

★ **Downtown Architecture:** In the early 20th century wealthy summer vacationers, industrialists, and stock market investors left their mark in Asheville's downtown, a district packed with art deco and beaux arts master-pieces (page 82).

★ **Biltmore Estate:** Asheville's most famous home is a symbol of Gilded Age grandeur. Across the property you'll find restaurants, a winery, trails, and gardens where it's easy to lose yourself for a day (page 82).

★ **Folk Art Center:** Learn about the master craftspeople of the southern Appalachians and purchase gorgeous handmade items such as traditional weaving, woodcarving, and fine-art furniture (page 88).

★ **Water Sports:** Whether you decide to stand-up paddleboard at dawn, Bellyak midday, or go for a relaxing float down the river in the afternoon, make time to get out on the water in Asheville (page 95).

★ **Zip-lining:** Get some adrenaline flowing on a monster ridge-to-ridge zip line in the Blue Ridge Mountains north of Asheville (page 96).

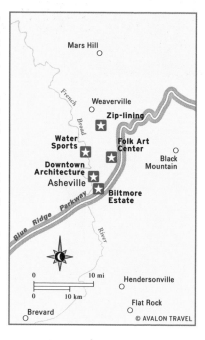

I f North Carolina wears the Blue Ridge and Smoky Mountains as a crown, then Asheville is the shining jewel at its center.

The allure of this place has been an open secret for more than a century. In the mid- to late 1800s, Asheville was a summertime retreat for the wealthy, but it wasn't until railroads arrived at the end of the 19th century that vacationers began visiting in earnest. Tens of thousands of wealthy and upwardly mobile farmers, war profiteers, and industrialists made their pilgrimages to Asheville, drawn by the rejuvenating qualities of the mountain air and cooler summertime temperatures. This was when George Vanderbilt, of the impossibly wealthy Vanderbilt dynasty, purchased more than 90,000 acres of land just south of downtown and began work on the Biltmore Estate, an architectural and horticultural marvel that's now open to the public.

One thing that drives Asheville is a creative spirit. Folk artists, musicians, and dancers have called the surrounding mountains home for as long as the city's been around. Generations of new artists, entrepreneurs, and performers have made their homes here, and the city has gained a reputation for innovation in many arts. On any given night, you might hear bluegrass or old-time music, electronic dance beats or outlaw country, rap or fusion jazz, or anything else from the banjo-picking, fiddle-playing, guitar-strumming street buskers. Artists and artisans, working in digital mediums and Appalachian traditions, hang their work side by side in Asheville's galleries. This, as well as the creative output by local chefs, bars, and brewers, has earned Asheville the nickname "Paris of the South."

And still Asheville grows. The youthful, counterculture energy of North Carolina's 11th-largest city continues to attract new residents. Artists are drawn to the large creative community. Some come to make their name on the dinner plate or in the pint glass, while others head for the outdoors. The Blue Ridge Parkway skirts the city to the south and east, the mountains lie to the north, and rivers flow through downtown. Great Smoky Mountains National Park is less than 90 minutes away. With these myriad riches, Asheville is thriving, a must-see city in the Southeast.

Previous: Luella's Bar-B-Que, Asheville; the porch of the Sourwood Inn. **Above:** busker in Asheville.

Asheville Area

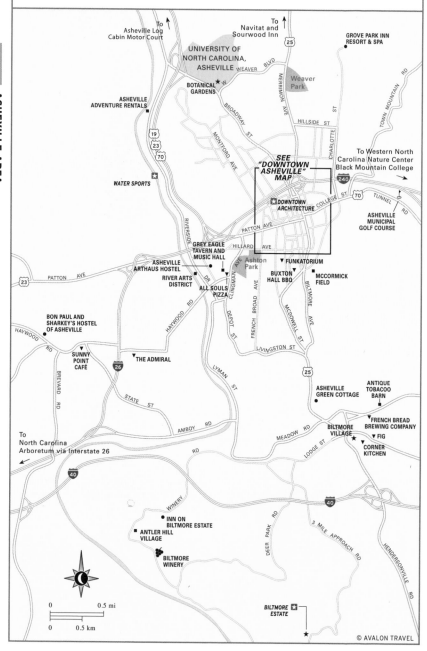

PLANNING YOUR TIME

Asheville's proximity to Great Smoky Mountains National Park (it's a little more than an hour to the south and west) makes it a fabulous gateway city to the most-visited national park in the United States. Using Asheville as a starting or ending point, or as a base of operations for day trips or overnights into the park, is an excellent plan. The city's diverse dining, lodging, and entertainment options make for a great mix of activities.

Seeing the sights in Asheville requires, at minimum, a long (and jam-packed) weekend; **4-5 days** is better. With four days, you'll have time to visit the Biltmore Estate, take in a brewery tour and one of the walking tours of downtown, drive the Blue Ridge Parkway, go for a river float, and take in some live entertainment. If you add in a fifth day, you can squeeze in a little more outdoor time to go whitewater rafting or take long a hike.

When to Go

In **winter,** your travel dollar will go a long way. Rooms are plentiful, and often discounted; dinner reservations at hot-ticket restaurants are easier to score; and the cocktails, beer, and wine still flow. Some of the best regional acts, such as Warren Haynes, roll through town and attractions like the Biltmore Estate, as well as museums, tours, and countless galleries, remain open for business. Hikers will have trails at the Biltmore Estate and in the nearby Great Smoky Mountains National Park to themselves. There will be snow, but it rarely closes the roads (with the exception of the Blue Ridge Parkway, which closes for long stretches in the winter).

In **spring**, wildflowers begin to liven up the landscape and warm-weather visitors appear. This is a prime time for wildflower hikes, driving the Blue Ridge Parkway, and for treks to nearby waterfalls. Spring also brings vibrancy back into the town as everyone shakes off the cold of winter.

Summer means cooler temperatures in the mountains. Free of the humidity and typical Southern summer heat, guests flock to Asheville for tubing or paddling on the rivers. Summer is also the time of festivals and events, including outdoor concerts and baseball games.

As stunning as the jewel-green summer mountains may be, **autumn**'s annual color show draws visitors in droves and fuels Asheville's **busiest season.** The fall

the Black Mountains in full autumn glory

color season is quite long, and visitors make their way from the Blue Ridge Parkway to the Smoky Mountains to little towns like Weaverville and Hot Springs to bear witness to the changing of the leaves. Restaurants are packed, breweries are bustling, and accommodations can be difficult to secure. So plan your fall trip early—it's worth it.

Asheville

SIGHTS

★ Downtown Architecture

As beautiful as Asheville's natural environment may be, the striking architecture is just as attractive. The Montford neighborhood, a contemporary of the Biltmore, is a mixture of ornate Queen Anne houses and craftsman-style bungalows. The Grove Park Inn, a huge luxury hotel, was built in 1913 and is decked out with rustic architectural devices intended to make vacationing New Yorkers and wealthy people feel like they were roughing it. In downtown Asheville is a large concentration of art deco buildings on the scale of Miami Beach. Significant structures dating to the boom before the Great Depression include the **Buncombe County Courthouse** (60 Court Plaza, built in 1927-1929), the **First Baptist Church** (Oak St. and Woodfin St., 1925), the **S&W Cafeteria** (56 Patton Ave., 1929), the **Public Service Building** (89-93 Patton Ave., 1929), and the **Grove Arcade** (37 Battery Park Ave., 1926-1929).

The **Jackson Building** (22 S. Pack Square, built in 1923-1924) is a fine example of neo-Gothic architecture with a disturbing backstory. According to legend, on the day of the stock market crash in 1929 that started the Great Depression, one of the wealthiest men in Asheville lost it all and leaped to his death from the building. Three or four (depending on who's telling the story) more of Asheville's wealthiest followed suit. What is known to be true is that there's a bull's-eye built into the sidewalk in front of the building as a morbid monument to the story.

★ Biltmore Estate

Much of downtown Asheville dates to the 1920s, but the architectural crown jewel, the **Biltmore Estate** (1 Approach Rd., 800/411-3812, www.biltmore.com, 9:30am-3:30pm daily Jan.-mid-Mar., 9am-4:30pm daily mid-Mar.-Dec., $40-75 adults, $20-38 ages 10-16, free under age 10, additional fees for activities) predates that by decades. It was built in the late 1800s for owner George Vanderbilt, grandson of Gilded Age robber baron Cornelius Vanderbilt. Like many of his wealthy Northern contemporaries, George Vanderbilt was first introduced to North

Asheville's architecture stands in both contrast and harmony with the Blue Ridge Mountains.

One Day in Asheville

Only have one day to devote to Asheville? Here are the city's must-see, must-do, and must-eat attractions:

MORNING

Start the day with some great breakfast grub from **Sunny Point Café** in West Asheville. Spend the morning **exploring boutiques and galleries** like those in the **Grove Arcade** and **Woolworth Walk**, taking time to admire examples of Asheville's notable **downtown architecture**, including the First Baptist Church and the Jackson Building.

AFTERNOON

At lunchtime, linger downtown for the **Eating Asheville** food tour, which begins at the Grove Arcade. **Buxton Hall Barbecue,** a few blocks off downtown on the South Slope, and **All Souls Pizza,** a six-minute drive from downtown in the River Arts District, are other good lunch options. After lunch, get a new perspective on the city by boarding the **LaZoom Comedy Tour** bus or by floating down the French Broad River with **Zen Tubing** or zip-lining over the forests north of Asheville with **Navitat.**

You could spend the afternoon at the **Biltmore Estate,** a three-mile drive from downtown. Enjoy the first part of your afternoon at Antler Hill Village for a wine tasting at the **Winery** and then lunch at the **Bistro,** but make sure to leave at least three hours to tour the house and gardens before they close at 4:30pm (3:30pm in winter).

EVENING

Head back downtown for the evening, kicking the night off with beer flights at **Wicked Weed Brewing** or cocktails from **Sovereign Remedies.** When you're ready for dinner, try **Table** for inventive American cuisine or **Cucina 24** for Italian. Walk dinner off with a stroll—a number of buskers will entertain you. Grab a nightcap at **The Imperial Life** or a chocolate at **French Broad Chocolates.** If you're in town on a Friday, check out the drum circle at **Pritchard Park.**

Carolina when he traveled to Asheville for the mountain air and nearby hot springs. He found himself so awestruck by the land that he amassed a tract of land south of Asheville where he would build his "country home" and enjoy the area's restive and healthful benefits. He engaged celebrity architect Richard Morris Hunt to build the manor, and because the land and the views reminded them of the Loire Valley, they planned to build the home in the style of a 16th-century French château. The resulting Biltmore Estate was the largest privately owned home in the country at the time of its completion. Vanderbilt also hired the esteemed Fredrick Law Olmsted, creator of New York City's Central Park, to design the landscape for the grounds, gardens, and surrounding forest, a project nine times the size of the New York project for which Olmsted is famous.

A three-mile-long approach road leads through manicured forests, revealing bits of the landscape and hiding the house until you are upon it, creating a sense of drama and wonder for arriving visitors. While the Biltmore Estate's original 125,000 acres are now greatly diminished—the estate comprises a little more than 8,000 acres today—it's easy to see just how big it was: standing on the South Terrace and looking south and west, everything in view was once part of the estate. A large tract of the land was sold to the federal government and has become part of the Pisgah National Forest; what remains is immaculately manicured.

Construction of the home was done

Downtown Asheville

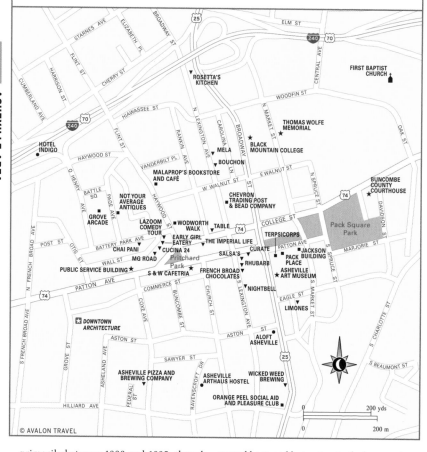

© AVALON TRAVEL

primarily between 1888 and 1895, though there were a number of projects that continued up through World War II (when part of the home was turned into a bunker to store part of the National Gallery of Art's collection). Many are astounded at how long it took to complete the home, but consider this: approximately 5,000 tons of stone were used to build it, there are 65 fireplaces and more than 250 rooms, the square footage is equal to nearly four acres, and the Banquet Hall is large enough to fit a 35-foot Christmas tree. For its time, the Biltmore was a technological marvel, with electricity, elevators,

central heat, and hot water. In the basement there's a heated pool, a gymnasium, and a bowling alley. But as astounding as the building itself may be, it's nothing compared to the art displayed here. There are paintings by Renoir, James Abbott Whistler, and John Singer Sargent; a collection of European antiques including Napoleon's chess set; and room upon room of masterwork in tiling, woodworking and carving, masonry, and stone carving.

George Vanderbilt found the concept of a self-sustaining estate appealing, and he included in the estate a working farm with

Asheville's "Bunk" History

This story starts in 1820 as Congress debated the issue of Missouri's statehood: Would it enter the union as a free state or a slaveholding state? The debate ground on for a month. Then, moments before the vote was to be called, Felix Walker, the representative from Asheville's district, brought the whole thing to a standstill with a long-winded, elaborate, hyperbolic speech. When his fellow members of Congress attempted to stop this interminable production, Walker refused, stating that he was speaking for his constituents, not for the benefit of his colleagues in the House. He was, he said, "speaking for Buncombe," referring to the county, pronounced "bunkum," of which Asheville is the seat.

"Speaking for Buncombe," and ultimately the words "bunkum" and "bunk," came to mean hollow political grandstanding. Today, nearly 200 years after Walker's verbose speech, you'll still hear news anchors, political pundits, bloggers, and talking heads refer to empty political rhetoric as "bunk."

crops, herds of cattle, a dairy, and all the farmers and workers required for such an operation. The Asheville neighborhood known as **Biltmore Village** was part of this mountain empire. If Vanderbilt stepped onto his estate today, he'd be happy to find that his vision of a self-sustaining estate endures. A vineyard (not open to the public) produces grapes that are processed at the estate's winery; a livestock breeding program produces fine stock; and a farm supplies more than 70 percent of seasonal and specialty vegetables to the estate's restaurants. Visitors can eat, shop, tour, explore, relax, and unwind without leaving the grounds, and there's easily enough here to fill a weekend.

Today the **Biltmore Winery** in **Antler Hill Village** operates in the estate's former dairy, vestiges of which include the industrial-farm rafters in the tasting room and the tile floor (designed for easy cleanup). Daily tours and complimentary wine tastings allow visitors to sample some award-winning wines and see how they're made. More than 500,000 people visit the tasting room annually, so expect a wait if you're here in high season. Tastings include something on the order of 20 wines (don't worry, they're small pours). You can also experience the Premium Wine Tasting ($3/pour or three pours for $8, complimentary for Biltmore Wine Club Members) of Biltmore's reserve and sparkling wines; there's also daily tastings of bubbly wine ($18) and pairings of red wine and chocolate ($20).

Antler Hill Village is also home to **Cedric's,** a brewery named after a beloved family dog, as well as a small museum, a souvenir shop, and a green to relax on. **River Bend Farm** is a beautiful compound that was once the hub of the estate's farming operation but now stands as a showpiece for traditional period crafts like woodworking and blacksmithing. Be sure to stop by the blacksmith's shop and watch master blacksmith Doc Cudd speak with considerable eloquence about the art of smithing as he hammers out everything from common nails to decorative leaves, flowers, and other pieces. Ask him to make the anvil sing and he'll happily oblige; he's one of a handful of smiths who know how to play the anvil as a musical instrument in the 18th- and 19th-century fashion. It's a beautiful, almost haunting sound you won't soon forget.

The **Equestrian Center** gives lessons and provides the opportunity to ride more than 80 miles of equestrian trails, many with sweeping views of the estate and glimpses of the main house that will take your breath away. Other ways to tour the estate include carriage rides; paved bike trails and mountain bike trails; canoes, kayaks, and rafts (the French Broad River bisects the estate); Segways; and, of course, on foot. You can even challenge your driving skills at the **Land Rover Experience Driving School.**

Most of the house is open to visitors on self-guided tours, while other sections—like the roof and some servants' areas—are accessible on behind-the-scenes tours. Admission cost for the Biltmore Estate varies by season and includes the house, gardens, and winery; activities such as horseback riding, rafting, and behind-the-scenes tours cost extra. Special events such as the Christmas Candlelight Tour (Nov.-Dec.) also have additional fees. Parking is free, and a complimentary shuttle takes you from parking lots to the house.

Botanical Gardens at Asheville

The **Botanical Gardens at Asheville** (151 W. T. Weaver Blvd., adjacent to UNC-Asheville campus, 828/252-5190, www. ashevillebotanicalgardens.org, dawn-dusk daily year-round, donation) is a 10-acre preserve for the region's increasingly threatened native plant species. Laid out in 1960 by landscape architect Doan Ogden, the gardens are an ecological haven. The many "rooms" are planted to reflect different environments of the mountains, including the Wildflower Trail, the Heath Cove, and the Fern and Moss Trail. Spring blooms peak in mid-April, but the gardens are an absolutely lovely and visually rich place to visit any time of year. Because of its serious mission of plant preservation, neither pets nor bicycles are allowed. Admission is free, but because the facility is entirely supported by donations, your contribution will have a real impact. You can coordinate a tour of the garden ($2 members, $3 non-members) with two weeks' advance notice. On the first Saturday in May, the **Day in the Gardens** brings food and music to this normally placid park, and garden and nature enthusiasts from all around come to tour and to buy native plants for their home gardens. There is also a **visitors center and gift shop** (10am-4pm Mon.-Sat., noon-4pm Sun.

Apr.-Oct., noon-4pm daily Nov.-Dec., closes for season Dec. 6-Mar.).

Western North Carolina Nature Center

Asheville, and western North Carolina generally, tend to be very ecologically conscious, as reflected in the **Western North Carolina Nature Center** (75 Gashes Creek Rd., 828/259-8092, www.wildwnc.org, 10am-5pm daily, closed Thanksgiving Day, Dec. 24-25, and Jan. 1, $10.95 adults, $9.95 seniors age 65 and up, $6.95 ages 3-15, free ages 2 and under, discount for Asheville residents). On the grounds of an old zoo—don't worry, it's not depressing—wild animals that are unable to survive in the wild due to injury or having been raised as pets live in wooded habitats on public display. This is the place to see some of the mountains' rarest species—those that even most lifelong mountain residents have never seen: cougars, wolves, coyotes, bobcats, and even the elusive hellbender. What's a hellbender, you ask? Come to the nature center to find out.

Black Mountain College

Considering the history of Black Mountain College from a purely numerical standpoint, one might get the false impression that this little institution's brief, odd life was a flash in the pan. In its 23 years of operation, Black Mountain College had just 1,200 students, only 55 of whom actually completed their degrees. But between 1933 and 1956, the unconventional school demonstrated an innovative model of education and community life.

The educational program was almost devoid of structure. Students had no set course schedule or requirements; they lived and farmed with the faculty, and no sense of hierarchy was permitted to separate students and teachers. Most distinguished as a school of the arts, Black Mountain College hired Josef Albers as its first art director when the Bauhaus icon fled Nazi Germany. Willem de Kooning taught here for a time, as did Buckminster Fuller, who

Thomas Wolfe, Native Son

Author Thomas Wolfe *(You Can't Go Home Again; Look Homeward, Angel)* grew up in an Asheville boardinghouse run by his mother and operated today as the **Thomas Wolfe Memorial** (52 N. Market St., 828/253-8304, www.wolfememorial.com, 9am-5pm Tues.-Sat., $5, $2 students). He described the town of "Altamont" (Asheville), his mother's boardinghouse "Dixieland," and the town's people so vividly in *Look Homeward, Angel* that the Asheville library refused to carry it, and Wolfe himself avoided the town for almost eight years. Even then, he only came back after his mother published an article titled "Return" in the Asheville newspaper.

In this passage from *Look Homeward, Angel,* Wolfe describes the excitement of approaching Asheville as a traveler.

The next morning he resumed his journey by coach. His destination was the little town of Altamont, twenty-four miles away beyond the rim of the great outer wall of the hills. As the horses strained slowly up the mountain road Oliver's spirit lifted a little. It was a gray-golden day in late October, bright and windy. There was a sharp bite and sparkle in the mountain air: the range soared above him, close, immense, clean, and barren. The trees rose gaunt and stark: they were almost leafless. The sky was full of windy white rags of cloud; a thick blade of mist washed slowly around the rampart of a mountain.

Below him a mountain stream foamed down its rocky bed, and he could see little dots of men laying the track that would coil across the hill toward Altamont. Then the sweating team lipped the gulch of the mountain, and, among soaring and lordly ranges that melted away in purple mist, they began the slow descent toward the high plateau on which the town of Altamont was built.

In the haunting eternity of these mountains, rimmed in their enormous cup, he found sprawled out on its hundred hills and hollows a town of four thousand people.

began his design of the geodesic dome while he was in residence. Albert Einstein and William Carlos Williams were among the roster of guest lecturers. I had the honor of working with and befriending poet Robert Creeley, one of the few people to get a degree here, and who taught here briefly before the school shut down in 1956, partly due to the prevailing anti-left climate of that decade.

The **Black Mountain College Museum and Arts Center** (56 Broadway, 828/350-8484, www.blackmountaincollege.org, 11am-5pm Mon.-Sat., free), an exhibition space and resource center devoted to the lauded college, is located in downtown Asheville. The downtown location keeps the spirit of the college alive by exposing more visitors to its historic and inspired-by-the-legacy contemporary works.

Asheville Art Museum

The **Asheville Art Museum** (2 S. Pack Square, 828/253-3227, www.ashevilleart. org, 10am-5pm Tues.-Sat., 1pm-5pm Sun., $8 adults, $7 students with ID, $7 over 60, free 5 and under) has been around since 1948, and in the intervening decades has helped enrich the art community of Asheville. The permanent collection includes an array of mediums and styles, ranging from photo portraits to ceramics to statuary to beautiful modern pieces. A large collection from the nearby experimental school, Black Mountain College, highlights works created by faculty and students.

★ Folk Art Center

Anyone with an interest in Appalachian handicrafts and folk art should stop by the **Folk Art Center** (Blue Ridge Parkway MP 382, 828/298-7928, 9am-5pm daily Jan.-Mar., 9am-6pm daily Apr.-Dec., free). Home to the Southern Highland Craft Guild, the Folk Art Center has around 30,000 square feet of space that includes three galleries, an auditorium, a research library, a tiny Blue Ridge Parkway info booth, and the Allanstand Craft Shop. Allanstand is the oldest continuously operated craft shop in the United States. Started in 1897 by a Presbyterian missionary, it maintains the same vision it had the year it was born: to preserve traditional art forms and raise the visibility of the arts and crafts of the Appalachian Mountains. Although the folk arts are well represented in beautiful pottery, baskets, weaving, and quilts, you'll also find the work of contemporary studio artists in an array of media, including gorgeous handcrafted furniture, clothing, jewelry, and toys. Hang out long enough and you may even see an artist at work. Every day, one or more members of the Southern Highlands Craft Guild is on hand to demonstrate their craft at the entrance to the Folk Art Center—whittling away at a chunk of wood with a pocketknife, spinning wool into yarn, or weaving or tying brooms. They'll be happy to explain their process and the history of their craft.

ENTERTAINMENT AND EVENTS
Nightlife
BARS AND CLUBS

Asheville is growing a reputation as a craft-cocktail destination to match its food renown. A big contributor to that movement is **The Imperial Life** (48 College St., 828/254-8980, http://imperialbarasheville.com, 4:30pm-close Wed.-Mon.), specializing in pre-Prohibition cocktails, a wine list that showcases lesser-known varietals, and small-batch spirits. They serve a limited menu of small plates made downstairs at **Table** (http://

tableasheville.com), a much-lauded restaurant under the same ownership.

Sovereign Remedies (29 N. Market St., 828/919-9518, www.sovereignremedies.com, 11am-2am Wed.-Mon., 4pm-2am Tues., $4-19) has quickly become a go-to for Asheville's cocktail lovers and those hankering for a small, delicious plate of food. Between the bartenders and some local foragers, Sovereign Remedies stays stocked with wild herbs, berries, fruit, and roots used to make cocktails or bitters, infuse or macerate various liquors, create shrubs (drinking vinegars; don't make that face, they're delicious), and use creatively in every way imaginable.

The Double Crown (375 Haywood Rd., 828/575-9060, www.thedoublecrown.com, 5pm-2am daily) has all the trappings of a dive bar, but serves legitimately good cocktails. They have an exceptional bourbon list, and the requisite beer selection stretches far beyond that of a tiny neighborhood bar. In addition to drinks, The Double Crown always has something going on: DJs (spinning actual records), karaoke, and live musical acts ranging from rock and rockabilly to country, soul, and gospel. It's well worth a stop, whether to sample some top-shelf bourbon, a cocktail, or a bottle of suds.

The vibe at **Banks Ave.** (32 Banks Ave., 828/785-1458, www.32banksave.com, 4pm-2am Mon.-Fri., 2pm-2am Sat., 1pm-2am Sun.) is of the "I don't give a damn, I'm having fun" variety. Graffiti on the walls, a Nintendo 64, impromptu pizza parties and cookouts, and odd holiday parties (like the Dead Celebrity-themed Halloween costume contest) bear witness to the laid-back attitude. For a real taste of how freewheeling this bar can be, ask one of the bartenders about their former name, Public School, and why they changed it.

Nightbell (32 South Lexington Ave., 828/575-0375, www.thenightbell.com, 6pm-12:30am Sun. and Wed.-Thurs., 6pm-2am Fri.-Sat.) is the latest from Katie Button, a 2014 nominee for the James Beard Rising Star Chef of the Year Award and one of the finest chefs in Asheville. This speakeasy-esque bar serves sophisticated, imaginative cocktails and some mighty fine nosh.

BREWPUBS AND TAPROOMS

Asheville has earned the title of Beer City, USA, for several years running—the beer scene here is off the hook. It seems like there's a brewery on every corner (or one planning to open there next month) and experimental brewers are introducing new styles, funky ingredients, and any little twist they can to get people talking. Loyal locals and pint hounds from all over frequent Asheville's bars, breweries, and pubs.

New Belgium Brewing (91 Craven St., 828/333-6900, www.newbelgium.com) opened a 500,000-barrel brewery in Asheville in spring of 2016. This huge operation will be the company's East Coast brewing headquarters for the foreseeable future, and the community has welcomed them with open arms. The facility includes a giant brewery and the **AVL Liquid Center** (11am-8pm Mon.-Sat., noon-8pm Sun.), more commonly known as a tasting room. Perched on a bluff overlooking the French Broad River, New Belgium took over a brownfield site—formerly utilized in heavy industry—and redeveloped it, building a new facility (for which they're expected to receive LEED certification). They donated a significant portion of land back to the city for use in extending the French Broad River Greenway. Brew fans can expect to taste Asheville-brewed Fat Tire, among others, at the Liquid Center.

Wicked Weed Brewing (91 Biltmore Ave., 828/575-9599, www.wickedweedbrewing.com, tasting room 3pm-11pm Mon.-Tues., 3pm-midnight Wed.-Thurs., 3pm-2am Fri.-Sat., 3pm-11pm Sun.; restaurant 11:30am-11pm Mon.-Tues., 11:30am-midnight Wed.-Thurs., 11am-1am Fri.-Sat., noon-11pm Sun.) has an excellent taproom and restaurant just a couple of blocks off Pack Square. Their tasting room features some two dozen beers, with Belgian red ales, fruit-forward sours, IPAs, and even a handful of porters and stouts. A few blocks away they've opened

the **Funkatorium** (147 Coxe Ave., 2pm-10pm Mon.-Thurs., noon-midnight Fri.-Sat., noon-10pm Sun.), a brewery featuring only sour and wild ales. There's bluegrass every Wednesday, a running club meets here on Thursdays, and they also serve some tasty bar snacks.

Hi-Wire Brewing (828/575-9675, www.hiwirebrewing.com) came to Asheville with one location on the **South Slope** (197 Hilliard Ave., 4pm-11pm Mon.-Thurs., 2pm-2am Fri., noon-2am Sat., 1pm-10pm Sun.) and quickly expanded to a spot near Biltmore Village they call the **Big Top** (2 Huntsman Place, 4pm-10pm Mon.-Thurs., 4pm-midnight Fri., noon-midnight Sat., 1pm-10pm Sun.; tours 5pm and 6pm Fri., hourly 2pm-5pm Sat., and 2pm and 3pm Sun.). They focus on lagers, pale ales, and IPAs, but their winter brew, the Strongman Coffee Milk Stout, is one of my favorites.

Burial Beer Co. (40 Collier Ave., 828/475-2739, www.burialbeer.com, 4pm-10pm Mon.-Thurs., 2pm-10pm Fri.-Sat., noon-8pm Sun.) produces some of Asheville's most exciting beers from its brewery/taproom on the south side of town. With a dozen taps open at any given time, Burial is able to show off its creativity. You'll find a lot of saisons and farmhouse ales on tap, as well as dubbels and Belgian-style stouts, but there's no shortage of IPAs, pilsners, blonde ales and other crisp, golden brews to taste. Tours ($8 for tasting tour, free for non-drinkers) are available in conjunction with Wicked Weed's Funkatorium through **South Slope Brewery Tours** (www.southslopebrewery-tours.com).

Located in an old warehouse in the River Arts District, **Wedge Brewing Company** (37 Paynes Way, Suite 001, 828/505-2792, www.wedgebrewing.com, 4pm-10pm Mon.-Thurs., 3pm-10pm Fri., 2pm-10pm Sat.-Sun.) has more than a dozen brews on tap, including pale ales, pilsners, and a Russian imperial stout flavored with raspberries. Their strong relationship with area food trucks makes this a great hangout for local beer and local grub with local beer enthusiasts any evening.

To sample a variety of Asheville's great

microbreweries, join a tour from **Asheville Brews Cruise** (828/545-5181, www.ashevillebrewscruise.com, from $59). The enthusiastic beer experts will shuttle you from brewery to brewery in the Brews Cruise van to sample some beer, learn about the growth of Asheville's beer scene, and gain some insight in the art and craft of brewing. On the tour, you'll visit **Asheville Pizza and Brewing Company** (675 Merrimon Ave., 828/254-1281, http://ashevillebrewing.com, 11am-midnight or later daily), where you can start off the evening with one of this pizzeria, microbrewery, and movie house's tasty beers and fortify yourself for the evening by filling up on good pizza. The **French Broad Brewing Company** (828/277-0222, www.frenchbroadbrewery.com, 1pm-8pm daily) is another popular local nightspot that's grown up around a first-rate beer-making operation, where you can choose from a varied menu that includes signature pilsners, lagers, and ales while listening to some good live music. The third destination on the cruise is Asheville's first microbrewery, the **Highland Brewing Company** (12 Old Charlotte Hwy., Suite H, 828/299-3370, www.highlandbrewing.com, tasting room 4pm-8pm Mon.-Thurs., 4pm-9pm Fri., 2pm-9pm

Sat., noon-6pm Sun.; tours 4:30pm and 5:45pm Mon.-Thurs., 4:30pm and 5:45pm Fri., hourly 2:30pm-6:30pm Sat., 2:15 and 4:15 Sun.). They've been making beer and raking in awards for well over a decade, and on first sip you'll understand why they're one of the Southeast's favorite breweries.

While it's not beer, **Urban Orchard Cider Company** (210 Haywood Rd., 828/774-5151, www.urbanorchardcider.com, 2pm-10pm Mon., 2pm-11pm Tues.-Thurs., noon-midnight Fri.-Sat., noon-10pm Sun.) is part of a new trend in craft brewing: cider. Urban Orchard is making some waves around Asheville because their cider is nothing like the cider you think you know, like the Sidra Del Diablo cider with smoked habanero pepper or the Ginger Champagne cider, with delicate bubbles and a ginger infusion. This stuff is good and the folks here are passionate about it, willing to explore a variety of styles and ingredients.

There are several brands of moonshine in North Carolina, but Asheville's Troy Ball, from **Troy & Sons** (12 Old Charlotte Hwy., Asheville, 828/575-2000, www.ashevilledistilling.com, tours 5pm and 6pm Fri.-Sat., free), uses an heirloom corn and a traditional recipe to make her much-talked-about moonshine.

the Orange Peel Social Aid and Pleasure Club

LIVE MUSIC

Great live music is the rule in Asheville—not just national touring acts, but regional and local bands that give the national acts stiff competition on any given night. Everywhere you turn you'll find buskers on street corners, solo guitarists in cafés, or a bluegrass trio set up on a restaurant's deck; at **Pritchard Park** (at Patton Ave., Haywood St., and College St.), a huge drum circle forms every Friday night. There are also formal music venues where you can hear rock, jam bands, bluegrass, funk, blues, country, rockabilly, alt-country, mountain swing, old-time music, electronica, and too many other genres to name.

My favorite spot for live music is the **Orange Peel Social Aid and Pleasure Club** (101 Biltmore Ave., 828/398-1837, www.theorangepeel.net, noon-midnight or later daily). They're billed as "the nation's premier live music hall and concert venue," and they can back that up with some powerful acts taking the stage, including Bob Dylan, Smashing Pumpkins, Bruce Hornsby, Mickey Hart of Grateful Dead fame, Mike Gordon from Phish, Chvrches, Beastie Boys, Flaming Lips, and My Morning Jacket. The Orange Peel is a cool concert hall with a great-big dance floor, great sound, and great history.

One of the best venues in town for roots music and eclectic small bands is the **Grey Eagle Tavern and Music Hall** (185 Clingman Ave., 828/232-5800, www.thegreyeagle.com). It's a small space set up more like a listening room than a bar or club, meaning folks come to listen to the music and interact with the performer rather than grab a beer and hop to the next bar.

Performing Arts

BALLET

Asheville's noteworthy ballet company, **Terpsicorps** (2 South Pack Sq., 828/252-4530, http://terpsicorps.org) performs for two brief but brilliant runs in the summer. Terpsicorps takes advantage of what is normally a slow season for other companies and hires some of the country's best dancers for a short-term stint in Asheville. Summer productions usually have three-night runs, so tickets sell out fast.

COMEDY

You may notice a giant purple bus zipping through the streets around Asheville, laughter and bubbles (yes, bubbles) coming from the windows. That's the **LaZoom Comedy Tour** (1½ Battery Park Ave., departs from 90 Biltmore Ave., 828/225-6932, www.lazoomtours.com, $24, must be at least age 13), delivering tours big in history and hilarity. The tour guides are outrageous—they're some of Asheville's weirdest (in a good way) people—and I guarantee you'll learn a thing or two (some history, a joke you may or may not want to tell your mom). They also offer the Haunted Comedy Tour (departing from 92 Patton Ave., $21), which adds in a supernatural note and tales of some of Asheville's spectral denizens. The Band & Beer Bus Tour ($29) departs from Tasty Beverage (162 Coxe Ave.) to visit a trio of area breweries for samples and some live local music.

The Altamont Theatre (18 Church St., www.thealtamont.com, show times and ticket prices vary) calls itself "Asheville's Best Listening Room" and they may be right. They host a variety of musical acts (country, soul, jazz, bluegrass, instrumental progressive space rock, you name it), spoken word performances, and comedians. Their comedy and improv shows are both smart and hilarious; comedian Cliff Cash, one of the funniest rising stars in the South, performs here on the regular. Since Asheville doesn't have a dedicated comedy club, The Altamont gladly fills that role.

Festivals and Events

Twice yearly, in late July and late October, the Southern Highland Craft Guild hosts the **Craft Fair of the Southern Highlands** (U.S. Cellular Center, 87 Haywood St., 828/298-7928, www.southernhighlandguild.org, 10am-6pm Thurs.-Sat., 10am-5pm Sun., $8 adults, under age 12 free). Since 1948 this event has brought much-deserved attention to the guild's more than 900 members, who live and work throughout the Appalachian Mountains. Hundreds of craftspeople participate in the event, selling all sorts of handmade items.

The biggest of Asheville's festivals and fairs (or at least the most anticipated), is the annual **Warren Haynes Christmas Jam** (www. xmasjam.com, mid-Dec.). Warren Haynes, longtime guitarist for The Allman Brothers Band, founding member of Government Mule, and Asheville native, invites a who's-who of musical acts to perform a benefit concert for Habitat for Humanity. The acts are generally biggies in the rock/jam world as well as bands on the rise. Buy tickets in advance, as the Christmas Jam tends to sell out quickly. In addition to the general admission tickets ($70), there are VIP packages ($399-699) that allow access to a side-stage viewing area, preshow shows, the Christmas Jam Friends & Family lounge and bar, a gift bag, and more.

The **Mountain Dance and Folk Festival** (www.folkheritage.org, 828/258-6101, ext. 345, ticket prices vary) is the nation's longest-running folk festival, an event founded in the 1920s by musician and folklorist Bascom Lamar Lunsford to celebrate the heritage of his native Carolina mountains. Musicians and dancers from western North Carolina perform at the downtown Diana Wortham Theater at Pack Place for three nights each summer. Also downtown, many of the same artists can be heard on Saturday evening at the city's **Shindig on the Green** concert series (Martin Luther King Jr. Park, 50 Martin Luther King Jr. Dr.).

SHOPPING
Antiques

For lovers of vintage, retro, and aged things, the **Antique Tobacco Barn** (75 Swannanoa River Rd., 828/252-7291, www.atbarn.com, 10am-6pm Mon.-Thurs., 9am-6pm Fri.-Sat., 1pm-6pm Sun. Mar.-Oct.; 10am-5pm Mon.-Sat., 1pm-5pm Sun. Nov.-Feb.) has more than 77,000 square feet of goodies to pick through.

This perpetual winner of the *Mountain XPress* "Best Antiques Store in Western North Carolina" has toys, art, tools, furniture, radios, sporting equipment, folk art, farm relics, oddball bric-a-brac, mid-century furniture, and all those great weird things you can only find in a collection this large. It takes a while to explore this humongous shop, so carve out some time.

Along Swannanoa River Road is the **Biltmore Antiques District** (120 Swannanoa River Rd.), a small shopping district that's packed with an intriguing group of antique shops. Some specialize in imports, others in lamps, European furniture, or fine jewelry. Exploring is always a good time because you never know what you'll find or where you'll find it.

Books, Toys, and Crafts

One of the social hubs of this city is **Malaprop's Bookstore and Café** (55 Haywood St., 828/254-6734, www.malaprops. com, 9am-9pm Mon.-Sat., 9am-7pm Sun.). This fun and progressive bookstore carries a deep selection of books that includes tomes by North Carolina authors and a particularly fine collection of regional authors. You'll find the requisite coffee bar and café with wireless Internet access, making it a particularly good spot to hang out. It's bright and comfortable, and the staff are well versed in all sorts of literature, so they can help you find a local author you'll enjoy reading. People in all walks of Asheville life come to Malaprop's, so expect to see creative dressers, the tattooed, business types, artists, students, and grannies.

Dancing Bear Toys (518 Kenilworth Rd., 800/659-8697, www.dancingbeartoys.com, 10am-7pm Mon.-Sat., noon-5pm Sun.) is located among the motels and chain restaurants out on US-70 (Tunnel Rd.), but inside it has the ambience of a cozy village toy shop. Dancing Bear has toys for everyone from babies to silly grown-ups: a fabulous selection of Playmobil figures and accessories; Lego, Brio, and other favorite lines of European toys; beautiful stuffed animals of all sizes;

all sorts of educational kits and games; and comical doodads.

A pair of great gem and crystal shops in Asheville fascinate me. Not only do they have some breathtaking minerals for sale, they also have fossils—fish, starfish, plants, even claws, teeth, and skulls. My favorite is **Cornerstone Minerals** (52 N. Lexington Ave., 828/225-3888, www.cornerstoneminerals.com, 11am-7pm Sun.-Thurs., 10am-9pm Fri.-Sat.); I like to stare at their sheets of fossil-imbued stone, while my wife always finds some cool bauble. The other spot is **Enter the Earth** (1 Page Ave. #125, inside the Grove Arcade, 828/350-9222, www.entertheearth.com, 10am-6pm Mon.-Sat., 11am-5pm Sun.), where they have some very impressive fossils and a good selection of jewelry using many of the stones and gems sold in the store.

The **Mast General Store** (15 Biltmore Ave., 828/232-1883, www.mastgeneralstore.com, 10am-6pm Mon.-Thurs., 10am-9pm Fri.-Sat., noon-6pm Sun.) is an institution in western North Carolina and beyond. They call themselves a general store, but they mean it in a very contemporary way. Cast-iron cookware, penny candies, and Mast logo shirts and jackets sit alongside baskets and handmade crafts. A good selection of outdoor clothing and equipment can get you outfitted for some time in the woods, or you can fill up a bag with candy and eat it while you drive the Blue Ridge Parkway.

Galleries

There are a number of galleries in downtown Asheville, and while most exhibit works from multiple artists, none can match the size of the **Woolworth Walk** (25 Haywood St., 828/254-9234, www.woolworthwalk.com, 11am-6pm Mon.-Thurs., 11am-7pm Fri., 10am-7pm Sat., 11am-5pm Sun., soda fountain closes 1 hour before the gallery), a two-story, 20,000-square-foot gallery featuring more than 160 local artists. Nearly every conceivable medium is represented, including digitally designed graphic prints, oil paintings, watercolors, jewelry, and woodworking.

This gallery is a favorite not just because it has a soda fountain but because the work on display is affordable as well as stunning.

American Folk Art and Framing (64 Biltmore Ave., 828/281-2134, www.amerifolk.com, 10am-6pm Mon.-Sat., noon-5pm Sun.) does a wonderful job of displaying contemporary Southern folk artists, including potters, painters, and woodcarvers, as well as helping the art-appreciating public learn more about local folk-art traditions and styles. They host six openings a year in the gallery, so work changes frequently, keeping the place bubbling with energy.

Shopping Centers and Districts
GROVE ARCADE

One of Asheville's shopping highlights is the 1929 **Grove Arcade** (1 Page Ave., 828/252-7799, www.grovearcade.com), a beautiful and storied piece of architecture that is now a chic shopping and dining destination in the heart of downtown. The expansive Tudor Revival building, ornately filigreed inside and out in ivory-glazed terra-cotta, was initially planned as the base of a 14-story building, a skyscraper by that day's standard. There are some fantastic galleries and boutiques, including **Mountain Made** (828/350-0307, www.mtnmade.com, 10am-6pm Mon.-Sat., 10am-5pm Sun.), a gallery celebrating contemporary art created in and inspired by the mountains around Asheville. Another favorite is **Alexander & Lehnert** (828/254-2010, www.alexanderandlehnert.com, 10am-6pm Mon.-Sat.), which showcases the work of two talented jewelers with different styles—Lehnert takes an architectural approach to designs, and Alexander chooses organic forms as inspiration. Not all stores in the Grove Arcade sell fine art and jewelry: at **Asheville NC Home Crafts** (828/350-7556, www.ashevillehomecrafts.com, 10am-6pm Mon.-Sat., noon-5pm Sun.) you can buy specialty yarn, patterns, hooks, and needles for all sorts of knitting, weaving, and crocheting projects, or you can buy a piece made by local artists. **Battery Park Book Exchange & Champagne Bar** (828/252-0020, 11am-9pm Sun.-Thurs., 11am-late Fri.-Sat.) has two things that go great together in a really relaxed atmosphere: wine and books. Outside the Grove Arcade, a row of shaded stalls house many great street artisans selling everything from soap to miniature topiaries.

RIVER ARTS DISTRICT

Along the Swannanoa River, many of Asheville's old warehouses and industrial buildings have been transformed into studio spaces, galleries, restaurants, and breweries in an area known as the **River Arts District** (www.riverartsdistrict.com). More than 160 artists have working studios here, and twice a year, during the first weekend of June and November, nearly every artist in the district opens their studios to the public for a two-day **Studio Stroll.** On the second Saturday of each month some of the studios (they rotate based on medium, so one month may be photography, the next clay, and so on) are open for **A Closer Look,** a day of artist demonstrations, classes, workshops, and creative activities.

Some studios are open daily, among them **Jonas Gerald Fine Art** (240 Clingman Ave., daily 10am-6pm), where the namesake artist specializes in abstract art that uses vivid colors and unusual composition to draw the viewer in. He works across many media, so there's a lot to see. **Odyssee Center for Ceramic Arts** (236-238 Clingman Ave., www.odysseyceramicarts.com, 9am-5pm Mon.-Sat., 1pm-5pm Sun.) is full of sculptors and teachers. Part of their mission is to promote artistic appreciation and advancement of ceramic arts; they hold regular classes, workshops, and talks led by master ceramic artists.

At the 1910 **Cotton Mill Studios** (122 Riverside Dr. at W. Haywood St., www.cottonmillstudiosnc.com, hours vary), several painters work alongside potters and jewelers. **Riverview Station** (191 Lyman St., http://riverviewartists.com, hours vary) is a circa 1896 building housing the studios of a wonderful array of jewelers, ceramicists, furniture designers, painters, and photographers. Another favorite gallery is **CURVE Studios & Garden** (6, 9, and 12 Riverside Dr., 828/388-3526, www.curvestudiosnc.com, most studios 11am-4pm daily). A fun, funky studio that has been around since before the River Arts District was a thing, and once a punk-rock club called Squashpile—you can't make up stuff like that—CURVE is home to encaustic painters, ceramic workers, jewelry designers, glass artists, fiber artists, and more. This is just a sampling of what's happening in the River Arts District; visit the website for detailed listings of the artists and their studios.

SPORTS AND RECREATION

Asheville is a "go out and do it" kind of town. It's not unusual to see mountain bikers, road riders, runners, hikers, flat-water kayakers, and their daredevil white water-loving cousins all on the streets in town. A number of gear shops call Asheville home, and access to trails, rivers, and mountain roads are all right here. The **Asheville Tourists** (30 Buchanan Place, 828/258-0428, www.milb.com), the Class A farm team of the Colorado Rockies, play here. They're the only spectator sport in town, unless you love high school sports.

Biking

Take a tour of Asheville by bicycle. If you're thinking "It's too hilly, I'll never be able to climb that," **Electro Bike Tours** (departs from Weaver Park's Merrimon Ave. entrance, 828/513-3960, http://electrobiketours.com, tours 10am daily, $55) can provide you with pedal-assisted bikes that make the hills easier and the flats seem like nothing at all. Rather than relying on a throttle, like a moped or electric scooter, these ingenious bikes use their power to make pedaling easier; you still have to work, just not as hard, to get where you're going. Start with the hill to the Grove Park Inn, the first stop on a two-hour tour of Asheville's historic and cultural sites.

Float down the French Broad River with Zen Tubing.

and is one of the oldest in the western part of the state. This Donald Ross-designed course is nearly 6,500 yards long from the championship tees and features a good mix of forgiving and narrow fairways, par-5 fairways begging for a birdie, and par-3 fairways that will challenge your ball placement.

Hiking

Ready for mountain air? Join **Blue Ridge Hiking Co.** (15 Hildebrand St., 828/713-5451, http://blueridgehikingco.com, $35-185) on a half-day, full-day, or overnight hike in the Pisgah National Forest. Founder Jennifer Pharr Davis has hiked more than 11,000 miles of long-distance trails and became the first woman to be the overall record holder for fastest through-hike of the Appalachian Trail: She hiked its 2,181 miles in 46.5 days. Don't worry, she and her guides don't go that fast on the trail; they like to slow down, enjoy the moment, and make sure everyone gets a look and feel for what they love about hiking.

★ Water Sports

Wai Mauna Asheville SUP Tours (tours depart from 159 Riverside Dr., 808/264-3005, www.waimaunaashevillesuptours.com, rentals $40, tours $65) is a natural fit for Asheville ("wai mauna" is Hawaiian for "mountain waters"). Wai Mauna offers four tours: the Sunrise Dawn Patrol, a midmorning tour, a midday paddle, and the Sunset Session. Many SUP outfitters ignore the two most beautiful parts of the day—dawn and dusk—but these guys embrace them. On the Dawn Patrol tour, the river is often shrouded in fog, the birds are waking up, and the water is perfectly still; it's a perfect time to paddle. All tours depart from the River Arts District and paddlers are shuttled to Hominy Creek, a few miles away; you then paddle downstream back to where you started.

The French Broad and Swannanoa Rivers offer a lot of opportunities to try your hand at stand-up paddleboarding. (It's much different than on a lake, marsh creek, or the ocean; you have to know how to read the river for

Golf

Golf in the mountains can be a challenge, with course layouts big on blind approaches and hard doglegs, but it pays off with beautiful views and long downhill shots that can make you feel like you hit it like a pro.

Play a round at the **Grove Park Inn Golf Club** (290 Macon Ave., 828/252-2711, www.groveparkinn.com, 18 holes, par 70, greens fees $65-140 peak season, $75-85 off-season, includes cart, discounts for juniors, late play, and off-season), where President Obama played a round during his 2010 stay. *Golf Digest* named this course one of the top 10 courses that are at least 100 years old, and it plays beautifully. This is a must-play course for serious golfers—not just because the views are spectacular, but also because the course contains so much history.

The **Asheville Municipal Golf Course** (226 Fairway Dr., 828/298-1867, www.ashevillenc.gov, 18 holes, par 72, greens fees $31-37, after 1pm $25, all greens fees include cart, tee-time reservation required) opened in 1927 underwater hazards and how to fall off correctly.) **Asheville Outdoor Center** (521 Amboy Rd., 828/232-1970, www.paddlewithus.com, lessons $65 for 1.5 hours, tours $35-65) provides introductory lessons to make sure you're safe on the river and rentals to make sure you have fun. They also offer tours ranging from a few to many miles, but it's all scenic and mostly downstream.

Tubing isn't a sport in so much as you simply recline in an inner tube and float from point A to point B, but it's a lot of fun. **Zen Tubing** (855/936-8823, www.zentubing.com, 10am-4pm daily, $20 adults, $15 ages 4-12, $5 cooler carrier; $5 same-day second trips) sends their tubers (what else would you call one who rides a tube?) on calm sections of the French Broad River. If you pick up a six-pack of your favorite beverage, book the cooler carrier tube to keep any snacks and beverages close at hand. Tube trips take a while, but you'll have plenty of company—the river is often mobbed by tubing enthusiasts. There are two locations: one in downtown Asheville (608 Riverside Dr.) and one in south Asheville (1648 Brevard Rd.).

Asheville Adventure Rentals (704 Riverside Dr., 828/505-7371, http://ashevilleadventurerentals.com, 10am-6pm Mon.-Thurs., 10am-6:30pm Fri.-Sun., rentals from $30 per day) specializes in gear that get you wet, namely stand-up paddleboards, kayaks, and Bellyaks. A Bellyak is a cross between a kayak and an ergonomically designed surfboard; you lie down and paddle like you're swimming, and take the river rapids head-on. It's a fun ride on the small but exciting rapids of the French Broad River when the stream is at normal levels; it's a thrilling ride when the river is running a little high. If you're equipped with your own paddleboard or kayak, Adventure Rentals rents helmets, dry suits, PFDs, kayak skirts, and more.

★ Zip-Lining

For a different perspective on the Asheville area, head north for 30 minutes along I-26 West and spend the day at **Navitat** (242 Poverty Branch Rd., Barnardsville, 855/628-4828 or 828/626-3700, www.navitat.com, 8am-5pm daily), where you can streak through the forest canopy on a pair of zip line courses like an overgrown flying squirrel. The **Blue Ridge Experience** (from $89) has the tallest zip line; it's an incredible 350 feet high (they say "don't look down," but please do). The longest zip line is more than 3,600 feet—that's a long ride. Two rappels, a pair of

the heart-pounding Blue Ridge Experience zipline at Navitat

sky bridges, and three short hikes provide interludes from all the zipping and flying, and there are plenty of opportunities for photos and action-camera videos. The **Moody Cove Adventure** ($99), a smaller course, has 10 zip lines up to 2,000 feet long, a pair of bridges, and two rappels. Combine the two courses ($159) into one giant day of adventure.

If you're tempted to zip line but want something a little less heart-pounding, try **The Adventure Center of Asheville** (1 Resort Dr., 877/247-5539, www.asheville-treetopsadventurepark.com, 9am-5pm Sun.-Wed., 8:30am-5:30pm Thurs.-Sat.), which has a number of high-flying adventures. Their **Treetops Adventure Park** ($49 adults, $44 ages 18 and under) has 60 challenges (read: rope swings, sky bridges, cargo nets to climb, short zip lines, leaps from tall platforms) spread over five different adventure trails, allowing you to face the trail that presents you with the best challenges. The **Zipline Canopy Tour** ($89 adults, $69 age 18 and under) has 11 zips, three sky bridges, and so many great views you'll forget about the zip lines. **Kid Zip** ($49 adults, $44 ages 18 and under) is a zip line course designed for kids ages 4-10. They also have the **KOLO Mountain Bike Park** ($19 adult full-day access, $14 youth full-day access, $8 2-hour access) and something called the **QuickJump** ($10 first jump, $5 additional jumps), where you can leap off a 65-foot tower and trust your harness to lower you safely to the ground.

Spas

After a day (or two) of playing hard in and around Asheville, you'll need to relax. The **Grove Park Inn Resort & Spa** (290 Macon Ave., 828/252-2711 or 800/438-5800, www.groveparkinn.com) has a spa known the world over and there are several places where you can get a massage. **Shoji Spa & Lodge** (96 Avondale Heights, 828/299-0999, www.shojiretreats.com, 10am-10pm Mon., 11am-8pm Tues.-Thurs., 10am-10pm Fri.-Sun., $41 one hour, $61 90 minutes, $72 two hours) does things a little differently. This Japanese-inspired spa has private outdoor hot tubs as well as coed hot tubs, saunas, and cold-plunge pools open to spa guests. The private hot tubs are big enough for groups of up to six, and each is perched on the side of the mountain, open on one side to give you a broad view of the mountain while staying out of sight from other guests. Shoji also offers massage treatments ($90-315), to which you can add public spa amenities for only $20. After a couple of long hikes, Shoji will help you relax.

On the Biltmore Estate

George Vanderbilt was drawn to Asheville by the mountain air and the glories of nature that surround the city. The **Biltmore Estate** (1 Approach Rd., 800/411-3812, www.biltmore.com) was once a huge estate of some 125,000 acres, almost every bit of it untamed. Landscape architect Frederick Law Olmsted groomed the forest around the house—the same forest you see today—but the rest was left a natural playground. Visitors can explore the forests, fields, trails, and waters of the Biltmore Estate and try their hand at sports and activities from the familiar (bicycling) to the exotic (the Land Rover Experience Driving School). The **Adventure Center** (800/411-3812, Antler Hill Village) can make reservations and point you in the right direction for any number of outdoor activities.

For starters, there are countless miles of bicycle trails on the **Biltmore Estate** (1 Approach Rd., 800/411-3812, www.biltmore.com, 9:30am-3:30pm daily Jan.-mid-Mar., 9am-4:30pm daily mid-Mar.-Dec., $40-75 adults, $20-38 ages 10-16, free under age 10). Bring your bike, or rent one in Antler Hill Village from the **Bike Barn** (800/411-3812, single-speed beach cruiser $15 per hour, mountain and hybrid bikes half-day and full-day $30-60 adults, $20-40 children, $50 tandem bikes, estate admission not included). Riding on paved roads is not allowed; they're too narrow to share with cars. Stick to the marked paths, which lead past prime photo spots and some of the most beautiful land on the estate.

Hiking on the Biltmore Estate (1 Approach Rd., 800/411-3812, www.biltmore.com, 9:30am-3:30pm daily Jan.-mid-Mar., 9am-4:30pm daily mid-Mar.-Dec., $40-75 adults, $20-38 ages 10-16, free under age 10) can mean anything from walking 2.5 miles of mulched paths in the manicured gardens to exploring the hills, meadows, streams, and riverbank on more than 22 miles of trails. None of the trails are rugged, so all you need is water, your camera, and maybe a walking stick.

Segway tours come in four flavors: a basic tour ($50) on a paved trail to the lagoon below the house; an off-road tour ($75) to a vista of the house past the lagoon; the westside tour ($100) to a seldom-seen side of the estate; and the advanced tour ($100), which follows the Deerpark Trail.

Equine enthusiasts can saddle up for an hour-long guided **horseback ride** ($60), a two-hour private trail ride ($160), or a private trail ride and picnic lunch ($230). Those who would rather sit back and relax can take carriage rides ($350 up to four guests) and wagon rides ($35).

Spend the day on the water with **guided raft trips** ($35 adults, $25 ages 12 and under) or a self-guided kayak trip ($25) on the French Broad River for a rare view of the estate. Novice anglers can sign up for a fishing lesson (from $125, kids' lessons available), but experienced anglers may opt for a daylong wade trip or drift boat trip ($350 for two guests).

If you're feeling really adventurous, learn to **shoot sporting clays** ($175-225). After a few lessons they'll have you knocking clay pigeons out of the sky. There's also a sporting clay course ($100) and a full-day shotgun sports clinic ($450).

The **Land Rover Driving Experience** gets you behind the wheel of a Land Rover with a lesson on off-road driving (1 hour $250, 2 hours $400). After your lesson, hit the trail (2 hours $400) or go out for a full day ($1,200) and master those off-road skills.

ACCOMMODATIONS

The **Asheville Bed & Breakfast Association** (www.ashevillebba.com) has a constantly growing membership of inns and B&Bs in the area, and they band together to promote getaways, tours, and seasonal packages. Check with them for any current specials.

Under $100

With so many neo-hippie types, college kids, dirtbags (it's not an insult, it's what rock climbers often call themselves), kayakers, hikers, and bikers coming through, it's no surprise to find a nice hostel nestled among the hotels and bed-and-breakfasts. At the **Asheville ArtHaus Hostel** (16 Ravenscroft Dr., 828/423-0256, http://aahostel.com, $50, bungalow with private bath $88) you'll find only private guest rooms and even a private bungalow. Reservations are available up to five months in advance, so it's easy to get a room if you know when you're traveling. At the hostel you'll find free waffles, coffee, and tea at make-your-own stations; free Wi-Fi; free parking; and downtown within walking distance.

Bon Paul and Sharky's Hostel of Asheville (816 Haywood Rd., 828/775-3283, www.bonpaulandsharkys.com, cash only) is a pleasant old white house with a porch and a porch swing, high-speed Internet access, and dorm-style bunks in women-only or coed shared rooms ($27) as well as camping ($20) in the yard. If you want a little more of a retreat, a private room with a TV and a queen bed ($72) and a cottage ($100) are available. Dogs must stay in the outdoor kennels.

$100-200

One of the most hospitable bed-and-breakfasts in Asheville is **Asheville Green Cottage** (25 St. Dunstans Circle, 828/707-6563 or 828/707-2919, www.ashevillegreencottage.com, $125-165 peak season, $95-135 off-season). This 1920s arts and crafts-style home is built of huge granite blocks and is simply decorated but cozy. Guest rooms are big enough, but breakfast is outstanding, and they can cater to special dietary needs. Asheville Green Cottage is a "healthy and green" bed-and-breakfast, meaning they're smoke-free, fragrance-free, and use natural products for cleaning. It's a great place to come home to after a day of exploring Asheville.

Just off the Blue Ridge Parkway north of Asheville is an inn that's a true retreat. The first time I saw the ★ **Sourwood Inn** (810 Elk Mountain Scenic Hwy., 828/255-0690, www.sourwoodinn.com, $155-200 inn rooms, $200 separate cabins), it charmed me so much that I made reservations for an anniversary weekend. Situated on the end of a ridgeline, the view is nearly 270 degrees from every balcony and bedroom window. There's no Wi-Fi or cell service, so you can truly unplug. There are a couple of miles of easy hiking trails, a pond, a bamboo grove, and some sculptures tucked in the woods nearby, but if you're feeling adventurous, there are options. The innkeeper's son-in-law happens to be a fly-fishing guide and an active hawker—he hunts with a hawk named Rocket Girl. Fishing and hawking packages are available; other specials include a Blue Ridge Parkway deal that includes fly-fishing, a massage, and horseback riding, as well as Biltmore Estate passes and wild food foraging. Call for directions—it's tricky to find.

★ **ASIA Bed and Breakfast Spa** (128 Hillside St., 828/255-0051, www.ashevillespa.com, $189-279) is one of my favorite places to stay in town. Every room has a big, comfortable bed and a two-person Jacuzzi tub; there's a sauna and cold shower for guests to use, and a European steam shower; breakfast is a healthy, filling affair; and, most importantly, the rooms are private and quiet. ASIA keeps a group of massage therapists and estheticians on call, so you can arrange for treatments of almost any kind on site. Throughout the house, comfortable seating areas make it easy to find a spot for breakfast or tea, or to just read or talk; my favorite spot is the tatami porch overlooking the Japanese garden at the front of the house.

Over $200

Hotel Indigo (151 Haywood St., 828/239-0239, www.boutiquehotel-asheville.com, $189-519) is shiny, modern, and steps away from downtown. The staff are attentive and courteous, and the concierges know the ins, outs, shortcuts, best restaurants and bars, and top townie things to see and do. As one of the tallest buildings in Asheville, the mountain views are spectacular from upper floors; keep that in mind when making a reservation.

If you've spent the day touring Biltmore House, viewing the incredible splendor in which a robber baron of the Gilded Age basked, it may be jarring to return to real life, unless you're Richard Branson or European royalty. You can soften the transition with a stay at the luxurious **Inn on Biltmore Estate** (866/336-1245, www.biltmore.com, $499-599 peak season, $259-399 off-season, suites up to $2,000). It's everything you'd wish for from a hotel in this location. The suites are beautifully furnished and luxurious, the views are magnificent, and the lobby, dining room, and library have the deluxe coziness of a turn-of-the-20th-century lodge. On the other hand, if you do happen to be Richard Branson or Queen Elizabeth and simply need a mountain getaway, consider the inn's **Cottage on Biltmore Estate** (from $1,600 per night). This historic two-room cottage was designed by Richard Howland Hunt, son of the mansion's designer, Richard Morris Hunt. Your own personal butler and chef come with the digs; call for rates. In December 2015, the Biltmore opened **Village Hotel on Biltmore Estate** (rooms from $279, packages from $313) in Antler Hill Village. The 209-room hotel is a testament to the ongoing and growing popularity of the Biltmore.

In the heart of downtown, **Aloft Asheville Downtown** (51 Biltmore Ave., 828/232-2838 or 866/716-8143, www.aloftashevilledowntown.com, $209-509) offers a hip spot to rest your head. There is a trendy bar serving rockstar cocktails, plush modern guest rooms, and fantastic city and mountain views from most rooms (others are poolside). Some of the best

Motor Courts

In the days of yore, before budget hotels became the norm, the motor court or cottage court was the stay-over of choice for middle-class travelers. Today, these motor courts and cottage courts are relics of the past and few remain, but the mountains of North Carolina still contain a handful of fine examples; in the Asheville area at least two are still operating today, providing travelers with retro accommodations. **Asheville Log Cabin Motor Court** (330 Weaverville Hwy., 828/645-6546, www.cabinlodging.com, 2-night minimum stay weekends, $85-245, two pets allowed, $15/night one pet, $25/night 2 pets) was constructed around 1930 and appears in the fantastic 1958 Robert Mitchum movie *Thunder Road*. The cabins have cable TV and wireless Internet access but no phones. Some are air-conditioned, but that's not usually a necessity at this elevation. Another great cabin court is the **Pines Cottages** (346 Weaverville Hwy., 828/645-9661, http://ashevillepines.com, $115-175, $15 per pet, up to 2 pets allowed). Billed as "A nice place for nice people," how could you resist staying here?

restaurants in Asheville are a few minutes' walk away, and the best live music in town is just a couple of blocks south.

The **Grove Park Inn Resort & Spa** (290 Macon Ave., 828/252-2711 or 800/438-5800, www.groveparkinn.com, $349-942 peak season, $177-755 off-season, spa and golf packages available) is the sort of place Asheville residents bring their out-of-town houseguests when giving them a grand tour of the city, simply to walk into the lobby to ooh and aah. The massive stone building—constructed by a crew of 400 who had only mule teams and a single steam shovel to aid them—was erected in 1912 and 1913, the project of St. Louis millionaire E. W. Grove, the name behind Grove's Tasteless Chill Tonic, a medicinal syrup that outsold Coca-Cola in the 1890s. You may see it in antiques shops; on the label is a picture of a wincing baby who looks like he's just been given a dose of the stuff.

The opening of the Grove Park Inn was cause for such fanfare that William Jennings Bryan addressed the celebratory dinner party. In the coming years, at least eight U.S. presidents would stay here, as would a glittering parade of early-20th-century big shots, among them Henry Ford, Thomas Edison, Eleanor Roosevelt, Harry Houdini, F. Scott Fitzgerald, Will Rogers, and George Gershwin. Even if you don't stay at the Grove Park while you are visiting Asheville, swing

by just to see it. You can drive right up to the front door, and if you tell the valets that you just want to go in and see the lobby, they'll probably be willing to watch your car for five minutes (a tip helps). The lobby is amazing, a cross between a Gilded Age hunting lodge and the great hall of a medieval castle. There are 14-foot fireplaces at each end, and the elevators, believe it or not, are inside the chimneys. It's easy to imagine flappers, foreign dignitaries, mobsters, and literati milling about the lobby with their martinis when this hotel was young.

You can also park your car and head inside for a cocktail or dinner at one of their many on-site establishments: **Vue 1913** (5pm-10pm nightly, $24-38) has French and American dishes that are well done but not particularly creative; **Edison craft ales + kitchen** (4pm-11pm Mon.-Thurs., 4pm-midnight Fri., 11am-midnight Sat., 11am-11pm Sun., $8-38) serves some high-quality bar food and craft beer; **Blue Ridge** (6:30am-10:30am daily, dinner 5pm-9pm Fri.-Sat., brunch noon-2:30pm Sun., breakfast $17-23, brunch $38, dinner $42) is a farm-to-table artisanal buffet (yes, I too am confused as to how artisanal and buffet work together); and the **Sunset Terrace** (11am-3pm and 5pm-10pm daily, $15-24 lunch, $22-59 dinner) and **Sunset Terrace Cocktail Lounge** (11am-9pm daily, $8-14). Each venue has phenomenal views, allowing you to have dinner or a glass of wine while watching the sun set.

Being a guest at the Grove Park is quite an experience. In addition to the spectacle of the lodge and its multiple restaurants, cafés, bars, and shops, for an additional charge guests have access to its world-famous **spa** (Mon.-Fri. $65, Sat.-Sun. $90). Nonguests can purchase day passes (Mon.-Thurs. $95). The pass gives access to the lounges, pools, waterfall, steam room, inhalation room, and outdoor whirlpool tub. The indoor pool is a fantastic place, a subterranean stone room with vaulted skylights and tropical plants. For extra fees ($109-500, most $200-300), guests can choose from a long menu of spa treatments: massages, facials, manicures, aromatherapy, and body wraps. For $70 you can have your aura photographed before and after the treatment to gauge the depth of your relaxation.

FOOD

No matter what you're craving, from Mediterranean to vegetarian, four-star to down-home, Asheville has the eateries that both embrace the Southern traditions of its mountain home and explore well beyond its borders. This is a town that clearly loves its food, with 13 active farmers markets, more than 250 independent restaurants, and 21 microbreweries in a city of fewer than 100,000 residents. Farmers work with restaurants to provide the highest-quality produce and meats, and artisanal bakers and cheese makers supply their tasty foodstuffs to restaurants across the price spectrum.

For a sampling of the best of what Asheville has to offer the gastronome, take a walking tour with **Eating Asheville** (828/489-3266, http://eatingasheville.com, daily tour $49, high-roller tour $59). Tours begin at the Grove Arcade (1 Page Ave.) and the Bier Garden (46 Haywood St.) and stop at six of Asheville's best farm-to-table restaurants for a taste of what they're cooking and provide two or three drink pairings as well as a talk about their food philosophy; sometimes tours meet the chef. Held on Saturday only, the deluxe high-roller tour visits six of the top restaurants and includes four or five beverage pairings (wine, beer, and craft cocktails); for just a few bucks more, it's the way to go. They also offer tours of six hot spots in West Asheville (tours about 2 hours, Fri.-Sat., $49), which has grown into a food destination unto itself.

Breakfast and Brunch

West Asheville's **Sunny Point Café** (626 Haywood Rd., 828/252-0055, www.sunnypointcafe.com, 8:30am-9:30pm Tues.-Sat., 8:30am-2:30pm Sun.-Mon., $10-17) serves three meals most days, but is so famous for its brunch that a line sometimes forms out the door. The breakfast menu is popular and served any time of day, even though the lunch and dinner menus are also well worth a trip. This is a great bet for vegetarians—the meatless options are imaginative and beautifully created. Whatever you get, order one of their angel biscuits; those things are tall, airy, and so good.

American

One of the best meals you'll eat in Asheville is at ★ **Rhubarb** (7 SW Pack Sq., 828/785-1503, www.rhubarbasheville.com, 11:30am-9:30pm Mon. and Wed.-Thurs., 11:30am-10:30pm Fri., 10:30am-10:30pm Sat., 10:30am-9:30pm Sun., shared plates $5-19, full plates $18-32). The menu is in constant flux based on seasonality, availability, and, as they say, "the whim of the chefs," but I've always found the food tremendously good—stellar even. The Local Lyonnaise salad features crispy trout sardines and smoky, wood-roasted potatoes; it's a thing of perfection. The mains encompass quite a range of flavors and techniques, such as goat cheese gnudi, a seared cauliflower "steak," and duck confit. Since everything's seasonal, expect some switch-ups on the sides and mains, but also expect an exceptional meal.

★ **The Admiral** (400 Haywood Rd., West Asheville, 828/252-2541, www.theadmiralnc.com, 5pm-10pm daily, small plates $10, entrées $28) has been a food destination since its opening in a humble cinderblock building in what they call "the wage-earning side of town." Blue-collar roots or no, they serve some distinguished and much-lauded New Southern food that keeps the kitchen on its toes with interesting techniques and seasonal ingredients. The restaurant is small yet cozy and chic, while somehow retaining a sort of dive-bar vibe (but in the best way). The cocktails aren't half-bad either.

Early Girl Eatery (8 Wall St., 828/259-9292, www.earlygirleatery.com, 7:30am-3pm Mon., 7:30am-9pm Tues.-Fri., 9am-9pm Sat.-Sun., $10-15) has caused a stir among area locavores and is gaining a following with visitors. More than half of the vegetables, meat, and fish used at Early Girl was raised or caught within 20 miles of the restaurant. The menu accommodates Asheville's large vegetarian and vegan contingent, but non-veg diners can feast on pan-fried trout with pecan butter, free-range chicken, or cheeseburgers made from hormone-free beef and topped with farmstead cheese, basil mayo, and all the fixings. Breakfast is served all day, and is among the best in Asheville. The multigrain pancakes are out of this world.

If you're in the mood for a killer hot dog, a bahn mi, or a Cuban sandwich that will make you consider proposing to whoever's behind the grill, head to **Ben's Penny Mart and Foothills Deli** (195 Hilliard Ave., 828/254-2367, www.benstuneup.com, 9am-midnight Mon.-Thurs., 9am-2am Fri.-Sat., $10-14). It's a tiny place and the menu is small, but every bite is perfection. Pick up a couple of beers on draft or in bottles or cans (or a can of Ben's Tune Up Sake) to have with your lunch.

In the River Arts District, **The Bull and Beggar** (37 Paynes Way, #007, 828/575-9443, www.the-bull-and-beggar.com, 5pm-10pm Sun.-Thurs., 5pm-11pm Fri.-Sat., $9-85) has become the dinner spot of choice for those in the know. With a menu that runs from a raw bar to a bone-in rib eye for two ($75), rich and filling French-inspired entrées complement a killer charcuterie platter and a list of $5 sides that are meal-worthy in and of themselves. On Monday night they serve a $6 burger; when I

asked a friend if we should go, she was rendered temporarily speechless by the memory of the previous week's burger.

Table (48 College St., 828/254-8980, http://tableasheville.com, lunch 11:30am-2:30pm Wed.-Sat., dinner at 5:30pm daily, brunch 10:30am-2:30pm Sun., lunch $8-14, brunch $6-14, dinner $19-34), a James Beard Award semifinalist, is upscale, interesting, innovative, and, above all else, delicious. They use ingredients like locally caught bass and mountain-raised pork and lamb, but you'll also find some unusual items, like sweetbreads or quail, on the menu. They're renowned for their charcuterie. Call for reservations and, if you're feeling bold, go with the chef's tasting menu, a selection of dishes that showcase the best this miniscule kitchen (you'll see it on your way in) has to offer.

The riverside **Smoky Park Supper Club** (350 Riverside Dr., 828/350-0315, www.smokypark.com, 2pm-late Tues.-Fri., 11:30am-late Sat., 11:30am-9pm Sun., small plates $5-16, large plates $8-27) cuts a striking figure on the banks of the French Broad—it's made entirely of shipping containers (the largest such restaurant in the United States when it opened), those industrial metal boxes loaded on cargo ships, trucks, and trains. As modern as the look may be, the menu is Appalachian through and through. They cook over wood here, so you'll find wood-roasted chicken and whole trout, grilled steaks and chops, and homey sides like creamed kale and butternut squash; they even do an amazing grilled cheese sandwich. On weekends they serve lunch, but through the week it's dinner only.

At **Local Provisions** (77 Biltmore Ave., 828/424-7815, www.localprovisionsasheville.com, 5:30pm-10pm Tues.-Sun., brunch 10:30am-2:30pm Sun., small plates $3-12, large plates $24-34), chef Justin Burdett honors and expands Southern food traditions. His innovative menu combines the flavors and ingredients of the South with those from near and far: sea urchin with beet and apple grace the menu along with buttermilk curds and whey. He keeps pushing, making kimchi and rabbit liver pâté and an assortment of terrines and sausages as well. Add to this a great (and affordable) wine list and you have the makings of an excellent meal.

Hot chicken, the peppery fried chicken that's a Nashville staple, has made its way to Asheville via **Rocky's Hot Chicken Shack** (1455 Patton Ave., 828/575-2260, www.rockyshotchickenshack.com, 11am-9pm Sun.-Thurs., 11am-10pm Fri.-Sat., $6-11). Like all hot chicken, Rocky's is served at a variety of spice levels, from plain (no spice, just fried chicken) and honey-style to the ghost pepper-sauced XX-Hot, the hottest item on the menu. (If this is your first hot chicken experience, start somewhere in the middle and work your way up.) There's a second Rocky's at 3749 Sweeten Creek Road (828/676-3222, 11am-9pm daily), in case you find yourself hungry in that part of town.

Asian

You'll find something unusual at **Ben's Tune Up** (195 Hilliard Ave., 828/424-7580, http://benstuneup.com, 4pm-2am Mon.-Fri., noon-2am Sat.-Sun., $9-14): a sake brewery. They're one of only a small group of sake brewers in the country, and their trio of sakes (more if they're feeling frisky or experimental) are mighty fine. Located in a former auto repair shop, their beer garden has enough eclectic art and odd industrial touches to honor the building's former purpose while still making it a cool spot to hang out, watch a country band, sip some sake, and order off the Japanese-inspired menu.

Gan Shan Station (143 Charlotte St., 828/774-5280, www.ganshanstation.com, 11:30am-2:30pm Mon. and Wed.-Sat., dinner 5pm-10pm Mon.-Sun., lunch $4-13, dinner $9-18) offers up a refreshing bit of fine dining to Asheville's world of Asian food. The menu is loaded with dishes that span nations and cuisines—from ramen (Japan) to bulgogi (Korea) to mapo doyfu (China) to citrus shrimp (Thailand). The real treat is the Chef's Table ($45, 48-hour reservation required), where you'll interact with the chefs from your kitchen-side table as they serve up dishes for the curious and adventurous eater.

I hope **Blue Dream Curry House** (81 Patton Ave., 828/258-2500, www.bluedreamcurry.com, 11:30am-9pm Mon.-Thurs., 11:30am-10pm Fri.-Sat., $7-12) becomes an Asheville staple. Menu options include a taco served on naan and pickled peanuts in a spicy, curried, and briny sauce. The curries are Japanese, Indian, Thai, and Peruvian, and they aren't afraid to offer a couple of meat options on the veggie- and vegan-centered menu.

Red Ginger Dim Sum and Tapas (82 Patton Ave., 828/505-8688, www.redginger-asheville.com, 11:30am-9pm Mon.-Thurs., 11:30am-10pm Fri., 11am-10pm Sat., 11am-9pm Sun., $4-18) specializes in Asian-style tapas and dim sum, delicious little Chinese dumplings that are steamed or fried and stuffed with savory fillings. While many diners are familiar with tapas (small, sharable plates), dim sum remains a bit of a mystery, especially as a main course. I recommend ordering several plates to share in order to explore a broad range of flavors and styles. Don't miss the Shanghai-style pork dumpling, shrimp rice roll, or Buddha bean curd roll. Their tapas, especially the smoked duck breast and steamed sea bass, do not disappoint.

Barbecue

What's a trip to North Carolina without barbecue? At **Luella's Bar-B-Que** (501 Merrimon Ave., 828/606-9024, www.luellasbbq.com, 11am-9pm Mon.-Thurs., 11am-10pm Fri.-Sat., noon-8:30pm Sun., $6.50-15), you can try the range of styles and sauces that make North Carolina 'cue distinct. Ribs, chopped pork, brisket, smoked wings, and sides like mac and cheese, fried okra, collard greens, and hush puppies are staples, but there's a surprising item on the menu: barbecued tempeh. (Tempeh is a cousin of tofu.) I'm a barbecue judge (really, I'm certified), so trust me when I say it's good—everything is here, from the grub to the vibe to the impressive array of local beer on draft.

When ★ **Buxton Hall Barbeque** (32 Banks Ave., 828/232-7216, www.buxtonhall. com, 11:30am-3pm and 5:30pm-10pm Tues.-Sun., $5-16) opened in August 2015, it was after months of anticipation. Chef Elliott Moss had been serving up 'cue at every event and in every parking lot in town, perfecting his technique while building this beautiful restaurant. Buxton is a blend of old-school barbecue at its best, and Moss spanned the Carolinas to create his menu. Chicken bog (rice, chicken, and sausage) from the South Carolina low country is right beside eastern North Carolina whole-hog barbecue and South Carolina barbecue hash and smoked sausages. All are accompanied by an excellent selection of classic barbecue sides.

French

Chef Michael Baudouin grew up in France's Rhône Valley, the son of a winemaker and an excellent cook. He brings his culinary heritage to Asheville at **Bouchon** (62 N. Lexington Ave., 828/350-1140, http://ashevillebouchon.com, from 5pm daily, small plates $6-20, entrées $18-25). Bouchon's "French comfort food" includes classics such as mussels frites (all you can eat Mon.-Wed.), French-style trout, and pan-seared duck breast with cherries. Delicious vegetarian options are available. If crepes are your thing, they also have **Creperie Bouchon** (62 1/2 Lexington Ave., 828/350-3741, www. creperiebouchon.com, 11am-9:30pm Mon.-Thurs., 11am-10:30pm Fri.-Sat., 11am-8pm Sun., $7-12). The creperie shares much of its menu with Bouchon, so expect similar appetizers, like those all-you-can-eat mussels.

Indian

Local favorite **Chai Pani** (22 Battery Park Ave., 828/254-4003, www.chaipani.net, lunch 11:30am-3:30pm Mon.-Sat., noon-3:30pm Sun., dinner 5pm-9pm Sun.-Thurs., 5:30pm-10pm Fri.-Sat., under $14) continues to win fans because of its cool atmosphere

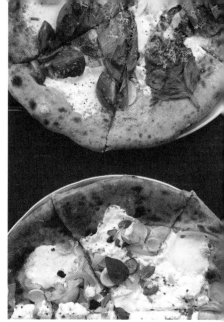

the pies at All Souls Pizza

and great food. The restaurant's name means "tea and water," a phrase that refers to a snack or a small gift. This restaurant is inspired by Indian street-food vendors and serves casual and affordable specialties from all over India.

★ **Mela** (70 Lexington Ave., 828/225-8880, www.melaasheville.com, lunch 11:30am-2:30pm daily, dinner 5:30pm-9:30pm Sun.-Thurs., 5:30pm-10pm Fri.-Sat., $10-15) is one of the best Indian restaurants in North Carolina. The elaborate menu offers dozens of choices, combining cuisines of both northern and southern India with great meat, seafood, and vegetable dishes. The restaurant is dark and elegant, but the prices are surprisingly low; you can put together a great patchwork meal of appetizers, which start at $2, along with soup and roti. Don't miss the samosas.

Italian and Pizza

★ **Cucina 24** (24 Wall St., 828/254-6170, http://cucina24restaurant.com, dinner from 5:30pm Tues.-Fri., from 5pm Sat.-Sun., $10-26) is, as executive chef Brian Canipelli says, "not a fettuccine alfredo-and-lasagna kind of place; we do cooking like it's done in Italy, but with North Carolina ingredients." I visit Cucina 24 every time I'm in Asheville, and every time I'm smitten with what Canipelli does in his kitchen. The pizzas are creative, accessible, and just a bit decadent (who microplanes black truffles over pizza?); the pastas are fresh, always elevated by interesting ingredients like sunchokes, trumpet mushrooms, pork cheeks, or smoked mackerel broth; and the charcuterie is made in-house. When we eat in the dining room, my wife and I go a little dressier, but stay more casual when eating at the bar; a good rule of thumb is to look as good as the food.

★ **All Souls Pizza** (175 Clingman Ave., 828/254-0169, www.allsoulspizza.com, lunch 11:30am-5pm Tues.-Sat., dinner 5pm-10pm daily, lunch $7-14, dinner $7-18) in the River Arts District has gotten creative with pizza in typical Asheville fashion. They mill their own flours and polenta from organic grains; source the meat, produce, and cheese close to Asheville; and everything else they can get locally, they do. The effort pays off in your first bite and you'll be hooked whether you go with a plain cheese pie; smoked shrimp, chilies, and mozzarella; country ham, egg, and mozzarella; or watercress, leeks, goat cheese, and mozzarella.

Latin American

Ask an Asheville resident for restaurant recommendations, and chances are **Salsa's** (6 Patton Ave., 828/252-9805, www.salsasnc. com, 11:30am-4pm Mon.-Sat. noon-4pm Sun., 5pm-9pm Sun.-Thurs., 5pm-9:30pm Fri.-Sat., lunch $10-15, dinner $15-22) will be one of the first names mentioned. Salsa's pan-Latin concoctions, from their famous fish burritos to exquisite cocktails, keep this tiny café jam-packed with locals and visitors. When the weather's good, it's fun to eat on their little street-side patio and watch the people go by.

Limones (13 Eagle St., 828/252-2327, http://limonesrestaurant.com, 5pm-10pm daily, brunch 10:30am-2:30pm Sat.-Sun., dinner $12-22) is delicious. Chef Hugo Ramírez, a native of Mexico City, combines his background in Mexican and French-inspired Californian food to create dishes that are as flavorful as they are memorable. However, if you're trying to work your way through the menu of margaritas, tequilas, and mescals, your recollection of what you ate may grow a little fuzzy.

Asheville's taco game is on point, and **Taco Billy** (201 Haywood Rd., 828/505-0088, www. tacobillyasheville.com, 7am-3pm Tues.-Sun., $2.50-4) is one of several fine taco joints, but with a twist: breakfast. This is a breakfast and lunch spot and their breakfast tacos (served all day, of course) are excellent. I recommend any of the Billy tacos: Billie Holiday (sausage, egg, and cheese); Billy Ocean (home fries, egg, and cheese); or Billy Joel (bacon, egg, and cheese). For lunch, the menu has everything from cumin sweet potato to fried chicken tacos, or you can build your own taco.

Spanish

★ **Cúrate** (11 Biltmore Ave., 828/239-2946, www.curatetapasbar.com, 11:30am-10:30pm Tues.-Thurs., 11:30am-11pm Fri.-Sat., 11:30am-10:30pm Sun., small plates $5-20) features the food of chef Katie Button, a James Beard Award semifinalist who cooked at legendary restaurant, elBulli, in Spain. She serves a Spanish tapas-style menu, so you'll be making a meal of a bunch of small plates and get to try a variety of flavors and textures. The *table de jamón* (a selection of three delicious and very different Spanish hams), and the *pulpo a'la gallega* (octopus and paprika with potatoes) are good dishes to share. There are also a number of vegan and gluten-free selections on the menu. The can't-miss street dish that people rave about is the *berenjenas la taberna*—fried eggplant drizzled in wild mountain honey and garnished with rosemary. This dish is incredible and can even serve as a final course if you like a savory-sweet dessert. There's a lot of energy in this restaurant, partially because a long bar faces the kitchen,

Foodtopia and Beer City, USA

From writers to musicians to artists, those with a creative streak have always found something inspiring in Asheville. In recent years, a new set of artists has emerged: **chefs, mixologists,** and **brewers** who are putting Asheville on the map for their creativity on the plate and in the glass.

Asheville's status as a "foodtopia" started in earnest in 2009, when the town won the coveted title of "Beer City, USA" (a title it held until 2013), was named "Best Craft Beer City in America," and was included in the *Huffington Post*'s Top 10 Undiscovered Local Food Cities. Since then it's only gotten bigger. With close to two dozen breweries downtown, some 80-odd local beers on tap at any given moment, and 250 independent restaurants, it's surprising that Asheville's food scene remained a secret as long as it did.

Once the word was out, the James Beard Award nominations included chefs and restaurants from Asheville, and more chefs wanted to come here to cook. Asheville now boasts a number of James Beard nominees, including Jacob Sessoms of **Table,** Katie Button of **Cúrate,** and Elliott Moss of **Buxton Hall Barbecue.**

Award-winners and nominees aren't the only foodies drawing attention to Asheville. A local character known as the Mushroom Man forages the surrounding forests for mushrooms, ramps, ferns, greens, berries, and roots, then sells his loot to restaurants in town. Stephen Steidle of **Eating Asheville** (828/489-3266, www.eatingasheville.com) leads walking tours of the town's best spots for food and drink, and the guys at **Asheville Brewery Tours** (828/233-5006, http://ashevillebrewerytours.com) help visitors find the tastiest brews in town.

putting everyone from chef Button to her expert kitchen brigade on display.

Vegetarian

When you've been at the Grey Eagle or the Orange Peel for a late show and you need to refuel with some good food, the lights are on at **Rosetta's Kitchen** (116 N. Lexington Ave., 828/232-0738, www.rosettaskitchen.com, 11am-2am Mon.-Sat., around $10). There's so much to recommend about this place: The food is very good, it's all vegetarian and mostly vegan, and it's made with local produce in season. They compost everything that makes its way back to the kitchen, recycle all their trash, and make sure their used vegetable oil goes to power biodiesel cars—it's Asheville's signature countercultural reinterpretation of the South. It's one of the best vegetarian places in town.

Desserts and Snacks

French Broad Chocolates (10 S. Pack Square, 828/252-4181, http://frenchbroad-chocolates.com, 11am-11pm Sun.-Thurs., 11am-midnight Fri.-Sat.) describes itself as "a sacred space for chocophiles." With a prominent location in Pack Square, hordes of chocophiles are getting in line to find out why this particular chocolatier is the talk of the town. The answer is simple: chocolate. Chocolate truffles, brownies, pastries, sipping chocolates, floats, bars, beans, and a laundry list of chocolate products nearly as long as the line here on a Friday night (and trust me, it's long). If you don't care for chocolate, get a non-chocolate dessert and sit at the table while your friends flip their lids over their bonbons. This is a true "bean-to-bar" chocolatier: they roast their own cacao in a rooftop solar roaster at their nearby factory and **tasting room** (21 Buxton Ave., 828/504-4996, noon-6pm Mon.-Sat., tours 2pm Sat.). It's getting closer to being a "farm-to-bar" chocolatier: The owners also own a cacao farm in Costa Rica, which they hope to harvest any season now.

The Gourmet Chip Company (43 1/2 Broadway St., 828/254-3335, www.gourmetchipcompany.com, 11am-6pm Sun.-Thurs., 11am-8pm Fri.-Sat., $5-9) has made me love potato chips again. They make chips fresh all day (and have a huge stack of potato sacks to prove it), topping them with some lovely and intriguing ingredients: goat cheese and sea salt, dehydrated apple cider vinegar and a balsamic reduction, dark chocolate and applewood-smoked bacon, buffalo sauce and blue cheese, honey and lavender. Served up in a paper cone, these are attractive dishes that are fun to eat. The only downside is that they're so good you'll want to eat them fast, which means both hands, which means you can't walk down the street as you gobble these delicious chips. Sit over them for a while and savor them anyway.

In Biltmore Village
In one of the historic cottages of Biltmore Village is the **Corner Kitchen** (3 Boston Way, 828/274-2439, www.thecornerkitchen. com, breakfast 7:30am-11am Mon.-Fri., brunch 9am-3pm Sat.-Sun., lunch 11:30am-3pm Mon.-Fri., dinner 5pm daily, breakfast $6-13, brunch $9-13, lunch $10-13, entrées $19-30). Head chef Joe Scully, first in his class at the Culinary Institute of America, counts among his illustrious former gigs New York's Waldorf Astoria and the United Nations, where he served as executive chef. He is joined in the Corner Kitchen by Josh Weeks, a young Carolina-born chef with an impressive résumé and expertise in Southern, French, and Pacific cuisines. They've put together an elegant menu that harmoniously combines home-style and haute cuisines. They also have a long, outstanding wine list; prices range $20-275 by the bottle, and a number of wines are available by the glass ($6-12).

Also excellent in Biltmore Village is **Fig** (18 Brook St., 828/277-0889, www.figbistro.com, lunch 11:30am-3pm daily, dinner 5:30pm-9pm Mon.-Sat., brunch 11:30am-3pm Sun., lunch $9-14, brunch $8-14, dinner $12-28). Chef William Klein worked at fine restaurants in France and San Francisco before returning to western North Carolina, where he feels his career began. At Fig, he has created an elegant menu that's French bistro through and through.

On the Biltmore Estate
There are no fewer than nine places to eat (plus snacks, ice cream, and coffee) on the Biltmore Estate (800/411-3812, www.biltmore.com, estate admission required to visit restaurants). The **Dining Room** (breakfast 7am-10:30am daily, breakfast buffet 7am-11am daily, dinner 5:30pm-9:30pm daily, reservations required, breakfast $5-18, buffet $20, tasting menus $58-85) is an elegant restaurant, led by chef David Ryba, featuring estate-raised Angus beef, mountain trout, Biltmore wines, and vegetables grown on estate gardens. The food is spectacular, and tables with a mountain view make the meal all that much better. Evening dress and reservations are recommended.

The **Biltmore Bistro** (in Antler Hill Village, adjacent to the winery, 11am-9pm daily, lunch $8-18, prix fixe lunch $25, dinner $19-40) has a well-rounded gourmet menu sourced from the Biltmore's own kitchen garden, locally raised heirloom crops, meat and seafood delicacies, and artisanal cheeses and breads. Lunch and dinner are dramatically different (wood-fired pizza at lunch, braised veal cheeks at dinner), but each menu features something from the wood-fired oven.

The dining room of the **Deerpark Restaurant** (11am-2pm Sat., 10am-2pm Sun., Sat. buffet $18, Sun. buffet $28) is a former barn designed by architect Richard Morris Hunt, now renovated to airy splendor with walls of windows. Expect hearty and homey meals based on Appalachian cuisine. Like the Deerpark, the **Stable Café** (lunch 11am-4pm daily, $19-33) was once livestock housing, and guests can sit in booths that were once horse stalls. This is a meat eater's paradise, with choices that include estate-raised Angus beef and pork barbecue with the house special sauce.

In the stable area near the house, both the **Bake Shop** (8:30am-6pm daily) and the **Ice Cream Parlor** (11am-6pm daily) serve fresh treats, and **The Courtyard Market** (11am-4pm daily) has hot dogs, salads, and snacks. The **Creamery** (11am-7pm Sun.-Thurs.,

10am-8pm Fri.-Sat.) is the place for sandwiches and hand-dipped ice cream in Antler Hill Village. **The Conservatory Café** (from noon daily), adjacent to the gardens, will keep you fed after a day admiring the roses. If you have a hankering for barbecue, a quick sandwich, some snacks, or a cold drink, the **Smokehouse** (noon-5pm Fri.-Sun.) in Antler Hill Village serves just what you need.

While you're in Antler Hill Village, check out **Cedric's Tavern** (11am-9pm daily, lunch $15-21, dinner $17-30). Named for George Vanderbilt's beloved Saint Bernard (you can see his huge collar on display at the entrance), Cedric's pays homage to pubs and taverns found in Britain, with a Southern twist. The fish-and-chips and scotch egg are both delicious. You can also grab a pint of Cedric's Pale or Brown Ale, both brewed by the Biltmore Brewing Company. Also in Antler Hill Village, the **Village Social** (in Village Hotel on the Biltmore Estate, 800/411-3812, breakfast 7am-11am, lunch and dinner 11am-10pm, late night 10pm-midnight, $6-35) focuses on small plates and tasting menus—all of which are seafood-centric. This a place to make a meal as light or as filling as you like.

TRANSPORTATION AND SERVICES
Car

Asheville lies at the crossroads of **I-40,** North Carolina's primary east-west highway, and **I-26,** a roughly north-south artery through the Southern Highlands. Splitting the difference, **US-19** runs at a diagonal, deep into the Smokies in one direction and into the northern Blue Ridge in the other. The Blue Ridge Parkway passes by just a few miles from downtown as it moves west-southwest toward Cherokee.

Air

The **Asheville Regional Airport** (AVL, 61 Terminal Dr., 828/684-2226, www.flyavl. com) is located south of the city in Fletcher, a 20-minute drive on I-26. Several airlines offer flights to Atlanta, Charlotte, and other U.S.

cities. Asheville's public bus system connects the airport with downtown Asheville. A taxi from the airport will run about $45.

Bus

There is a **Greyhound station** (2 Tunnel Rd., 828/253-8451, www.greyhound.com) in Asheville. Asheville's extensive public bus system, **ART** (www.ashevillenc.gov, 6am-11:30pm Mon.-Sat., $1, $0.50 seniors), connects most major points in the metropolitan area, including the airport, with downtown. Check online for routes and schedules.

To Great Smoky Mountains National Park

From Asheville it's easy to get to Great Smoky Mountains National Park (GSMNP). In just over an hour you can be in Cataloochee, at the north end of the park, to camp, hike, and watch for elk in a serene mountain cove; to get there take I-40 west to Exit 20 and follow the signs. You can also take I-40 west into Tennessee, then follow the Foothills Parkway to US-321 and skirt the edge of GSMNP to **Gatlinburg,** Tennessee, and the entrance to the park (a trip of about 90 minutes). From Gatlinburg, you can make a loop back to Asheville by taking Newfound Gap Road across GSMNP to Cherokee, North Carolina (about 2.5 hours), and then back to Asheville via US-441 to US-19 to I-40, a total loop of about 3.5 hours and some 175 miles.

You can also head straight to **Cherokee** from Asheville and enter GSMNP via Newfound Gap Road there. It's an hour drive following I-40 west to exit 27, then taking US-19 south to US-441, which carries you right into Cherokee.

Alternately you can take the more scenic, but much longer, route and get to Cherokee via the **Blue Ridge Parkway.** This route is only 83 miles, but it takes 2-2.5 hours. If you want to go this way, head south out of Asheville along US-25 and pick up the Blue Ridge Parkway about 5.5 miles out of town; turn south on the Parkway and drive it until you reach Cherokee and GSMNP. And, of course, you can reverse the course if you're making that grand loop; you can return to Asheville via the Blue Ridge Parkway by picking it up in Cherokee and driving north.

Services

The **Asheville Visitors Center** (36 Montford Ave., near I-240 exit 4C, 828/258-6129) can set you up with all the maps, brochures, and recommendations you could need. Other sources are **Explore Asheville** (www.exploreasheville.com) and the **Asheville Area Chamber of Commerce** (www.ashevillechamber.org). The **Blue Ridge National Heritage Area** (www.blueridgeheritage.com) has a number of valuable trip-planning resources.

For planning a trip to the Smoky Mountains, you'll find many resources through **Great Smoky Mountains National Park** (GSMNP, 865/436-1200, www.nps.gov/grsm); of course Asheville knows its stuff about the Smoky Mountains too, so you'll find a number of trip-planning tools to the nation's most popular national park through the city's visitor services.

Listen to public radio at **WCQS** (88.1 FM) and **WNCW** (88.7 FM). **WTMT** (105.9 FM) and **WOXL** (98.1 FM) are music stations.

Mission Hospital (509 Biltmore Ave. and 428 Biltmore Ave., 828/213-1111, www.missionhospitals.org) in Asheville has two campuses and two emergency departments.

Around Asheville

Throughout the mountains around Asheville you'll come across towns official and unincorporated, some just collections of houses at a wide spot on a mountain road, others established towns with deep histories and more than a little creative juice flowing in their collective blood. Carved out of the forest, Black Mountain, Weaverville, and Madison County draw visitors all year long to soak up some of the same mountain air that made many of these places famous retreats for the wealthy or heady spaces where artists could discover inspiration. Whatever the reason for visiting, these towns have personalities, histories, cultures, and environments distinct enough to allow the truly curious to discover a small town (or two) full of surprises.

BLACK MOUNTAIN

Named for a onetime train depot, the town of Black Mountain sits 15 miles west of Asheville and is one of several bedroom communities serving the city. At one time, Black Mountain's claim to fame was the experimental Black Mountain College and its intellectual and artistic legacy. The school is long gone and the Black Mountain College Museum and Arts

Center is located in Asheville where it's visible to a much larger audience, but some of the artistic residue is still around in the form of the Lake Eden Arts Festival, or LEAF, which takes place on the former college campus.

Sights

Step into the **Swannanoa Valley Museum** (223 W. State St., 828/669-9566, www.history.swannanoavalleymuseum.org, 10am-5pm Tues.-Sat. Apr.-Oct., $5) to learn about the history of this area, including its settlement by the Cherokee people, early industrialization, and the shutdown of the Beacon Blanket Factory. The museum offers something a little different: hikes, and not just short ones. The **Swannanoa Rim Explorer Series** (hikes $30/members, $50/nonmembers, series of 11 hikes $280/members, $500/nonmembers) and **Valley History Explorer Hiking Series** (hikes $20/members, $30/nonmembers, series of seven hikes $140/members, $210/nonmembers) take museum members and guests on a series of hikes that reveal the history, geography, and rugged beauty of the Swannanoa Valley. Some of these hikes are difficult—steep, long,

Around Asheville

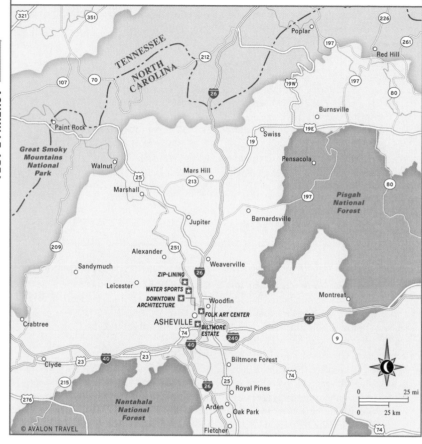

© AVALON TRAVEL

exposed in places—and others are geared toward beginners; check with the museum to register and get information on difficulty and schedules.

The **Black Mountain Center for the Arts** (225 W. State St., 828/669-0930, http://blackmountainarts.org, 10am-5pm Mon.-Fri.) is a gallery and performance space in the heart of town. Once the town hall, the Center for the Arts now houses art classes and summer camps for kids and adults, workshops and talks, performances (of all sorts: concerts, dance, poetry, storytelling, live theater), and gallery openings.

Entertainment and Events

Pisgah Brewing Company (150 Eastside Dr., 828/669-0190, www.pisgahbrewing.com, 4pm-9pm Mon.-Wed., 2pm-10pm Thurs.-Fri., noon-10pm Sat., 2pm-9pm Sun., open late for concerts, cash only) is both a brewpub and a music venue, featuring an eclectic mix of bands from roots music to rock. Pisgah was the Southeast's first certified organic brewery, and several beers are on tap year-round, including their pale ale, porter, and stout; a long list of seasonal brews rotates through the year and a growing list of specialty brews, like their sour brown ale, are gaining a loyal following.

Tours of the brewery are offered at 2pm and 3pm Saturday, but you can stop in and try a beer anytime they're open.

Black Mountain Ciderworks (104 Eastside Dr., #307, 828/419-0089, www.black-mountainciderworks.com, 3pm-8pm Mon. and Wed.-Fri., 2pm-8pm Sat.) is one of several spots across the state making cider and one of only a select few to make mead (that's a fermented honey beverage that should make you think of vikings and Beowulf). Their ciders aren't cloyingly sweet or closer to carbonated apple juice than an alcoholic beverage; rather, they're on the dry side and tend to be complex in flavor. At any given time, they're pouring a half-dozen of their ciders and meads, and many are blended to make some interesting concoctions. In summer, they'll throw basil into a mix of mead and cider, or blend apple cider and cherry mead, or go for it and try something completely different by adding blueberry and cardamom, fresh ginger, lavender, quince, or rose.

In May and October, Black Mountain is the scene of the **Lake Eden Arts Festival** (377 Lake Eden Rd., 828/686-8742, www.theleaf.org), better known as LEAF. Based around roots music—and there are some amazing performers here every year—LEAF is also a festival of visual arts, poetry, food, and even the healing arts. It's an amazing scene, and it takes place, appropriately, at Camp Rockmont, once the campus of Black Mountain College, the short-lived but historically important avant-garde institution that was home to a number of influential American artists and writers.

Shopping

Black Mountain Books (103 Cherry St., 828/669-8149, 11am-5pm Mon.-Sat., 11am-3pm Sun.) specializes in rare and out-of-print titles and is a great place to find unusual volumes on North Carolina, Black Mountain College, the Southern Appalachians, and even 18th- and 19th-century England and Scotland.

There are several galleries in Black Mountain, so you'll have your choice of where to browse and where to buy. **Seven Sisters Craft Gallery** (117 Cherry St., 828/669-5107, www.sevensistersgallery.com, 10am-6pm Mon.-Sat., noon-5pm Sun.) has been around for more than 30 years and carries large-scale photos, oil paintings by local and regional artists, and a host of styles, mediums, and price points. Stop in at **Sourwood Gallery** (110 Broadway, 828/669-4975, www.

the Black Mountains near Asheville

sourwoodgallery.com, 11am-3pm Mon.-Tues., 10am-5pm Wed.-Sat., 1pm-4pm Sun.), a little co-op gallery featuring paintings, jewelry, wood carvings and turned wood, photography, and other fine art by local artists. Styles and skill levels vary from artist to artist, but there's solid and reasonably priced work.

Recreation

Black Mountain Golf Club (17 Ross Dr., 828/669-2710, www.blackmountaingolf.org, 18 holes, par 71, greens fees $20-24 walking, $27-40 with cart) is something of a legend. Not because Donald Ross designed the front nine or because the Black Mountains surrounding the course make for a breathtaking round, but because it's the home of one of the longest holes in the world. In fact, that hole was once the longest in the world. The par 6 (yes, par 6) 17th hole measures an unbelievable 747 yards; a friend of mine said of the hole, "don't bother bringing your short game."

Accommodations

The **Inn Around the Corner** (109 Church St., 800/393-6005, www.innaroundthecorner.com, $140-195) is a classic bed-and-breakfast in a lovely 1915 home with a huge front porch. Just about every room has a great view, but the best is from the porch bed, where you'll fall asleep under the gaze of the mountains and wake when the birds start their day.

Arbor House of Black Mountain (207 Rhododendron Ave., 828/357-8525, www.arborhousenc.com, $150-230), a four-room bed-and-breakfast, hosts travelers year-round, but like most places in the area, peak season coincides with the turning of the leaves every fall. Views from the inn are wide and beautiful, especially when the leaves are out, but book early for leaf season.

Food

Berliner Kindl German Restaurant (121 Broadway, 828/669-5255, http://berliner-kindl.homestead.com, 11am-8pm Mon.-Sat., 11:30am-3pm Sun., $9-28) serves traditional German food like schnitzel, a variety of sausages, and the sides you'd expect: fried potatoes, German potato salad, sauerkraut, and red cabbage. They make their own sauerkraut in-house.

Over on Church Street you'll find the **Black Mountain Bakery** (102 Church St., 828/669-1626, 8am-4pm Tues.-Sat., under $10), a little café where you can order a quick soup and sandwich as well as a dessert or a cookie for the road. **Blue Ridge Biscuit Company** (601 W. State St., 828/357-8501, 7am-2pm Tues.-Fri., 8am-3pm Sat., under $10) is another good option for breakfast or lunch. They make massive biscuits, and though you can get yours with all sorts of breakfast meats and sausage gravy, I recommend trying the shiitake mushroom gravy for something a little different.

Transportation and Services

From Asheville, Black Mountain is about 15 miles east on I-40 (take Exit 70 or Exit 64).

The best visitor information for Black Mountain is at **ExploreAsheville** (www.exploreasheville.com); select Black Mountain as the region when looking at categories like shopping or dining. The **Black Mountain and Swannanoa Chamber of Commerce** (www.blackmountain.org) maintains a list of member businesses and has a small bit of visitor information on its site.

WEAVERVILLE

Less than 10 miles north of Asheville, Weaverville served as a vacation town for wealthy city and Piedmont dwellers in the late 1800s, though it had been settled by a handful of families since the 1780s. At one time, a pair of grand hotels—the Dula Springs Hotel and Blackberry Lodge—welcomed well-heeled and notable visitors like author O. Henry. The town never grew to be much more than a bucolic getaway, and today, with a population hovering around 2,500, Weaverville holds onto its former identity even as it grows into a bedroom community for Asheville.

Sights

The **Dry Ridge Museum** (41 N. Main St.,

828/250-6482, 10am-2pm Sat., free) holds a collection of artifacts, letters, and photos telling the history of Weaverville. It's small and has odd hours, but may be of interest to local-history buffs.

A few miles down the road is the birthplace of North Carolina's Civil War governor, Zebulon T. Vance (if ever there was a Civil War governor's name, that's it). The **Vance Birthplace** (911 Reems Creek Rd., 828/645-6706, www.nchistoricsites.org, 9am-5pm Tues.-Sat.) has a reconstructed log house as well as a toolhouse, smokehouse, springhouse, slave cabin, and a few more re-created structures. Tours of the home are available at the bottom of the hour.

Shopping

There are a lot of great potters in western North Carolina, but Rob and Beth Mangum of **Mangum Pottery** (16 N. Main St., 828/645-4929, www.mangumpottery.com, 9am-5pm Mon.-Fri., 10am-4pm Sat.) are two of the most innovative. They make beautiful earthy-colored dinnerware and mugs to satisfy the practical side of life, and they also build the most unexpected things out of pottery—ceramic clocks, ceramic furniture, ceramic musical instruments that really play—all in the most Seussian shapes and colors.

Maggie B's Wine & Specialty Store (10-C S. Main St., 828/645-1111, www.maggiebswine.com, 10am-6:30pm Tues.-Wed. and Sat., 10am-8pm Thurs.-Fri.) is a wine and specialty food shop operated by a husband and wife who know what tastes good. Maggie B's has an excellent selection of wine and beer, and an assortment of goods and snacks to make for a perfect picnic. If you're here and you're hungry, they do have a menu of sandwiches and salads ($5-11) and wine and beer by the glass.

The artwork at **MIYA Gallery** (20 N. Main St., 828/658-9655, www.miyagallery.com, 8am-5pm Mon.-Sat.) includes fine art, jewelry, furniture, and sculpture. More than 90 area artists and craftspeople have their work on display here. Pick up, or just admire leather books, exquisite and experimental wooden vessels, and fine photo prints of mountain scenes.

Recreation

Curtis Wright Outfitters (24 N. Main St., 828/645-8700, www.curtiswrightoutfitters.com, 10am-6pm Mon.-Sat.) keeps a store stocked with fly-fishing gear, clothing, tackle, and supplies. They offer a range of guided fishing trips ($200/half day wading, $300/full day wading, $350/half-day float trip) on area streams and rivers. You can also hunt grouse for a half day ($295) or full day ($395), or take part in one of their fly-fishing schools ($175) or classes ($75) and hone your technique or learn to tie flies.

Golfers will want to visit the **Reems Creek Golf Club** (36 Pink Fox Cove Rd., 800/406-3936, www.reemscreekgolf.com, 18 holes, par 72, greens fees $23-45 Mar.-Nov., $23-34 Nov.-Mar., rental clubs available). This course has appeared on *Golf Digest*'s "Places to Play" list in part because it's so beautiful, but also because of the challenges a mountain course like this delivers.

Accommodations

Dry Ridge Inn Bed and Breakfast (26 Brown St., 828/658-3899, www.dryridgeinn.com, $119-179) has eight guest rooms in a former parsonage built in 1849. Rooms feature king or queen beds, a gas fireplace, and reliable Wi-Fi. And there's a fridge stocked with complimentary beverages on the main floor. Breakfast is served either in the dining room or on the patio. Weather permitting, have breakfast outside and feel that fresh mountain air that made this town a vacation spot for generations.

The Inn on Main Street Bed and Breakfast (88 S. Main St., 828/645-4935 or 877/873-6074, www.innonmain.com, $139-179) offers an eco-friendly place to rest your head. They use no cleaning chemicals or deodorizers in the inn, all bath products are natural, and they cook their vegetarian meals using as many organic ingredients as possible.

There are five rooms in the main house and a pair in a separate cottage; the rooms are comfortable and homey without being too saccharine.

Food

A few doors down from Mangum Pottery you'll find **Well Bred Bakery & Café** (26 N. Main St., 828/645-9300, www.well-bredbakery.com, 7:30am-7pm Mon.-Thurs., 7:30am-8pm Fri., 8am-8pm Sat., 8am-7pm Sun.), which sells soups, sandwiches, quiche, and salads as well as a dazzling array of artisanal breads and elaborate desserts. They promise "karma-free coffee" (I think that means fair-trade), and even sell the *New York Times,* so you don't have to go into crossword-puzzle withdrawal on your trip.

If you're in Weaverville and need pizza, **Blue Mountain Pizza and Brew Pub** (55 N. Main St., 828/658-8777, www.bluemountainpizza.com, 11am-9pm Tues.-Thurs. and Sun., 11am-10pm Fri.-Sat., $7-24) is your spot. The building dates to the 1820s and now houses a two-barrel brewing system, meaning the brewmasters get to experiment a lot, often with positive results. Blue Mountain Pizza serves specialty pizzas, calzones, stromboli, subs, and salads. Their Henny Penny Pizza is a barbecued chicken pizza with red onion and bacon, and the Marge is simply olive oil, roma tomatoes, fresh mozzarella, and basil.

Stoney Knob Cafe (337 Merrimon Ave. 828/645-3309, www.stoneyknobcafe.com, 11am-9pm Mon.-Thurs., 11am-9:30pm Sat., 9:30am-3pm Sun., lunch $10-13, dinner $15-32, brunch $5-14) serves dishes representative of cuisines the world over, and surprisingly, does a good job with every dish they serve. If your party wants pizza, tacos, and stir-fry, they can deliver; if you want a tasty filet mignon, they have that too.

Transportation and Services

Weaverville is just 10 miles north of Asheville along a very easy drive. Simply follow US-70W/US-19N/US-23N north, then turn right on Weaver Boulevard.

The **Weaverville Business Association** (www.visitweaverville.com) provides visitor information online. You can also find visitor information at **Explore Asheville** (www.exploreasheville.com).

MADISON COUNTY

North of Asheville, Madison County is a world unto itself. The wild mountain terrain is dotted with hot springs and towns no bigger than inkblots on a map, but still this county, which shares a border with an equally wild corner of Tennessee, draws visitors. Some come for the solitude, others the hot springs, others the rafting and to explore the great outdoors; still others come for the music. As is true all along the Appalachian Range and especially in the Blue Ridge Mountains, music plays an important role in the identity of the place. In most towns you'll find a stage, porch, coffee shop, or gas station where bluegrass musicians will gather to play, carrying on the long-held traditions of the people here.

Entertainment and Events

Mars Hill, a tiny college town, is a center of mountain culture thanks to Mars Hill College. The **Bascom Lamar Lunsford "Minstrel of the Appalachians" Festival** (early fall, 828/689-1571, www.bascomlunsfordfestival.wordpress.com, $10 adults, $5 children) is a nearly 50-year-old annual gathering of some of the best mountain musicians, dancers, and craftspeople from this hotbed of folk traditions. Mars Hill College is also the home of the **Southern Appalachian Repertory Theatre** (Owen Theater, 44 College St., 828/689-1239, http://sartplays.org), a highly regarded ensemble presenting a range of contemporary drama, musicals, and family productions. SART's stage is in the Owen Theater, a great-looking old Baptist church on the Mars Hill College campus.

Many other venues in Madison County towns feature live bluegrass and old-time music. **Zuma Coffee** (10 S. Main St., Marshall, 828/649-1617, www.zumacoffee.blogspot.com, 7am-6pm Mon.-Wed.,

7am-9pm Thurs.-Fri., 9am-6pm Sat., under $10) has a free bluegrass jam session every Thursday starting at 7pm and serves up a good cup of coffee. **The Depot** (282 S. Main St., Marshall, 828/206-2332), a former railroad depot building, has free concerts every Friday starting at 6:30pm. And the **Madison County Arts Council** (90 S. Main St., Marshall, 828/649-1301, www.madisoncountyarts.com) wouldn't be worth their salt if they didn't host a few concerts, but lucky for you, they have plenty. The Arts Council puts on shows at their headquarters on Main Street and at the **Ebbs Chapel Performing Arts Center** (271 Laurel Valley Rd., Mars Hill, 828/689-3858, www.ebbschapelauditorium.com); check the schedule for shows, times, and prices.

Sports and Recreation

On a 4,700-foot mountaintop above Mars Hill, the **Wolf Ridge Ski Resort** (578 Valley View Circle, 800/817-4111, www.skiwolfridgenc.com, 9am-4:30pm and 6pm-10pm Tues.-Sat., 9am-4:30pm Sun.-Mon. Dec.-Mar., $24-71 adults, $20-61 students and ages 5-18, free under age 4, rentals $19-34) has more than 80 acres of prime skiing and snowboarding slopes. It is also the home of the Snow Sports School, which offers private and group lessons for all ages of beginning and intermediate winter sports enthusiasts. There are multiple lifts, two lodges to relax in, and multiple hearty dining options. The attached **Scenic Wolf Resort** offers year-round cabin accommodations ($300-550 in season), a huge indoor heated pool, and numerous recreational activities.

Sandy Bottom Trail Rides (1459 Caney Fork Rd., Marshall, 828/649-3464 or 800/959-3513, www.sandybottomtrailrides.net, 10am, noon, and 2pm daily, 1 hour $35, 2 hours $65, 3 hours $85), based at a 100-year-old family farm, leads horseback treks deep into the forest to an early-19th-century garnet mine. They'll also carry you in style in a horse-drawn buggy, if you prefer.

There are plenty of white-water rafting opportunities in the area, with several guide companies to choose from. **Hot Springs Rafting Co.** (22 NW Hwy. 25/70, 877/530-7238, www.hotspringsraftingco.com, rafting $40-65, funyak $30-35/day, unguided rafting $30-35/day) keeps you on the river right around Hot Springs. Their guided rafting trips are quite the thrill, but the unguided trips and funyaks (think white-water raft meets inflatable kayak) can give you a satisfying day on the water. **French Broad Rafting and Ziplining** (US-25/70, Marshall, 800/570-7238, www.frenchbroadrafting.com, white-water rafting $51-75, flat-water rafting $30-46, zip-lining $79) can get you equipped and ready for a guided or unguided rafting trip on the French Broad River, which has both white-water and calm sections. Or get your adrenaline rush in the trees on a zip-line course that mixes zip lines, rappels, and short hikes to make a unique mountain experience.

Accommodations

Defying that worn-out stereotype of mountain isolation, Madison County has for centuries been a destination for vacationers because of its natural hot springs. Going back at least to the mid-18th century—and, according to tradition, long before the first European settlers arrived—the springs have had a reputation for curative powers. A succession of grand hotels operated at Hot Springs, all long since burned down. In one of the area's odder historical moments, the resort served as an internment camp for German prisoners during World War I, mainly commercial sailors and members of an orchestra who had the misfortune of being in the United States when the war broke out.

Modern visitors can still take a dip in the mineral springs. **Hot Springs Resort and Spa** (US-25/70, at the entrance to the town of Hot Springs, 828/622-7676, www.nchotsprings.com, suites $109-300, cabins $50-72, camping $24-60) is a much simpler affair than the old hotels; it's not a luxury destination but a place where you can lodge or camp for the night and soak in the famous

100°F water. Spa services run $50-130, and there's a series of outdoor mineral baths. Baths are open Monday-Thursday noon-10pm and Friday-Sunday 10am-midnight, and range in price from $20/person to $55 for the bathhouse; rates drop after 6pm.

The **Mountain Magnolia Inn** (204 Lawson St., Hot Springs, 828/622-3543 or 800/914-9306, www.mountainmagnoliainn. com, $100-230) provides lodging in an ornate 1868 home and in nearby creekside cabins. The inn's dining room is a nice gourmet restaurant (breakfast for guests daily, dinner for guests and non-guests 5:30pm-9pm Thurs.-Mon., $15-45) that features locally raised organic produce, meats, cheeses, and wines.

Appalachian Trail hikers and those who like to play hard and live cheap should take notice of **Laughing Heart Lodge** (289 NW Hwy. 25/70, Hot Springs, 828/622-0165, www.laughingheartlodge.com). Here you'll find several types of accommodations. First, the hostel ($15 bunk room, $25 single private room, $40 double private room), which was built in 1974 but still offers a modicum of comfort and privacy; then, the lodge ($100-125), which has seven rooms, each with a private bath; and, finally, the cabin ($120-150).

Food

The **Smoky Mountain Diner** (70 Lance Ave., Hot Springs, 828/622-7571, www.smokymountaindinerhotsprings.com, 6am-8pm Mon.-Sat., 6am-4pm Sun., breakfast $1-15, lunch and dinner $5-17) is one-part diner, one-part your granny's kitchen table. Country staples like corn bread, pinto beans, chicken livers, and pork chops are on the menu, as are biscuits, pancakes, French toast, omelets, and even pizza. If you're so inclined, they have all-you-can-eat pinto beans for $5.

The bar food at **Iron Horse Station** (24 S. Andrew Ave., Hot Springs, 866/402-9377, www.theironhorsestation.com, 11:30am-9pm Sun.-Thurs., 11:30am-10pm Fri.-Sat., lunch under $10, dinner $6-20) isn't the bar food you'd expect to find at a small-town joint with

a name like this. Sure, there's onion rings and fried green tomatoes, but also a tofu napoleon, penne pasta (which you can get with blackened tofu), and fresh rainbow trout. You can stay here, too, in one of four rooms ($75-160), each named after a different type of Pullman car from the heyday of railroads.

In Marshall, **Sweet Monkey** (133 Main St., Marshall, 828/649-2489, www.sweetmonkeybakery.com, 9am-3pm Mon., 9am-9pm Wed.-Sat., 10am-4pm Sun., under $15) is gaining a reputation for good pizza and exceptional baked goods. Their menus—they serve breakfast, lunch, and dinner here—are heavy on the bread and big on flavor, which is perfect after a day of white-water rafting or when you have a hankering for a cookie.

Transportation and Services

To get to Madison County and the towns of Marshall and Hot Springs, you'll want to head north out of Asheville along US-25/US 70. Take exit 19A for Weaverville/Woodfin, but continue on US-25/US-70. You'll reach Marshall first, a 20-mile drive from Asheville; Hot Springs is another 16 miles north, putting it 36 miles from Asheville. Mars Hill is a 20-minute drive north from Asheville via US-23/US-19. Follow US-25/US-70 out of Asheville and stay on this route past Weaverville, where it will turn into US-23/US-19; take exit 11 onto NC-213 to get to Mars Hill.

The **Madison County Tourism Administration** (www.visitmadisoncounty. com) site covers all the towns in the county and is therefore comprehensive. If you'd like to get more specific, try the **Hot Springs Tourism Association** (www.hotspringsnc. org) for details on the town of Hot Springs; or the town of **Marshall** (www.townofmarshall.org) for information that's more municipal than touristy. **Mars Hill**'s website (www.townofmarshill.org) is also geared more toward municipal information than tourist interests, but there is some information that visitors may find helpful.

Southern Blue Ridge and Foothills

Look for ★ to find recommended
sights, activities, dining, and lodging.

Highlights

★ **Chimney Rock:** Hike or take an elevator ride to the top of this 315-foot geological beauty (page 121).

★ **Sierra Nevada Brewery:** Sample brews, hear a free concert, enjoy dinner, and learn how breweries are becoming more environmentally responsible at this showpiece from a craft beer giant (page 125).

★ **Carl Sandburg Home National Historic Site:** Poet Carl Sandburg called North Carolina home, and you can tour the place that inspired his later work (page 126).

★ **North Carolina Arboretum:** Explore more than 400 acres of natural and landscaped gardens, including a massive collection of azaleas and bonsai trees, and miles of hiking and walking trails (page 136).

★ **Pisgah Ranger District:** This 150,000-acre section of the Pisgah National Forest encompasses the Cradle of Forestry Museum, Shining Rock Wilderness, Sliding Rock, Cold Mountain, and many other favorite outdoor destinations (page 143).

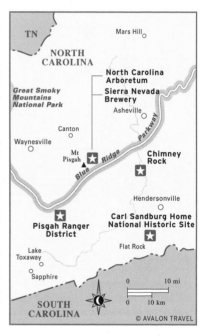

The mountains south of Asheville have an air of enchantment to them—the area gives the impalpable sense of having had a spell cast upon it.

No doubt a parapsychologist could assign a name to this atmosphere; it has a weird energy that makes it seem as likely that you'll encounter a fairy or an alien as a postal worker. There are some quantifiable symptoms of this peculiarity. For one, Polk County has its own climate. Called the Thermal Belt, the meteorological pocket formed on this sheltered slope of the Blue Ridge has distinctly milder summers and winters than the surrounding areas. In the 19th century the area became a favorite summering spot for the Charleston elite and other Southerners of the plantation class. Some old houses and inns remain as vestiges of this genteel past.

In January 1874, Bald Mountain, north of Chimney Rock, began to rumble; it grew louder until, by the spring of that year, the mountain shook with such force that windows and crockery in valley homes shattered. A smoking, hissing crack opened in the side of the mountain, causing residents to fear a volcanic eruption. Many moved away or found religion. The shaking and rumbling eventually settled down. A crew of spelunkers a generation later concluded that the mountain was hollow and that enormous boulders sometimes became dislodged inside, showering into the caves below and causing the enormous booms. At least that's one theory.

Chimney Rock itself was the scene of bizarre phenomena in the first decade of the 1800s. Locals and visitors began to report witnessing spectral gatherings, crowds of people gathered on top of the rock and rising together into the sky. In the fall of 1811 multiple witnesses saw, on different occasions, two armed cavalries mounted on winged horses battling in the air over Chimney Rock, their gleaming swords clashing audibly. Whichever phantom cavalry triumphed in that battle, the rock is now maintained by the state of North Carolina and climbed daily by hundreds of visitors, none of whom have reported sightings of any spectral cavalry, horse droppings, or flashing sabers.

Previous: Looking Glass Falls; fall color along the Blue Ridge Parkway. **Above:** pony, Mill Spring.

Southern Blue Ridge and Foothills

GEORGIA

TENNESSEE

SOUTH CAROLINA

NORTH CAROLINA

Great Smoky Mountains National Park

Pisgah National Forest

Pisgah National Forest

Mt Mitchell State Park

Little Switzerland

Franklin

Bryson City

Cherokee

Dillsboro

Sylva

Maggie Valley

Waynesville

Canton

Asheville

Marshall

Mars Hill

Weaverville

Black Mountain

Marion

Rutherfordton

Columbus

Tryon

Saluda

Hendersonville

Flat Rock

Brevard

Highlands

Cashiers

Sapphire

Lake Toxaway

Gneiss

Waterville

WOLF

Lake Lure

Chimney Rock

END OF THE BLUE RIDGE PARKWAY

RICHLAND BALSAM

PISGAH RANGER DISTRICT

CRADLE OF FORESTRY

NORTH CAROLINA ARBORETUM

SIERRA NEVADA BREWERY

CHIMNEY ROCK

CARL SANDBURG HOME NATIONAL HISTORIC SITE

Sliding Rock

Looking Glass Falls

Dry Falls

Bridal Veil Falls

White Water Falls

French Broad River

Blue Ridge Pkwy.

0   10 mi
0   10 km

© AVALON TRAVEL

PLANNING YOUR TIME

The small towns in this region benefit from Asheville day-trippers, Great Smoky Mountains National Park visitors, and a loyal and growing group of fans who have discovered the charm, beauty, and zest for life that permeates this area.

Plenty of people visit the Southern Blue Ridge to unplug for a week or so, breathe in that mountain air, and escape the heat of the Piedmont and coastal plains for the cooler climes of higher elevations. It's possible to get an overview of the area in **3-4 days.** Spend one night in Chimney Rock or Lake Lure and explore the park, then head west to Brevard where you can hike and hunt for waterfalls between shopping and dining in Saluda, Flat Rock, and Hendersonville. Spend at least one day driving and hiking along the Parkway before a final night in Waynesville. Outdoor enthusiasts will want to spend more time here to dig into their chosen activity and the same goes for those seeking a little culture; the music and theater scenes can be lively.

When to Go

Summer is a popular time to visit, as the mountain elevations bring cooler temperatures and generally lower humidity, providing relief from the sun-soaked Piedmont and coast. Through summer, the mountains are richly green and driving along the Blue Ridge Parkway offers plenty of chances to take in the emerald-green hills marching out of sight in any direction. In late summer, the region's apple orchards ripen from the end of July to mid-September. Summer has the potential for pop-up thunderstorms and subsequent flash flooding; keep an eye on weather forecasts.

Autumn is by far the busiest season, as leaf lovers pack every hotel, B&B, and resort around, driving the Parkway and every scenic back road to get their fill of perfect fall foliage. In summer and fall, reserve your room or cabin well in advance to ensure you have a place to stay, and plan for slightly longer waits at the better restaurants.

Winter is slower and snowier, but there's a certain charm to the place when there's a dusting (or even an inch or two) of the white stuff on the ground. From late fall through early spring, prepare for snow, or even ice, and know how to drive in less-than-perfect conditions. The Blue Ridge Parkway will close for winter weather as needed, but many of the surrounding roads experience similar conditions, so drive with caution.

Spring is an excellent time to explore the waterfalls, as seasonal rain and snowmelt make for larger water volume and more impressive falls.

Chimney Rock and Hendersonville

Chimney Rock and Hendersonville are both easy drives from Asheville. To the south and east, Chimney Rock and the town of Lake Lure are named for a pair of North Carolina's natural wonders: Lake Lure and Chimney Rock. The mountains are rugged here and from the top of Chimney Rock, Lake Lure is a lovely shining jewel among the folds of the hills. This is the site of several memorable filming locations, such as *The Last of the Mohicans* and *Dirty Dancing.*

CHIMNEY ROCK AND LAKE LURE
★ Chimney Rock

Chimney Rock State Park (US-64/74A, Chimney Rock, NC at Blue Ridge Parkway MP 384.7 via US-74A East, 800/277-9611, www.chimneyrockpark.com, ticket plaza open 8:30am-5:30pm daily Mar.-Oct., 8:30am-4:30pm daily Nov., 10am-4:30pm Fri.-Tues. early-Dec.-Christmas Eve, 10am-4:30pm Christmas-New Year's Eve, 10am-4:30pm Fri.-Tues. Jan.-late Mar., $15 adults,

$7 ages 5-15, 4 and under free) is just one of the many geological beauties you'll find along the Blue Ridge Parkway corridor. The 315-foot tower of stone that is Chimney Rock stands on the side of the mountain. To get to the top of the chimney, you can take a 26-story elevator ride, or hike the **Outcroppings Trail,** a 0.25-mile trail nicknamed "The Ultimate Stairmaster." No matter how you get there, the view is spectacular.

There are a number of additional dizzying views to take in and mountain-hugging trails to hike in Chimney Rock State Park. The **Needle's Eye** and **Opera Box** are rock formations that offer spectacular views. The **Hickory Nut Falls Trail** takes you to the top of the 400-foot Hickory Nut Falls via a moderately difficult 0.75-mile trail. One of the most recognizable views is on the **Skyline-Cliff Trail** loop, a strenuous two-hour hike that will take you to some places you may recognize from the 1992 film *The Last of the Mohicans.* There are also kid-friendly trails. Bring your little ones along on the 0.6-mile **Woodland Walk,** where animal sculptures and "journal entries" from Grady the Groundhog wait to be discovered. A trail map covering the entire park is available at the park's website (www. chimneyrockpark.com).

Chimney Rock is more than just hiking trails. In November, Santa rappels down the tower in a pre-Christmas display of his chimney-navigating prowess, but year-round you'll find rock climbers in the park for bouldering, top-rope, and multi-pitch climbs. Want to try but don't know the terms? **Fox Mountain Guides** (888/284-8433, www.foxmountainguides.com, lessons from $45 for two hours, $160-195 for half- and full-day novice climbs) will gear you up and show you the ropes.

Nearby **Rumbling Bald Mountain** (Boys Camp Rd., Lake Lure) was recently made part of Chimney Rock State Park, and climbers couldn't be happier. Here you'll find more than 1,500 bouldering "problems" (a form of low-altitude, ropeless climb that often traverses a rock face) to solve (solving it means traversing it successfully). Currently, only the south face is open to climbers and no commercial climbing guides are allowed to operate there.

Sports and Recreation
LAKE LURE

Lake Lure, a 720-acre man-made highland lake, was created in the 1920s. Several local outfitters will guide you or set you up for a day on the lake or on area rivers. Try **Lake**

Chimney Rock

Lure Adventure Company (442 Memorial Hwy., 828/625-8066, www.lakelureadventurecompany.com, 9am-7pm daily) for ski trips ($140 per hour), fishing (half-day $250), to ride around (from $65 per hour), or kayaking and stand-up paddleboarding (rentals from $19 per hour, tours $34 adults, $29 children). For a relaxed sightseeing tour on the lake, **Lake Lure Tours** (next to Lake Lure Town Marina, 877/386-4255, www.lakelure.com, tours depart hourly from 11am daily Apr.-May and Sept.-Oct., from 10am June-Aug., call for times Mar. and Nov., $15-30 adults, $7-10 under age 12), which offers dinner and sunset cruises as well as daytime jaunts.

TRYON INTERNATIONAL EQUESTRIAN CENTER

Mill Spring, about 15 minutes south of Lake Lure on NC-9, is home to a huge equestrian center hosting competitions, horse shows, lessons, and rides year-round. **Tryon International Equestrian Center** (TIEC, 4066 Pea Ridge Rd., Mill Spring, 828/863-1000, www.tryon.coth.com) puts on free hunter-jumper shows and competitions, hosts concerts and events, and has everything riders, spectators, and equine enthusiasts could want all on one property. Choose from eight on-site restaurants including **Legends Grille** (828/863-1122, 4pm-9pm Wed., 11am-9pm Thurs. and Sun., 11am-11pm Fri.-Sat., $13-34), an upscale eatery serving steaks and seafood; **Roger's Diner** (828/863-1113, 8am-9pm Mon.-Thurs., 7am-9pm Wed.-Sun., breakfast around $7, lunch and dinner $7-14), serving breakfast and traditional diner fare; and **Blue Ginger Sushi & Noodles** (828/863-1121, 11am-7pm Thurs. and Sun., 11am-9pm Fri.-Sat., around $9). There's also a coffee shop, snack bar, pizza oven, and sandwich-centric café.

Since riders and show enthusiasts travel from far and wide, TIEC has lodging for horse and rider. The **Stable House Inn** (828/863-1015, $125) has 50 rooms, each with two queen beds; the **Tryon River Cabins** have one- ($185), three- ($750), and five-bedroom cabins

($1,000) available, each with weekly rental discounts; as well as several RV pads ($43).

GOLF

There are two golf courses at **Rumbling Bald Resort** (112 Mountains Blvd., Lake Lure, www.rumblingbald.com): the Bald Mountain Golf Course and Apple Valley Golf Course.

Bald Mountain Golf Course (828/694-3042, 18 holes, par 72, greens fees from $30 late Nov.-late Mar., $33-59 late Mar.-late Nov.) makes the most of the bald rock faces that give the course its name and allows you some beautiful views of them as they tower overhead. You may recognize the 16th hole, a picturesque par 3 where a couple of scenes from *Dirty Dancing* were shot.

At **Apple Valley Golf Course** (828/694-3042, 18 holes, par 72, greens fees from $30 late Nov.-late Mar., $33-59 late Mar.-late Nov.), you'll find a set of links that's been called one of the most beautiful mountain courses to play. This is especially true in fall, when the hillsides surrounding the course are in full blaze.

Accommodations

The 1927 **Lake Lure Inn and Spa** (2771 Memorial Hwy., 888/434-4970, www.lakelure.com, from $109) is a grand old hotel that was one of the fashionable Southern resorts of its day. Franklin Roosevelt and Calvin Coolidge stayed here, as did F. Scott Fitzgerald. The lobby is full of strange antiques that are the picture of obsolete opulence—a Baccarat chandelier much older than the hotel and a collection of upright disc music boxes, up to eight feet tall, that were all the rage before the invention of the phonograph. The Lake Lure Inn has been restored beautifully and is equipped with two restaurants, a bar, and a spa.

In 1937, the **Lodge on Lake Lure** (361 Charlotte Dr., Lake Lure, 828/625-2789 or 800/733-2785, www.lodgeonlakelure.com, $180-310) opened as a retreat for North Carolina highway patrolmen and their families. In 1990, it opened to the public with 17 guest rooms and an excellent restaurant. Tree Tops Restaurant (6pm-9pm Wed.-Mon., reservations required) serves a prix fixe menu ($65/two diners) of three to five appetizers, entrées, and desserts. The menu has a strong focus on seasonal ingredients and the restaurant sources much of its product from local and regional farms. Try the rainbow trout (caught daily) and anything with mushrooms.

Rumbling Bald Resort on Lake Lure (112 Mountains Blvd., Lake Lure, 828/694-3000 or 800/260-1040, www.rumblingbald.com) has studios ($85-110), condos ($145-205), motor coach facilities ($50-60), and vacation homes ($165-590) in a quiet mountain cove. On the resort's property are a few miles of hiking and biking trails (bike rentals from $15/hour), as well as a variety of water activities: pontoon boats (from $75/hour); kayaks, canoes, paddleboats, and stand-up paddleboards (from $20/hour); and scenic cruises ($24 adults, $21 ages 4-12, free under 4). There's also a fitness center, golf, and tennis.

Rumbling Bald has several restaurants to choose from, the best of which is Lakeview Restaurant (828/694-3045, lunch 11:30am-2:30pm daily late Mar.-early Sept., dinner and bar 5pm-late Tues.-Sat. Apr.-late Nov., lunch $8-17, dinner $12-32). There's also a pizza place and seasonal dinner cruises ($55, $65 with wine service). Call or check online for a schedule.

Food

In addition to the dining options at Rumbling Bald, the Lodge on Lake Lure, and TIEC, there are a few other spots worth checking out.

Medina's Village Bistro (430 Main St., Chimney Rock, 828/989-4529, www.medinasvillagebistro.com, 7am-3pm Sun.-Mon., 7:30am-9pm Wed.-Sat., breakfast $3-8, lunch $4-11, dinner $8-22) is a great spot for breakfast with the locals. They pack the joint, read the local paper, talk local politics a little too loudly, and generally inhabit the place as only locals can; they're a friendly bunch, though. The cinnamon rolls are out-of-this-world good.

Dining at La Strada at Lake Lure (2693 Memorial Hwy., Lake Lure, 828/625-1118, www.lastradaatlakelure.com, 11:30am-late daily, lunch $6-24, dinner $10-24) is Italian-American through and through. The menu is packed with pizza and pasta, and many of the classics—chicken parmesan, lasagna, chicken alfredo—appear alongside daily specials that use ingredients a little closer to home. You're bound to see plenty of rock climbers carbing it up here as they prepare for a day on the rock face.

At the Rutherfordton County North Carolina Airport, about 10 minutes south, the 57 Alpha Café (622 Airport Rd., Rutherfordton, 828/286-1677, www.57alpha.com, 11am-3pm Tues.-Sun., around $10) serves up enchiladas, burritos, quesadillas, and a legendary burger. Called the "Hundred Dollar Hamburger," it's a whopper; it earned its name not for premium ingredients, but for the $10 cost of the burger and the $90 in fuel pilots would spend flying in for lunch.

Transportation and Services

The drive from Chimney Rock to Asheville is a curvy, 40-minute haul along US-74 to where it meets I-240. You'll pass beneath the Blue Ridge Parkway about 35 minutes (20 miles) outside Chimney Rock. Hendersonville lies 18 miles west, a 30-minute drive along US-64, which you will pick up in the nearby town of Bat Cave, three miles west of Chimney Rock.

The main hospital in Rutherfordton is Rutherford Hospital (288 S. Ridgecrest Ave., Rutherfordton, 828/286-5000, www.rutherfordhosp.org).

HENDERSONVILLE AND VICINITY

An easy 30-minute drive from Asheville, Hendersonville is a small, comfortable city with a walkable downtown filled with boutiques and cafés. It's also the heart of North Carolina's apple industry. Hundreds of orchards cover the hillsides of Henderson County and all along the highway, long packinghouses bustle in late summer as they process more than three million tons of apples. There are also many shops and produce stands run by members of old orchard-owning families, where you can buy apples, cider, preserves, and many other apple products.

Sights

One of North Carolina's cool small transportation museums is located at the Hendersonville Airport. The **Western North Carolina Air Museum** (130 Gilbert St., 828/698-2482, www.wncairmuseum.com, 10am-5pm Sat., noon-5pm Wed. and Sun. Apr.-Oct., noon-5pm Sat.-Sun. and Wed. Nov.-Mar., free) houses a collection of more than a dozen historic small aircraft, both originals and reproductions. Most are from the 1930s and 1940s, though some are even older; all are wonderfully fun contraptions to explore.

★ SIERRA NEVADA BREWERY

Sierra Nevada Brewery (100 Sierra Nevada Way, Mills River, 828/681-5300, www.sierranevada.com, 11am-9pm Mon.-Thurs., 11am-10pm Fri.-Sat., noon-9pm Sun.) is about 20 minutes from Hendersonville, midway between that city and Asheville, and it's a beer lover's playground. They have tours of the brewery (on the hour 11am-3pm Mon.-Thurs.,

11am-4pm Fri.-Sat., and noon-4pm Sun.), tours showing off their sustainable practices (2:30pm Fri.-Sat.), and a three-hour Beer Geek Tour (their name, not mine, $30, 2:30pm Thurs.), as well as plenty of beer to sample. There's a fantastic little restaurant ($9-28) on site and an indoor and outdoor space for concerts and special events.

Shopping

Hendersonville's downtown **Curb Market** (221 N. Church St. at 2nd Ave., 828/692-8012, www.curbmarket.com, 8am-2pm Tues., Thurs., and Sat.) has been in operation since 1924. Here you can buy fresh locally grown fruits, vegetables, and flowers; fresh-baked cakes, pies, and breads; jams, jellies, and pickles made in local home kitchens; and the work of local woodcarvers, weavers, and other craftspeople.

While in the Hendersonville area, keep an eye out for brightly colored folk painting-adorned packages of **Immaculate Baking Company** (www.immaculatebaking.com) cookies. Besides making totally delicious cookies, this Hendersonville-based company helps support the work of visionary outsider artists throughout the South; they're "cookies with a cause."

Main Street in Hendersonville

Accommodations

Pinebrook Manor (2701 Kinuga Rd., 828/698-2707, www.pinebrookmanor.com, $165-245) has four rooms named after literary figures, and their pricing reveals something about the owners' literary tastes. The hosts are top-notch, the whole place is lovely, and the breakfast is much better than the typical B&B quiche.

Melange Bed & Breakfast Inn and Gardens (1230 Fifth Ave. W., 828/697-5253, www.melangebb.com, $179-225), just a short walk from downtown, is the sort of place you don't want to leave. The six comfy rooms are tastefully decorated, making guests feel at home. Let them know if you have special dietary needs and they'll do their best to accommodate you with an option as delicious and filling as every other breakfast they serve.

There are some chain hotels in Hendersonville, but a good alternative is **Cedarwood Inn** (1510 Greenville Hwy., 828/692-8284 or 800/832-2072, www.cedarwood-inn.com, $90-150). It may not look like much from the outside, but it is, in many ways, beyond its appearance, a throwback to those family motels of the 1950s and '60s. They hit that experience (minus the kitsch) right on the head. It's clean, comfortable, and cheap, so why look elsewhere?

Food

★ **Umi Japanese Fine Dining** (633 N. Main St., 828/698-8048, www.umisushinc.com, lunch 11am-3pm Mon.-Fri. and noon-3pm Sat.-Sun., dinner 4:30pm-9:30pm Mon.-Thurs., 4:30pm-10pm Fri., 3pm-10:30pm Sat., and 3pm-9pm Sun., $8-27) surprised me. I didn't expect to find some of the best sushi in North Carolina here, but I did. Every roll is close to perfect—their sushi chef and his fellow rollers take fish deliveries three to four times weekly. Sure, you can get beef teriyaki or miso salmon, but why when the rolls are so good? They also have a nice sake menu.

West First Wood-Fired (101B First Ave., 828/693-1080, www.flatrockwoodfired.com, lunch 11am-2pm Mon.-Sat., dinner from 5pm Mon.-Sat., lunch $6-17, dinner $6-20) has great pizza, as well as some excellent entrees, that gets creative without getting weird. Try the Greek lamb pizza or goat cheese pizza, or if pizza isn't doing it for you, opt for fresh veggies and pappardelle or the braised skirt steak.

Transportation and Services

The Hendersonville area is an easy drive from Asheville, with Hendersonville less than 30 minutes down I-26. **Asheville Regional Airport** (AVL, 61 Terminal Dr., 828/684-2226, www.flyavl.com), south of Asheville, is very convenient to this region; several airlines have flights to Atlanta, Charlotte, and other U.S. cities.

Maps and guides are available at the **Hendersonville and Flat Rock Visitors Information Center** (201 S. Main St., Hendersonville, 800/828-4244, www.historichendersonville.com). In Hendersonville, the primary hospital is **Pardee Hospital** (800 N. Justice St., Hendersonville, 866/790-9355, www.pardeehospital.org).

FLAT ROCK
Sights

When you're in these mountains, you're in apple country. **Sky Top Orchards** (3403 Greenville Hwy., 828/692-7930, www.skytoporchard.com, 9am-6pm Aug. 1-Dec. 1) is a pick-your-own orchard with 22 varieties of apples to pick, as well as fresh cider, jams and jellies, and awesome apple cider donuts. Be sure to bring cash when you visit, as their card reader can't always be counted on.

★ CARL SANDBURG HOME NATIONAL HISTORIC SITE

Just south of Hendersonville is the historic village of Flat Rock. Founded in the early 19th century as a vacation spot for the Charleston plantation gentry, Flat Rock retains a delicate, cultured ambience created many years ago. Many artists and writers have lived in this area, most famously Carl Sandburg, whose house, Connemara, is preserved as the **Carl Sandburg Home National Historic Site**

Carl Sandburg's Home

In 1945, American poet Carl Sandburg moved his family to the picturesque mountains of North Carolina. He wasn't seeking inspiration for his writing, he was simply seeking the best place for his wife to raise her herd of prize-winning Chikaming goats. At the 264-acre Connemara Farm, he found both.

This is where Sandburg wrote around one-third of his body of work; received his second Pulitzer Prize, the International United Poets Laureate award, and the Presidential Medal of Freedom; and passed away at the age of 89. Today you can experience the solitude and muse this poet, journalist, storyteller, folk singer, and goat raiser found at the **Carl Sandburg Home National Historic Site** (81 Carl Sandburg Ln., Flat Rock, parking area at 1800 Little River Rd. across from the Flat Rock Playhouse, 828/693-4178, www.nps.gov/carl, 9am-5pm daily, closed Thanksgiving, Christmas, and New Year's Day, house tour $5 adults, $3 seniors ages 62 and over, free for 15 and under).

Tour the house and see more than 65,000 artifacts, including more than 12,000 books and the desk and office where Sandburg worked. The farm still operates a small dairy and the National Park Service raises goats like the ones Mrs. Sandburg raised; you can find their milk in specialty stores in Flat Rock.

Connemara and the property are crowded in fall, as the more than five miles of hiking trails that crisscross the farm come alive with leaf peepers. It's worth the stop in any season, however, as spring and summer wildflowers and winter's snow complement Sandburg's literary legacy.

Reaching Connemara and the Carl Sandburg Home NHS is easy from both Asheville and the Blue Ridge Parkway. From Asheville, head south out of town on McDowell Street/US-25; at Biltmore Forest, merge onto Hendersonville Street/US-25 and continue along this road. Merge on US-74/I-26 East and follow the signs to Flat Rock and the historic site. From the Blue Ridge Parkway, exit at Milepost 388.8 and turn south on Hendersonville Road and follow the same route. Expect a drive of around 45 minutes and 27 miles from downtown Asheville, 30 minutes and 22 miles from the Blue Ridge Parkway.

(81 Carl Sandburg Lane, 828/693-4178, www.nps.gov/carl, 9am-5pm daily, house tour $5 adults, $3 over age 61, free under age 16). Sandburg and his family lived here for more than 20 years, during which time he wrote and won the Pulitzer Prize for *Complete Poems,* and no doubt observed bemusedly as his wife and daughters raised champion dairy goats (a herd of goats lives on the grounds today). Half-hour tours take visitors through the house to see many of the Sandburgs' belongings. There is a bookstore in the house, and more than five miles of trails through the property. As a poet whose first steps were in the mountain clay, I have a soft spot for this place, and it's easy for me to see what Sandburg found so inspiring and appealing about the quiet, the air, and the space; take a moment to sit and reflect while you're here and try writing a couple of lines of your own.

Entertainment and Events

A second literary landmark stands in the village: the **Flat Rock Playhouse** (2661 Greenville Hwy., 828/693-0731, www.flatrockplayhouse.org). Now the state theater of North Carolina, the Flat Rock Playhouse's history dates to 1940, when a roving theater company called the Vagabonds wandered down from New York and converted an old gristmill in the village into a stage. They returned every summer for the next few years, entertaining the locals with plays held in a succession of locations, from the old mill to a circus tent, eventually constructing a permanent theater. They now have a 10-month season, drawing more than 90,000 patrons each year.

Shopping

You'll find quite a few nice galleries and studios in Flat Rock along a strip called Little

Rainbow Row. One place that jumps out is the anchor of Little Rainbow Row, **The Wrinkled Egg** (2710 Greenville Hwy., 828/696-3998, www.thewrinkledegg.com, 10am-5:30pm Mon.-Sat., noon-5:30pm Sun.). This weird little store sells custom care packages for kids heading off to Scout camp, equestrian camp, religious camp, and whatever summer camps kids go to these days. It's a fun place to stop to get a little something for the kids in your life.

Sweet Magnolia Gallery (2720 Greenville Hwy., 828/697-2212, www.sweetmagnoliagallery.com, 11am-5pm Tues.-Sat., 12:30pm-5pm Sun.) carries some stunning jewelry and is the flagship store for Melinda Lawton Jewelry. In addition to Lawton's designs, you'll find vintage pieces for an intriguing mix of styles, stones, and prices.

Food

Flat Rock's a pretty small town, but there are a couple of eateries of note. For barbecue, grab a table at **Hubba Smokehouse** (2724 Greenville Hwy., 828/694-3551, www.hubbahubbasmokehouse.com, 11am-3pm Tues.-Wed., 11am-5:30pm Thurs., 11am-7pm Fri.-Sat., $4-13). They serve a range of sauces that encompass North and South Carolina styles and throw in a little Texas for good measure. Many claim the 'cue here is so good you can eat it naked (without sauce, not without pants), but I'm a sauce lover, so you'll have to decide for yourself. **Flat Rock Village Bakery** (2710 Greenville Hwy., 828/693-1313, www.flatrockwoodfired.com, 7am-5pm Mon.-Wed., 7am-7pm Thurs.-Sun., $4-14) is the parent of Hendersonville's West First Wood-Fired; they serve pizzas, sandwiches, salads, and baked goods. Stop in for a snack or a full meal—they've got you covered on both fronts.

Transportation

Hendersonville and Flat Rock are close neighbors, separated by a drive of nine miles along NC-225/Greenville Highway.

SALUDA AND VICINITY

Just east and south of Hendersonville, bordering South Carolina, Polk County is home to several interesting little towns, most notably Tryon and Saluda, along with a lot of beautiful mountain countryside. In Saluda you'll find a tiny downtown laid out along the old Norfolk Southern Railway tracks. The tracks at Saluda are the top of the steepest standard-gauge mainline railroad grade in the United States. This county's history abounds with exciting stories of runaway trains that derailed at spots like "Slaughterhouse Curve," and more than two dozen railroad workers have been killed on this grade.

Entertainment and Events

For one weekend every July, Saluda busts at the seams with visitors to the **Coon Dog Day Festival** (800/440-7848, www.saluda.com). Hundreds of beautiful, highly trained dogs from all over the region come to town to show off in a parade and trials, while the humans have a street fair and a 5K race.

The town's **Top of the Grade Concert Series** (www.saluda.com) runs from May to September and brings in artists for one free concert every month. Genres range from rock to country to Americana; check online for the current schedule. Like any good North Carolina town, Saluda holds a **Town BBQ—** called the Pig Out—in September; if you're the type to mingle with the locals, this is the perfect chance.

Sports and Recreation

Equestrian life plays a growing role in Polk and the surrounding counties of North Carolina's southern mountains. The **Foothills Equestrian Nature Center** (3381 Hunting Country Rd., Tryon, 828/859-9021, www.fence.org), known as FENCE, occupies 380 beautiful acres along the border with South Carolina. The equestrian center has stables for 200 horses and two lighted show rings. FENCE hosts cross-country, three-day, A-rated hunter and jumper, dressage, and many other equestrian events throughout the year. The annual Block House Steeplechase has been held in Tryon for 60 years, and FENCE has hosted the event for 20 of those years. FENCE also offers regular hikes and bird-watching excursions on its lovely property.

The Gorge (166 Honey Bee Dr., Saluda, 855/749-2500, www.thegorgezipline.com, $95) gives you a treetop view of the mountains and Green River Gorge as you zip-line from tree to tree. There are 11 zip lines, three rappels, and a heart-pounding sky bridge on this course that descends 1,100 feet in total. It is one of the best zip lines in the state; if adrenaline is your thing, check it out.

Food

For such a tiny town, there are an awful lot of eating places in Saluda. Just stand in the middle of Main Street and look around; there are several choices, and you won't go wrong at any of them. The **Saluda Grade Café** (40 Main St., 828/749-5854, http://saludagradecafe.com, lunch 11am-3pm Tues.-Sat., dinner 5pm-9pm Wed.-Sat., 11am-7pm Sun., $11-25) serves food representing a variety of cuisines, including comfort food meatloaf and low-country shrimp and grits; the small menu manages to have a little bit of everything on it. Finding something to eat isn't hard, but steer toward the pasta, as it's house-made.

Wildflour Bakery (173 E. Main St., 828/749-9224, http://wildflourbakerync.com, 8am-3pm Mon.-Sat., 10am-2pm Sun., Pizza Night 5pm-8pm Fri., breakfast and lunch $2-8, Pizza Night $6-22) stone-grinds wheat every morning to make absolutely delicious breads. Breakfast and lunch are served, making this a great place to fill up before a day of kayaking or hiking. Don't miss Friday Pizza Night, where they serve up regular or thin-crust (and even gluten-free) pies with your choice of toppings, along with 10 specialty pizzas. You can bring your own wine or beer on Pizza Night, so order a pie or two, crack open a local brew, and settle in for a little while.

BREVARD

Brevard is the pleasant seat of the improbably named Transylvania County, a county that's mountainous and beautiful in a gothic forest sort of way (not a Dracula sort of way). As you might expect, Halloween is a big deal in this town. Brevard is also known for sheltering a population of rather startling and odd-looking white squirrels. The local legend about their origin goes that their ancestors escaped from an overturned circus truck in Florida in 1940 and made their way to Brevard as pets. More likely, say researchers, is that they came from an exotic pet breeder in Florida, and were acquired by a Brevard-area family. In any case, the white squirrels escaped into the wild of Transylvania County, and you'll probably see their descendants in the area when you visit.

Entertainment and Events

The **Brevard Music Center** (349 Andante Ln., 828/862-2100, www.brevardmusic.org) has attracted the highest-caliber young musicians for more than 70 years for intensive summer-long classical music instruction. Throughout the summer, Brevard Music Center students, as well as visiting soloists of international fame, put on a world-class concert series, performing works from Tchaikovsky to Gilbert and Sullivan.

Shopping

A center for a very different sort of music is **Southern Comfort Music** (16 W. Main St., 828/884-3575, www.celestialmtnmusic.com, 10am-5:30pm Mon.-Fri., 10am-4pm Sat.). Among more usual musical items, this nice little shop carries two lines of locally made instruments: Cedar Mountain Banjos, of the open-backed, old-time variety, are beautifully crafted and ring clear and pretty, while local builder Lyle Reedy hand-makes fiddles from a variety of fine woods; his instruments have a deep, biting sound loved by fiddlers. Musicians and woodworkers alike will enjoy a stop at this Main Street shop.

DD Bullwinkel's (50 S. Brevard St.,

828/862-4700, www.ddbullwinkels.com, 10am-7pm Mon.-Thurs., 10am-8pm Fri.-Sat., 11am-6pm Sun.), attached to Rocky's Grill & Soda Shop, is hard to pass by. They sell a variety of casual outdoor gear, T-shirts, and gadgets. It's a great spot to pick up a Brevard souvenir.

At **O. P. Taylor's** (16 S. Broad St., 828/883-2309, www.optaylors.com, 10am-6pm Mon.-Sat., noon-5pm Sun.), you'll find a toy shop loaded with Lego and Playmobil toys, board and card games for the family, gags and gifts, and playthings old and new. This is a fun shop, especially if you're traveling with kids or bringing back a gift for them.

The White Squirrel Shoppe (2 W. Main St., 828/877-3530, www.whitesquirrelshoppe.com, 10am-5:30pm Mon.-Thurs., 10am-6pm Fri.-Sat., 1pm-5pm Sun.) is one of those quaint souvenir emporiums that has a bit of everything. Need a candle that smells like cookies? Want some hand towels embroidered with Brevard's legendary white squirrel? They have it all. The shop is charming and the owners are nice; it's the kind of place where I buy a little something for my mom or mother-in-law when I'm in town.

Brevard is also home to a number of artists, and if you're here for a quick bite and then it's back to the Parkway, take the time to stick your head in **Number 7 Fine Arts and Crafts Cooperative** (12 E. Main St., 828/883-2294, www.number7arts.com, 10am-5pm Mon.-Sat., 1pm-4pm Sun.). This gallery has featured works by a diverse group of around 25 Transylvania County artists for more than 15 years. Many of the works are inspired by and created in the midst of the phenomenal local landscape.

Accommodations

Slip back in time at the ★ **Sunset Motel** (523 S. Broad St., 828/884-9106, www.thesunsetmotel.com, $75-120). This kitschy motel is a throwback to the days of the classic roadside motel experience: it's cheap, comfortable, and has chairs right outside your door so you can visit with your neighbors (and it has the best

modern convenience—free Wi-Fi). The staff is exceedingly friendly and ready to help with suggestions for places to eat and things to do. You can add on tickets to the Brevard Music Center, waterfall tours, and more when you book your room, so it's super-convenient. And for film buffs, Robert Mitchum stayed here when he was filming *Thunder Road.*

The **Campbell House Bed and Breakfast** (243 W. Main St., 800/553-2853, www.campbellhousebrevard.com, from $159) was renovated in 2014 after a few years of neglect. The new owners didn't just return the house to its former beauty, they surpassed it. The five rooms feature queen beds and private baths and, though none are suites, all are spacious. Though other accommodations in town are bicycle-friendly, Campbell House is the home of bicycle enthusiasts. One of the innkeepers is an avid bicyclist and uses Brevard as a base from which to ride.

The **Inn at Brevard** (315 E. Main St., 828/884-2105, www.theinnatbrevard.com, $150-225) is spacious, beautiful, and kid-friendly. Their 14 rooms are well appointed and they serve a full breakfast.

Camping

Davidson River Campground (Davidson River Circle, reservations 800/444-6777, local information 828/862-5960, www.recreation.gov, open year-round, sites $22-44) is just outside Brevard in the Shining Rock Wilderness Area. There are around 160 sites, some with river frontage, and all have access to hot showers and flush toilets; each site comes equipped with a picnic table, fire ring, and grill. It's the most convenient campground for exploring the hiking and fishing in the area, as well as checking out the waterfalls here.

Ash Grove Mountain Cabins and Camping (749 East Fork Rd., 828/885-7216, www.ash-grove.com, tents and RVs $27-44, cabins $115-165) occupies 14 mountaintop acres just 10 minutes outside of Brevard. This retreat is open year-round, unlike others in the area, so you can experience all four seasons in this lovely spot. The cabins are quaint

Rocky's Grill & Soda Shop in Brevard

and cozy and the tent and RV sites are well maintained. Common areas include a bonfire pit, a few lawn games, and a tiny waterfall.

Just 12.5 miles south of downtown Brevard, **Black Forest Family Camping Resort** (280 Summer Rd., Cedar Mountain, 828/884-2267, www.blackforestcampground.com, Mar. 15-Nov. 15, limited facilities in winter, tent sites $32, RV sites $37, RV with full hookup $39-43, cabin $55) has 100 campsites that are level and, more importantly, shaded. Nearby you'll find hiking, fishing, rock climbing, and mountain biking; on-site, you'll find a playground complete with horseshoe pits, a large heated swimming pool, and a video arcade. There's also free Wi-Fi.

Food

The Falls Landing Eatery (23 E. Main St., 828/884-2835, www.thefallslanding. com, 11:30am-3pm Mon., 11:30am-3pm and 5pm-9pm Tues.-Sat., $13-27) is a spot popular among locals. They specialize in seafood (foreshadowed by the rainbow trout on their sign), and their North Carolina trout sautéed in lemon butter and bourbon is particularly good. Don't discount their burgers, steaks, or lamb chops, though, because they deliver on flavor and value.

★ **Hobnob Restaurant** (192 W. Main St., 828/966-4662, www.hobnobrestaurant. com, lunch 11:30am-2:30pm daily, dinner 5pm-9pm daily, brunch 11am-2:30pm Sun., lunch $7-17, dinner $7-32, brunch $9-18) is one of the best places to eat in Brevard, and not just because the food is good, but because it's interesting. The sweet chili beurre blanc served with pan-seared salmon, the seafood lasagna, and the fried green tomato caprese salad keep the menu accessible and fun.

One of the top restaurants in Brevard is ★ **The Square Root** (33 Times Arcade Alley, 828/884-6171, www.squarerootrestaurant.com, lunch 11am-4pm Mon.-Sat., dinner 5pm-9pm daily, brunch 11am-3pm Sun., lunch around $10, dinner around $20, brunch around $10). Inside, the exposed brick walls create a warm room where the food is more like delicious art. Something as simple as a burger and onion rings comes out as a tower of food, and fine dinner entrées, like the five-spice tuna or the filet mignon, are almost too pretty to eat. Almost.

For a quick bite or a shake, malt, or ice cream soda, check out **Rocky's Grill & Soda Shop** (50 S. Broad St., 828/877-5375, www. ddbullwinkels.com, 10am-7pm Mon.-Thurs., 10am-8pm Fri.-Sat., 11am-6pm Sun., lunch around $8). This place has been around since 1942, and the nostalgic counter with its line of chrome stools takes you back to the heyday of this soda fountain. Enjoy a malt, milk shake, ice cream soda, root beer float, and even an egg cream (try one if you've never had one). It's a must stop, especially as a reward after a morning hike or bike ride.

There are two breweries in Brevard, and both should be on any beer lover's itinerary. **Oskar Blues Brewery** (342 Mountain Industrial Dr., 828/883-2337, www.oskarblues. com, noon-8pm daily) was born in Colorado, but chose Brevard as the home of their East

Coast brewery thanks to its small-town vibe, proximity to awesome mountain biking, and ease of distribution. Tour the brewery (4pm Mon.-Thurs., hourly 2pm-5pm Fri.-Sun.) and grab a taste of one of their brews; my friends are partial to Pinner Throwback IPA and Mama's Little Yella Pils (a pilsner), but I prefer the Old Chub Scotch Ale.

Brevard Brewing Company (63 E. Main St., 828/885-2101, www.brevard-brewing.com, 2pm-11pm Mon.-Thurs., noon-midnight Fri.-Sat., 2pm-10-pm Sun.) specializes in German-style lagers and pilsners, though they also brew IPAs, dunkels, and some seasonal specialties. The taproom is open and friendly, but they don't serve food (you're welcome to bring some in from elsewhere).

Transportation and Services

From Hendersonville, Brevard is a short jog west on US-64, a drive of 35 minutes. From Asheville, the drive to Brevard is 35 miles (45 minutes) following I-40 to I-26; then take NC-280 west to the small mountain town.

Maps and guides are available at the **Transylvania County Tourism Development Authority** (35 W. Main St., 800/648-4523, www.visitwaterfalls.com). In Brevard, the main hospital is **Transylvania Community Hospital** (90 Hospital Dr., 828/884-9111, www.trhospital.org).

Dupont State Forest

Transylvania County is known as the Land of Waterfalls, and with more than 250 in the area, the moniker is well earned. About 10 miles south of Brevard, **Dupont State Forest** (US-276, 828/877-6527, www.dupontforest.com) has more than 90 miles of hiking trails crisscrossing its 10,000 acres. Some of Transylvania County's most beautiful waterfalls are located within the forest and are accessible on foot via moderate or strenuous forest trails or, with special permits and advance reservation for people with disabilities, by vehicle. Visitors should use caution, wear bright-colored clothing, and leave that bearskin cape at home from

Hooker Falls in Dupont State Forest

September through December, when hikers share the woods with hunters.

Many of Dupont State Forest's hiking and mountain-biking trails are rugged forest paths; others, like those that lead to a trio of waterfalls—**Hooker, Triple, and High Falls**—are wide, maintained avenues through the woods. That's not meant as a criticism of the hike to Triple Falls or High Falls (that trail is steep and hot and challenging to plenty of folks who traverse it), but it's not a lace-up-your-boots-for-a-day-of-mountaineering kind of trail. In spring and summer it can be a hot, sweaty affair (bring water), but the views are more than worth it. After this longer hike, make the shorter one to the lower Hooker Falls and go for a swim in the crisp mountain water. Already cool, it will feel downright cold—and quite refreshing—on a hot day.

HIGHLANDS AND VICINITY

This part of the country is blessed with some beautiful waterfalls, some of which are easily visited. **Whitewater Falls** (Hwy. 281, at the state line, south of Highlands, $2 per vehicle), at over 400 feet, is reported to be the highest waterfall east of the Rockies. An upper-level viewing spot is located at the end of a wheelchair-accessible paved trail, while a flight of more than 150 steps leads to the base of the falls. The falls are a fabulous sight, but remember to stay on the trails; several visitors have fallen to their deaths when they left the trail to get a different perspective. A much smaller but still very beautiful waterfall is **Silver Run Falls** (Hwy. 107, 4 miles south of Cashiers), reached by a short trail from a roadside pullout. **Bridal Veil Falls** (US-64, 2.5 miles west of Highlands) flows over a little track of road right off US-64. You'll see a sign from the main road where you can turn off and actually drive behind the waterfall, or park and walk behind it. Another falls that you can walk through is **Dry Falls** (US-64, between Highlands and Franklin, $2 per vehicle), reached by a small trail off the highway; the path curves right into and behind the 75-foot waterfall.

Sports and Recreation

Gorges State Park (Hwy. 281 S., Sapphire, 828/966-9099, http://ncparks.gov) is a lush mountain rain forest that receives 80 inches of precipitation annually. The steep terrain rises 2,000 vertical feet in four miles, creating a series of rocky waterfalls and challenging trails. This 7,500-acre park is the only state park west of Asheville, and it's a sight, with a collection of waterfalls and a fantastic concentration of rare and unique plant and animal species. You'll find a number of rugged trails for hiking, mountain biking, and horseback riding, and there are streams filled with rainbow and brown trout as well as smallmouth bass. Primitive camping (free) is permitted in designated areas.

There are plenty of other places to go for a hike. At **High Hampton Inn and Country Club** (1525 Hwy. 107 S., Cashiers, 800/334-2551, www.highhamptoninn.com), you'll find eight trails of varying difficulty; the most challenging are the hikes to the peak of Chimney Top Mountain and of Rock Mountain. **Rock Mountain,** the smaller of the two at 4,370 feet, is a moderate-to-strenuous hike of 90 minutes to the summit. The trail is well marked and well maintained, and there are only a couple of challenging spots on your trip to the summit. **Chimney Top Mountain,** the taller of the two at 4,618 feet, is strenuous, especially if you push it at the suggested pace of 90 minutes to

the Honeymoon Cabin at High Hampton Inn and Country Club

the top; stretch it out to two hours and it's a bit easier. This trail takes you through some rhododendron thickets, where the plant creates a tunnel around the trail, and encounters a couple of small rock scrambles. These scrambles are easier going up than coming down, so be careful, especially if you're hiking solo. Once you reach the summit of Chimney Top, you'll see why that effort was worth it: it's a million-dollar view. Be careful at the top because it can get windy and there are some pretty severe exposures (read: cliffs) at a few points.

Accommodations and Food

The 3,500-foot-high town of Cashiers ("CASH-ers") is home to the **High Hampton Inn and Country Club** (1525 Hwy. 107 S., 800/334-2551, www.highhamptoninn.com, 2-night minimum, from $203), a popular resort for generations of North Carolinians. This was originally the home of Confederate general Wade Hampton, the dashing Charlestonian cavalryman. The lodge, a big old 1930s wooden chalet with huge cozy fireplaces in the lobby, is surrounded by 1,400 acres of lakeside woodlands, with an 18-hole golf course, a good buffet-style restaurant (dinner jacket requested in the evening), clay tennis courts, and a fitness center that features a climbing tower.

Southern Blue Ridge Parkway

The Blue Ridge Parkway runs along the ridgelines from central Virginia to Cherokee, North Carolina. When it reaches Asheville, it skirts the city and makes a sweeping arc until it turns northward on its final run to the southern terminus. The landscape north of Asheville is rugged and the peaks the tallest in the East. As you move farther south along the Parkway, you pass by Cold Mountain, the peak memorialized by novelist Charles Frazier and the subsequent film; Richland Balsam, the highest point on the Parkway; and vistas that include Looking Glass Rock, Devil's Courthouse, and a few waterfalls.

BLUE RIDGE PARKWAY VISITOR CENTER (MP 384)

The **Blue Ridge Parkway Headquarters** (MP 384, 828/271-4779, www.nps.gov/blri) are working park offices and offer very little to visitors. For an overview of the Blue Ridge Parkway, a gift shop, and as much information as you can handle regarding what to do, where to go, and how to get there on the Blue Ridge Parkway, try the **Blue Ridge Parkway Visitor Center** (828/298-5330, 9am-5pm daily, free). There is a 22-foot-long interactive map, displays on the history and heritage of the Parkway, and a great video (it runs about 25 minutes and is worth the wait and the watch) that will give you a better idea about the Parkway, but the real help comes from the desk operated by the Blue Ridge National Heritage Area (www.blueridgeheritage.com). They have information on the numerous cultural sites and happenings along the Parkway, and can provide you with directions and ideas for stops and side trips.

This building is notable for being certified Leadership in Energy Efficient Design (LEED) Gold by the U.S. Green Building Council. Energy-saving features include active/passive heating and cooling, a living roof planted with sedum, and other features designed to reduce everything from water use to nighttime lighting. All of this is in keeping with the founding principles that guided the construction of the Blue Ridge Parkway, the principles that said that the structures and buildings found in the park would have a natural look, blend in with their environments, and be kind to the earth nearby.

Southern Blue Ridge Parkway

© AVALON TRAVEL

Bryson City
Cherokee
Great Smoky Mountains National Park
SOUTHERN END
Cherokee Indian Reservation
BIG WITCH GAP OVERLOOK
HEINTOOGA OVERLOOK
Pisgah National Forest
Maggie Valley
Dellwood
WATERROCK KNOB VISITOR CENTER
RICHLAND BALSAM
PISGAH RANGER DISTRICT
Waynesville
DEVIL'S COURTHOUSE TRAIL
Blue Ridge Parkway
Cold Mountain 6,030ft.
Canton
Nantahala National Forest
GRAVEYARD FIELDS OVERLOOK
LOOKING GLASS ROCK OVERLOOK
CRADLE OF FORESTRY OVERLOOK
COLD MOUNTAIN OVERLOOK
Mt. Pisgah 5,721ft.
Pisgah National Forest
Cherokee National Forest
Brevard
LAKE POWHATAN
NORTH CAROLINA ARBORETUM
SIERRA NEVADA BREWERY
CARL SANDBERG HOME NATIONAL HISTORIC SITE
CHIMNEY ROCK
Asheville

0 25 km
0 25 mi

Hiking

VISITOR CENTER LOOP TRAIL

Distance: 1.5-mile loop
Duration: 45 minutes
Elevation gain: 50 feet
Difficulty: easy to moderate
Trailhead: near the far end of the visitors center parking lot, near the bus and RV parking area

This popular trail was built by volunteers from the Carolina Mountain Club and Friends of the Blue Ridge Parkway. It is a loop that incorporates part of the Mountains-to-Sea Trail. Not far in, you'll enter a bit of a clearing and begin to descend into the woods. Here, you'll find a rhododendron thicket and see that the ground is covered in English ivy. If you look close (and you should), you'll see poison ivy leaves here and there. Be wary, as poison ivy is everywhere on this hike. But the trail is well traveled, so if you stick to the path, you should remain rash-free.

As you near the half-mile mark, you'll need to cross the Blue Ridge Parkway. Be quick and be safe when you do. After crossing, you have a clear hike until you reach the 0.75-mile mark when you reach the top of a small rise. Take a drink and a picture, and head on down the trail until you reach the fork where the Mountains-to-Sea Trail breaks off. This is 1.1 miles in, so you're close to the end. (If you continued on the Mountains-to-Sea Trail, in 2.5 miles you'd reach the Folk Art Center.) Continue on, pass under the parkway via a stone culvert, and stroll back to the starting point.

★ NORTH CAROLINA ARBORETUM (MP 393)

The enormous **North Carolina Arboretum** (100 Frederick Law Olmsted Way, 828/665-2492, www.ncarboretum.org, 8am-9pm daily Apr.-Oct., 8am-7pm daily Nov.-Mar., bonsai exhibition garden 9am-5pm daily, parking $12) is considered by many to be one of the most beautiful in the country. The 434 natural and landscaped acres back into the Pisgah National Forest, just off the Blue Ridge Parkway. Major collections include the National Native Azalea Repository, where you can see nearly every species of azalea native to the United States, as well as a number of hybrids. The special Bonsai Collection is where staff horticulturists care for more than 200 bonsai plants, many of their own creation.

Walking areas range from easy to fairly rugged, but with 10 miles of hiking and biking trails, you will find one that suits your skill level. Bicycles and leashed dogs are permitted on many of the trails. To learn more about the history of the arboretum, the plants themselves, and the natural history of the region, join one of the **guided tours** (1pm Tues. and Sat.). These two-mile walk-and-talk tours happen rain or shine, so dress for the weather. The arboretum also has a very nice café, the **Savory Thyme Café** (11am-4pm Tues.-Sat., noon-4pm Sun., $4-9), and a gift shop, **Connections Gallery** (11am-4pm daily).

LAKE POWHATAN (MP 393)

At mile marker 393, the Blue Ridge Parkway crosses over the French Broad River. Exit here, at Brevard Road/NC-191, and you're not far from the **Lake Powhatan Recreation Area and Campground,** the **Bent Creek Experimental Forest,** the **Shut-in Trail,** and Asheville's **Zen Tubing.** Stop and hike or bike the day away, then go for a relaxing float on the river before retiring to your campsite.

Lake Powhatan Recreational Area

Lake Powhatan Recreational Area and Campground (375 Wesley Branch Rd., Asheville, 877/444-6777 for reservations, 828/670-5627 for local information, www.recreation.gov, open Apr.-Nov., campsites $22/single campsite, $44/double, RV hookups campsite fee plus $3/water and sewer, $6/electric, $9 combined; dump station $10-50, day use $2/person) is surrounded by the 6,000-acre Bent Creek Experimental Forest and miles of **mountain biking** and **hiking** trails. There are 97 **campsites** here, each with experimental forest east of the Mississippi, and the research done here has helped sustain or rehabilitate hundreds of thousands of acres of forest in the United States.

As cool as an experimental forest is, the thing that draws most visitors here are the **hiking** and **mountain biking** trails, many of which allow **horseback riders** as well. Before you set off on any trail, note if it allows your chosen mode of exploration. And remember to bring water, your camera, bug spray, and, if you can, a bag for any litter you find on the trail.

Hiking
HOMESTEAD TRAIL
Distance: 1 mile one-way
Duration: 30 minutes
Elevation gain: 30 feet
Difficulty: easy
Trailhead: near the campsites on the shore of Lake Powhatan

The Homestead Trail takes you along the shores of Lake Powhatan, past the dam, and then downstream beside Bent Creek. It's a flat, easy hike, despite a couple of footbridges and wet patches, and offers several opportunities for great photos of the lake, especially in the fall.

SMALL CREEK TRAIL
Distance: 0.5 miles one-way
Duration: 15 minutes
Elevation gain: 150 feet
Difficulty: easy to moderate
Trailhead: on the Homestead Trail

On the Homestead Trail, when you pass the beach and cross Small Creek, the trail splits. Stay left for Homestead, but go right to explore the Small Creek Trail and connect to Deerfield Loop. Though Small Creek is short, it does gain a little elevation as it rises through rhododendron and mountain laurel thickets.

DEERFIELD LOOP TRAIL
Distance: 0.8-mile loop
Duration: 25 minutes
Elevation gain: 250 feet

nearing the summit on a Blue Ridge Parkway trail

a picnic table, tent pad, and fire ring; a bathhouse outfitted with hot showers and flush toilets; and a lifeguard-protected beach and swimming lake. Downtown Asheville is just 10 minutes away, good for when you're hungry for something you didn't cook yourself, if you're here for a concert, or if you just want to go out on the town. Quiet hours begin at 10pm nightly, at which time the gates are closed and locked. If you plan on being out after the gates are closed, be sure to let someone know and you can make accommodations to get back in.

Bent Creek Experimental Forest
Surrounding Lake Powhatan is the **Bent Creek Experimental Forest** (1577 Brevard Rd., Asheville, 828/667-5261, www.srs.fs.usda.gov/bentcreek/). You may be wondering what exactly is an experimental forest. Well, it's a designated forest that's part of ongoing research on silvicultural practices that help in the development of new forest management techniques. Bent Creek is the oldest federal

Difficulty: easy to moderate

Trailhead: off Small Creek Trail or near the start of Homestead Trail

This short loop can be made longer by combining parts of Homestead and Small Creek Trails, but on its own, it's a quick workout with a couple of steep spots (not too steep; they'll just slow you down a bit). There is a portion where the trail ducks into a mountain cove, traversing a steep slope and a slippery spring or seep as it does so. Use caution in spots where it's wet or steep and you'll do just fine.

PINE TREE LOOP TRAIL

Distance: 2-mile loop

Duration: 1 hour

Elevation gain: 200 feet

Difficulty: easy to moderate

Trailhead: near Wesley Branch Road after it crosses Bent Creek but before it reaches Lake Powhatan

This two-mile loop takes you up the hill above Bent Creek through a mixed forest of hardwoods and the rhododendron that grows everywhere here. As you climb, you'll cross one of Bent Creek's feeder streams before gaining a little more elevation and then passing by the headwaters of this stream about halfway up the mountain. As you return, you'll find a couple of places where the trees open up, especially in spring and fall, to reveal the valley you're in. For the last leg of this trail, you join with Deerfield Loop until you return to Lake Powhatan.

LOWER SIDEHILL TRAIL

Distance: 3.5 miles one-way

Duration: 1.5-2 hours

Elevation gain: 400 feet

Difficulty: moderate

Trailhead: near Boyd Branch Trailhead parking area on Bent Creek Gap Road

Directions: Bent Creek Gap Road is the continuation of Wesley Branch Road. As you leave the campground at Lake Powhatan, turn left after you cross Ledford Branch at the place where you meet Wesley Branch Road. This will put you on Bent Creek Gap Road; the trailhead is just over one mile away.

The Lower Sidehill Trail is hilly but not too difficult. It follows a number of old roads—logging and forestry roads, most likely—as it climbs smaller hills on its north end before hitting a steeper section on the south end. Along the way it passes through a range of forest types, from hardwoods to dry oak and pine to moist hemlock and other cove-found hardwoods like sycamore. You'll also see more of the mountain laurel and rhododendron that loves this area. This trail feels pretty remote, even though you're never far from a road or either end of the trail.

Once you reach the south end of the trail, you can reverse direction or walk back along Bent Creek Gap Road, a pleasant, flat stroll through the woods alongside the namesake creek.

Shut-In Trail

Shut-In Trail is an old one, dating back to around 1890 when George Vanderbilt established this trail to link his hunting lodge at Buck Springs, just below the summit of Mount Pisgah, to his Biltmore Estate. When the Blue Ridge Parkway came through, parts of the trail were lost, but the pieces that remain follow the original track. The trail earns its name from the "tunnels" the path forms through the dense rhododendron and mountain laurel thickets, giving it a close, "shut-in" feeling.

You can use this trail as a long-distance hike, but considering there's no overnight camping along the Parkway, it would be brutal. At 16.3 miles with around 3,000 feet of elevation gain, to tackle the whole trail in one go is a feat best left to ultra-hikers and long-distance trail-runners. Here, the trail is broken down into hikeable sections, using the access points to Shut-In Trail along the Blue Ridge Parkway as convenient shuttle points and starting areas:

FRENCH BROAD RIVER TO WALNUT COVE OVERLOOK

Distance: 3.1 miles one-way

Duration: 2-2.5 hours

Elevation gain: 800 feet

Difficulty: moderate to strenuous
Trailhead: just off the exit at MP 393.6
Directions: There is a very small parking area on the exit ramp, but you may want to park at the Bent Creek River and Picnic Park, a few hundred yards south on NC-191 from the Parkway ramp. There, a short trail (only a few hundred feet long) takes you to the Shut-In Trail.

This first segment of the Shut-In Trail isn't as shut in by the rhododendron thickets as the rest of the trail, and, in fact, the forest here is quite open. The Mountains-to-Sea Trail follows the Shut-In Trail all the way to Mount Pisgah, so you may encounter some thru-hikers.

About 0.25 mile into the Shut-In Trail, you'll find your first "tunnel" through the mountain laurel. When you emerge, it's time to ascend. The trail is steep but manageable as it climbs to an old road. In the late fall, winter, and early spring, you can see the river from here. The road continues to climb, then gradually descends into a hardwood forest. At just over a mile in, you'll encounter a second road; bear left and follow this road up to another road (at 1.6 miles in) and descend to mile 1.8, where you'll turn onto yet another road that parallels the Blue Ridge Parkway.

Two miles in, you'll encounter your last left turn and immediately the road will begin a series of switchbacks as it climbs the mountain. Be wary of poison ivy here, as it tends to be prolific. As you descend from these heights, you'll find the road and trail are broad and tree-lined, giving the sense of a lush, manicured forest. Continue through these woods until you reach the Blue Ridge Parkway at 3.1 miles in. A right turn on the Parkway takes you to Milepost 396.4 and the Walnut Cove Overlook.

WALNUT COVE OVERLOOK TO SLEEPY GAP OVERLOOK
Distance: 1.8 miles one-way
Duration: 1.25-1.5 hours
Elevation gain: 200 feet
Difficulty: moderate
Trailhead: MP 396.4 at the Walnut Cove Overlook

You're past the roads on this part of the Shut-In Trail. Here, the trail is, well, more trail like, so take a little more care with how and where you step. For the first 0.75 miles, be wary of the poison ivy, which grows quite heartily here. At 1.25 miles in, you'll come to an intersection. This is the Grassy Knob Trail, connecting the Shut-In Trail to part of the Bent Creek trail system. Keep to the left and continue on to cross a small creek—it may be dry in summer months—then another, even smaller water feature before you enter the final tunnel of mountain laurel. Once on the other side, you're not far from the Sleepy Gap Overlook at Milepost 397.3.

SLEEPY GAP OVERLOOK TO CHESTNUT COVE OVERLOOK
Distance: 0.9 miles one-way
Duration: 45-60 minutes
Elevation gain: 600 feet
Difficulty: moderate to strenuous
Trailhead: MP 397.3 at the Sleepy Gap Overlook

Here, you'll find that the hardwoods are enormous, taking on proportions that may surprise you. They remind me of the Forest Moon of Endor from *Return of the Jedi*. This short trail has a steep ascent and descent around 0.6 miles in, but the end point—Chestnut Cove Overlook at Milepost 398.3—isn't far.

CHESTNUT COVE OVERLOOK TO BENT CREEK GAP
Distance: 2.8 miles one-way
Duration: 1.5-1.75 hours
Elevation gain: 200 feet
Difficulty: strenuous
Trailhead: MP 398.3 at the Chestnut Cove Overlook

When starting this trail from Chestnut Cove Overlook you may be wondering which are the chestnut trees. You'll be hard pressed to find one, as a blight introduced from Asia destroyed the trees by the end of the 1930s. Chestnuts made up around 25 percent of the forest in many areas, and it's hard to imagine the richness of these woods if they'd survived.

Here, the Shut-In Trail earns its name. The thickets of mountain laurel and rhododendron form tunnels and passageways for much of the trail as it descends into Chestnut Cove. The effect is one of isolation. Though you're close to the Parkway and not far from civilization, the sounds of the forest overtake the intermittent road sounds and you feel very remote.

For the first 1.5 miles, give or take, you'll find yourself on a slow, gradual descent that takes you in and out of the "tunnels" and patches of hardwood forest. At 1.1 miles in, you'll encounter a woods road; stay to the left and cross a creek at 1.4 miles, then it's back into the "tunnels" for the long ascent out. You'll cross two more streams, at 2 and 2.4 miles, and continue on through the rhododendron tunnels. As you near the 2.8-mile mark, you'll find Forest Service Road 479 and Bent Tree Gap. Blue Ridge Parkway Milepost 400.3 is just to the left.

BENT CREEK GAP TO BIG RIDGE OVERLOOK

Distance: 4 miles one-way
Duration: 2.5-2.75 hours
Elevation gain: 700 feet
Difficulty: strenuous
Trailhead: MP 400.3 Bent Creek Gap

This section combines three smaller, more strenuous sections of the Shut-In Trail. The first runs from Bent Creek Gap to the Beaver Dam Gap Overlook at Milepost 401.7, and it provides a truly wide view of the countryside.

The trail ascends from Forest Service Road 479 near the Bent Creek Experimental Forest Sign; a short way in—about 250 feet— you'll turn onto an old road. A half mile in, you'll pass a spring with some cold and tasty water, but if you're there at the end of an especially dry or hot summer, you'll be out of luck. Continue climbing until you summit Ferrin Knob, where you have a great view to the northeast. At 1.5 miles in, you'll find yourself in the midst of a wildflower-choked gap. Enjoy it for a moment before descending to the Beaver Dam Gap Overlook at Milepost 401.7.

From here to the Stoney Bald Overlook is only 0.9 miles, but it's a tough stretch. The

trail sticks close to the Parkway, but rises and falls quite steeply. Expect about 300 feet of elevation gain and loss as you crest knobs and ridges. A quarter mile in, be mindful of the poison ivy, but pay some attention to the exquisite craftsmanship that went into the rock cribbing stabilizing the hillside along the trail as you crest a high point. Descend to a low point where you'll find violets and other wildflowers, and then ascend again. Once you reach the ridgeline at 0.7 miles in, you'll descend the final 0.2 miles through switchbacks lined with buttercups and orchids to the Stoney Bald Overlook at Milepost 402.6.

On the final leg of this segment, the trail is more of the same: a couple of steepish sections and some wildflowers. You'll ascend immediately on this trail, and continue to climb for 0.4 miles until you reach the top of a knoll and descend. At 0.7 miles, you'll cross the Blue Ridge Parkway (be careful) and continue through until you reach the Big Ridge Overlook at Milepost 403.6.

BIG RIDGE OVERLOOK TO THE MOUNT PISGAH TRAILHEAD

Distance: 4.2 miles one-way
Duration: 2.75-3 hours
Elevation gain: 1,100 feet
Difficulty: moderate to strenuous
Trailhead: Big Ridge Overlook at MP 403.6

The final leg of the Shut-In Trail is made up of three segments. The first two are easier than the last, but the payoff is worth the effort. Keep in mind, though, that you can stop at any of the overlooks to shorten your hike if you're running low on daylight.

From the Big Ridge Overlook to Mills River Valley-Elk Pasture Gap is a pretty easy 1.1 miles. The first half of the trail is mostly flat, but 0.5 miles in you begin a steady, and increasing, ascent. Along the way, you'll pass assorted wildflowers and even blueberries (if they're in season, try a few). A narrow ridgeline awaits at 0.8 miles in.

Like the last segment, this one features one short but steep ascent; the rest of the elevation gain is hardly noticeable. A little more than a quarter mile in, you'll pass a spring where you can refill your water bottle. Closer to the end of the section, you'll find some great trail-building work in the rock walls supporting the trail. Imagine hauling the stone to build that wall on your back. The trail just got a little easier, didn't it? Take a break at Mills River Valley-Elk Pasture Gap at Milepost 404.5; the toughest section is ahead.

If you're itching to get to Mount Pisgah, skip a couple of sections and jump right to Elk Pasture Gap. Here, at the Mills River Valley-Elk Pasture Gap (MP 404.5), you're at an elevation of about 4,200 feet. You'll climb to around 5,000 in under two miles, so get ready. Is it worth it? You bet. The views of Mount Pisgah and other peaks and valleys are worth framing (especially in fall), and there are a couple of berry patches along the way.

You'll start climbing immediately once you leave Mills River Valley-Elk Pasture Gap. Climb steadily for 0.35 miles to where you reach the top of a knob. Then descend to a wide, flat gap. There is another steep ascent at 0.7 miles, with a break at 0.8 miles for a photo op of Mills River Valley to the east. Continue climbing until you begin to level out near the large patch of wild berries. The next 0.2 miles are relatively level, but then you climb again, and hard. As the elevation changes, so does the vegetation. The plants are smaller and scrubbier here than they were just a few hundred feet below. When you reach the ridgeline at 1.5 miles, you'll be rewarded with a view to the east and Mount Pisgah above and to your right. Climb a small knob (with the scantest of views from the top) and descend into a thicket of mountain laurel, and then hike another 0.3 miles to the Mount Pisgah Trailhead parking area at Milepost 407.6. This is the proverbial end of the Shut-In Trail.

Water Sports

Zen Tubing (1648 Brevard Rd., 855/936-8823, www.zentubing.com, 10am-4pm daily, $20 adults, $15 ages 4-12, $5 cooler carrier, same-day second trips $5) operates two float trips: one from their base in Asheville, the other from this facility near Lake Powhatan and the Bent Creek Experimental Forest. The floats are fantastic—you get your tube and one for a cooler, then hop on the shuttle to a spot upriver. Once you get in the water, you have nothing to do but reapply your sunscreen and relax as you float down to Zen's spot and your car. I've floated both of Zen's routes and this one is considerably less crowded, but no less fun.

MOUNT PISGAH (MP 408.6)

At one time, Mount Pisgah was owned by the Vanderbilts, and their estate stretched from the Biltmore Estate, some 16 miles distant in Asheville, to this 5,721-foot summit. The mountain and the land between here and the Biltmore were used as a private hunting retreat. Accessing Mount Pisgah from the Blue Ridge Parkway is easy. At Milepost 408.6, you'll find the **Mount Pisgah Campground** and, across the Parkway, the **Pisgah Inn.**

Hiking

A network of trails and connectors circle Mount Pisgah. The two below are highly recommended.

MOUNT PISGAH SUMMIT TRAIL
Distance: 2.6 miles round-trip
Duration: 2-2.5 hours
Elevation gain: 750 feet
Difficulty: moderate to strenuous
Trailhead: Mount Pisgah Trailhead (MP 407.7)

The view from the summit of Mount Pisgah is well worth the effort you'll put into getting up here. It can be strenuous, especially if you're not in the best shape, but it's hikeable if you take your time. Note that the elevation gain is about 200 feet in the first half of the hike and a little more than 500 in the second half. At times, this trail is steep.

You'll start the hike on Little Pisgah Mountain, where you'll eventually crest a ridge between Little Pisgah and Mount Pisgah. This is where it gets more difficult and many people turn back. Ahead, the trail follows the ridgeline and becomes a bit steeper before it cuts away from the ridge onto a very steep section with several difficult step-ups and rocky sections that are a little nerve-racking if you're not an experienced hiker. This is the steepest section, so if you can do this, you've pretty much summited.

After this steep section, you'll enter a mountain laurel tunnel that's long and rocky. The trail turns, switches back, and follows a new ridge to the summit as it passes through an impressive stand of beech trees.

Once on top, you'll see the transmission tower for WLOS-TV and an observation deck. Though the deck is nice, it and the giant metal tower pull you out of the nature moment and into the modern world, but the view from here is spectacular. To the west, you'll see the Shining Rock Wilderness and Cold Mountain (at the northern end) and, on clear days, the Smoky Mountains in the distance. To the north is Asheville, the Craggy Mountains, Mount Mitchell, and if you're keen-eyed, the Biltmore Estate.

BUCK SPRING TRAIL

Distance: 6 miles one-way
Duration: 4 hours
Elevation gain: 500 feet
Difficulty: easy to moderate
Trailhead: behind the Pisgah Inn

This trail runs from the Pisgah Inn down the mountain to US-276, making for a long 12-mile out-and-back—and the back part is all uphill, so keep that in mind as you're planning how far to go and how much water to bring with you.

Some folks have called this an ideal walking path or the perfect hike. After a short section of moderately steep trail, things even out and the grade becomes so gradual that you won't notice that you're descending. Don't expect mountain vistas on this hike; it's all downhill and never really pops out to a bald or clearing with any kind of view. It does, however, have more than a dozen stream crossings, meaning the little waterfalls, pools, and cascades you'll see, many ringed with rich beds of ferns, moss, and wildflowers, will more than make up for the lack of views.

Hike the trail as far as you want, but remember that it is all uphill on the way back, so it will take a little longer and tax you a little more, but most everyone should be able to enjoy a nice long, peaceful hike in the woods on this trail.

Accommodations

Up on the Blue Ridge Parkway above Waynesville and quite close to Asheville is the fantastic **Pisgah Inn** (MP 408.6, 828/235-8228, www.pisgahinn.com, Apr.-Oct., $145-260), which is much like Skyland and Big Meadows on Virginia's Skyline Drive, with motel-style accommodations surrounding an old lodge with a large family-style dining room and a Parkway gift shop. The inn is on a nearly 5,000-foot-high mountaintop, so the view is sensational. Trails lead from the inn to short, pretty strolls and challenging daylong hikes. The on-site restaurant has a mesmerizing view and an appetizing and varied menu of both country cooking and upscale meals. The guest rooms are simple but comfortable, each with their own balcony and rocking chairs overlooking the valley. Rooms have a TV but no telephone. The Pisgah is a perfect spot for resting, reading, and porch-sitting, but it's quite kitschy; I hope someone helps restore it to its potential.

Camping

The **Mount Pisgah Campground** (MP 408, Canton, reservations 877/444-6777, local information 828/648-2644, www.recreation.gov, early May-late Oct., campsites $16-19) has more than 60 tent-only and RV campsites. Note that although there are some modern amenities like flush toilets and drinking water, there is no electricity, water, or sewer hookups for RVs. Also, take caution with food storage and disposal because black bears frequent the area.

Food

Despite the shortcomings of the accommodations, the **Pisgah Inn Restaurant** (MP 408.6, 828/235-8228, www.pisgahinn.com, 7:30am-10:30am, 11:30am-4pm, and 5pm-9pm daily Apr.-Oct., $3-27) dishes up some tasty grub. Breakfast ranges from light to hearty, depending on what you want and what you're up to that day; lunch ranges from salads to barbecue to burgers; and dinner runs the gamut from steaks and mountain trout to chicken pot pie and the Pisgah Pasta—garlic and white wine cream sauce, fresh tomatoes, mushrooms, and spinach over pasta, served plain or with chicken or shrimp.

COLD MOUNTAIN OVERLOOK (MP 412)

Cold Mountain is a massif everyone in these parts has known about for years, but one that was popularized in the rest of the world by Charles Frazier's 1997 novel *Cold Mountain* and the 2003 Academy Award-winning film of the same name. Frazier set his historical novel in the land of his kin, and based characters on his ancestors, but one of the largest, most looming characters is certainly the mountain and the land around it. View the famed mountain from the Cold Mountain Overlook at Milepost 411.8, or, even better, from Milepost 412.2. Pull off at the Wagon Gap Road parking area (you may recognize Wagon Gap from the book) and walk north along the Parkway a short distance for a fantastic view of the mountain. When you look at it, you may say, "It didn't look like this in the movie." That's because the film was shot in Romania, not western North Carolina.

The 6,030-foot Cold Mountain has a well-earned name. This section of the Parkway is closed for much of the winter and often well into spring. According to Blue Ridge Parkway sources, most closures are from November through March and sometimes well into April. Be sure to check the closure map (www.nps.gov/blri; click the Road Closures link).

For another great look at Cold Mountain, you can hike to the top of Mount Pisgah via the Mount Pisgah Summit Trail. And you can do more than just admire Cold Mountain from a distance—you can climb it. There's no direct access to the trail from the Parkway, but you can reach it from the Art Loeb Trail.

★ PISGAH RANGER DISTRICT

Wending through the mountain roads between Waynesville and Brevard, and easily accessible from the Blue Ridge Parkway at Milepost 412, US-276 carries you right into the **Shining Rock Wilderness,** a part of the larger **Pisgah National Forest.** Is it worth the drive? You bet. As part of the 79-mile **Forest Heritage Scenic Byway** (a loop that twice crosses the Parkway as it circles the Pisgah National Forest), it's simply spectacular. Continue down the scenic byway to reach the town of Brevard, just 18.5 miles off the Parkway. From the Parkway, it will take you around 30 minutes of driving along this beautiful, waterfall-laced road to reach downtown Brevard. Simply follow US-276 South to US-64 West and you're there.

Before you turn off the Blue Ridge Parkway and onto the Forest Heritage Scenic Byway, stop at Milepost 411 at the **Cradle of Forestry Overlook.** Here you can see **Looking Glass Rock,** a smooth, bald bit of near-white rock that's quite distinct as it shines through the surrounding green. In the fall, it's a sight, especially when the trees are in their full blaze of color.

Sights
PISGAH RANGER STATION

Just south of the Blue Ridge Parkway and north of Brevard in the town of Pisgah Forest is the **Pisgah Ranger Station** (US-276, Pisgah Forest, 828/877-3265, www.fs.usda.gov, 8am-5pm daily mid-Apr.-mid-Nov., 8am-4:30pm daily mid-Nov.-mid-Apr.) of the Pisgah National Forest. The forest covers 500,000 acres, which is a large swath of western North Carolina, but this 157,000-acre ranger district has many of the forest's favorite attractions. A good topographic map of the ranger district is available from National Geographic (www.natgeomaps.com/ti_780). In the ranger district are more than 275 miles of hiking trails and several campgrounds; the most easily accessible is **Davidson River Campground** (828/877-3265, reservations at www.recreation.gov, year-round, $22-44), which is 1.5 miles from the Brevard entrance. It has showers and toilets.

CRADLE OF FORESTRY

If you have kids with you, make sure you stop at the **Cradle of Forestry** (US-276, Pisgah Forest, 828/877-3130, www.cradleofforestry. com, 9am-5pm daily mid-Apr.-early Nov., $5 adults, free for 15 and under). This museum and activity complex commemorates the rise of the forestry profession in the United States, which originated here at a turn-of-the-20th-century training school in the forests once owned by George Washington Vanderbilt, master of Biltmore. Plow days and living-history days throughout the year give an interesting glimpse into this region's old-time methods of farming and frontier living. Self-guided trails lead through the woods to many interesting locations of this campus of America's first school of forestry. Most of what's here is geared toward little ones.

SLIDING ROCK

Not to be confused with Shining Rock, **Sliding Rock** (off US-276, 7.2 miles from the Parkway) is an easily accessible waterfall and swimming spot with a parking lot ($2 fee), bathhouse, and lifeguards (10:30am-6pm daily Memorial Day-Labor Day). You can actually ride down the 60-foot waterfall, a smooth rock face (not so smooth that you shouldn't wear sturdy britches) over which 11,000 gallons of water rush every minute into the chilly swimming hole below. How chilly? It's a breathtaking 55°F in the summer. Given its proximity to the Cradle of Forestry—it's just four miles south—it's worth a stop with a car full of kids, especially if they are adventurous, even daredevilish, and outdoorsy.

Looking Glass Falls

LOOKING GLASS FALLS

This is the land of waterfalls, and here's a chance to see a beaut. The 60-foot **Looking Glass Falls** (off US-276, 9.3 miles from the Parkway) plunges over a granite face into a deep, and cold, swimming hole. Looking Glass Falls is both kid-friendly and **wheelchair accessible** (at least to the upper overlook); that and its proximity to the Blue Ridge Parkway make it the perfect quickie waterfall. There are a number of beautiful waterfalls in North Carolina and this is one of the best. The proportions of the falls and the lush vegetation around it are reminiscent of Oahu's Waimea Falls.

Hiking
LOOKING GLASS ROCK TRAIL
Distance: 6.2 miles round-trip
Duration: 4 hours
Elevation gain: 1,650 feet
Difficulty: moderate to strenuous
Trailhead: on Forest Road 475, just south of Looking Glass Falls

Directions: Just down the road from Looking Glass Falls, heading toward Brevard, you'll pass National Forest Road 475 on your right. Turn here. In less than a half mile you'll reach the Looking Glass Rock trailhead. This is a great out-and-back hike. There's only one trail at the trailhead, and it goes straight to the top of Looking Glass Rock, making this a fairly easy trail to follow. The elevation gain will test your legs as you ascend and again when you descend. Bring plenty of water and a snack, and dress appropriately for the weather.

The trail opens beside a small stream. Cross it and ascend through a hemlock forest. After crossing the creek, you'll top a small ridge and head into a cove on the other side. Here you'll find a larger stream with a few pretty, but small, cascades. Continue climbing.

Soon after you find the second stream, you'll encounter the first of many switchbacks. Notice that the forest has grown sparser and the view has opened up. As you climb higher, the trees will get shorter, with one notable exception that we'll get to in a moment. Soon the switchbacks will shorten, becoming tighter and more frequent as you climb up a small ridge.

When you're about a mile in, you'll reach a left-hand switchback with a large, magnificent Carolina hemlock at the tip. Behind the tree, the view opens up a bit more, revealing cliffs on the north face of the mountain. Be extremely careful if you go around the hemlock to ogle the cliffs; there's a sheer, very dangerous, 30-foot drop right behind the tree.

As you start to ascend again, you'll find that the cliffs you saw from the hemlock switchback form a sort of ring around the mountain. The trail gets steeper and rockier. This route is just about the only way up this mountain, save scaling the near-vertical cliffs. The next set of switchbacks leads through this steep slope covered with Carolina hemlocks. These are different from the hemlocks at the start of the trail. In fact, the Carolina hemlock is only found in a small area around the Blue Ridge and Smoky Mountains in five states. Soon, though, these trees will all be dead due to an insect infestation.

After passing a campsite at the midway point of the hike, you'll enter an area where rhododendron and mountain laurel are more dominant. As the trail moves off the edge of the ridge you're following, you'll find a helipad painted with a large "H." It seems out of place, but even stranger is the carved signature Max Wilson left on the rock here, accompanied by the two dates he climbed to this rock in the 1930s and 1950s. The final push to the top of the mountain is steep and rocky, so watch your footing.

The round, flat summit is rather anticlimactic. For the real reason you came up here, walk a few more yards and pop out of the oak and rhododendron forest onto the top of the cliffs. The view is among the best in the area, but be careful—the surface can be slick.

LOOKING GLASS ROCK OVERLOOK (MP 417)

This overlook offers an impressive view of Looking Glass Rock, a mountain that's mostly bare rock that shines in the sun kind of like a looking glass.

Hiking

SKINNY DIP FALLS TRAIL

Distance: 0.8 miles round-trip

Duration: 45 minutes

Elevation gain: 210 feet

Difficulty: moderate to strenuous

Trailhead: MP 417, across the Parkway from the Looking Glass Rock Overlook

This is a short hike with a tantalizing name, and if you're here during the right time of year and there's no one around, you can participate in your own au natural swimming session at the base of the falls. If you do decide to dip more than a toe in the water, know that it's cold.

Start the hike by crossing the Parkway and ascending through a forest of oak, maple, and birch trees. Climb a set of steps and cross the Mountains-to-Sea Trail onto an old roadbed. Take this all the way to the falls. There are only a few spots where the trail gets rough with wet areas, eroded bits, and the typical rocks and roots, but other than that, the trail's about as easy as you'll find around here.

Cross a couple of bridges and go down another steep set of steps and you're here. The Yellowstone Prong runs right by that trail and the three-tiered falls, each around 10 feet high, plunges down the cliffs. This is your chance to strip, dip, then drip-dry on one of the small beaches or flat rocks.

GRAVEYARD FIELDS OVERLOOK (MP 418.8)

The East Fork Overlook at Milepost 418.3 gives you a great look back over the Shining Rock Wilderness. Look until you've had your fill and then head down the road a half mile to Milepost 418.8 and the Graveyard Fields Loop Trail.

Graveyard Fields takes its name not from a literal graveyard (though if you've been vigilant, at several places along the Parkway you'll have seen little country churches and fence-ringed graveyards alongside them), but rather from the stumps left standing after decades of logging and a couple of raging forest fires. After the last, name-giving fire in 1942, the charred stumps looked like tombstones, hence the name.

Hiking
GRAVEYARD FIELDS LOOP TRAIL
Distance: 2.2 miles round-trip
Duration: 1.5 hours
Elevation gain: 300 feet
Difficulty: easy to moderate
Trailhead: MP 418.8

The Graveyard Fields Loop Trail is easy and picturesque, and spur trails lead to two waterfalls, so during peak times (read: wildflower season and autumn), you may find parking at the trailhead to be difficult.

The trail begins on a paved trail through a thicket of mountain laurel and rhododendron. Soon the pavement ends and the trail begins in earnest, crossing a small creek and then a rock outcropping with a small cave. This part of the trail is prone to eroding, so watch your step. Cross the river on the footbridge ahead and turn right on a short spur trail to the first waterfall, Yellowstone Falls, also called Lower Falls. Notice that the rock behind the falls is golden in the right light, giving the falls their name. As you retrace your steps back to the footbridge, grab a handful of wild blueberries if they're in season.

Don't cross the bridge or your hike will be far too short. Instead, continue following the river upstream. Here, you're in the area known as Graveyard Fields. It's a wide expanse, dotted with wildflowers and berry bushes (wild blueberries, gooseberries, and blackberries), and is very pretty when the light is right.

Stay on this trail until you reach an intersection about 1.4 miles in. If you follow the trail to the right, you'll be on a path that's about 0.75 miles long, unmaintained, and steep. What's at the end? Upper Falls, an impressive sight and one worth seeing, but only if you're up to the task of following a potentially difficult trail. If you do head to Upper Falls it will add a little time to your hike, as you must go up and then back down this steep section of trail.

The left-hand path at this intersection loops back to the trailhead, crossing the river, part of which you'll need to boulder-hop or wade. Continue on the trail. When you reach a long log bridge over a marshy area, you're almost back to the start.

DEVIL'S COURTHOUSE (MP 422.4)

According to Cherokee legend, this spot was the home of a giant, slope-eyed spirit named Judaculla. He's something like the Cherokee version of Sasquatch, so be ready to snap a picture if you find him holding court on this distinct rocky outcropping. Whether he's here or not, this little hike is well worth the effort.

Hiking
DEVIL'S COURTHOUSE TRAIL
Distance: 0.9 miles round-trip
Duration: 45 minutes

Elevation gain: 150 feet
Difficulty: moderate to strenuous
Trailhead: MP 422.4

About half of this trail is paved, the other half is steep. After you pass through the spruce-fir forest, you'll pop out onto the gnarly rock outcropping that is Devil's Courthouse. It's a great place to watch for hawks and eagles riding the thermals in the valley below. It's also a great vantage point in general, providing a 360-degree view of the surrounding land. Markers in the rock help you identify landmarks. Stay inside the designated area, though; if you don't, you risk a 200-foot sheer drop off the Courthouse.

COLD MOUNTAIN (MP 423.2)

Cold Mountain may not be the tallest (though it is more than 6,000 feet high) in the Blue Ridge, but its name is the most recognizable, thanks to Charles Frazier, novelist and native of western North Carolina. His novel, *Cold Mountain,* and the subsequent film adaptation, takes place here during the Civil War (and is based somewhat on his family history) and made the mountain known to those outside the region. You can view Cold Mountain from the Parkway (back at MP 411, 412, and many others) and from the summit of Mount Pisgah, but you can't drive to it. To reach the summit, or even its lower slopes, you'll have to hike in. It's tough, but beautiful, and as one of the highest peaks in the area, the views are well worth the effort.

Hiking

COLD MOUNTAIN SUMMIT HIKE VIA THE ART LOEB TRAIL

Distance: 10.6 miles round-trip
Duration: 6-7 hours
Elevation gain: 2,800 feet
Difficulty: strenuous
Trailhead: Daniel Boone Scout Camp
Directions: Take the exit at Parkway MP 423.2 and follow NC-215 North for 13 miles. Turn right onto Little East Fork Road. Go 3.8 miles to the Daniel Boone Scout Camp. After you pass the last building, the trailhead is on the left.

Getting to the trailhead for the Cold Mountain summit hike seems like a hike in and of itself, but once you set foot on the trail, all of that disappears. Bring plenty of water, weather-appropriate clothing (including something a little warmer for near the summit), something to eat (you'll be out here all day), a light, and a map.

Leaving the trailhead behind, you'll ascend via a series of switchbacks 1.1 miles to a ridgeline (and the first campsite if you're overnighting it). Two miles in, you'll cross Sorrell Creek (and pass another campsite). As the trail continues to rise, you'll pass through some rich land. Keep your eyes out for wildflowers, especially trillium. At 3.8 miles in, turn left at Deep Gap, where you'll find another campsite. From here, you're only 1.5 miles from the summit. The primo campsite is near the summit, but be aware it's chilly up here, even in the summer when temperatures can dip into the 50s at night.

The summit of Cold Mountain is treecovered and viewless, but make a stop there anyway so you can say you summited. If you backtrack 10 or 12 yards down the trail, you'll see a small spur trail that leads to a rock ledge. Here's where you'll find your million-dollar view: a 180-degree panorama to the south.

The summit trail is not marked, but it is well traveled and pretty obvious. But any time you go into the woods for a hike, especially an unmarked one, bring a detailed topographic map with you. You'll be able to find maps at any of the outdoor outfitters in Asheville and at many of the gift shops along the Blue Ridge Parkway.

RICHLAND BALSAM OVERLOOK (MP 431.4)

The last dozen miles of the Parkway prior to this point have been the highest on the route, and you're about to reach the apex. At 6,047 feet, Richland Balsam is the **highest point on the Parkway.** At the Haywood-Jackson Overlook at Milepost 431 (6,020 feet), you get expansive views to the south and west where long lines of mountains march off into the blue distance, and, on the closer hills, the mountainsides are so thick with dark green conifers that they seem black.

Hiking
RICHLAND BALSAM SELF-GUIDING TRAIL

Distance: 1.4-mile loop
Duration: 1.25 hours
Elevation gain: 270 feet
Difficulty: moderate
Trailhead: MP 431

The summit of Richland Balsam is at 6,292 feet, so you have a little climb ahead of you. Begin your hike on a short section of paved trail at the end of the parking area. Continue until you reach the loop trail intersection. Stay right and begin a steeper ascent. Along the way, you'll pass several benches where you can rest or snap a picture or two, but the best opportunities for photos are near the summit.

A little over a half mile in, you'll reach the summit. Stop, look around, take a deep breath of fir-scented air, and begin your descent. A mile in, you'll reach a break in the trees that gives you a glimpse of the land to the east. Push on through the tunnel formed by evergreen boughs, and when you reach the bench, take a long look at the excellent view here. Follow the trail back to the intersection, bear right, and you're back at the parking lot.

WATERROCK KNOB (MP 451.2)

The **Waterrock Knob Visitor Center** (828/775-0975, 10am-5pm daily May-Sept.) is a small affair. A tiny gift shop, restrooms with pit toilets but no running water, and a parking area with a fabulous view of the sunset of the Smokies round out the offerings. There is a trail that takes you out to Waterrock Knob, a picturesque spot drawing its name from a cool stream where hunters would come to fill waterskins or canteens. It's a beautiful hike that I highly recommend.

Hiking
WATERROCK KNOB TRAIL

Distance: 1.2 miles round-trip
Duration: 1 hour
Elevation gain: 600 feet
Difficulty: strenuous
Trailhead: MP 451.2 at the Waterrock Knob Visitor Center

This trail is short but surprisingly strenuous, as it's all uphill (until you come back, then it's all downhill, which is even more difficult). While many visitors will take the quarter-mile

hiking to the top of Waterrock Knob

paved trail to a platform with a great view of its own, for the best vista, keep climbing.

As you follow the trail beyond the platform, the paving falls away and it turns into a typical dirt trail. The view keeps opening up the farther you go. You'll pass through huckleberry brambles, as well as blackberries and blueberries (ripe in late summer), and picture-perfect rock outcroppings.

In a few spots you may have to scramble over some rocks for the best views or pictures, and so long as you're careful, it's worth it. At the summit you'll find a bench where you can rest your legs and soak in the scenery.

Follow the trail a few steps more and you'll come to another rock outcropping where you'll have views of Clingmans Dome (6,643 ft.), Mount LeConte (6,593 ft.), and Mount Guyot (6,621 ft.), the highest peaks in Great Smoky Mountains National Park to your west.

SOCO GAP (MP 455.7)

When you reach the 4,570-foot Soco Gap, you're on the edge of the Qualla Boundary and Cherokee country. The overlook here is less of an overlook and more of a parking area, at least until the National Park Service clears a few trees. Don't worry about views, though: As you round some of the big sweeping turns on the descent toward Cherokee and the end of the Blue Ridge Parkway, you'll have plenty more views to take in.

BIG WITCH GAP OVERLOOK (MP 461.9)

This intriguing spot brings with it the potential to see the namesake Big Witch, the Anglicized name of a famous Cherokee medicine man who lived in these parts for more than 90 years. Here, at the Big Witch Gap Overlook, you have an excellent view of the Great Smoky Mountains. If you're here at the right time of day or year, you'll see why they call them the Great Smoky Mountains—the fog and mist rise like tendrils of smoke from what seems like every cove and hollow in these hills.

SOUTHERN END (MP 469.1)

Congratulations, you made it to the end of (or, depending on your perspective, the beginning of) the Blue Ridge Parkway. At Milepost 469.1, you'll intersect US-441 just a mile or so from Cherokee to the south and east, and Great Smoky Mountains National Park to the north and west. This is the time to pull off, get out of the car, and snap a selfie in front of the Blue Ridge Parkway sign at the southern end of the route. After that, it's on to Cherokee for a meal, a massage, and some blackjack.

Waynesville and Vicinity

Waynesville, just 30 miles west of Asheville and about 30 miles east of Cherokee, is the very definition of the word quaint. Writers have compared it to a Norman Rockwell painting, its storybook Main Street bustling with shops and lined with brick sidewalks and iron lampposts. This is an artistic little community where the art and craft galleries and studios are seemingly endless. In nearby Cullowhee, Western Carolina University is one of the mountain region's leading academic institutions, as well as the location of the Mountain Heritage Center museum and Mountain Heritage Day festival.

SIGHTS

One interesting stop in Waynesville is the **Museum of North Carolina Handicrafts** (49 Shelton St., 828/452-1551, www.sheltonhouse.org, 10am-4pm Tues.-Sat. May-Oct., $6 adults, $5 students, free ages 5 and under). Consisting of a farmhouse, barn, and gardens, the museum opened in 1980 and shows off the work of Native American and North

Waynesville

Carolina heritage artists. This means mountain musical instruments, ceremonial items and crafts from Native American tribes, basketry, woodcarvings, quilts, and even antique farm tools. Tours of the museum are guided, so you'll hear plenty of stories to go with the items you see.

SHOPPING

Waynesville's downtown can keep a gallery-hopper or shopper happy for hours. Main Street is packed with studio artists' galleries, cafés and coffee shops, and a variety of boutiques.

Books and Specialty Items

Blue Ridge Books & News (152 S. Main St., 828/456-6000, www.blueridgebooksnc.com, 9am-6pm daily) is a nice bookstore specializing in regional-interest titles and good coffee. A number of prominent Southern authors come through here to read and sign books; check the shop's schedule online to see whose book tour is coming through town, and ask about signed copies while you're there.

Good Ol' Days Cigars (46 N. Main St./145 Wall St., 828/456-2898, www.goodoldaysci-gars.com, 11am-5pm Mon.-Sat.) offers a large selection of fine tobacco and smoking products—cigars as well as pipes, loose tobacco, and rolling papers—and a lounge in which to enjoy them.

One of the several locations of **Mast General Store** (63 N. Main St., 828/452-2101, www.mastgeneralstore.com, 10am-6pm Mon.-Sat., noon-6pm Sun. spring-fall, hours vary in winter) is here in Waynesville. While the stores are perhaps best known among vacationers for making children clamor for the candy kept in big wooden barrels, they have an even larger selection of merchandise for adults, including camping gear, such as top-brand tents, cookware, and maps and outdoors-oriented upscale clothing and shoes by Columbia, Teva, Patagonia, and Mountain Hardwear.

Galleries

Waynesville's galleries are many and varied, although the overarching aesthetic is one of studio art with inspiration in the environment and folk arts. **Twigs and Leaves** (98 N. Main St., 828/456-1940, www.twigsandleaves. com, 10am-5:30pm Mon.-Sat., 1pm-4pm Sun., hours vary seasonally) carries splendid art furniture that is both fanciful and functional, pottery of many hand-thrown and hand-built varieties, jewelry, paintings, fabric hangings, mobiles, and many other beautiful and unusual items inspired by nature.

Art on Depot (250 Depot St., 828/246-0218, 10am-5pm Thurs.-Tues., 10am-6pm Wed.) is a working pottery studio and gallery where local and regional artists exhibit and sell their work. Artistic creations for sale include decorative and functional pottery by the resident potter and many of her contemporaries as well as paintings, jewelry, sculpture, and a few pieces by area fiber artists.

Studio Thirty Three (822 Balsam Ridge Rd., 828/452-4264, www.studio33jewelry. com, by appointment) carries the work of a very small and select group of fine jewelers from western North Carolina. Their retail and custom inventory consists of spectacular handcrafted pieces in a variety of styles and an array of precious stones and metals. This is a must-see gallery if you have a special occasion coming up. The gallery describes its stock as ranging in price from "$65 to $16,000," and most items cost upward of $2,000. Even if you're not about to mark a major life event or spend that kind of money just for fun, it's worth stopping in to gaze at all that sparkle.

ACCOMMODATIONS

Waynesville has quite a selection of luxury inns. The **Andon-Reid Inn** (92 Daisey Ave., 800/293-6190, www.andonreidinn.com, $145-205, no children or pets) is a handsome turn-of-the-20th-century house close to downtown with five tranquil guest rooms, each with its own fireplace, and a sumptuous breakfast menu that might include sweet-potato pecan pancakes and pork tenderloin, homemade corn bread with honey butter, or the intriguing baked lemon eggs. With advance notice they can cater to special dietary needs.

In the community of Balsam, seven miles southwest from Waynesville, the ★ **Balsam Mountain Inn** (68 Seven Springs Dr., Balsam, 800/224-9498, www.balsammountaininn.net, $100-230, no pets) has stood watch for a century in a haunting location—an imposing old wooden hotel with huge double porches overlooking a rather spooky little railroad platform and the beautiful ridges of Jackson and Haywood Counties beyond. The interior has barely changed since its earliest days, paneled in white horizontal beadboard throughout with 10-foot-wide hallways said to have been designed to accommodate steamer trunks. The one telephone is at the front desk, and there are no TVs, so plan to go hiking or to sit on the porch before dining in the downstairs restaurant, and then curl up and read in the library. There is, incongruously, fast Wi-Fi. Among the inn's reported ghosts is a woman in a blue dress, said to originate in room 205 but to come and go elsewhere on the second floor. This inn has a few rough edges, but the atmosphere can be found nowhere else.

For absolute tip-top luxury, try **The Swag** (2300 Swag Rd., 800/789-7672, www.theswag. com, $495-850). Superb guest rooms and cabins of rustic wood and stone each have a steam shower, and several have saunas, wet bars, and cathedral ceilings. The menu is decidedly country and upscale, two things you wouldn't think go together, but they do, and quite nicely. The inn is at 5,000 feet elevation in a stunning location at the very edge of Great Smoky Mountains National Park.

FOOD

Waynesville's ★ **Frogs Leap Public House** (44 Church St., 828/456-1930, http://frogsleappublichouse.com, 11:30pm-2:30pm Tues.-Sat., 5pm-9pm Tues.-Thurs., 5pm-10pm Fri.-Sat., lunch $7-18, dinner $8-29) serves an interesting menu that's quite sophisticated, yet not afraid of its Southern roots. Dishes like the wood-grilled sirloin tip in a bourbon-shallot demi-glace or the spicy Korean pork belly sliders show an adventurous spirit that diners appreciate, not just because it's ambitious, but because it's excellent.

If you're just passing through town and need a jolt of good strong coffee, visit **Panacea** (66 Commerce St., 303 S. Main St., 828/452-6200, http://panaceacoffee.com, 7am-5pm Mon.-Thurs., 7am-11pm Fri., 8am-11pm Sat., $5-11) in the funky Frog Level neighborhood downhill from downtown. The proprietors give back to their community, and trade fairly with the communities that supply their coffee. They stock beans, blends, and brews from all around the world.

The ever-popular **Bogart's** (303 S. Main St., 828/452-1313, www.bogartswaynesville. com, 11am-9pm Sun.-Thurs., 11am-10pm Fri.-Sat., $7-23) is locally famous for its filet mignon, though their local trout also has a good reputation. The menu is huge but very steakhouse; vegetarians will have a tough time, although a few dishes, like the chipotle black bean burger and the grilled Portobello salad, provide options.

TRANSPORTATION AND SERVICES

Waynesville is easy to reach from either I-40 or the Blue Ridge Parkway. On I-40, take Exit 27 and turn south; downtown is about 7 miles away. From Blue Ridge Parkway Milepost 423.4, follow US-276 north for 30 minutes right into town. From Milepost 443.1, turn onto US-74 E/US-23 N and zoom into Waynesville from the west in about 10 minutes. Asheville lies 31 miles to the east; Cherokee and Great Smoky Mountains National Park are only 27 miles west.

The **Haywood County Tourism Development Authority** (44 N. Main St., 800/334-9036, http://visitncsmokies.com/) has a wealth of information about visiting Waynesville and the surrounding towns. **MedWest Haywood** (262 Leroy George Dr., Clyde, 800/4243672, www.haymed.org), accessible from the Lake Junaluska exit off US-23/US-74, is the region's hospital.

Cherokee and Maggie Valley

Look for ★ to find recommended sights, activities, dining, and lodging.

Highlights

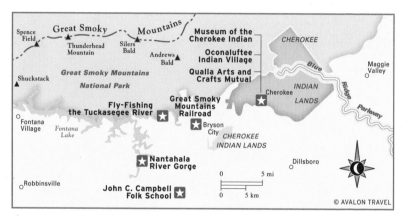

★ **Museum of the Cherokee Indian:** The Cherokee people have lived in the Smoky Mountains for thousands of years. This excellent museum tells unforgettable tales of their history (page 160).

★ **Qualla Arts and Crafts Mutual:** Ancient craft traditions still thrive among Cherokee artists in western North Carolina. At the Qualla Mutual, visitors to the Eastern Band's seat of government can learn about and purchase the work of today's masters (page 161).

★ **Oconaluftee Indian Village:** Demonstrations in traditional cooking, flint knapping for arrowheads and spearpoints, and ritual dance give visitors a glimpse into 18th-century tribal life at this re-created Cherokee Indian village (page 161).

★ **Great Smoky Mountains Railroad:** See the Blue Ridge in its deepest summer green or a blaze of autumn color on a rail tour departing from the historic depot in Bryson City (page 170).

★ **Nantahala River Gorge:** So steep that in some places the water is only brushed by sunlight at high noon, this gorge is an unbeatable place for white-water rafting (page 170).

★ **Fly-Fishing the Tuckasegee River:** Several outfitters can hook anglers up for a great day on the Tuckasegee River, which conveniently flows right through Bryson City (page 171).

★ **John C. Campbell Folk School:** For nearly a century the Folk School has been a leading light in promoting American craft heritage, nurturing new generations of artists, and securing the future of Appalachian artistic traditions (page 177).

A sense of otherworldliness and of magic rises up from these hills like the mist that evokes the Smoky Mountains.

Maybe it's the way the land is folded and rumpled like a quilt at the foot of the bed, or perhaps it's some element of Cherokee mythology come to life. After all, this is the ancestral home of the Cherokee people and the present home of the Eastern Band of the Cherokee Indians; it's possible that something in these hills and hollows remains, imprinted from their collective memories. In towns like Cherokee, the magic is thick, but it's also present in Bryson City, throughout the Nantahala National Forest, and along Maggie Valley, calling to visitors and enchanting them year after year.

The town of Cherokee sits on the Qualla Boundary at the edge of Great Smoky Mountains National Park. Make no mistake, this isn't a reservation; it's ancestral Cherokee land. They're quite proud of the small group of forefathers who refused relocation and the travesty of the Trail of Tears, choosing instead to hide in these hills, wage a guerilla war, and ultimately win the right to set up a Cherokee government.

Other towns here abut the national park or are just a few miles away, and the Cherokee influence is felt everywhere you go. An altogether lovely place, the mountains are tall, the roads winding, and the streams downright picturesque. It's a place people are proud to call home, whether their family has been here for 10 years or 10,000.

PLANNING YOUR TIME

To make the most of your time, spend **two days** in Cherokee, (one for the casino, one for the cultural sights), set aside at least **one day** to visit the national park, and use **one day** for exploring the small towns. If camping is your thing, there are plenty of campsites in the park and some very good ones on the outskirts; if it's not, there are lovely B&Bs and funky older hotels around. A more luxurious experience can be had at Harrah's Cherokee Casino.

When to Go

Autumn is prime time to visit the Smoky Mountains and the towns in this part of North

---

Previous: fall color on the mountains; the Tuckasegee River in Bryson City. **Above:** stacked firewood.

Cherokee and Maggie Valley

© AVALON TRAVEL

Fontana Village

Robinsville

129

Nantahala River Gorge

Nantahala

To JOHN C. CAMPBELL FOLK SCHOOL

19
74

28

NANTAHALA RIVER GORGE

Shuckstack 4,020ft

Appalachian

Spence Field 4,900ft

Thunderhead Mountain 5,530ft

Fontana Lake

Trail

Silers Bald 5,607ft

Clingmans Dome 6,643ft

Great Smoky

Andrews Bald 5,860ft

Mountains

Cades Cove

RICH MTN RD

RICH MTN

321

Townsend

LITTLE RIVER RD

Little River

To Knoxville

ELKMONT

Sugarland Mtn

NEWFOUND GAP

Great Smoky Mountains National Park

Mt LeConte 6,593ft

Appalachian

Charlie's Bunion 5,900ft

Trail

Mt Guyot 6,621ft

FLY-FISHING THE TUCKASEGEE RIVER

GREAT SMOKY MOUNTAINS RAILROAD

Bryson City

28

DEEP CREEK

19

CHEROKEE INDIAN LANDS

Pisgah National Forest

441

Dillsboro

441

MINGUS MILL

Newfound Gap 5,046ft

441 RD

SMOKEMONT

Mingus Falls

Cherokee

MUSEUM OF THE CHEROKEE INDIAN

OCONALUFTEE INDIAN VILLAGE

QUALLA ARTS AND CRAFTS MUTUAL

CHEROKEE INDIAN LANDS

BLUE RIDGE

BALSAM MOUNTAIN

BALSAM MTN RD

Mt Sterling 5,835ft

CATALOOCHEE

COVE CREEK RD

441

23
74

PKWY

Maggie Valley

THE STOMPIN' GROUNDS

WHEELS THROUGH TIME MOTORCYCLE MUSEUM

19

To Asheville

0   5 mi
0   5 km

Carolina. As leaves on the trees change—first at the highest elevations, then creeping down the mountains week by week—the Blue Ridge Parkway sees heavy traffic and these little mountain towns bustle with people. Generally, this is during October, but it can start as early as mid-September and last as late as mid-November. Regardless of Mother Nature's schedule, it can be difficult to get a hotel room in October without advance reservations.

During **winter,** this area will see significant snowfall at times and correspondingly low temperatures. This is when Great Smoky Mountains National Park receives its lowest visitation levels and many businesses shutter for the season or reduce their hours. However, it's no less charming a time to visit. Hiking the winter woods is a favorite of many an outdoors enthusiast. Some **roads may close** temporarily during winter, like the Blue Ridge Parkway and Newfound Gap Road, which bisects the national park and leads to Gatlinburg, Tennessee.

Spring sees the return of visitors as the mountains come alive with wildflowers and the year's first leaves. **Summer** brings on another flower show, with flame azaleas, mountain laurel, and rhododendron all blooming from April through July. Water activities like tubing and white-water rafting offer the chance to cool off after long hikes or a good ride on a mountain bike. Fly-fishing is popular year-round, with hundreds of miles of trout streams on the Qualla Boundary (where you'll need a tribal permit to fish).

Maggie Valley

Maggie Valley is a vacation town from the bygone era of long family road trips in wood-paneled station wagons. Coming down the mountain toward Maggie Valley you'll pass an overlook that, on a morning when the mountains around Soco Gap are ringed by fog, is surely one of the most beautiful vistas in the state.

SIGHTS

In a state with countless attractions for automotive enthusiasts, Maggie Valley's **Wheels Through Time Museum** (62 Vintage Lane, 828/926-6266, www.wheelsthroughtime. com, 9am-5pm Thurs.-Mon. Apr.-late Nov., $12 adults, $10 over age 65, $6 ages 5-12, free under age 4) stands out as one of the most fun. A dazzling collection of nearly 300 vintage motorcycles and a fair number of cars are on display, including rarities like a 1908 Indian, a 1914 Harley-Davidson, military motorcycles from both world wars, and some gorgeous postwar bikes. This collection, which dates mostly to before 1950, is maintained in working order—almost every one of the bikes is revved up from time to time, and the museum's founder has been known to take a spin on one of the treasures.

Bluegrass music and clogging are a big deal in this town. The great bluegrass banjo player Raymond Fairchild is a Maggie native, and after his 50-year touring and recording career, he and his wife, Shirley, are now the hosts of the **Maggie Valley Opry House** (3605 Soco Rd., 828/926-9336, www.raymondfairchild. com, 8pm Mon.-Fri. June-Oct.). In season, you can find bluegrass and country music concerts and clogging exhibitions most every night.

RECREATION
Hiking

Near Maggie Valley, the mountains become rough. Located on the valley floor, the town of Maggie Valley is surprisingly short on trails, and what trails there are can be quite strenuous. There's the 2.6-mile stroll around **Lake Junaluska,** but other than that, the majority of the trails are found at the crest of the mountains, along the Blue Ridge Parkway. To the east of Maggie Valley,

Maggie Valley

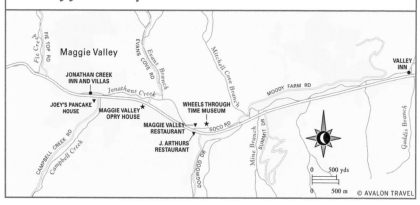

the mountains are a little more forgiving and there are many trails of various intensities and lengths, but in the immediate area, you'll have to take the Heintooga Spur Road, a connector road between the Parkway and Great Smoky Mountains National Park, to a mile-high campground, picnic area with unparalleled views, and the **Flat Creek Trail.** On Heintooga Spur Road, you'll pass into Great Smoky Mountains National Park proper and be treated to no fewer than five stunning overlooks, the best of which is the Mile High Overlook, offering a glimpse of Clingmans Dome, Mount LeConte, Mount Kephart, and Mount Guyot.

FLAT CREEK TRAIL

Distance: 5 miles round-trip
Duration: 3 hours
Elevation gain: 250 feet
Difficulty: moderate
Trailhead: Heintooga Ridge picnic area off Heintooga Spur Road, accessible at MP 458.2

Though named the Flat Creek Trail, you will find a waterfall—the 200-foot Flat Creek Falls, a beautiful but difficult-to-see cascade—along the path. The main trail is easy, with little elevation gain or loss until you turn off onto the short spur trail that takes you to the falls. The falls trail is steep and slick, so be careful if you decide to explore in this area.

Heavy logging at the turn of the 20th century opened the forest up and allowed a thick swath of grass to grow here. Today, much of the grass remains and the forest seems to rise from it like an island in a sea of green. It's a strange sight.

Winter Sports

Maggie Valley's **Cataloochee Ski Area** (1080 Ski Lodge Rd., off US-19, 800/768-0285, snow conditions 800/768-3588, www.cataloochee. com, lift tickets $20-65, rentals $21-30) has slopes geared to every level of skier and snowboarder. Classes and private lessons are taught for all ages.

At Cataloochee's sister snow-sports area, **Tube World** (US-19, next to Cataloochee Ski Area, 800/768-0285, www.cataloochee.com, $25, must be over 42 inches tall, late Nov.-mid-Mar.), you can zip down the mountain on inner tubes, and there's a "Wee Bowl" area for children (call ahead, $5).

ACCOMMODATIONS AND FOOD

The main drag through Maggie Valley (Soco Rd./US-19) is lined with motels, including some of the familiar national chains. Among the pleasant independent motels are **The Valley Inn** (236 Soco Rd., 800/948-6880, www.thevalleyinn.com, in-season rates vary, from $39 off-season) and **Jonathan Creek Inn and Villas** (4324 Soco Rd., 800/577-7812, www.jonathancreekinn.com, from $90), which has creekside rooms with screened-in porches.

★ **Joey's Pancake House** (4309 Soco Rd., 828/926-0212, www.joeyspancake.com, 7am-noon Fri.-Wed., about $8) has been flipping flapjacks for travelers and locals alike since 1966. The pancakes, waffles, and country ham are so good that lines form on the weekends—get here early.

J. Arthurs Restaurant (2843 Soco Rd., 828/926-1817, www.jarthurs.com, lunch noon-2:30pm Fri.-Sun., early-bird dinner 4:30pm-6pm daily, early bird $17, dinner from 4:30pm daily, $15-25) is a popular spot locally for steaks, which are the house specialty; they've been serving them up for more than 25 years. The restaurant also has a variety of seafood and pasta dishes, but there are few vegetarian options.

A Maggie Valley dining institution that's been around since 1952 is **Maggie Valley Restaurant** (2804 Soco Rd., 828/926-0425, www.maggievalleyrestaurant.net, 7am-9pm daily May-Oct., breakfast $1-10, lunch and dinner $5-12). Expect comfort-food classics—meatloaf, meatloaf sandwiches, something called a chuck wagon, pork chops, biscuit sandwiches, grits, bottomless coffee, and even buttermilk—along with one of the best pieces of fresh fried trout you'll find in these mountains.

TRANSPORTATION

US-19 is the main thoroughfare in these parts, leading from Asheville to Great Smoky Mountains National Park. If you're taking your time between Asheville, Boone, or parts north, the Blue Ridge Parkway is a beautiful, but slow, drive to this part of the state. Maggie Valley is also a reasonably short jog off I-40 via exits 20, 24, and 27.

Cherokee and the Qualla Boundary

The town of Cherokee is a study in juxtapositions: the cultural traditions of the Cherokee people, the region's natural beauty, a 24-hour casino, and community-wide preparation for the future. Cherokee is the seat of government of the Eastern Band of the Cherokee, who have lived in these mountains for centuries. Today, their traditional arts and crafts, government, and cultural heritage are very much alive. The Qualla ("KWA-lah") Boundary is not a reservation, but a large tract of land owned and governed by the Cherokee people. Institutions like the Museum of the Cherokee Indian and the Qualla Arts and Crafts Mutual provide a solid base for the Eastern Band's cultural life. As you drive around, take a look at the road signs: Below each English road name is that same name in Cherokee, a beautiful script created by Sequoyah, a 19th-century Cherokee silversmith. This language, once nearly extinct, is taught to the community's youth

and there is a Cherokee language immersion school on the Qualla Boundary. However, this doesn't mean the language is not in danger; few Cherokee people speak it fluently.

The main street in Cherokee is a classic cheesy tourist district where you'll find "Indian" souvenirs—factory-made moccasins, plastic tomahawks, peace pipes, and faux bearskins. In a retro way, this part of Cherokee, with its predictable trinket shops and fudgeries, is charming; check out the garish 1950s motel signs with comic-book caricatures outlined in neon, blinking in the night.

Aside from its proximity to Great Smoky Mountains National Park and the Blue Ridge Parkway, the biggest draw in town is Harrah's Cherokee Casino, one of the largest casino-hotels in the state and home to a world-class spa. The 24-hour entertainment opportunities attract visitors from far and wide, some of whom stay on the property the whole time,

Cherokee

To
Great Smoky Mountains National Park and
Blue Ridge Parkway

TSALI BLVD

DR

WASHINGTON

JOSEPH

ACQUONI RD

OCONALUFTEE
INDIAN VILLAGE ✪

QUALLA ARTS AND
CRAFTS MUTUAL ✪

MUSEUM OF THE ✪
CHEROKEE INDIAN

(1361)

Fair
Grounds

441

Oconaluftee River

B1A HWY 1390

B1A HWY 316

0   200 yds
0   200 m

441 19

19

TSALAGI RD

To
Harrah's Cherokee
Casino and Hotel

© AVALON TRAVEL

cherokeemuseum.org, 9am-7pm Mon.-Sat., 9am-5pm Sun. late June-Aug., 9am-5pm daily Sept.-May, $10, $6 ages 6-12, free under age 5) was founded in 1948 and was originally housed in a log cabin. Today, it is a well-regarded modern museum and locus of community culture. In the exhibits that trace the long history of the Cherokee people, you may notice the disconcertingly realistic mannequins. Local community members volunteered to be models for these mannequins, allowing casts to be made of their faces and bodies so that the figures would not reflect an outsider's notion of what Native Americans should look like; the mannequins depict real people. The Museum of the Cherokee Indian traces the tribe's history from the Paleo-Indian people of the Pleistocene, when the ancestral Cherokees were hunter-gatherers, through the ancient days of Cherokee civilization, and into contact with European settlers.

A great deal of this exhibit focuses on the 18th and 19th centuries, when a series of tragedies befell the Cherokee as a result of the invasion of their homeland. It was also a time of great cultural advancement, including Sequoyah's development of the script to write the Cherokee language. The forced relocation of Native Americans called the Trail of Tears began near here, along the North Carolina-Georgia border, in the early 19th century. A small contingent of Cherokees remained in the Smokies at the time of the Trail of Tears, successfully eluding, and then negotiating with, the U.S. military, who were trying to force most of the Native Americans in the Southeast to move to Oklahoma. Those who stayed out in the woods, along with a few others who were able to return from Oklahoma, are the ancestors of today's Eastern Band, and their history is truly remarkable.

A favorite part of the museum are the stories, legends, and myths described on placards throughout the museum. There's the story of a boy who became a bear and convinced his entire clan to become bears also. There's one about Spearfinger, a frightening creature that some say still lives in these woods. And there

while others take a break from the slap of cards and the flash of slot machines to experience the natural and cultural wonders of Cherokee.

Take everything you see—the casino, the tacky tourist shops, and the stereotyping signs—with a grain of salt, as they don't represent the true nature of the Cherokee people and their long history.

SIGHTS
★ Museum of the Cherokee Indian

The **Museum of the Cherokee Indian** (589 Tsali Blvd., 828/497-3481, www.

are tales about Selu, the corn mother, and Kanati, the lucky hunter. Cherokee member and contemporary writer Marilou Awiakta has written widely about Selu, tying the past and present together with taut lines of thought that challenge our views on culture and technology.

★ Qualla Arts and Crafts Mutual

Across the street from the museum is the **Qualla Arts and Crafts Mutual** (645 Tsali Blvd., 828/497-3103, http://quallaartsandcrafts.com, 8am-6pm Mon.-Sat., 9am-5pm Sun.), a community arts co-op where local artists sell their work. The gallery's high standards and the community's thousands of years of artistry make for a collection of very special pottery, baskets, masks, and other traditional art. As hard as it is to survive as an artist in a place like New York City, artists in rural areas such as this have an exponentially more difficult time supporting themselves through the sale of their art while maintaining the integrity of their vision and creativity. The Qualla co-op does a great service to this community in providing a year-round market for the work of traditional Cherokee artists, whose stewardship of and innovation in the arts are so important. The double-woven baskets are especially beautiful, as are the carvings of the masks representing each of the seven clans of the Cherokee people (the Bird, Deer, Longhair, Blue, Wolf, Paint, and Wild Potato).

★ Oconaluftee Indian Village

Oconaluftee Indian Village (778 Drama Rd., 828/497-3481, http://visitcherokeenc.com, open Mon.-Sat. May-mid-Oct, gates open and tours begin at 10am, tours run every 15 minutes until 4pm when the box office closes, village closes after final tour, usually around 5pm, $19 adults, $11 children, free 5 and under) is a re-created Cherokee village tucked into the hills above the town. Here, you'll see how the tribe lived in the 18th century. Tour guides in period costumes lead groups on walking lectures with stops at stations where you can see Cherokee cultural, artistic, and daily-life activities performed as authentically as possible. From cooking demos to flint knapping (for arrowheads and spearpoints) to wood carving and clay work, you'll get a look at how the Cherokee lived centuries ago. The highlight of the tour is the ritual dance demonstration showing half a dozen dances and explaining their cultural significance.

Harrah's Cherokee Casino

The Eastern Band of the Cherokee operates **Harrah's Cherokee Casino and Hotel** (777 Casino Dr., 828/497-7777, www.harrahscherokee.com, 24 hours daily). This full-bore Vegas-style casino has more than 3,800 digital games and slot machines along with around 150 table games, such as baccarat, blackjack, roulette, and a poker-only room. Inside the casino complex is a 3,000-seat concert venue where acts like Alicia Keys and the Black Crowes have performed, as well as a huge buffet and a grab-and-go food court next to the casino floor. Unlike in the rest of the state, smoking is allowed on the casino floor, though certain areas have been designated as nonsmoking. If you're a nonsmoker, it may take some patience. Inside the hotel portion of the casino are a restaurant, a Starbucks, and the **Mandara Spa,** which offers salon and spa services such as massages and facials.

ENTERTAINMENT

Of the several outdoor dramas for which North Carolina is known, among the longest running is Cherokee's *Unto These Hills* (Mountainside Theater, 688 Drama Rd., adjacent to Oconaluftee Indian Village, 866/554-4557, www.visitcherokeenc.com, 8pm Mon.-Sat. May 30-Aug. 15, $20-23 adults, $10-13 ages 6-12, free under age 6). For more than 60 summers, Cherokee actors have told the story of their nation's history, from ancient times through the Trail of Tears. Every seat in the house is a good seat at the Mountainside Theater, and the play is certainly enlightening. If you're gun-shy or

The Story of the Cherokee

The Cherokee believe that the mountains of western North Carolina have been part of their homeland dating back to at least the last ice age (some 11,000 years ago). By the time Spanish soldiers encountered the Cherokee in the 1540s, the tribe controlled around 140,000 square miles across the southern United States, living in log cabins in towns and villages throughout their territory. They farmed corn, squash, and beans (known as "The Three Sisters"); hunted elk, deer, and bear; and prospered in peacetime and warred with other tribes periodically.

During the first two centuries of earnest European contact, the Cherokee were peaceful and hospitable with the colonists they encountered. Through the course of those 200 years, strings of broken treaties and concessions by the Cherokee had shrunk their once-vast empire dramatically. When President Andrew Jackson insisted that all Indians in the Southeast be moved west of the Mississippi, the real trouble began.

As Jackson's forced march and relocation of the Cherokee and other tribes, known as the **Trail of Tears,** pressed on, a small group of Cherokee avoided relocation by becoming North Carolina citizens. A band of resistance fighters stayed behind near modern-day Cherokee, hiding in the hills, hollows, and caves high in the mountains. These holdouts would become the core of the **Eastern Band of Cherokee Indians.** Unable to own any land, the Cherokee turned to an adopted tribe member to purchase and hold land in his name. He did so, and in 1870, the Cherokee formed a corporation and took control of that land, which they called the **Qualla Boundary.**

Today, the Eastern Band of the Cherokee Indians has nearly 15,000 members (their counterparts in Oklahoma number 10 times as many), many of whom live within the 82-square-mile Qualla Boundary. Tribe members are fiercely proud of their heritage, traditions, stories, and language. An afternoon spent at the **Museum of the Cherokee Indian,** the **Qualla Arts and Crafts Mutual,** and the **Oconaluftee Indian Village,** followed by an evening showing of *Unto These Hills,* will give you a more complete understanding of their history.

easily startled, be warned: There is some cannon fire and gunfire in the play.

Hear stories, learn dances, and interact with Cherokee storytellers at the **Cherokee Bonfire** (Oconaluftee Islands Park, Tsalagi Rd. and Tsali Blvd., where US-19 and US-441 intersect, 800/438-1601, www.visitcherokeenc.com, 7pm and 9pm Fri.-Sat. May-Sept., free, including marshmallows). Bring your bathing suit and some water shoes to the bonfire; afterward, you may want to go for a wade or a quick dip in the Oconaluftee River, which is wide, rocky, and fun.

RECREATION

I'd be in trouble with my dad if I didn't mention that you can—no, must—ride go-karts at **Cherokee Fun Park** (1897 Tsali Blvd., 828/497-5877, www.cherokeefunparknc.com, 10am-10pm Sun.-Thurs., 10am-11pm Fri.-Sat. summer, hours vary seasonally, single rider

$8, doubles $12). A family tradition for as long as I remember, we would strap ourselves into a go-kart and hurtle around a track—and, boy, do they have a track at Cherokee Fun Park. You can't miss it as you're driving to or from Great Smoky Mountains National Park; there's an insane three-level corkscrew turn on one track and a pro track inside where you can drive faster-than-usual carts. And there's mini golf ($8).

Fishing

Cherokee has more than 30 miles of streams, rivers, and creeks ideal for fishing. Add to that the fact that the Eastern Band owns and operates a fish hatchery that releases around 250,000 trout into these waters every year and you have the perfect mix for fantastic fishing. Unlike the rest of North Carolina, you don't need a North Carolina fishing license; you need a **Tribal Fishing Permit** (www.

fishcherokee.com, 1 day $10, 2 days $17, 3 days $27, 5 days $47), sold at a number of outlets in Cherokee. You'll find brook, brown, golden, and rainbow trout, and it's fly-rod-only, so you have to have your cast down pat if you want to bring in a big one. There are both catch-and-release and catch-and-keep waters in the Qualla Boundary, but if you want to fish outside the boundary, where several streams and the Oconaluftee River have great fishing, you need a North Carolina or Tennessee fishing permit. Tennessee permits are only valid inside Great Smoky Mountains National Park boundaries in North Carolina.

Golf

The **Sequoyah National Golf Club** (79 Cahons Rd., Whittier, 828/497-3000, www.sequoyahnational.com, 18 holes, par 72, greens fees from $55), five miles south of Cherokee in Whittier, is a stunning mountain golf course. Making the most of the contours and elevation, the course offers tee boxes with breathtaking views of the fairways and the Smoky Mountains. The course record is 62, an impressive feat on a normal course, but here it's something else. Holes like number 12, a par 5 that plays uphill the whole way, present the usual par-5 difficulties combined with steep elevation gain, and number 15, a par 4 that entices golfers to play over aggressively and drop a ball short of the fairway and into the woods, test a golfer's club knowledge and course IQ. This is a tough course for first-timers because so many of the holes have blind approaches, doglegs, or both, but it's enjoyable enough.

Water Sports

For fun on the water, try **Smoky Mountain Tubing** (1847 Tsali Blvd., 828/497-4545, http://cherokeetubeandraft.com, 10am-6pm daily, weather permitting, $10). They do only one thing: rent tubes on which you'll drift down the river and splash your friends. Smoky Mountain Tubing has mountains of tubes, so rent one and float down the Oconaluftee River for two or three hours. They have a fleet of shuttle buses to pick you up a few miles downstream.

ACCOMMODATIONS

Cherokee has many motels, including a **Holiday Inn** (376 Painttown Rd., 828/497-3113, www.ihg.com, from $90) and an **Econo Lodge** (20 River Rd./US-19, 828/497-4575, www.choicehotels.com, from $70, pets allowed).

Sequoyah National Golf Club

★ **Harrah's Cherokee Casino Resort** (777 Casino Dr., 828/497-7777, www.harrahscherokee.com, $100-500) is without a doubt the best place to stay in Cherokee. The rooms are spacious, comfortable, and well kept; there's the casino and a number of dining options an elevator ride away; and the spa provides an added layer of amenities you don't find at other hotels in town. At the higher floors, the view of the mountains is spectacular.

There's something about visiting a place and living where the residents live, and ★ **Panther Creek Cabins** (Wrights Creek Rd., 828/497-2461, www.panthercreekresort.com, cabins $100-150) gives you that chance with your choice of eight cabins, ranging from private two-person affairs to larger lodges that could easily sleep you and seven others in four beds. These quaint cabins are quiet, just outside of downtown Cherokee, and comfortable.

FOOD

The arrival and expansion of Harrah's Cherokee Casino (777 Casino Dr., 828/497-7777, www.harrahscherokee.com) brought with it a bevy of restaurants. **Ruth's Chris Steak House** (dinner 5pm-10pm Mon.-Thurs., 5pm-11pm Fri.-Sat., lounge 4pm-11pm Mon.-Thurs., 4pm-midnight Fri.-Sat., lounge and dinner 4pm-9pm Sun., $60) is here, and like its other locations, serves a variety of steaks and chops, a handful of seafood dishes, and more than 220 wines.

Brio Tuscan Grille (828/497-8233, 11:30am-10pm Sun.-Thurs., 11:30am-11pm Fri.-Sat., $20-40) is a fine Italian restaurant specializing in dishes from northern Italy. This isn't a spaghetti-and-meatballs kind of place; it's more refined, with dishes like lasagna Bolognese al forno, lobster and shrimp ravioli with crab insalata, Tuscan grilled pork chops, and bistecca alla Fiorentina. The ambience is nice, the wine list is nicer, and the food is great.

What's a casino without a buffet? Anyone can find something that satisfies at **Chef's Stage Buffet** (4:30pm-10pm Mon.-Thurs., 4:30pm-11pm Fri.-Sat., 1pm-10pm Sun., $26; seafood buffet Sun.-Fri., $32), where four chefs run four distinct micro-restaurants. There's everything here: Asian dishes, Latin, Italian, seafood, Southern, barbecue, a salad bar you could land an airplane on, and desserts for days. A second buffet option is the **Selu Garden Café** (7am-2:30pm daily, around $15), which offers up a hearty breakfast every day, a slightly more upscale brunch on weekends (11:30am-2:30pm Sat.-Sun.), and a bottomless soup and salad bar.

Downstairs in Harrah's, just off the casino floor, is an airport-style food court that includes the **Winning Streaks Deli** (11am-11pm daily, $10), a deli serving hot and cold sandwiches and panini made with Boar's Head meats and cheeses; grab-and-go sandwiches are available 24 hours daily. There is also **Pizzeria Uno Express** (11am-11pm Sun.-Thurs., 11am-2am Fri.-Sat., around $10), serving thin-crust pizza, calzones, and pasta dishes; **Noodle Bar** (6pm-2am Mon.-Thurs., 5pm-3am Fri.-Sat., 5pm-2am Sun., around $18), serving Asian dishes like ramen and dim sum options; **Johnny Rockets** (24 hours daily, around $10), serving burgers, sandwiches, fries, milk shakes, and breakfast; and a **Dunkin' Donuts Express** (24 hours daily, around $5) that has doughnuts and coffee. The food court also has a variety of snacks and drinks available 24 hours daily.

Just outside of the town of Cherokee is **Granny's Kitchen** (1098 Painttown Rd., 828/497-5010, www.grannyskitchencherokee.com, breakfast 7am-11am daily June-Aug. and Oct. and Fri.-Sun. Apr.-May, Sept., and Nov.; lunch and dinner 11am-8pm daily mid-Mar.-Nov., breakfast $8, lunch $8.50, dinner $12), a country-buffet restaurant where you can get some of the best fried chicken in North Carolina. You won't find Granny here; Granny is actually a man who likes to joke, "no one wants to eat at grandpa's, so I became granny."

TRANSPORTATION AND SERVICES

Cherokee is located on a particularly pretty and winding section of US-19 between Maggie Valley and Bryson City, 2.5 miles south of the southern terminus of the Blue Ridge Parkway. From the cultural center of Cherokee, the Blue Ridge Parkway is only six minutes north along US-441, and Great Smoky Mountains National Park only a few minutes beyond. US-441—called Newfound Gap Road within the national park—bisects the park, connecting Cherokee with the Tennessee towns of Gatlinburg and Pigeon Forge; it's about a 45-minute drive to reach Gatlinburg.

The **Cherokee Welcome Center** (498 Tsali Blvd., 800/438-1601, www.visitcherokee-enc.com, 8am-8pm daily) can help you with tickets, directions, and things to do and see.

There's one radio station in Cherokee, and that's **WNCC** (101.3), a country station, though you can pick up distant stations with a wider selection.

SYLVA

The small town of Sylva, about 15 miles south of Cherokee, is crowned by the pretty Jackson County Courthouse, a stunning building with an ornate cupola, kept under wistful watch by the requisite courthouse-square Confederate monument. Visitors should stop by the **Jackson County Visitor Center** (773 W. Main St., 800/962-1911, www.mountainlovers. com) or visit them online to learn more about the communities here.

Sights

Sylva's most photogenic, and therefore most-photographed, building is the **Historic Courthouse** (310 Keener St.). Perched on a hill overlooking West Main Street, it's a beautiful sight. A long white stairway leads to the classical revival building built in 1914; along the way is a fountain, statue, and beautiful view of downtown. In 1994, court operations moved to the Justice Center, and today the Jackson County Genealogical Society, the Jackson County Historical Association, the Jackson County Arts Council, and the Jackson County Public Library call the building home.

South of Sylva, the mysterious **Judaculla Rock** (off Caney Fork Rd., www.judacul-larock.com) has puzzled folks for centuries. The soapstone boulder is covered in petroglyphs, estimated to be at least 500 years old. The figures and symbols and squiggles are clearly significant, but as of yet are not understood. I'm fascinated with petroglyphs,

the Historic Courthouse in Sylva

and these are some of the most mysterious I've encountered. The soft rock has eroded and the pictures are not as clear as they were in generations past, but many of them can still be discerned.

To reach the rock, drive south on Highway 107 eight miles past the intersection with Sylva's Business US-23. Make a left on Caney Fork Road/County Road 1737 and drive 2.5 miles to a gravel road. Turn left, and in just under 0.5 mile you'll see the rock on the right, and a parking area on the left.

Entertainment

For a cocktail and a fancy bar snack, head to **The Cut Cocktail Lounge** (610 W. Main St., 828/631-4795, 5pm-2am Mon.-Fri., noon-2am Sat.-Sun., food served until close). The Cut has the perfect dive-bar feel, but they serve an upscale drink. House-made bitters and infusions, top-shelf liquor, and a creative bent ensure good drinks, and their menu—small and snack-centered as it may be—is just right for this onetime barber shop (hence the name). They serve brunch on Saturday and Sunday (noon-4pm, around $10) and quite often have some sort of "slow-cooker special," which may be a soup or stew, maybe chicken and dumplings, who knows? Come for a drink, stick around for the conversation, or claim a table and play a hand of cards or a round on a board game.

Shopping

Sylva's City Lights Bookstore (3 E. Jackson St., 828/586-9499, www.citylightsnc. com, 9am-9pm Mon.-Sat., 10am-3pm Sun.) is hardly a knockoff of the monumental Beat establishment in San Francisco with which it shares a name. Instead, it's a first-rate small-town bookstore with stock that has the novelty sought by vacationers and the depth to make regulars of the local patrons. In addition to the sections you'll find in any good bookstore, their books include regional interest, folklore, nature, recreation guides, history, and fiction and poetry by Appalachian and Southern authors.

Accommodations

The **Blue Ridge Inn** (756 W. Main St., Sylva, 828/586-2123, from $110) is a great place to stay in Sylva. Located at the far end of downtown, it's an eight-minute walk to the breweries at the other end of town and a three-minute walk to dining spots like Lulu's and City Lights Cafe. The rooms are comfortable and priced right, and the staff is exceptionally polite.

Food

The North Carolina mountains are experiencing a booming organic foods movement, and you'll find eco-aware eateries throughout the area. ★ **Lulu's On Main** (612 W. Main St., 828/586-8989, www.lulusonmain. com, 11:30am-8pm Mon.-Thurs., 11:30am-9pm Fri.-Sat., $11-19) is one of the most acclaimed restaurants in the area. The menu is American gourmet at heart with splashes of Mediterranean and Nuevo Latino specialties. Try the walnut-spinach ravioli or the raspberry rum pork loin. There are plenty of vegetarian options.

At **Evolution Wine Kitchen** (506 W. Main St., 828/631-9856, www.evolutionwinekitchen.com, 9am-9pm Mon.-Wed., 9am-midnight Thurs.-Sat., $5-30), they have a full-service wine shop, a wine bar, and a little restaurant. You can get a sandwich or salad, and they have a great charcuterie board if you want to linger over a glass or two. If you don't know wine that well, relax; they also have tastings and classes (check the schedule).

City Lights Café (3 E. Jackson St., 828/587-2233, www.citylightscafe.com, 8am-9pm Mon.-Sat., 9am-3pm Sun., breakfast $2-8, lunch and dinner $5-12), located downstairs from the bookshop of the same name, has some excellent crepes, a mighty good biscuit, and fun burritos, as well as wine and beer. It's a cool, casual spot to dine and relax with a book and a bottle of wine, or to see a small local play.

Soul Infusion (628 E. Main St., 828/586-1717, www.soulinfusion.com, 11am-late Mon.-Fri., noon-late Sat., $5-10) is a cozy hippie-gourmet teahouse in an old house on Main Street. You can get very good burritos, sandwiches, pizza, wraps, more than 60 kinds of tea, and even more selections of bottled beer. On weekends and some weeknights, local blues, folk, reggae, and experimental musicians put on a show. Seize the opportunity to hear some of the talent in this musical region.

BREWERIES

There are a trio of breweries and an excellent bottle shop in town. The bottle shop, **Tonic Craft Beer Market** (625 W. Main St., 828/586-2929, www.tonicdelivers.com, noon-10pm Mon.-Sat., noon-7pm Sun.), has a small selection of beer on tap and a much larger selection in bottles. Expect to discover some unusual and often hard-to-find beer here, including a (relatively) huge choice of sours and wild ales. They have a cozy little bar and a couple of spots inside and out where you can sit, sip, and enjoy.

The first time I tasted a beer from **Innovation Brewing** (414 W. Main St., 828/586-9678, www.innovation-brewing.com, 2pm-midnight Mon.-Thurs., noon-midnight Fri.-Sat., noon-11pm Sun.) I knew they were going places. They've racked up accolade after accolade since their opening. On tap they keep 22 beers, 10 of which (a few IPAs, a stout or porter or two, and other styles) are always on tap; the rest are seasonal and specialty brews including a sour and saison. Non-drinkers and designated drivers will enjoy their very spicy house-made ginger ale. If you're hungry, the resident food truck, **Cosmic Carry-Out** (828/506-2830, 2pm-9pm Mon.-Tues., noon-9pm Wed.-Sun., under $10), serves burgers, fries, and veggie burgers.

The **Sneak E Squirrel** (1315 W. Main St., 828/586-6440, 2pm-midnight daily) keeps a dozen or so brews on tap at any given moment, and they're not afraid to experiment with flavors or styles. Among the brews I've sampled are a cherry vanilla stout, a beer that tasted like gingersnaps, and a rich, malty English strong ale. Their kitchen serves a small menu of nachos, fries, burgers, and sandwiches ($5-9) to complement the libations.

In downtown Sylva is **Heinzelmannchen Brewery** (545 Mill St., 828/631-4466), which specializes in beer styles from brewmaster Dieter Kuhn's home region in Germany. Choices include a honey blonde ale, a delicious pilsner, a brown ale, and their Black Forest Stout, a dark, creamy draft. You may be wondering what a Heinzelmannchen is—they're helpful gnomes that live in the Black Forest. Around here, they stop by to help with the beer at night while everyone's asleep.

Transportation

Sylva lies 19 miles southwest of Waynesville along US-74, known as the Great Smoky Mountain Expressway; take exit 83 and you'll be in town in just over a mile. Asheville is an hour northeast along US-74 and I-40; Cherokee and the entrance to Great Smoky Mountains National Park is only 25 minutes north via US-74 and Highway 441.

DILLSBORO

Next door to Sylva is Dillsboro, a river town of rafters and crafters. **Dogwood Crafters** (90 Webster St., 828/586-2248, www.dogwoodcrafters.com, 10am-6pm daily Mar.-Dec., 11am-4pm Fri.-Sun. Jan.-Feb.), in operation for more than 30 years, is a gallery and co-op that represents around 100 local artists and artisans. While the shop carries some of the ubiquitous country-whimsical stuff, mixed in is the work of some very traditional Blue Ridge weavers, potters, carvers, and other expert artisans, making the shop well worth a visit.

In November, Dillsboro's population grows by approximately 5,000 percent when potters and pottery lovers descend on the town for the annual **Western North Carolina Pottery Festival** (828/631-5100, www.wncpotteryfestival.com). This juried pottery show features more than 40 potters, a street fair, and the Clay Olympics. The Clay Olympics are timed competitions to make the tallest cylinder or widest bowl, as well as blindfolded

Western North Carolina Fly-Fishing Trail

Jackson County is the home of the first and only Fly-Fishing Trail in the country; it includes 15 spots on some of the best trout waters in the Smokies where you can catch rainbow, brook, and brown trout, and even the occasional golden trout. Because of its proximity to many mountain communities, the Fly-Fishing Trail has become the epicenter of fly-fishing in the region. Easy access to these waters, convenient complimentary maps (available at www.flyfishingtrail.com and http://mountainloversnc.com), and the excellent support the trail receives make it a choice spot for trout fishing no matter which community you're visiting.

Top spots include **Panthertown Creek,** where a two-mile walk from the end of Breedlove Road (Hwy. 1121) leads you to what some have called the "Yosemite of the East" because of its picturesque rocky bluffs. You'll catch more brook trout than you may have thought possible on this three-mile stream, which is catch-and-release only.

For an "urban" fishing experience, try the **Tuckasegee River** as it passes through Dillsboro. You can park and fish at a number of places between Dillsboro Park and the Best Western River Escape Inn, and you run a good chance of catching a large rainbow or brown trout.

The **Lower Tuckasegee River,** running from Bakers Creek Bridge to Whittier along US-19/74, is around 10 miles of excellent fishing for rainbow and brown trout as well as smallmouth bass.

Fly-Fishing Trail cofounder Alex Bell, who knows the waters of western North Carolina intimately, operates **AB's Fly Fishing Guide Service** (828/226-3833, www.abfish.org, half-day wading trips $150/1 person, $225/2 people, $300/3 people, full day with lunch, $225/1 person, $300/2 people, and $375/3 people; full-day float trips with lunch $350/1 or 2 people). AB's supplies tackle and waders if you need them, as well as extensive lessons in proper casting, water reading, and fly selection, but you're responsible for securing your own North Carolina fishing license and trout stamp.

---

pot-making. It's odd, but the crowd and the artists get into it, making the one-day festival worth seeing.

Sports and Recreation

Dillsboro River Company (18 Macktown Rd., 866/586-3797, www.northcarolina-rafting.com, 10am-6pm daily May-Sept., last float trip 2:30pm, rentals $5-30, guided trips $22-40), across the river from downtown Dillsboro, will set you afloat on the Tuckasegee River, a comparatively warm river with areas of Class II rapids. (It's pronounced "tuck-a-SEE-jee" but is often referred to simply as "the Tuck.") Dillsboro River Company rents rafts, "ducks," and inflatable and sit-on-top kayaks. If you'd like to hire a river rat, guides will be happy to lead you on tours twice daily, and for an extra fee you can share a boat with the guide. There are minimum weight restrictions for these watercraft, so if you are traveling with children, call ahead to ask if the guides think your young ones are ready for the Tuckasegee.

Accommodations

Of the many historic inns in this region, one of the oldest is Dillsboro's **Jarrett House** (100 Haywood St., 828/586-0265 or 800/972-5623, www.jarretthouse.com, from $129, includes full country breakfast). The three-story 1880s lodge was built to serve railroad passengers, and today it's once again a busy rail stop, now for the Great Smoky Mountains Railroad's excursion trains. The guest rooms have old-fashioned furniture, air-conditioning, and private baths, but the only TV is in the lobby.

The **Best Western Plus River Escape Inn & Suites** (248 WBI Dr., 828/586-6060, www.book.bestwestern.com, $95-210) is a surprisingly great hotel. While most chain hotels are nondescript, this one really steps it up with a well-kept, modern interior and rooms with balconies overlooking the river.

Food

The ★ **Jarrett House** (100 Haywood St., 800/972-5623, www.jarretthouse.com, 11:30am-2:30pm and 4:30pm-7:30pm Tues.-Sun., under $15) is famous for its dining room, an extravaganza of country cooking based on the staples of country ham and red-eye gravy. You can order many other mountain specialties, including fried catfish, fried chicken, sweet tea, biscuits, and for dessert the daily cobbler or vinegar pie (a strange but tasty pie that's similar to a pecan pie without the pecans and with vinegar). There are few options for vegetarians, but if you like heavy Southern fare, you'll think you're in heaven. You can also eat at **Coach's Bistro** ($15-20), a little restaurant serving up more modern dishes in a more modern setting; menu items range from homey bites to roast beef and mashed potatoes.

Haywood Smokehouse (403 Haywood St., 828/631-9797, www.haywoodsmokehouse. com, 11am-9pm Tues.-Sat., $8-26) is a funky little barbecue shack serving some fine western North Carolina 'cue, craft beers, and house-made smoked barbecue sauces. The menu's small, but if it's pork or chicken and it can be barbecued, it's here. The Haywood Smokehouse is biker-friendly, so don't be surprised if you see a line of Harleys outside.

Transportation

Dillsboro is only 1.8 miles west of Sylva; you can get there by following West Main Street out of town. US-23/US-441 runs through Dillsboro and provides easy access to the region from the south (Atlanta, Georgia, is 2.5 hours away) and connects the town to US-74. From Exit 81 on US-74, Dillsboro is a mile away.

CULLOWHEE

The unincorporated village of Cullowhee ("CULL-uh-wee"), located on Highway 107 between Sylva and Cashiers, is the home of Western Carolina University (WCU). The university's **Mountain Heritage Center** (Hunter Library, WCU campus, 828/227-7129, www.wcu.edu, 10am-4pm Fri.-Mon., 10am-7pm Thurs.) is a small museum with a great collection that will fascinate anyone interested in Appalachian history. The permanent exhibit *Migration of the Scotch-Irish People* is full of artifacts like a 19th-century covered wagon, wonderful photographs, homemade quilts, linens, and musical instruments. The Mountain Heritage Center also hosts two traveling exhibits in addition to the permanent installation as well as the annual **Mountain Heritage Day** (www. mountainheritageday.com, late Sept.) festival, which brings together many of western North Carolina's best and most authentic traditional musicians and artisans in a free festival that draws up to 25,000 visitors.

Cullowhee is only 6 miles south of Sylva along NC-107, a trip of about 10 minutes.

Bryson City and the Nantahala Forest

To look at the mountains here, you'd think that the defining feature in this part of North Carolina would be the surrounding peaks, but that is only half right. This is a land dominated by water. Smoke-thick fog crowds valleys in the predawn hours. The peaks stand ringed in clouds. Moss, ferns, and dense forests crowd the edges of rivers and streams. All of it—the mountains, the mist, the ferns, the fog—makes it feel like you've stepped into a fairy tale when you're in the Nantahala Gorge. According to Cherokee stories, a formidable witch called Spearfinger lived here, as did a monstrous snake and even an inchworm so large it could span the gorge.

The Nantahala River runs through the narrow gorge, attracting white-water enthusiasts to the rapids. Nearby Bryson City is a river town whose proximity to the cataracts makes it a favorite haunt for rafters, kayakers, and other white-water thrill seekers. If you approach Bryson City from the north on US-19, you're in for a strange sight: The banks of the Tuckasegee River are shored up with crushed cars.

SIGHTS
★ Great Smoky Mountains Railroad

The **Great Smoky Mountains Railroad** (GSMR, depots in Bryson City and Dillsboro, 800/872-4681, www.gsmr.com, from $50 adults, $29 children) is one of the best and most fun ways to see the Smokies. On historic trains, the GSMR carries sightseers on excursions from two to several hours long, through some of the most beautiful scenery in the region. Trips between Dillsboro and Bryson City, with a layover at each end for shopping and dining, follow the banks of the Tuckasegee River, while round-trips from Bryson City follow the Little Tennessee and Nantahala Rivers deep into the Nantahala Gorge. Many other excursions are offered, including gourmet dining and wine- and beer-tasting trips. There are Thomas the Tank Engine and the Little Engine That Could trips for kids, and runs to and from river-rafting outfitters.

SPORTS AND RECREATION
★ Nantahala River Gorge

The stunningly beautiful Nantahala River Gorge lies just outside Bryson City in the Nantahala National Forest. Nantahala is said to mean "land of the noonday sun," and there are indeed parts of this gorge where the sheer rock walls above the river are so steep that sunlight only hits the water at the noon hour. Eight miles of the Nantahala River flow through the gorge over Class II-III rapids. The nearby Ocoee River is also a favorite of rafters, and the Cheoah River, when there are controlled water releases, has some of the South's most famous and difficult Class III-IV runs.

OUTFITTERS AND TOURS

The Nantahala River Gorge supports scores of river guide companies, many clustered along US-19 west. Because some of these rapids can be quite dangerous, be sure to call ahead and speak to a guide if you have any doubts as to your readiness. If you are rafting with children, check the company's weight and age restrictions beforehand.

Endless River Adventures (14157 US-19 W., near Bryson City, 800/224-7238, www.endlessriveradventures.com) gives

The Nantahala River is a popular area for hiking and water sports.

white-water and flat-water kayaking instruction, rentals, and guided trips on the Nantahala, Ocoee, and Cheoah Rivers. They'll be able to suggest a run suited to your skill level. **Carolina Outfitters** (715 US-19, Topton, 800/468-7238, www.carolinaoutfitters.com) has several package outings that combine river trips with horseback riding, bicycling, panning for gems, and riding on the Great Smoky Mountains Railroad. **Wildwater Rafting** (10345 US-19 W., 12 miles west of Bryson City, 828/488-2384, www.wildwaterrafting.com) offers river guide services and leads **Wildwater Jeep Tours** ($50-110 adults, $40-90 children), half- and full-day Jeep excursions through back roads and wilderness to waterfalls and old mountain settlements.

You can explore the mountains around Bryson City with the **Nantahala Outdoor Center** (13077 US-19 W., Bryson City, 828/785-4836, www.noc.com, 9am-5pm daily, from $30), which offers a variety of adventure options that include white-water rafting, stand-up paddleboarding on the flat-water sections of the river, hiking, mountain biking, and zip-lining. Half-day, full-day, and overnight trips are possible, and excursions like the Rapid Transit combine a relaxing morning train ride with an afternoon rafting trip.

★ Fly-Fishing the Tuckasegee River

The Smoky Mountains, especially the eastern grade of the Smokies, are laced with streams perfect for fly-fishing. Anglers from all over come here to float, wade, camp, fish, hone their fly-tying craft, and learn the finer points of fly-fishing. The Tuckasegee River flows right through downtown Bryson City, and many of its feeder streams and creeks are ideal spots to throw a line.

For fly-fishers who don't need a guide, a number of streams around are packed with fish, but be sure to inquire about regulations for individual streams; some may be catch-and-release, while a neighboring stream could be catch-and-keep. Some streams have regulations about the types of hooks you can use. Once you're ready to put your line in the water, try **Hazel Creek** on the north shore of Fontana Lake, where you'll find pristine waters and a good number of fish. Other nearby creeks, like **Eagle Creek** and any of the feeder creeks that empty into the lake, are prime spots as well.

GUIDES

Fontana Guide Service (3336 Balltown Rd., Bryson City, 828/736-2318, www.fontanaguides.com, $200-500 full-day trips, price depends on group size) has a number of options depending on season, interest, and skill level, including options to fish in the national park. In addition to fly-fishing excursions, they also offer kayak fishing, bass and lake fishing, as well as night fishing in select spots.

Fly Fishing the Smokies (Bryson City, 828/488-7665, www.flyfishingthesmokies. net) has a number of guides and options for a day or more of fishing. Wade the streams with them for a half-day (1 person $150, 2 people $175) or full-day (1 person $200, 2 people $250) outing, try a float trip (half-day $225 per boat, full-day $300 per boat), or go backcountry camping and fly-fishing in Great Smoky Mountains National Park ($500-850 per person). They also go bass fishing on nearby Fontana Lake (half day $225, full day $300).

A top fishing guide in the Bryson City area is **Steve Claxton's Smoky Mountain Adventures** (Bryson City, 828/736-7501, http://steveclaxton.com), who specializes in leaving civilization behind in favor of camping, catching wild mountain trout, and getting a true taste of the wilderness. Three-day, two-night camping trips for 5-7 people run around $400 per person, and four-day, three-night trips are $450-500 per person. They also offer daylong fishing trips (1 person $225, 2 people $250, 3 people $300).

Nantahala Fly Fishing Co. (Robbinsville, 828/479-8850 or 866/910-1013, www.flyfishnorthcarolina.com, guided trips and private lessons half day $150 1 angler, $75 per additional person, full day $300 1 or 2 anglers, $75 per additional person) provides guided trips for fly-rod fishing, but if you've never held one of these odd fishing rods in your hand, they also provide a fly-fishing school ($300 for 2 days) and private instruction. Best of all, they have a "No Fish, No Pay" guarantee.

Hiking

Great Smoky Mountains National Park has more than 800 miles of wilderness trails, and with around 40 percent of the park located in Swain County, more trails than you could hike in a week are within striking distance of Bryson City. **Deep Creek Loop** is a four-mile loop that passes two waterfalls on an easy, mostly flat, track. You can also take the strenuous **Deep Creek Trail** to Newfound Gap Road, a 14.2-mile one-way hike that will require a return ride. The **Noland Creek Trail** is a fairly easy six-mile trail near the end of the Road to Nowhere (a failed road-building project from the 1930s and 1940s). At the end of the Road to Nowhere, just past the tunnel, is the **Goldmine Loop Trail,** a three-mile track that's beautiful and enjoyable.

Golf

Smoky Mountain Country Club (1300 Conleys Creek Rd., Whittier, 828/497-7622, www.carolinamountaingolf.com, 18 holes, par 71, greens fees 18 holes $59, 9 holes $35, includes cart, discounts for students, seniors, and off-peak play, club rentals $10) is a mountain golf course where nearly every hole has views that will distract you from the sport; an aggressive player will find rewards on several holes. While some of the greens are open, many are well guarded by bunkers and contours that make greenside chipping tricky, especially if you haven't played much in the mountains.

ACCOMMODATIONS

The ★ **Folkestone Inn** (101 Folkestone Rd., 828/488-2730 or 888/812-3385, www.folkestoneinn.com, $120-169) is one of the region's outstanding bed-and-breakfasts, a roomy

1920s farmhouse expanded and renovated into a charming and tranquil inn. Each room has a balcony or porch. Baked treats at breakfast include shortcake, kuchen, cobblers, and other delicacies. An 85-year-old hotel listed in the National Register of Historic Places, the **Fryemont Inn** (245 Fryemont St., Bryson City, 828/488-2159 or 800/845-4879, www.fryemontinn.com, mid-Apr.-late Nov., $110-283 with meals, late-Nov.-mid-Apr. $115-225 no meal service) has a cozy, rustic feel with chestnut-paneled guest rooms and an inviting lobby with an enormous stone fireplace.

Some river outfitters offer lodging, which can be a cheap way to pass the night if you don't mind roughing it. The **Rolling Thunder River Company** (10160 US-19 W., near Bryson City, 800/408-7238, www.rollingthunderriverco.com, no alcohol permitted) operates a large bunkhouse with beds ($10-12 per person per night) for its rafting customers. **Carolina Outfitters** (715 US-19, Topton, 828/488-6345, www.carolinaoutfitters.com) has a number of accommodations available ($50-100), including two-room cabins, two-bedroom apartments, and three-bedroom cabins suitable for a large group. Many of the outfitters also offer camping on their properties.

Camping

Among the nicest camping options available in the Nantahala National Forest is **Standing Indian Campground** (90 Sloan Rd., Franklin, 877/444-6777, www.recreation.gov, Apr.-Nov., $16). Standing Indian has a nice diversity of campsites, from flat grassy areas to cozy mountainside nooks. Drinking water, hot showers, flush toilets, and a phone are all available on-site, and leashed pets are permitted. At 3,400 feet in elevation, the campground is close to the Appalachian Trail.

Deep Creek Tube Center and Campground (1090 W. Deep Creek Rd., Bryson City, 828/488-6055, www.deepcreekcamping.com, Apr. 3-Oct. 30, camping $23-50, cabins $69-195) has more than 50 campsites and 18 cabins, as well as access to

Deep Creek, where you can go tubing (tube rentals $5 per day). The creek runs right by many campsites. You can also go gem "mining" here, a great mountain tradition; they sell bags and buckets of gem-enriched dirt in the camp store. The best part is that the facility is within walking distance of Great Smoky Mountains National Park.

FOOD

The **Cork & Bean Bistro** (24 Everett St., 828/488-1934, www.theeveretthotel.com, 4:30pm-8pm Tues., 11am-8pm Wed.-Thurs., 11am-8:30pm Fri., 9am-8:30pm Sat., 9am-3pm Sun., $9-36) serves three excellent meals daily, using local and seasonal ingredients to create updated takes on familiar dishes or regional specialties. The trout cakes (or any preparation of locally sourced trout) are outstanding, as is any venison dish, but you can't go wrong with a burger either.

The Appalachian Trail passes only a few feet from **River's End Restaurant** (13077 Hwy. 19 W., 828/488-7172, www.noc.com, 8am-7pm Sun.-Thurs., 8am-8pm Fri.-Sat., $6-20) at the Nantahala Outdoor Center. Given its proximity to the trail (really a footbridge over the river, but on the trail nonetheless) and to the center's rafting, paddling, hiking nexus, it's a popular spot for outdoorsy sorts. The menu reflects this with dishes like the Sherpa bowls (rice, veggies, and optional meat) that are packed with protein, calories, and carbs to fuel you through a day on the trail.

For a hearty steak, check out **Jimmy Mac's Restaurant** (121 Main St., 828/488-4700, www.jimmymacsrestaurant.com, 11:30am-9pm daily, $8-30). In addition to steak, they serve beef, elk, and buffalo burgers and seafood. Service is fantastic; let them know you're there for a special occasion and they'll treat you even better.

TRANSPORTATION

Bryson City can be reached via US-19, if you're coming south from Maggie Valley and Cherokee. US-74 also passes close by for easy access from the east or the west. Since Bryson City is less than 20 minutes from Cherokee, it's a good base from which to explore the national park via Newfound Gap Road, the Blue Ridge Parkway, and the southwestern edge of GSMNP.

Robbinsville and the Valley Towns

Between Robbinsville and the Georgia state line is another region at the heart of Cherokee life. Snowbird, not far from Robbinsville, is one of the most traditional Cherokee communities, where it's common to hear the Cherokee language and the arts, crafts, and folkways are flourishing. The burial site of Junaluska, one of the Eastern Band's most prominent leaders, is here.

As moving as it is to see the memorial to one of the Cherokee heroes, the town of Murphy is forever linked to tragedy for the Cherokee people and a dark incident in American history—the Trail of Tears. Around 16,000 Cherokee people, including warriors and clan leaders, men, women, children, the elderly, and the infirm, were forced to leave their homes in North Carolina, Tennessee, and Georgia; they were arrested and marched under guard to Fort Butler, here in Murphy, and from Fort Butler they were forced to walk to Oklahoma. You'll find the names of these people, many of whom died along the way, inscribed in Cherokee on a memorial at the L&N Depot in Murphy.

In addition to places of historical significance in Cherokee culture, this far southwestern corner of North Carolina has other compelling sights. Brasstown, a tiny village on the Georgia state line, is the home of the John C. Campbell Folk School, an artists' colony nearly a century old, where visitors can stroll among studios and along trails and stop in to a gallery-shop for some of the most beautiful crafts you'll find in the region. Back up toward Robbinsville, the relentlessly scenic Cherohala Skyway crosses 43 miles of the Cherokee and Nantahala National Forests. This road is a major destination for motorcyclists and sports-car drivers as well as daytrippers and vacationers.

ROBBINSVILLE

The whole southwestern corner of North Carolina is rich with Cherokee history and culture, and the Robbinsville area has some of the deepest roots of great significance to the Cherokee people. In little towns and crossroads a few miles outside Robbinsville, several hundred people known as the Snowbird community keep alive some of the oldest Cherokee ways. The Cherokee language is spoken here, and it's a place where some of the Eastern Band's most admired basket makers, potters, and other artists continue to make and teach their ancient arts. If you're visiting and want to enjoy an adult beverage, you'd better bring your own, as Graham County is North Carolina's one and only dry county.

Sights

Outside Robbinsville in the ancient Stecoah Valley is an imposing old rock schoolhouse built in 1930 and used as a school until the mid-1990s. It has been reborn as the **Stecoah Valley Center** (121 Schoolhouse Rd., Stecoah, 828/479-3364, www.stecoah-valleycenter.com), home of a weaver's guild, a native plants preservation group, a concert series, several festivals, and a great **Gallery Shop** (828/497-3098, 10am-5pm Mon.-Sat. Mar.-Oct., 10am-5pm Mon.-Fri. Nov.-Dec., closed Jan.-Feb.) of local artisans' work. Concerts in the Appalachian Evening summer series, featuring area musicians, are preceded by community suppers of traditional mountain cuisine.

On Robbinsville's Main Street is the **Junaluska Memorial** (Main St., 0.5 miles north of the Graham County Courthouse,

828/479-4727, 9am-5pm Mon.-Sat. Apr.-Oct., call for hours Nov.-Mar.), where Junaluska, a 19th-century leader of the Eastern Band of the Cherokee, and his third wife, Nicie, are buried. The marker was dedicated in 1910 by the Daughters of the American Revolution, and the gravesite is maintained by the Friends of Junaluska, who also operate the **Junaluska Museum** (828/479-4727, 9am-5pm Mon.-Sat. Apr.-Oct., call for hours Nov.-Mar., free) on the same site. At the museum you'll find ancient artifacts from life in Cheoah thousands of years ago. There are also contemporary Cherokee crafts on display, and outside you can walk a path that highlights the medicinal plants used for generations in this area.

Down a winding country road 14 miles outside Robbinsville, **Yellow Branch Pottery and Cheese** (136 Yellow Branch Circle, Robbinsville, 828/479-6710, www.yellowbranch.com, noon-5pm Tues.-Sat. Apr.-Nov. or by appointment) is a beautifully rustic spot for an afternoon's excursion. Bruce DeGroot, Karen Mickler, and their herd of Jersey cows produce prizewinning artisanal cheeses and graceful, functional pottery. Visitors are welcome at their farm and shop.

Entertainment and Events

Every year on the Saturday of Memorial Day weekend in late May, the Snowbird Cherokee host the **Fading Voices Festival** in Robbinsville. The festival features a mound-building ceremony along with typical festival attractions—music, dancing, storytelling, crafts, and lots of food—but in the deeply traditional forms carried on by the Snowbird community. Contact the Junaluska Museum (828/479-4727) for more information.

Sports and Recreation

The **Joyce Kilmer Memorial Forest** (Joyce Kilmer Rd., off Hwy. 143 west of Robbinsville, 828/479-6431, www.grahamcountytravel.com) is one of the largest remaining tracts of virgin forest in the eastern United States, where 450-year-old tulip poplar trees have grown to 100 feet tall and 20 feet around. The

Junaluska

One of the most important figures in the history of the Eastern Band of the Cherokee is Junaluska, who was born near Dillard, Georgia, in 1776. During the wars against the Creek Indians from 1812 to 1814, the Cherokee people fought beside U.S. forces, and it's said that the fierce young Junaluska saved the life of Andrew Jackson at the battle of Horse Shoe Bend in Alabama.

Twenty years later, Jackson, by then president, repaid Junaluska's bravery and the loyalty of the Cherokee people by signing the Indian Removal Act, which ordered that they, along with four other major Southern nations, be forced from their homelands and marched to the new Indian Territory of Oklahoma. Junaluska traveled to Washington and met with Jackson to plead for mercy for the Cherokee nation; his pleas were ignored, and in 1838, Junaluska joined 16,000 members of the Cherokee nation who were force-marched close to 1,000 miles to Oklahoma. Midway across Tennessee, he led a failed escape attempt and was captured and chained; he completed the march in leg irons and manacles. It was during this time that Junaluska supposedly said, "If I had known what Andrew Jackson would do to the Cherokees, I would have killed him myself that day at Horse Shoe Bend." In 1841 he was finally able to leave Oklahoma and made the 17-day trip to North Carolina on horseback.

He spent his final years in Cherokee County, on land granted to him by the state of North Carolina. He and his third wife, Nicie, are buried at Robbinsville, at what is now the Junaluska Memorial and Museum. His grave was originally marked according to Cherokee tradition—with a pile of stones—but in 1910 the Daughters of the American Revolution commissioned a marker for his gravesite. During the dedication ceremony, Reverend Armstrong Cornsilk delivered a eulogy in the Cherokee language:

He was a good man. He was a good friend. He was a good friend in his home and everywhere. He would ask the hungry man to eat. He would ask the cold one to warm by his fire. He would ask the tired one to rest, and he would give a good place to sleep. Juno's home was a good home for others. He was a smart man. He made his mind think well. He was very brave. He was not afraid.

Juno at this time has been dead about 50 years. I am glad he is up above [pointing upward]. I am glad we have this beautiful monument. It shows Junaluska did good, and it shows we all appreciate him together—having a pleasant time together. I hope we shall all meet Junaluska in heaven [pointing upward] and all be happy there together.

forest stands in honor of Joyce Kilmer, a soldier killed in action in France during World War I. His poem, "Trees," inspired this living memorial. The only way to see the forest is on foot, and a two-mile loop or two one-mile loops make for an easy hike through a remarkable forest.

The Joyce Kilmer Memorial Forest abuts the Slickrock Wilderness Area, and **Slickrock Creek Trail** is one of its longest trails. This 13.5-mile (one-way) trail starts out easy, but the final 5-5.5 miles are fairly strenuous. *Backpacker* magazine has named this one of the toughest trails in the country, in part

because the hike can be made into a 21.7-mile loop by connecting with the **Haoe Lead, Hangover Lead,** and **Ike Branch** trails. Be forewarned that this is a big trip, but it's rewarding, with views of waterfalls (the first is only a few miles in, on the easy part) and rhododendron thickets. Its name is apt: The rocks here can be incredibly slick.

The trailhead for the **Hangover Lead South Trail** is adjacent to the parking area at Big Fat Gap (off Slick Rock Rd., about 7 miles from US-129). The trail is only 2.8 miles long, but it's strenuous. The payoff is the view from the Haoe Lead summit at 5,249 feet. There are backcountry campsites here, and the rule is to keep campsites 100 yards from streams and follow Leave No Trace guidelines.

A handy collection of trail maps for Joyce Kilmer Memorial Forest, Slickrock Creek, Snowbird Back Country, and Tsali Recreation Area are available from the Graham Chamber (http://grahamchamber.com). The maps provide a rough idea of the locations and routes of these trails, but they are not a replacement for topographic maps, which you should have with you while on any of these rugged or isolated trails.

Accommodations

The **Snowbird Mountain Lodge** (4633 Santeetlah Rd., 11 miles west of Robbinsville, 800/941-9290, http://snowbirdlodge.com, $240-470) was built in the early 1940s, a rustic chestnut-and-stone inn atop a 3,000-foot mountain. The view is exquisite, and the lodge is perfectly situated amid the Cherohala Skyway, Lake Santeetlah, and the Joyce Kilmer Forest. Guests enjoy a full breakfast, picnic lunch, and four-course supper created from seasonal local specialties.

Another pleasant place to stay near Robbinsville is the **Tapoco Lodge Resort** (14981 Tapoco Rd., 15 miles north of Robbinsville, 828/498-2800, www.tapocolodge.com, Thurs.-Sat. Nov.-Sept., daily Oct., rooms and suites $239-329, cabins $149-249). Built in 1930, the lodge is in the National Register of Historic Places, and it has the feel of an old-time hotel. Guest rooms in the main lodge and surrounding cabins are simple but comfortable, and the resort overlooks the Cheoah River, a legendary run for rafters when occasional controlled releases of water form crazy-fast rapids. The on-site **Jasper's Restaurant** (dinner from 5:30pm Thurs.-Sat., $26-46) serves fine Appalachian food, while the pub **SlickRock Grill** (11am-late daily, $9-23) is perched over the river.

Angels Landing Inn Bed & Breakfast (94 Campbell St., Murphy, 828/835-8877, www.angelslandinginn.wordpress.com, $88-105) is one of the only B&Bs in town.

Fortunately, the folks are friendly and the price is right. **Mountain Ivy Rentals** (56 Airport Rd., 2.5 miles east of Robbinsville, 8258/735-9180, www.mountainivy.com, 2-night minimum, $125) has one log-sided cabin that sleeps six and is steps away from great trout fishing in the stream that runs alongside the cabin. An indoor fireplace and a space outside for a campfire help make it cozy in any season. The garage is handy for motorcycle travelers, as it gives them a place to secure trailers, bikes, and other gear.

At the **Simple Life Campground** (88 Lower Mountain Creek Rd., 828/788-1099, www.thesimplelifecampground.com, Mar.-Nov., cabins $28-108, RVs $24-42, tents $14) the cabins, RV sites, and tent sites have access to hot showers and Wi-Fi. This campground is near the Cherohala Skyway, Joyce Kilmer Memorial Forest, and Lake Santeetlah.

If you're RVing your way through the Smokies, the six-acre **Teaberry Hill RV Campground** (77 Upper Sawyers Creek Rd., 828/479-3953, http://teaberryhill.com, $45) is one of the nicest campgrounds you'll find, with large pull-through sites to accommodate any size RV. Amenities include 50-amp electrical hookups, water and sewer, and Wi-Fi access.

HAYESVILLE, BRASSTOWN, AND MURPHY

Between Hayesville and Brasstown, you can get a really good sense of the art that has come out of this region over the years. These three small towns are along the Georgia border on US-64.

Murphy River Walk

The **Murphy River Walk** in Murphy is a three-mile trail along the Hiwassee River and Valley River, winding from Konehete Park to the Old L&N Depot. A beautiful walk (and a great way to stretch your legs after a long ride) through this charming, tiny town, the River Walk gives you the chance to see Murphy up close and personal.

After your walk along the river, take a look at some of the antique stores in Murphy. A popular stop is **Linger Awhile Antiques and Collectibles** (46 Valley River Ave., 321/267-2777, 10am-5pm Tues.-Sat.).

★ John C. Campbell Folk School

One of North Carolina's most remarkable cultural institutions, the **John C. Campbell Folk School** (1 Folk School Rd., Brasstown, 800/365-5724, www.folkschool.org) was created by Northern honeymooners who traveled through Appalachia 100 years ago to educate themselves about Southern highland culture. John C. and Olive Dame Campbell, like other high-profile Northern liberals of their day, directed their humanitarian impulses toward the education and economic betterment of Southern mountain dwellers. John Campbell died a decade later, but Olive, joining forces with her friend Marguerite Butler, set out to establish a "folk school" in the Southern mountains that she and John had visited. She was inspired by the model of the Danish *folkehøjskole,* workshops that preserved and taught traditional arts as a means of fostering economic self-determination and personal pride in rural communities. Brasstown was chosen as the site for this grand experiment, and in 1925, the John C. Campbell Folk School opened its doors.

Today, thousands of artists travel every year to this uncommonly lovely remote valley, the site of an ancient Cherokee village. In weeklong and weekend classes, students of all ages and skill levels learn about the traditional arts of this region, such as pottery, weaving, dyeing, storytelling, and chair caning, as well as contemporary and exotic crafts such as photography, kaleidoscope making, bookmaking, and paper marbling. The website outlines the hundreds of courses offered every year, but even if you're passing through the area on a shorter visit, you can explore the school's campus. Visitors are asked to preserve the quiet atmosphere of learning and concentration when viewing the artist studios, but you can have an up-close look at some of their marvelous wares in the school's **Craft Shop** (bottom floor of Olive Dame Campbell Dining Hall, 8am-5pm Mon.-Wed. and Fri.-Sat., 8am-6pm Thurs., 1pm-5pm Sun.), one of the nicest craft shops in western North Carolina. Exhibits about the school's history and historic examples of the work of local artists of past generations are on display at the **History Center** (8am-5pm Mon.-Sat., 1pm-5pm Sun.), next to Keith House.

There are several nature trails on campus that thread through this lovely valley. Be sure to visit the 0.25-mile **Rivercane Walk,** which features outdoor sculpture by some of the greatest living artists of the Eastern Band of the Cherokee. In the evenings you'll often find concerts by traditional musicians, or community square, contra, and English country dances. A visit to the John C. Campbell Folk School, whether as a student or a traveler, is an exceptional opportunity to immerse yourself in a great creative tradition.

Clay County Historical and Arts Council Museum

Hayesville's Old Clay County Jail, built in 1912, is now home to the **Clay County Historical and Arts Council Museum** (21 Davis Loop, Hayesville, 828/389-6814, www.clayhistoryarts.org, 10am-4pm Tues.-Sat. late May-early Sept., call for hours early Sept.-late May). This is a small and extremely interesting museum with varied collections, including the medical instruments of an early country doctor; an original jail cell complete with a file hidden by a long-ago prisoner, discovered during renovations; an old moonshine still; a collection of beautiful Cherokee masks; and a remarkable crazy quilt embroidered with strange and charming illustrations.

Accommodations

Harrah's Casino in Cherokee opened a sister location here in Murphy in late 2015. **Harrah's Cherokee Valley River Casino & Hotel** (777 Casino Pkwy., Murphy, 828/422-7777, www.caesars.com, from $179) has 300 rooms in a seven-story hotel, and a huge gaming floor: 50,000 square feet containing 70 table games and more than 1,000 slot machines. As the rooms go, they're quite comfortable (borderline luxury), but remember that smoking is permitted at the casino, so be sure to request a non-smoking or smoking room, based on your preference.

At time of publication, the dining options were limited to Nathan's Famous Hot Dogs (open 24 hours), Panda Express (11am-11pm Sun.-Thurs., 11am-2am Fri.-Sat.), Earl of Sandwich (11am-11pm Sun.-Thurs., 11am-2am Fri.-Sat.), Papa John's Pizza (11am-11pm Sun.-Thurs., 11am-2am Fri.-Sat.), and Starbucks (6am-11pm Sun.-Thurs., 6am-1am Fri.-Sat.). Still, who comes to a casino to eat? The table games are fun and it's going to be interesting to watch this casino grow.

Food

Herb's Pit Bar-B-Que (15896 W. US Hwy. 64, Murphy, 828/494-5367, www.herbspitbarbque.com, 11am-8pm Wed., Thurs., and Sun., 11am-9pm Fri. and Sat., $2-24) is the western terminus of the North Carolina Barbecue Trail and should be your first (or last) stop on it. Here you can sample more than the 'cue that pitmasters in the deep mountains make—you can also order plates of tasty fried trout and chicken.

Tiger's Department Store (42 Herbert St., Hayesville, 828/389-6531, 9:30am-6pm Mon.-Sat., under $10) may be a surprise as a dining option, but in addition to clothing and gear, this store has an old-fashioned soda counter that provides some tasty refreshments.

The Copper Door (2 Sullivan St., Hayesville, 828/389-8460, http://thecopperdoor.com, 5pm-10pm Mon.-Sat., $16-48) is an upscale joint serving a nice selection of seafood, steaks, and other meat-centric dishes, but they can accommodate vegetarians and vegans. This elegant restaurant is run by a chef from New Orleans, and his influence is all over the menu, from crawfish to mussels to other French- and creole-inspired creations. In 2011 and 2012 they received *Wine Spectator* magazine's Award of Excellence.

TRANSPORTATION

This is the southwestern-most corner of North Carolina, in some places as close to Atlanta as to Asheville. Robbinsville is located on US-129 about 30 miles (40 minutes) southwest of Bryson City. Hayesville and Brasstown are easily reached via US-64, which closely parallels the Georgia border. Robbinsville, Hayesville, and Brasstown are all less than a two-hour drive from Asheville.

Great Smoky Mountains National Park

Look for ★ to find recommended
sights, activities, dining, and lodging.

Highlights

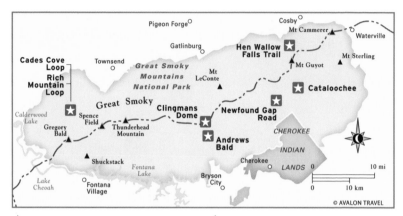

© AVALON TRAVEL

★ **Newfound Gap Road:** Bisecting Great Smoky Mountains National Park, this 33-mile route offers plenty of long views, short hikes, and streamside driving (page 186).

★ **Clingmans Dome:** From this third-highest peak in the eastern United States, set in a dramatic alpine environment, you'll have an astounding view of up to 100 miles on a clear day (page 188).

★ **Andrews Bald:** Hike to one of the prettiest high-altitude meadows in the Smokies (page 191).

★ **Hen Wallow Falls Trail:** An easy out-and-back day hike leads to one of the loveliest waterfalls in the park (page 198).

★ **Cataloochee:** Camping in this secluded valley—with its Milky Way views, solitude, and frequent elk sightings—is bliss (page 200).

★ **Cades Cove Loop:** The most-visited spot in Great Smoky Mountains National Park offers plenty of wildlife viewing and the largest collection of intact historic structures in the park (page 205).

★ **Rich Mountain Loop:** Hike up, up, up into the hills for a gorgeous view of Cades Cove (page 207).

The Smokies draw more than 10 million visitors annually and it's easy to see why: These mountains are laced with hiking trails, rivers, and waterfalls and populated with diverse wildlife.

Straddling the North Carolina/Tennessee state line, Great Smoky Mountains National Park's 521,085 acres are just about equally split between the two states. The slightly larger North Carolina side of the park is wilder and less developed than the Tennessee side, but throughout the park you'll find places so remote and so isolated they've remained undisturbed by humans for untold lengths of time. You'll also find places like Cades Cove, a wide, secluded valley that was home to some of the first pioneers to push west into Tennessee and now sees droves of visitors in autumn.

GSMNP comprises more than 800 square miles of cloud-ringed high peaks and rain forest. There are tens of thousands of species of plants and animals that call the park home, with 80 species of reptiles and amphibians alone, which is why the park is sometimes called the Salamander Capital of the World. More than 200 species of birds nest here, and 60-plus mammals roam these hills.

The nonprofit organization Discover Life in America (www.dlia.org) has been conducting an All-Taxa Biodiversity Inventory, a census of all nonmicrobial life forms in the GSMNP; as of 2016 they had discovered more than 970 species of plants and animals previously unknown to science. The deep wilderness is an awesome refuge for outdoor enthusiasts, and the accessibility of the park's absolutely ravishing scenery makes it ideal for visitors of all ability levels and nearly all interests.

PLANNING YOUR TIME

Many visitors to Great Smoky Mountains National Park (GSMNP) devote only one day to the park. They drive Newfound Gap Road, take a short hike along the way, and circle Cades Cove before moving on. To do justice to the park, give the area at least **three days.** Spend one day in the Cataloochee Valley, and then devote another day or two to savoring

Previous: a stream through the Smoky Mountains; sunset over the Smokies. **Above:** a sign warns of curves on Newfound Gap Road.

Great Smoky Mountains National Park

© AVALON TRAVEL

Nantahala National Forest

SKYWAY

Lake Cheoah

Santeetlah Lake

TWENTYMILE

Gregory Bald 4,948ft

CADES COVE LOOP

RICH MOUNTAIN LOOP

RICH MTN
(CLOSED IN WINTER)

FOOTHILLS PKWY

Fontana Village

129

Robbinsville

Shuckstack 4,020ft

Appalachian

Spence Field 4,900ft

RICH MTN RD

Townsend

321

28

Fontana Lake

Thunderhead Mountain 5,530ft

LITTLE RIVER

Little River RD

Nantahala River Gorge

Nantahala

19

74

28

Silers Bald 5,607ft

Andrews Bald 5,860ft

CLINGMANS DOME

ELKMONT

SUGARLAND VISITOR CENTER

Pigeon Forge

West Prong Little Pigeon River

Bryson City

DEEP CREEK

ANDREWS BALD

Clingmans Dome 6,643ft

NEWFOUND GAP ROAD

NEWFOUND

Gatlinburg

441

321

416

Little

CHEROKEE INDIAN LANDS

Nantahala National Forest

74

19

441

Cherokee

OCONALUFTEE VISITOR CENTER

SMOKEMONT

Mt. LeConte 6,593ft

GREENBRIER

Newfound Gap 5,048ft

Newfound Gap RD

Mt Guyot 6,621ft

HEN WALLOW FALLS TRAIL

Cosby

441

Dillsboro

Sylva

CHEROKEE INDIAN LANDS

BALSAM

BLUE

BALSAM MOUNTAIN

BALSAM MTN RD

CATALOOCHEE

Trail

COSBY

Mt Sterling 5,835ft

BIG CREEK

Mt Cammerer 5,025ft

32

40

74

23

72

19

0   5 km
0   5 mi

Smoky Mountain Blooms and Foliage

You'll find the most abundant display of spring wildflower blooms in mid-to-late April. Keep in mind that the dates for wildflower blooms and fall color displays are only guidelines. A number of factors contribute to peak timing of blooms and changing leaves. Check with park officials for the best times and places to experience the finest each season has to offer. At the highest elevations, **leaves begin to change** during the first two weeks of **October,** creeping down the mountains and ending in late October or early November.

- **Catawba rhododendron:** Grows at elevations above 3,500 feet; blooms in June.

- **Flame azalea:** This wild shrub blooms at lower elevations in April and May, at higher elevations through June and early July.

- **Mountain laurel:** Blooms from early May through June.

- **Rosebay rhododendron:** Blooms in lower elevations in June and July.

the sights of Newfound Gap Road, including Clingmans Dome and Cades Cove.

Lodging within the park is limited to camping—unless you want to hike to the rustic LeConte Lodge—so your best bets for hotels, inns, cabins, and B&Bs are the Tennessee towns of Gatlinburg, Pigeon Forge, and Knoxville.

The seasons have a major impact on visitation to GSMNP. Crowds arrive for the blooming of wildflowers in spring, and every autumn the park grows thick with visitors and even thicker with a blaze of red, yellow, and burgundy leaves on each mountainside.

When to Go

To get a sense of the variability of the weather in GSMNP, keep in mind that the elevation ranges from under 1,000 feet to over 6,600 feet. At Clingmans Dome, the highest elevation in the park, the average high temperature is only 65°F in July, and only in June-August can you be sure that it won't snow. If ever there were a place for wearing layers of clothing, this is it. No matter what season the calendar tells you it is, be on the safe side and pack clothing for the other three seasons too. Keep these extremes in mind in terms of safety as well: a snowstorm can bring two feet of snow at high elevations, and it's not at all unusual for the weather to be balmy at the foot of the mountain and icy at the top. At times the temperature has fallen to -20°F. Roads can be closed in the winter if the weather gets bad or restricted to vehicles with snow chains or four-wheel drive.

SPRING

Spring wildflowers begin to appear in late **March**, peaking in mid-to-late **April**. Azaleas, mountain laurels, and rhododendrons put on the best show during summer, blooming first at lower elevations and then creeping up the mountains. Flame azalea is a funny plant, peaking in different areas as the microclimates dictate; the shrubs are ablaze with color **April to July**. Mountain laurel overlaps with blooms in **May-June,** and rhododendron shows its color in **June-July**.

SUMMER AND FALL

The **most crowded times** in the park are from **mid-June** to **mid-August** and all of **October**. During fall, spots like Newfound Gap Road and Cades Cove can become absolutely lousy with cars (expect bumper-to-bumper traffic as you loop Cades Cove), and the hiking trails are crowded with picture-takers. If fall color is on your agenda, consider spending more time exploring the back roads, long hikes, and seldom-seen corners of the park's extreme north and south ends.

The mountaintops are the first to show autumn's arrival in early October, with colors then bleeding down until mid-to-late October and early November, when trees from the foot to the crest of the mountains are aflame with color. Summer heat can alter the schedule for blooms and fall colors, as can rainfall levels; visitors can call Great Smoky Mountains National Park or check regional websites to find out how the season is progressing.

WINTER

Winter can be an excellent time to visit the park, especially if there's been a dusting of snow. With fewer crowds and maintained roads like Cades Cove Loop and Newfound Gap Road, the mountains, trails, streams, and historic structures here can be a lonely, lovely sight. However, the Blue Ridge Parkway closes in winter due to ice and snow, and Newfound Gap Road can be a nerve-wracking drive in inclement weather. Several other roads in the park are closed in the winter, although closing dates vary. Among these are Balsam Mountain, Clingmans Dome, Little Greenbrier, Rich Mountain, and Round Bottom Roads and the Roaring Fork Motor Nature Trail. Find out current conditions by calling the park's weather information line (865/436-1200, ext. 630).

Exploring the Park

Great Smoky Mountains National Park (GSMNP, 865/436-1200, www.nps.gov/grsm) was the first—and the largest—of three National Park Service units established in the southern Appalachians. The park was founded in 1934, followed in 1935 by the Blue Ridge Parkway and in 1936 by Shenandoah National Park. These sister facilities include some 600 miles of contiguous road and close to 800,000 acres of land, all of it acquired from private landholders, and all of it standing testament to the wild, rugged beauty of the Appalachian Mountains and the people who helped tame these places.

GSMNP itself is the most-visited National Park, with around 10 million visitors each year. In the 521,085-acre park, you'll find 800 miles of hiking trails, including 70 miles of the Appalachian Trail; 16 mountains over 6,000 feet; 2,100 miles of mountain streams and rivers; and an astoundingly diverse set of flora and fauna.

More than 17,000 species have been documented here, including more than 100 species of native trees, 1,500 flowering plant species, 200 species of birds, 66 types of mammals, 67 native species of fish, 39 varieties of reptiles, and 43 species of amphibians. And that's not even counting the mushrooms, mollusks, and millipedes. Researchers believe an additional 30,000-80,000 species may exist. No other area of a similar size in a similar climate can boast a higher number of species. A multitude of factors are believed to have contributed to this astounding number, including the wide elevation range (from 875 to 6,643 feet), which provides quite a variance in temperature, as well as the fantastic growing conditions created by summer's high humidity and abundant rainfall (apart from the Pacific Northwest, these are the rainiest mountains in the country). Plus, as some of the oldest mountains in the world—it is believed they were formed some 200-300 million years ago—the Smokies have seen a number of dramatic changes. During the last ice age (10,000 years ago), the glacial intrusion into the United States didn't reach the Smokies, making them a refuge for species of plants and animals displaced from homes farther north.

VISITORS CENTERS

Begin your exploration of GSMNP with a stop at one of the park's four visitors centers. You'll find rangers who know the trail and road conditions as well as what's blooming where. You can also grab detailed maps and trail guides.

Oconaluftee Visitor Center

If you're entering GSMNP from the North Carolina side, Oconaluftee Visitor Center (1194 Newfound Gap Rd., Cherokee, NC, 828/497-1904, www.nps.gov/grsm, 8am-4:30pm daily Dec.-Feb., except Christmas Day, 8am-5pm daily Mar., 9am-6pm daily Apr.-May, 8am-7:30pm daily June-Aug., 8am-6:30pm daily Sept.-Oct., 8am-5pm daily Nov.), just two miles north of Cherokee on US-441/ Newfound Gap Road, is the best place to begin your tour.

Clingmans Dome Visitor Contact Station

Along Newfound Gap Road, you'll find the turnoff to Clingmans Dome and the Clingmans Dome Visitor Contact Station (Clingmans Dome Rd., off Newfound Gap Rd., 25 miles from Cherokee, NC, and 23 miles from Gatlinburg, TN, 865/436-1200, www.nps.gov/grsm, 10am-6pm daily Apr.-Oct., 9:30am-5pm daily Nov.). Clingmans Dome is the highest peak in GSMNP and features a fantastic viewing platform. At the visitor contact station, you'll find information on the park, a bookstore, and restrooms.

Sugarlands Visitor Center and Park Headquarters

The busiest information center in the park is also the first stop for visitors entering the park from Tennessee. Sugarlands Visitor Center and Park Headquarters (1420 Old TN-73 Scenic, Gatlinburg, TN, 865/436-1200, www.nps.gov/grsm, 8am-4:30pm daily Dec.-Feb., except Christmas Day, 8am-5pm daily Mar., 9am-6pm daily Apr.-May, 8am-7:30pm daily June-Aug., 8am-6:30pm daily Sept.-Oct., 8am-5pm daily Nov.) is located just inside the park, only two miles from Gatlinburg. Here you'll find the usual visitors center information as well as a 20-minute film introducing you to the park.

Cades Cove Visitor Center

In Cades Cove, about halfway around the ever-popular Loop Road, is the Cades Cove Visitor Center (Cades Cove Loop Rd., 865/436-1200, www.nps.gov/grsm, 9am-4:30pm daily Dec.-Jan., except Christmas Day, 9am-5:30pm daily Feb. and Nov., 9am-6:30pm daily Mar. and Sept.-Oct., 9am-7pm daily Apr. and Aug., 9am-7:30pm daily May-June). Indoor and outdoor exhibits illustrate Southern mountain life and culture, and there are a number of historic structures to photograph and explore.

Backcountry Information Office

The knowledgeable folks at the Backcountry Information Office (865/436-1297, 8am-5pm daily) are a good first resource when planning a hiking or backcountry camping trip. There are more than a dozen shelters and around 100 backcountry campsites sprinkled throughout the park at convenient intervals. Those on multiday hikes or interested in backcountry camping can reserve tent sites and shelter space (www.smokiespermits.nps.gov, permits $4/person/night) up to 30 days in advance of their trip. Hikers, campers, anglers, and equestrians are asked to follow Leave No Trace practices.

Field Schools

Two Tennessee-based organizations affiliated with GSMNP offer ways to get to know the park even better. The Smoky Mountain Field School (865/974-0150, www.outreach. utk.edu) teaches workshops and leads excursions to educate participants in a wide array of fields related to the Smokies. One-day classes focus on the history and cultural heritage of the park, the lives of some of the park's most interesting animals, folk medicine and cooking of the southern Appalachians, and much more. Instructors also lead one-day and overnight hikes into the heart of the park. This is a great way to discover the park far beyond what you would be able to do on your own, so check their schedule and sign up for a class that interests you.

The **Great Smoky Mountains Institute at Tremont** (9275 Tremont Rd., Townsend, TN, 865/448-6709, www.gsmit.org) teaches students of all ages about the ecology of the region, wilderness rescue and survival skills, and even nature photography. Many of the classes and guided trips are part of Road Scholars, kids' camps, or teacher-training institutes; however, there are also rich opportunities for unaffiliated learners.

PARK ENTRANCES

There are three main entrances to Great Smoky Mountains National Park. Each is easily accessed from a nearby gateway town:

- From **Cherokee, North Carolina,** drive two miles north along US-441 into the park.

- From **Gatlinburg, Tennessee,** follow US-441 south two miles into the park.

- From **Townsend, Tennessee,** take TN-73 three miles east into the park.

In addition to the main entrances, there are 17 other points at which to enter the park via automobile. The majority of these are gravel roads of varying states of maintenance and requiring varying degrees of driving confidence and skill, but if you're up for an adventure, you can find some beautiful corners of the park along these routes.

GSMNP is unusual among the National Parks System in that it has **no entrance fee,** so if you see a Friends of the Smokies donation box and you're so inclined (or so moved by what you see around you), toss a few bucks their way.

DRIVING TOURS
★ Newfound Gap Road

While many visitors use this 33-mile road that bisects Great Smoky Mountains National Park as a mere thruway, it's actually one of the prettiest drives you'll find anywhere. This curvy road alternates between exposed and tree-enclosed, and a number of scenic overlooks provide spectacular views of the Smokies. Stop at one that has a trail (more than half of them do) and take a short walk into the woods, or eat a picnic lunch at one of the mountainside overlooks. Whatever you do on this road between Cherokee and Gatlinburg, take your time and enjoy the ride.

Rich Mountain Road

Rich Mountain Road is a photographer's dream. Running north from Cades Cove

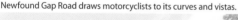
Newfound Gap Road draws motorcyclists to its curves and vistas.

over Rich Mountain to Tuckaleechee Cove and Townsend, this one-way gravel road provides stunning views of Cades Cove. For eight miles the road makes its way through an oak-dominated hardwood forest. Don't try this in the family sedan or your economy rental; use a truck or SUV instead because the road does become steep once it passes outside park boundaries.

If you're stuck with the rental or you aren't confident in your off-road driving abilities, you can always enjoy similar views on the 8.5-mile Rich Mountain Loop hike. The hike is a great way to see Cades Cove without the high-season gridlock.

Foothills Parkway

It's not in the park, but the **Foothills Parkway** is a great scenic drive that gives you high-elevation views without the same traffic you'll find on more popular routes in the park proper. The Foothills Parkway is reached via US-321, 5.5 miles from Townsend. The 17-mile road has plenty of places to pull off to picnic or take in the view. There's one short hike here at Look Rock, a 0.5-mile stroll to an observation tower.

Newfound Gap Road

Easily the most heavily traveled route in the Smokies, Newfound Gap Road (US-441) connects Cherokee with Gatlinburg and sees thousands of visitors a day. Newfound Gap Road is the perfect introduction to GSMNP: Contour-hugging curves, overlooks with million-dollar views, easy hikes right off the roadway, and a 3,000-foot elevation change give you a great overview of these mountains and this spectacular park. During peak times in the summer and fall, it's not uncommon to encounter a traffic jam or two along this 33-mile scenic route, especially when bears are taking their time crossing the road.

Newfound Gap Road earned its name in 1872 when Swiss geographer Arnold Henry Guyot determined that a newly found gap was the lowest pass through the Great Smoky Mountains. Lower in elevation and easier to access than the former passage at Indian Gap, 1.5 miles away, the name Newfound Gap was soon used to refer to the entire route.

SIGHTS
Oconaluftee Visitor Center

As you begin your trip along Newfound Gap Road from the North Carolina side, your first stop will probably be the "Welcome to Great Smoky Mountains National Park" sign, but the **Oconaluftee Visitor Center** (1194 Newfound Gap Rd., Cherokee, NC, 828/497-1904, www.nps.gov/grsm, 8am-4:30pm daily Dec.-Feb., except Christmas Day, 8am-5pm daily Mar. and Nov., 9am-6pm daily Apr.-May, 8am-7:30pm daily June-Aug., 8am-6:30pm daily Sept.-Oct.), just two miles north of Cherokee on US-441/Newfound Gap Road, will likely be the second stop you make. You can pick up a park map, grab the schedule of ranger-led programs, and see exhibits on the people who called these hills home long before the park was in existence. The visitors center and adjacent comfort station are LEED Gold certified.

Mountain Farm Museum

Next to the visitors center is **Mountain Farm Museum** (sunrise-sunset daily year-round, free), which showcases some of the finest farm buildings in the park. Most date to the early 1900s and among them are a barn, apple house, and the Davis House, a log home built from chestnut wood and constructed before the American chestnut blight decimated the species. This collection of structures is original to the area and dates back to the turn of the 20th century. Though the barn is the only structure original to this site, the other buildings were moved here from inside and adjacent to the park and arranged much like the typical farm of the era would have been laid out. If you visit during peak times, you'll see costumed living-history interpreters demonstrating the day-to-day chores that would've occurred on this farm: preparing meals, sowing, maintaining and harvesting the garden, taking care of the hogs, and the like.

Deep Creek Valley Overlook

The Deep Creek Valley Overlook, 14 miles from the Oconaluftee Visitor Center (and 16 miles from Sugarlands Visitor Center if coming from the other direction), is one of the most popular overlooks in the park for good reason. From here you'll have a long view of the mountains, which roll away from you for as far as you can see.

Oconaluftee River Valley Overlook

Halfway through Newfound Gap Road is the Oconaluftee River Valley Overlook, a spot where you can spy the deep cut of the valley formed by the Oconaluftee River. This place is ideal for a picnic, so if you're hungry and you've brought your blanket and something to eat, spread out and relax for a few minutes.

Newfound Gap

One of the most-visited overlooks is at Newfound Gap. This is the highest elevation on Newfound Gap Road, at 5,048 feet, and though the views here are fantastic, the first thing you'll probably notice is the Rockefeller Memorial, a simple stone terrace that straddles the Tennessee/North Carolina state line and commemorates a $5 million gift made by the Rockefeller Foundation to acquire land for the park. In 1940, President Franklin D. Roosevelt dedicated the park from this site. Plan to spend a little time here, especially early in the morning or near sunset. At sunset, you can see the Smokies' namesake haze settling into the folds and wrinkles of the mountains, and in the early morning, the mountains emerge from a blue haze in a subtle display of color that's been the subject of many a postcard and computer desktop background.

★ Clingmans Dome

At 6,643 feet, Clingmans Dome is the third-highest mountain in the eastern United States, and the highest in the Great Smoky Mountains. A flying saucer-like observation tower at the end of a long, steep walkway gives 360-degree views of the surrounding mountains, and on a clear day that view can be as

Clingmans Dome

The Appalachian Trail

The 2,184-mile Appalachian Trail (AT) runs from Georgia to Maine, with 95.5 miles within North Carolina and another 200 straddling the border of North Carolina and Tennessee. This section is a high climb, with many peaks over 5,000 feet and gaps brushing 4,000 feet, but the fantastic balds (natural and agricultural areas devoid of trees) along the trail here—like Cheoa Bald and Max Patch—are big draws for day hikers and segment hikers, and having vistas this beautiful this early in the long journey helps through-hikers retain their focus and determination to reach their goal.

The Appalachian Trail cuts a path through the Nantahala National Forest, regarded by many as one of the best sections of the southern portion of the trail, before crossing the hills of the southern Blue Ridge and following the crest of the Smokies along the Tennessee border. This section of the trail is rated between a 3 and a 6 on the AT's 10-point scale, which means the trail varies from moderate elevation changes on well-graded trails to strenuous and short but steep climbs to extended climbs that last hours, as well as short sections with difficult footing. For through-hikers, who often have years of trail experience, the path here isn't as difficult as it may be for some day or even overnight hikers.

Finding a day hike isn't hard west of Asheville, especially in the deeper mountains along Great Smoky Mountain National Park. Driving the Newfound Gap Road from the town of Cherokee into Tennessee, go about 16 miles from the Oconaluftee Visitors Center to the Newfound Gap parking lot. There is a trailhead to the left of the overlook. Take the moderate four-mile hike to **Charlies Bunion,** a peak along the AT with a very odd name. You'll gradually gain around 1,600 feet in elevation, but if you bring a picnic lunch, you'll have a lovely dining spot.

far as a hundred miles. More often, though, it's misty up here in the clouds, and Clingmans Dome receives so much precipitation that its woods are actually a coniferous rain forest. The road to the summit is closed December 1-March 31, but the observation tower remains open for those willing to make the hike. To get to Clingmans Dome, turn off Newfound Gap Road 0.1 mile south of Newfound Gap, and then take Clingmans Dome Road (closed in winter), which leads 7 miles to the parking lot. The peak is near the center of the park, due north from Bryson City, North Carolina.

Campbell Overlook

The **Campbell Overlook** is only three miles from the Sugarlands Visitor Center, and it's home to one of the best views of Mount LeConte you'll find along the road. LeConte is an interesting mountain. At 6,593 feet, it's the third-highest peak in the Smokies, but it's the tallest mountain east of the Mississippi in that it rises more than a mile from the foot of the mountain to the summit.

Sugarlands Visitor Center

The **Sugarlands Visitor Center** (1420 Old TN-73 Scenic, Gatlinburg, TN, 865/436-1200, www.nps.gov/grsm, 8am-4:30pm daily Dec.-Feb., except Christmas Day, 8am-5pm daily Mar., 9am-6pm daily Apr.-May, 8am-7:30pm daily June-Aug., 8am-6:30pm daily Sept.-Oct., 8am-5pm daily Nov.) is the most popular visitors center in the park due to its proximity to Gatlinburg. There's the usual visitors center stuff—maps, guidebooks, a few gift items, some snacks—and it's also the origination point for the 1.9-mile Gatlinburg Trail.

RECREATION
Hiking

Great Smoky Mountains National Park contains hundreds of miles of hiking trails, ranging from family-friendly loop trails to strenuous wilderness treks. Before embarking on any of these trails, obtain a park map and talk to a park ranger to ascertain trail conditions and gauge whether it's suited to your hiking skills.

No dogs or other pets (other than service animals) are permitted on park trails, except the Gatlinburg Trail and Oconaluftee River Trail, though they are allowed in front-country campsites and picnic areas, so long as they remain on-leash.

OCONALUFTEE RIVER TRAIL

Distance: 3 miles round-trip
Duration: 45 minutes
Elevation gain: 70 feet
Difficulty: easy
Trailhead: Oconaluftee Visitor Center, or just outside of Cherokee on US-441

This trail by the Oconaluftee River runs from the visitors center to the outskirts of Cherokee. It's great for walking or jogging and is one of two paths in GSMNP where you can walk your dog or ride your bike. Flat save for a bridge or two and a few gentle rises, the Oconaluftee River Trail is a lovely walk. In the spring the banks of the Oconaluftee are blanketed with wildflowers, and throughout the year you may see a herd of elk crossing the river at any number of places. Bring bug spray because it can get a bit buggy right by the river on a still day.

APPALACHIAN TRAIL TO MOUNT LECONTE VIA THE BOULEVARD

Distance: 15.6 miles one-way
Duration: 7-8.5 hours
Elevation gain: 3,000 feet
Difficulty: strenuous
Trailhead: Appalachian Trail trailhead at the Newfound Gap Road Overlook

This is a tough hike. The trail largely follows the crest of the mountains, and thus rises and falls several times with some significant elevation gains and losses.

From the start, the trail climbs. For 2 miles you'll be on a steady incline, but there are views aplenty to give you a little boost. At 1.7 miles, just before you come to the junction with Sweat Heifer Creek Trail, you'll have a good look at Mount LeConte to the north. At 2.8 miles, The Boulevard forks off to the left.

Continue along The Boulevard, ignoring the sign for the Jump-Off Trail (you can hike that one-mile trail on the return trip if you want). Soon you'll drop down to an elevation around 5,500 feet, after which the trail bounces back and forth between 5,500 and 6,000 feet until you begin to properly climb Mount LeConte and make your way to the lodge there and the 6,593-foot summit.

CHARLIES BUNION

Distance: 8.1 miles round-trip
Duration: 7-8.5 hours
Elevation gain: 1,700 feet
Difficulty: strenuous
Trailhead: Appalachian Trail trailhead at the Newfound Gap Road Overlook

Originally named Fodderstack, the rock formation of Charlies Bunion earned its new name when two men, Charlie Conner and Horace Kephart, were hiking here. According to legend, they stopped to rest at Fodderstack and Conner removed his boots and socks, revealing a bunion that Kephart felt resembled the rocks around them. Impressed, Kephart promised Charlie that he'd get the name of this place changed on official maps in honor of the bunion.

The first leg of this trail follows the Appalachian Trail and The Boulevard to Mount LeConte. From the start, the trail climbs. For 2 miles you'll be on a steady incline, but there are views aplenty to give you a little boost. At 1.7 miles, just before you come to the junction with Sweat Heifer Creek Trail, you'll have a good look at Mount LeConte to the north. At 2.8 miles, The Boulevard forks off to the left; continue straight to reach Charlies Bunion.

The Icewater Spring Shelter, aptly named for the cold spring that flows out of the mountain here (treat the water before you drink it), is just 0.25 miles from the junction and is a good spot to rest. From the spring, continue a little less than a mile to a short spur trail on your left that leads out to the rock outcrop known as Charlies Bunion.

★ ANDREWS BALD

Distance: 3.5 miles round-trip
Duration: 3 hours
Elevation gain: 1,200 feet
Difficulty: moderate
Trailhead: Clingmans Dome parking area at the end of Clingmans Dome Road

The highest grassy bald in GSMNP, Andrews Bald is a beautiful sight at the end of a nearly two-mile hike from Clingmans Dome. Balds are simply meadows found higher up on the mountain than you'd expect, and this one is absolutely lousy with flame azalea and rhododendron blooms in the summer.

Before recent trail renovations, the Andrews Bald hike had some of the most rugged sections of rocky trails in the park, but thanks to the Trails Forever program, work crews fixed drainage issues, rebuilt parts of the trail, and even built a few stairways from native rocks and trees. Now the hike is easier and safer and leads to a spectacular view of the Smoky Mountains. A bonus: The hike is just long enough to discourage some potential hikers, but it's still short enough to be doable by everyone in your party.

The Forney Ridge Trail starts in a spruce-fir forest that was once beautiful, but is now unfortunately dead or dying. That's because the forest has been ravaged by a tiny bug—the balsam woolly adelgid—which devours Fraser firs. However, there is a certain beauty in the white bones of the tree trunks jutting up from the land. Don't worry though, the views get considerably better in a short time. Around 1.6 miles into the hike you'll reach the edge of Andrews Bald, where the forest opens up into a fantastic panorama. In spring and summer, you'll find a proliferation of wildflowers, flame azalea, and rhododendron.

ALUM CAVE BLUFF TO MOUNT LECONTE

Distance: 5 miles one-way
Duration: 3-3.5 hours
Elevation gain: 2,560 feet
Difficulty: moderate with strenuous sections
Trailhead: Alum Cave Trailhead

As one of the most popular hikes in the park, this trail receives a lot of wear-and-tear. Repair work is ongoing through 2016, which means the **trail is closed** (7am-5:30pm Mon.-Thurs.) as work crews perform much-needed maintenance. Though work will focus on the upper part of the trail (from the Bluffs to the summit of Mount LeConte), the trail is open weekends-only to keep hikers and workers safe. If you're visiting midweek and want to do a LeConte day hike, head up via Rainbow Falls Trail instead.

The trail starts off fairly gently as it climbs up to Arch Rock. Alum Cave Creek runs alongside the trail for a while, and here you'll have the chance to snap pictures of several cascades and beautiful rhododendron thickets (which bloom in late June and July). You'll reach Arch Rock, which is less arch and more natural tunnel, around 1.5 miles in.

Here the trail begins to climb more steeply. A set of stone steps leads out of Arch Rock and the forest changes from hemlock and hardwood to spruce and fir trees. In another half mile you'll reach Inspiration Point, where the view opens onto one of the mid-elevation balds.

When you reach Alum Cave Bluffs, you're halfway to Mount LeConte. The rock formations aren't caves, but rather deep overhangs that create an impressive shelter from the rain. The Smokies receive more than 85 inches of rain a year, yet the majority of the soil under the bluffs remains dry and dusty, an arid spot in one of the wettest forests in the nation.

Most hikers turn around at Alum Cave Bluffs, but if you're pushing on to Mount LeConte, the path steepens and grows more challenging as you gain elevation. The trail narrows to a set of rock ledges where steel cables have been bolted into the mountain for use as a handhold. The drop may be precipitous, but the views are fantastic. Soon, the trail intersects with Rainbow Falls Trail, leading you to the summit of Mount LeConte in short order.

If you plan on hiking to Mount LeConte and back in a day or spending the night at the lodge, it's in your best interest to arrive early so you can get a parking space.

CHIMNEY TOPS

Distance: 4 miles out and back
Duration: 3.5 hours
Elevation gain: 1,400 feet
Difficulty: strenuous
Trailhead: Chimney Tops trailhead on Newfound Gap Road

This popular hike leads to an outstanding view from its namesake pinnacles. The trail has suffered some severe storm damage in the past few years past, and was closed intermittently until a Trails Forever team completed repairs, fixing drainage issues, installing or refreshing rock steps and staircases, and building elevated turnpikes, as well as other laborious methods to mitigate the impact from hikers and mother nature.

Chimney Tops takes its name from the twin knobs that rise from a ridge like chimneys. These rocky summits are rare in the Smokies, but that's not the draw—what brings people up this steep, challenging trail is the 360-degree view. And it's incredibly steep, gaining nearly 1,000 feet in the last mile. To reach the pinnacles, the actual Chimney Tops, requires a very steep scramble over bare rock, which can be dangerous, and it's easier to climb up than to come back down.

Many people explore the first few hundred yards of this trail because it's right off Newfound Gap Road. The cascades, pools, and boulders found along Walker Camp Prong are picturesque and good for wading and sunbathing. As you climb, you'll cross Road Prong, another stream, twice. Just after the second crossing the trail splits, with one part following Road Prong and the other heading to Chimney Tops. Stay right and head to the chimneys.

After a brief ascent, the trail steepens quite significantly. Take a breather here before tackling this long, straight climb. The trail continues and narrows as you walk the ridgeline. Soon, you'll be at the foot of the Chimney Tops and you'll see a sign from the National

mountain stream near Chimney Tops

Park Service warning you to proceed at your own risk. Heed this sign, as the last bit of "trail" to the summit is a scramble that doesn't require any specialized equipment but is quite risky if you're inexperienced in such terrain.

GATLINBURG TRAIL

Distance: 3.8 miles round-trip
Duration: 2 hours
Elevation gain: 20 feet
Difficulty: easy
Trailhead: Sugarlands Visitor Center

This is one of only two trails in the park to allow **pets** and **bicycles** (the other is the Oconaluftee River Trail in Cherokee). More of a walk than a hike, the Gatlinburg Trail follows the West Prong Little Pigeon River and Newfound Gap Road for most of the trip. It's pretty and not especially challenging, but the optional walk to Cataract Falls—a few hundred yards up Cove Mountain Trail, which splits off the Gatlinburg Trail near the trailhead—can provide some photo opportunities and a pretty, easy-to-reach waterfall.

Horseback Riding

Three commercial stables in the park offer "rental" horses (about $30/hour). **Smokemont** (828/497-2373, www.smokemontridingstable.com) is located in North Carolina near Cherokee. Two are in Tennessee: **Smoky Mountain** (865/436-5634, Gatlinburg, TN, www.smokymountainridingstables.com) and **Cades Cove** (10018 Campground Dr., Townsend, TN, 865/448-9009, http://cadescovestables.com).

ACCOMMODATIONS AND CAMPING

As big as GSMNP may be, there are few places to stay within the boundaries—and nearly all of them are either campsites or backcountry shelters. The lone exception is LeConte Lodge, a collection of cabins and small lodges with a central dining room/lodge. It's only accessible by hiking in, so you have to be dedicated to stay there.

LeConte Lodge

Just below the 6,593-foot peak of Mount LeConte is the only true lodging in GSMNP, the ★ **LeConte Lodge** (865/429-5704, www.lecontelodge.com, Mar. 21-Nov. 22, adults $140, children ages 4-12 $85, includes lodging, breakfast, and dinner). Like the mountain's summit, the lodge is accessible only via the network of hiking trails that crisscross the park. And if the accessibility limitation isn't rustic enough for you, this collection of cabins has no running water or electricity. What it does have is views for days and the seclusion of the Smoky Mountains backcountry.

For the most part the environs harken back to the lodge's 1934 opening. LeConte Lodge has no hot showers. In every cabin there is a bucket for a sponge bath—which can be surprisingly refreshing after a hot day on the trail—that you can fill with warm water from the kitchen, though you need to supply your own washcloth and towel. There are a few flush toilets in a separate building, and the only lights, aside from headlamps and flashlights, are kerosene lanterns. Your room does come with two meals: dinner and breakfast. Both are served at the same time every day (6pm for dinner and 8am for breakfast), and feature food hearty enough to fuel another day on the trail.

The lodge doesn't lack for charm, but it does for comfort, so if you're the five-star-hotel, breakfast-in-bed type, this may not be the place for you. Catering to hikers who are happy to have a dry place to sleep and a bed that's more comfy than their sleeping bag, it's short on luxury amenities, and rooms are, in truth, bunk beds in small, drafty cabins. But if you're a hiker or if you just love to have a completely different experience when you travel, this is a one-of-a-kind accommodation. Make reservations well in advance because the lodge books pretty quickly up to a year in advance, especially during peak weekends and all throughout the fall color bonanza.

RESERVATIONS

Accommodations for LeConte Lodge are made via **lottery** (www.lecontelodge.com). The lottery is quite competitive, but it's easy to enter; simply go to their website and fill out the online form, including your desired dates and the number in your party. If your application is chosen in the lottery, you will receive an invoice with your accommodation information. Booking information for the following season becomes available online in mid-summer, so keep an eye out and get your application in early.

If you want to stay at LeConte Lodge, but you're late to the lottery party, try to get on the **wait list.** The process is the same, but the dates are limited—typically weeknights—and the larger cabins are all that's available.

You can try one other method: **calling** (865/429-5704). Cancellations made with less than 30-day notice skip the wait-list and are instead offered to the first inquiry that matches availability. Frequent calls are a good way to snag these last-minute reservations.

GETTING THERE

The **Roaring Fork Motor Nature Trail** at the foot of Mount LeConte is the starting point for a trio of hiking trails that lead to LeConte Lodge. **Bull Head Trail** is a 6.8-mile trip from the trailhead to the lodge, as is **Rainbow Falls Trail.** (Bull Head and Rainbow Falls Trails share a trailhead at the designated parking area on the Motor Nature Trail.) **Trillium Gap Trail,** the trail used by the lodge's pack llamas, passes by the beautiful Grotto Falls on its 6.7-mile route (the trailhead is at the Grotto Falls parking area on the Motor Nature Trail). Each of these three trails requires a four-hour hike to reach the lodge from the trailhead.

Three other trails lead to Mount LeConte from various points in the park. Alum Cave Trail (5 miles one-way) enters from Newfound Gap Road; it's the shortest and easiest to access, but it's also the steepest. On top of that, trail maintenance will keep this route closed (Mon.-Thurs.) through 2016. You're better off using Rainbow Falls or Trillium Gap Trails until trail maintenance is complete.

Alternately, The Boulevard connects the Appalachian Trail to LeConte Lodge (13.2 miles from Newfound Gap Overlook). The Boulevard is relatively easy with little elevation change, but there's the issue of exposure on this trail—the rock path has more than a few dizzying drops right beside the trail. This, combined with the fact that it comes in from the Appalachian Trail, deters most day- or overnight-hikers from use. Brushy Mountain Trail (11.8 miles round-trip) leads to the summit from the Porters Creek Trailhead off Greenbrier Road. Despite the significant elevation change, this is a relatively easy trail.

Camping

Smokemont Campground (877/444-6777, www.recreation.gov, year-round, $17-20) is just off Newfound Gap Road, 3.2 miles from the Oconaluftee Visitor Center. There are 142 total sites available between tent campsites and RV sites. It's located on the banks of the Oconaluftee River and thus can get quite buggy, so be prepared.

Eastern Smokies

The eastern side of GSMNP was settled before the western side, so you'll find plenty of coves and hollows with historic structures or the ruins of cabins, barns, and other buildings in the fields and woods and along creek banks and floodplains. There are also several herds of elk here, introduced several years ago in an attempt to revive the species that once roamed these hills.

ROARING FORK
Roaring Fork Motor Nature Trail
5.5 MILES ONE-WAY

One of the most beautiful drives in GSMNP is the **Roaring Fork Motor Nature Trail.** This one-way loop passes through rhododendron thickets and dense hardwood forests as it follows the old roadbed of the Roaring Fork Community. To get here, turn onto Historic Nature Trail-Airport Road at traffic light #8 in Gatlinburg and follow the signs. Before you reach the trail, you'll drive a short distance on Cherokee Orchard Road, which runs through what was an 800-acre commercial orchard in the 1920s and '30s; shortly after the orchard, you'll be at the head of the trail and have the chance to purchase an inexpensive tour booklet from a roadside exhibit.

The roadbed here was built by hand in the 1850s, which explains both its narrowness and serpentine route. Around 25 families lived here, and though it may look quaint and primitive to our eyes, a few of the homes had running water thanks to the system of troughs—some of which are still

Roaring Fork and Greenbrier Cove

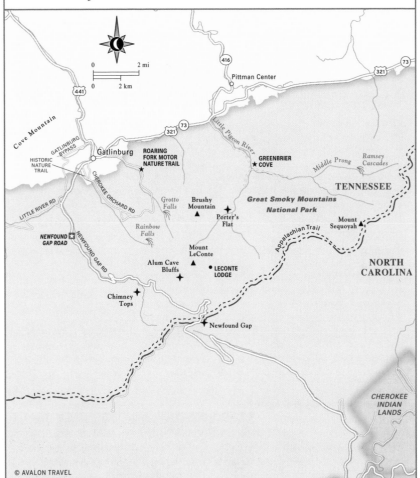

© AVALON TRAVEL

standing—that carried water right to the houses.

As the road climbs through the forest, roll down your windows and take in a few deep breaths of that fresh, cool mountain air. There is a pair of **overlooks,** though they're overgrown and in poor repair. When you stop, take in the silence. You'll soon find yourself surrounded by the sounds of nature: wind, birds calling, streams rumbling and echoing through the forest.

Be sure to stop at the cabins still standing here. **Ogle Place,** a two-room cabin surrounded by rhododendrons; **Ephraim Bales Cabin,** which is smack in the middle of a boulder field; and **Alfred Regan Cabin,** which has an amazing trough system still in place, are all worth spending a few minutes exploring and photographing.

Hiking

There are three waterfalls within hiking

distance of the Motor Nature Trail: **Rainbow Falls** (the most popular of the hikes), **Grotto Falls,** and **Baskins Falls.** If you're not up for a hike, **Thousand Drips Falls** (sometimes called the Place of a Thousand Drips) is just off the road. In wet times, it's a great cascade plummeting down the mountain; during drier times it's much tamer but still serene.

RAINBOW FALLS TRAIL

Distance: 5.4 miles round-trip
Duration: 3.5-4 hours
Elevation gain: 1,700 feet
Difficulty: strenuous
Trailhead: Roaring Fork Motor Nature Trail, 3.3 miles from Gatlinburg traffic light #8, at the Rainbow Falls and Bull Head Trail parking area

This trail is strenuous due to how steep and rocky it is and how slick it can become in places where the trail nears the water and as you get closer to the falls.

As you leave the parking area, you'll cross Trillium Gap Trail and begin to climb alongside LeConte Creek. Follow the trail as it goes through a couple of switchbacks and then crosses the creek on a log bridge. Here you'll enter a stretch where some impressive trees stand. Soon you'll cross LeConte Creek again. At this crossing you can see Rainbow Falls above you. Continue up the trail to a spot just below the falls.

Here LeConte Creek plunges 80 feet to the rocks below. During that plunge, the water becomes more of a heavy mist, giving us the name Rainbow Falls. Though you can get some good photography from the trail, there are other interesting shots to be had from different angles around the falls. Be aware that if you scramble around the falls, the rocks are slick and you could slip and hurt yourself, and with a 2.7-mile hike back to the car, who wants to do that? If you decide to explore the area around the falls, use caution and stay safe.

You may notice that the Rainbow Falls Trail continues on past the waterfall itself. It is possible to take this trail to the summit of Mount LeConte, but that is a strenuous, steep, full-day hike of close to 14 miles.

GROTTO FALLS TRAIL

Distance: 2.6 miles round-trip
Duration: 2-2.5 hours
Elevation gain: 585 feet
Difficulty: moderate
Trailhead: Roaring Fork Motor Nature Trail, about 2 miles into the trail, Grotto Falls parking area on the left

From the parking area, you'll follow a short, unnamed spur before joining Trillium Gap

fall color near Roaring Fork Motor Nature Trail

Trail, which leads to Grotto Falls before continuing to the top of Mount LeConte. As you hike, you'll notice the path is hard packed—that's because this trail is the resupply route for LeConte Lodge and it sees quite a bit of traffic from llama trains carrying supplies up to the lodge. If you're lucky, you'll see one of these trains.

The forest was once composed largely of hemlock trees, but thanks to a nasty little bug—the hemlock woolly adelgid—many of these trees are dead or dying. Even though some of the trees are being ravaged, the forest is still thick, and opens dramatically where the stream plunges 25 feet to form Grotto Falls.

The most intriguing part of Grotto Falls is the grotto. Trillium Gap Trail passes behind the falls thanks to a hefty rock overhang. It makes for some interesting photographic opportunities and, because of this, is one of the most popular waterfall hikes on this side of the park.

BASKINS FALLS TRAIL

Distance: 3.2 miles round-trip
Duration: 3 hours
Elevation gain: 950 feet
Difficulty: strenuous
Trailhead: Roaring Fork Motor Nature Trail, on the left near the Jim Bales Place

This 30-foot waterfall is like a little secret hidden along the popular Roaring Fork Motor Nature Trail. Seldom visited, it's almost a forgotten hike, meaning you can have the falls to yourself.

As soon as you start the hike, you'll pass a cemetery before making a climb up to a ridgeline. A steep descent from the ridge will take you to Baskins Creek. Cross the creek (be careful, especially in high water) and make the steep climb over another ridge. From here you can see what's left of an old chimney standing in the woods. Just beyond a tiny, wildflower-filled meadow is the side path leading to the base of the falls. On the right side of this trail is an old homesite, followed by a steep descent down to the falls.

Many hikers will turn around here and

return to their car, but it is possible to continue along this trail another 1.5 miles and arrive near the entrance to the Motor Nature Trail. If you do this, know that you will have a 3-mile walk along the road back to your car.

GREENBRIER COVE

Greenbrier Cove, like many other coves in the park, was once home to a mountain community. This area was settled in the early 1800s, and families farmed, trapped, and hunted the land until the establishment of the national park. This cove has an interesting footnote: Dolly Parton's ancestors, Benjamin C. and Margaret Parton, moved here in the 1850s and their descendants left when the park was formed.

Greenbrier is stunning, especially in spring. The cove is known as a wildflower hot spot, but don't underestimate the beauty of this place in any season.

Hiking
RAMSEY CASCADES TRAIL

Distance: 8 miles out and back
Duration: 5.5 hours
Elevation gain: 2,375 feet
Difficulty: strenuous
Trailhead: Ramsey Cascades Trailhead at the Greenbrier park entrance, six miles east of Gatlinburg off US-321

Ramsey Cascades is the tallest waterfall in GSMNP, spilling 100 feet in a series of steps before collecting in a pool at the base. As if that wasn't reason enough to undertake this hike, this section of the park is known as a wildflower paradise, so a springtime visit is highly recommended.

The first portion of this trail is a continuation of the gravel road you took to the parking area. You'll soon cross Little Laurel Branch and almost immediately after, the Middle Prong of Little Pigeon River via a long footbridge. If you've timed your hike with the wildflower bloom, the next half mile will be a riot of color.

The hiking here is easy until you reach the 1.5-mile mark, where the Jeep trail you're on ends. To the left (north) is the Greenbrier Pinnacle Trail, a trail that's not maintained by the park; Ramsey Cascades Trail continues on through a thicket of rhododendron.

Past this point you find yourself on a trail where roots and rocks are more the norm, so watch your footing. Continue along this trail; it will turn steep, you'll cross the Ramsey Prong and a side stream, and you'll know you've arrived when you hear the waterfall. The final approach is rocky and slick, with a lot of scrambling, so use caution. When you've taken in all of the Ramsey Cascades you can handle, simply reverse course to the trailhead.

BRUSHY MOUNTAIN TO MOUNT LECONTE

Distance: 11.8 miles out and back
Duration: 6-7 hours
Elevation gain: 3,000 feet
Difficulty: moderate
Trailhead: Porters Creek Trailhead on Greenbrier Road, six miles east of Gatlinburg off US-321
Directions: From traffic light #3 in Gatlinburg (junction of US-441 and US-321), travel east on US-321. Drive six miles and then turn right on Greenbrier Road (which becomes a gravel road). At the fork in the road 3.1 miles in, continue straight 1 mile to the Porters Creek Trailhead.

The first mile or so of this trail follows an old gravel road, the Porters Creek Trail. In spring, trillium are profuse here. You'll pass a cemetery and several stone walls and then cross a footbridge at a fork in the road. Turn left at the fork. You'll meet another fork 100 yards or so down the trail, at which you turn right onto Brushy Mountain Trail.

The trail continues on 4.5 miles, climbing some 2,500 feet as it does. At 5.5 miles, you'll meet Trillium Gap Trail. Go left on the Trillium Gap Trail and you'll reach Mount LeConte. Turn right and you can reach the summit of Brushy Mountain in 0.6 mile.

COSBY

For the first half of the 20th century, Cosby was known as the moonshine capital of the world. The national prohibition on liquor turned many locals to making their own. When scientists and workers began to come to Oak Ridge to work on secret military ventures like the Manhattan Project, they weren't accustomed to Tennessee's dry county laws, and the demand for moonshine skyrocketed. Today there isn't much by way of moonshine production in town, and most of the visitors come here for the national park.

Cosby's present reputation is as a friendly town with one of the lesser-used park entrances. That's good for you, because when autumn leaves begin to change and the crowds pack Gatlinburg and clog the easy-to-access trails along Newfound Gap Road, you can head to Cosby. In town you'll find a few restaurants and a handful of cabin rentals, but the park is the real treasure.

Hiking

★ **HEN WALLOW FALLS TRAIL**

Distance: 4.4 miles out and back
Duration: 3.5 hours
Elevation gain: 900 feet
Difficulty: moderate
Trailhead: Gabes Mountain Trailhead, across the road from the Cosby Campground picnic area

From the outset, Gabes Mountain Trail is a steady climb on a path that's at times rugged. Follow this trail until you see a sign for the side trail leading to the waterfall (2.1 miles into the hike). The 0.1-mile side trail is a little steep, but not problematically so.

Hen Wallow Falls tumbles 90 feet into a small pool below, where there are plenty of salamanders to see. The falls themselves are only 2 feet wide at the top, but fan out to 20 feet at the bottom; during dry months, the falls are still pretty, but less wow-inducing.

To get back to the trailhead, just retrace your steps.

MOUNT CAMMERER TRAIL

Distance: 11.2 miles out and back
Duration: 7-7.5 hours
Elevation gain: 2,740 feet

Difficulty: strenuous

Trailhead: Low Gap Trailhead, just beyond the Cosby Campground amphitheater area

Park in the group parking area and walk along the road to where it curves into the B-Section of the campground. Just before campsite 92 you'll see a trailhead; follow it a short distance until it crosses Cosby Creek, then turn right on Low Gap Trail. From here, the trail climbs a little less than three miles up the mountain via a series of winding switchbacks until you reach the Appalachian Trail.

Turn left to join the Appalachian Trail for 2.1 miles. The first mile of this is more level, so it gives you a chance to catch your breath or make up some time. You'll know when you reach the junction with the Mount Cammerer Trail because the Appalachian Trail descends to the right; you want to stay straight. The summit is 0.6 miles from where you leave the Appalachian Trail.

At the summit is a stone fire tower built in the 1930s and restored by volunteers throughout the years. The view from the deck here is awesome—it's one of the best in the park.

Camping

Cosby Campground (471 Cosby Campground Road A, Cosby, TN, 423/487-2683, www.recreation.gov, Apr.-Oct., $14) has 157 sites for tents and RVs. Despite being home to the park's third-largest campground, Cosby is known as the quietest of the park's gateways. There are a number of trails that originate from the campground.

BIG CREEK

Big Creek is the site of another beautiful and seldom-visited front-country campground and one of the best hikes for inexperienced backpackers and day hikers. The Big Creek Trail is more of an easy creekside walk than a hike, but it's long enough to make you feel accomplished when you're done. In addition to the long out-and-back that is Big Creek Trail, there are options for extending the hike into longer overnighters.

Hiking
BIG CREEK TRAIL
Distance: 10.6 miles round-trip
Duration: 5-6 hours
Elevation gain: 600 feet
Difficulty: easy
Trailhead: Big Creek Picnic Area off I-40 at the Waterville exit (exit 457)

Big Creek Trail follows an old motor road built by the Civilian Conservation Corps (CCC) in the 1930s, so it's smooth and wide, with a very gentle grade for its entire length. The difficult part of this trail is the distance, so be sure to bring plenty of water and something to eat.

Roughly a mile in, you'll see Rock House, an impressive rock cliff just off the trail that has sheltered more than a few loggers, CCC workers, hunters, and hikers from a rainstorm. Just beyond Rock House is Midnight Hole. Here, Big Creek flows through a narrow chute in the rock and drops six or seven feet into a deep, dark pool before flowing on.

Two miles in, you'll see Mouse Creek Falls, a 35-foot cascade that drops right into Big Creek. It's a fantastic spot to sit, relax, take some pictures, and enjoy the woods. It's also a great spot to turn around if you have younger or older hikers with you who may not be up for the whole 10-mile trip.

Push on past Mouse Creek Falls and you'll come upon Brakeshoe Spring. In another 2.5 miles you'll reach Walnut Bottoms and Campsite 37. This is one of the best campsites in the park if you're going to make this hike an overnighter. Once you're here, it's time to retrace your steps back to the trailhead.

Camping
The **Big Creek Campground** (off Rte. 284/Mt. Sterling Rd., 12 sites, first-come first-served, Apr.-Oct., $14) is located off Route 284. Amenities include a ranger station, pay phone, restrooms, a picnic area, and a group camp as well as equestrian sites. Trailheads to Baxter Creek Trail, Big Creek Trail, and the Chestnut Branch of the AT lead from the campground.

CATALOOCHEE VALLEY

Nestled in the folds of the mountains and encircled by 6,000-foot peaks, the Cataloochee Valley was settled in the early 1830s. This isolated valley on the northeastern edge of GSMNP was home to two communities—Big and Little Cataloochee—and more than 1,200 people in 1910. By the 1940s all but a few were gone, having left the valley for hills and hollows nearby. Today this is one of the more beautiful spots in the national park, and a few historic structures are all that remains of the communities that thrived here, save a few memories and stories written down.

Cataloochee Valley is not far from I-40, but it can be a little difficult to find because the signage directing you here is poor at best. From I-40, take Exit 20 onto US-276. Take an immediate right onto Cove Creek Road. The condition of the road—it's alternately gravel and paved—and the narrow, winding route will make you doubt you made the right turn, but you did. Zigzag up this road for about 12 miles and suddenly it will open up into the wide, grassy expanse that is Cataloochee Valley. Before you begin your descent into the valley, stop at the overlook just past the intersection with Big Creek Road. From here you can marvel at the valley sweeping away

before you and the mountains rising up all around.

The valley is open to vehicle traffic from 8am to sunset, so keep that in mind if you're visiting without plans to camp. Though less visited than other areas, like Cades Cove on the western side of the park, Cataloochee sees its fair share of visitors. Most arrive in the evenings shortly before sunset to see the elk grazing in the fields. If you don't plan on camping and you'd rather avoid the crowds, as small as they may be, visit in midday and take a hike and see if you can find the elk in the woods; it's where they go to escape the heat.

★ Cataloochee

There are four prominent structures still standing in Cataloochee Valley: two homes, a school, and a church. A few other structures and ruins, cemeteries, fences, and walls remain throughout the valley as well. The most prominent building is the **Palmer Chapel and Cemetery.** The chapel was built in 1898, and it's been some time since there's been a regular service here. Today the chapel sees sporadic use, the most regular being the annual reunion of the descendants of some of the oldest Cataloochee families. Descendants of the Barnes, Bennett, Caldwell, Noland, and

elk near the Palmer Chapel in Cataloochee

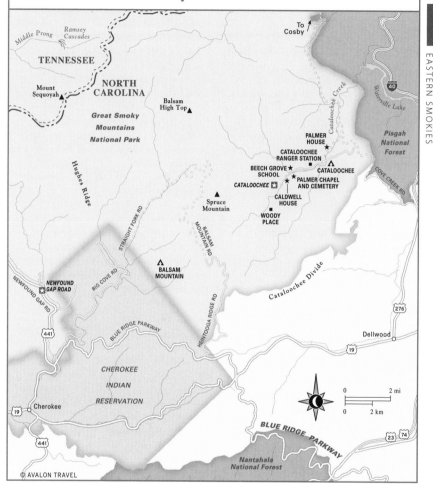

Cataloochee Valley

Palmer families gather here to eat, hold a short church service, and maintain the cemetery. Throughout the year there are some great opportunities to capture the chapel in all sorts of lighting, weather, and seasonal conditions.

Across the road is the **Beech Grove School,** the last of three schools to serve the children of the valley. It's empty save for a few artifacts. Beech Grove School operated on a very different school schedule than we're familiar with: The only regular school sessions were held from November to January, sometimes February and rarely into March. This odd schedule was built around the seasons, which freed children for planting and harvesting, as well as hunting and preserving food—staple activities for many living in the mountains

Just up the road is the **Caldwell House.** We know from records that the owner, Hiram Caldwell, was prosperous, but you could tell that just by comparing this 1906 home with the other historic homes in the park, which are, by and large, log cabins. The Caldwell House is frame-built (similar to houses now) with paneling on the interior walls.

The final structure is the **Palmer House,** located off Big Creek Road, not far from the Cataloochee Ranger Station. This was once a log home—two, actually, connected by a covered walkway called a dog trot—but as the owners came into money in the early 1900s they began making improvements and remodeling the home. They covered the exterior and interior with weatherboarding and began using fancy wallpaper in some rooms (scraps of the wallpaper are there today). When the son inherited the property, he remodeled it, adding rooms to the home and operating it as a boardinghouse. Renters were primarily anglers who came to fish in the three miles of stocked trout stream the family owned.

Hiking
BOOGERMAN TRAIL
Distance: 7.4-mile loop
Duration: 3.5-4 hours
Elevation gain: 1,050 feet
Difficulty: moderate
Trailhead: just past Cataloochee Campground

This trail isn't named for some fearsome and mythical creature from the woods; it's named for Robert "Boogerman" Palmer, the former owner of much of the land along this hike. Palmer is rumored to have earned his nickname in school, where he told his teacher that he wanted to be "the Boogerman" when he grew up. This trail is anything but fearsome, and in summer you'll likely see a few other hikers; if it's solitude you're seeking, hit the trail during the shoulder seasons.

Start the hike by crossing Palmer Creek. Follow Caldwell Fork upstream for nearly a mile and you'll come to Boogerman Trail. Turn left onto the trail and begin a gentle climb. When you reach a lower ridgeline, the path levels out, then descends through a grove of pine trees before ascending again. Soon, the trail makes a steep ascent to another level ridge. This section features some of the

largest trees, mostly poplars, that you'll see on this hike.

As you continue on this short ridgeline section, you'll encounter some signs of human settlement, the first of which is a stone wall. Continue your descent and cross the stream you're following a few times, passing more rock walls along the way. If the wildflowers aren't too high, you may spot a large, strange piece of metal just off the trail. It's the remnant of some sort of homesteading equipment, perhaps a sluice gate for a water flume, or maybe a piece from a sawmill. Whatever it is, it's alien here.

When you pass the decayed remains of a cabin, you're close to the junction with Caldwell Fork Trail. At Caldwell Fork Trail, turn right and cross Snake Branch (the stream you've been following) and soon thereafter, Caldwell Fork. You'll cross Caldwell Fork several more times before reaching the junction with Boogerman Trail and the path back to the trailhead.

Camping
The ★ **Cataloochee Campground** (877/444-6777, www.recreation.gov, Mar.-Oct., $20, reservations required) has 27 tent and RV sites. There is a horse camp with seven sites not far up the valley; down the valley there's a group campground with three sites and room for much larger parties. This highly recommended campsite is one of the most secluded you'll find in the front country.

BALSAM MOUNTAIN ROAD
14 MILES, 1.5 HOURS

Since most of the crowds who visit GSMNP use Newfound Gap Road exclusively, it's nice to find a route that's less traveled and possibly more beautiful. One such route is Balsam Mountain Road, a lovely drive where you may be lucky to see 10 other cars.

Accessible only from the Blue Ridge Parkway near Soco Gap, the road traverses 14 miles of ridgeline. To reach Balsam Mountain

The Return of Native Elk

Elk are native to the mountains of North Carolina and Tennessee, but overhunting decimated their population across the region. In North Carolina, the last elk was believed to have been killed in the late 1700s; in Tennessee, the mid-1800s. In 2001, the National Park Service reintroduced elk to the park by bringing 25 elk to GSMNP from Land Between the Lakes National Recreation Area in Kentucky. The next year they brought in another 27 animals. Today, they believe somewhere between 150 and 200 elk live in the park.

The majority of the elk can be seen in the **Cataloochee Valley,** though a small herd does live near the **Oconaluftee Visitor Center** and **Smokemont Campground** and can be seen wading across the river and grazing in the fields and forest there.

Adult males, called bulls, weigh 600-700 pounds, while females, referred to as cows, are around 500 pounds. Some bulls have antlers five feet across. They're territorial, and bulls do sometimes see humans as a threat and may charge. It's best to watch the elk from a safe distance. In GSMNP it is illegal to approach elk within 50 yards (150 feet) or any distance that disturbs or displaces the animals.

At certain times of year, you may see calves walking close by their mothers. Never approach or touch a calf. If an elk calf feels threatened and its mother is not nearby, its natural defense is to lie down and be still. It may look orphaned, but mom's within earshot, so back away slowly.

Elk are most active in the early morning and evening, much like deer. Also like deer, their diet is primarily grass, bark, leaves, and acorns. There are no natural predators of elk in the Smokies today, though sick, injured, and young elk are sometimes targets of opportunity for black bears, coyotes, or even the boldest of bobcats.

Road, turn off the Parkway at **Milepost 458** and follow Heintooga Ridge Road to the Heintooga Overlook and Picnic Area; here the road changes names to Balsam Mountain Road, and turns to gravel.

As soon as it turns into Balsam Mountain Road, it becomes one-way, so you're committed to follow it to its end. This will take about 1.5 hours (if you don't stop to hike or take in the scenery), primarily because the gravel road forces you to slow down. It's narrow but well maintained, so you can drive most cars along the route. If you're in doubt of the road's condition or are concerned about your vehicle's clearance, check online (www.nps.gov/grsm) for road closures and advisories.

Balsam Mountain Road is an excellent place to see **spring wildflowers,** summer rhododendron, and **fall leaves.** At these times, traffic may pick up, but the idea of a gravel road discourages enough visitors to keep this road the one less traveled.

When you've driven about 13 miles along Balsam Mountain Road, it becomes two-way again. Here, it begins to follow Straight Fork, which will lead you right onto Straight Fork Road, which cuts through the Cherokee Indian Reservation to US-441.

Camping

The ★ **Balsam Mountain Campground** (Heintooga Spur Rd., MP 458.2, first-come first-served, May-Oct., $14) is the highest campground in Great Smoky Mountains National Park at 5,310 feet. This primitive campground has 43 sites for tents and RVs, with a dedicated tents-only section. Amenities include an amphitheater, restrooms, and a ranger station with nearby access to Round Bottom Picnic Area and the Flat Creek trailhead. It's a beautiful, isolated campground that's often overlooked because it's slightly off the beaten path; that, in addition to the fact that it's a primitive campground (read: no showers), means that for most of the year you won't have many neighbors here. Plus, if you're driving a vehicle you feel comfortable driving on forest roads, the Balsam Mountain Road (sometimes called Round Bottom Road) continues on from the campground, making a nice trip through the forest down to Cherokee (it takes about two hours).

An equestrian-friendly campground at **Round Bottom Horse Camp** (Straight Fork-Round Bottom Rd., 865/436-1261, www.nps.gov/grsm or reserve at www.recreation.gov, Apr.-Oct., $20) has five campsites, stalls, and bedding for horses. Its location north of Cherokee, just inside the park and far up narrow Big Cove Road, makes it perfect for long rides with larger groups.

Western Smokies

The western Smokies are a bit wilder than the eastern Smokies. As pioneers moved in from the east, they first settled the coves and hollows there, then found passes through the Smokies and settled there. The mountains are tall and steep, and the valleys deep, and where there are coves and meadows, they're broad, rich-soiled places that, before the national park, were home to several small communities.

LITTLE RIVER ROAD
Elkmont
At the Elkmont Campground, only eight miles from Gatlinburg, drifts of male **fireflies** rise up from the grass to flash their mating signal, but they don't do so as individuals—they blink in coordinated ways that still baffle researchers. For a two-week window every summer (often early to mid-July, but it depends on a variety of factors), their nightly light show delights crowds. It starts slowly, with only a few of these insects showing off. Then more join in, and more until they reach a crescendo. Slowly, they begin to synchronize until, at the peak, whole fields may flash all at once, giving you a sudden and startling blink of light and just as sudden darkness. Or they may flash in waves moving around the fields and hillsides. Or large groups may appear to flash their lights at one another and wait in the darkness for a response. Whatever the reason for their display, the synchronous fireflies are amazing little creatures. Nineteen species of fireflies live in GSMNP, but these are the only fireflies in the park to synchronize their flashing.

The synchronous fireflies may have been one of the reasons the Wonderland Park Hotel was built here in Elkmont. In 1908, the little logging town of Elkmont was born, and in 1912, the Wonderland Park Hotel was built. Cottages dotted the hillsides and bottoms. Once the park was established, cottage owners were granted lifetime leases on their property, and family members continued to renew the leases at 20-year intervals until the early 1990s. The Wonderland Park Hotel and the cottages were at one time slated for demolition, but the **Elkmont Historic District** is now listed in the National Register of Historic Places. The hotel collapsed in the early 2000s, and the Park Service has visions of restoring a few of the remaining cottages, but work has yet to begin in earnest.

Hiking
LAUREL FALLS TRAIL
Distance: 2.5 miles round-trip
Duration: 1.5-2 hours
Elevation gain: 400 feet
Difficulty: easy to moderate
Trailhead: parking area 3.9 miles west of Sugarlands Visitor Center on Little River Road

As the shortest and possibly easiest waterfall hike in Great Smoky Mountains National Park, Laurel Falls is the most popular of such hikes. The trail is paved and the grade is gentle (after you get past a short, steep section at the start of the trail), and the falls are a little over 1.3 miles from the trailhead.

Prepare to be dazzled when you reach the falls. Laurel Falls drops 75 feet in a wide, picture-perfect cascade. It's a gorgeous spot to

The Firefly Lottery

Viewing the synchronous fireflies at Elkmont is deservedly popular—so much so, that in 2016, the park instituted a lottery system to control access and limit traffic congestion. The new lottery assigns parking passes and provides shuttle transportation during the eight days of the event (late-May to early June). Hopeful visitors can apply online during the three days the **lottery** (877/444-6777, www.recreation.gov, limit one pass per household, passes are free, $1.50 application fee) is open; applicants will have two dates to choose from. Once the lottery closes, results become available about a week later. Up to 1,800 parking passes will be made available (about 225 cars per day). The lucky winners will receive a parking pass for Sugarlands Visitor Center; after parking at your assigned arrival time, you'll board the shuttle to Elkmont and back.

In 2016, the lottery opened on April 29 and closed May 2. Successful applicants received notices of their passes by May 10. At time of publication, it remains to be seen whether the lottery system was successful, or the resulting impact on attendance. While there are other places within the park to see fireflies—pretty much any meadow or grassy area—only Elkmont has the synchronous fireflies.

photograph, but you have to be there early in the day to get a shot of the falls without people in it.

Camping

The **Elkmont Campground** (434 Elkmont Rd., Gatlinburg, TN, 865/430-5560, www.recreation.gov, $17-23) has 220 campsites, 55 of them along the Little River, with front-row seats to the firefly light show for those here at the right time. This is the largest of the campgrounds in GSMNP, and one of the most visited. In addition to the firefly show and the attraction of Little River, this site also serves as a good base for exploring the area.

Elkmont Campground Concessions (www.elkmontcampgroundconcession.net, 4pm-8pm daily Mar. 8-May, 9am-9pm daily June-Aug. 15, 4pm-8pm daily Aug. 16-Oct., 4pm-6pm daily Nov.) has a handful of snack foods and beverages as well as firewood, ice, and a few camping items.

CADES COVE

Easily the most popular auto tour loop in Great Smoky Mountains National Park, Cades Cove receives around two million visitors a year. They come for the scenery—a long, wide, grassy-bottomed valley surrounded by undulating mountains—to see the handful of preserved homesteads and historic structures,

and because it's one of the park's best, and most reliable, spots to see wildlife.

★ Cades Cove Loop
11 MILES, 2-4 HOURS

The **Cades Cove Loop** is approximately 11 miles long, but in summer and especially in fall when the leaves are at their best, expect to spend two hours or more on this one-way road through the valley floor—and that's if you don't stop to photograph the wildlife or explore the historic structures. If you're the curious type or find the light is perfect for taking pictures, you can easily double the amount of time you spend here. When you do stop, be sure to pull off the road and leave enough room for traffic to pass. One source of traffic jams in Cades Cove is visitors who stop in the middle of the road to ooh and aah at the wildlife and scenery.

The popularity of this drive is very well deserved. In the hours around dawn and dusk, wildlife is especially active. Vast herds of white-tailed deer are the most common sight (I once tallied 50 in a field before I quit counting), but black bears are also frequently spotted. The bears like to cozy up to the apple trees that dot the cove, and you'll occasionally spot them and their cubs napping or eating in the branches.

You may notice that the fields look

especially manicured. They are, to an extent. Far from being mown and maintained like a golf course, the fields in Cades Cove are allowed to run wild, but only so wild. The National Park Service maintains the fields and fences, mowing, repairing, and reseeding as necessary to keep the valley looking much like it did when settlers lived here.

To take this lovely-in-any-season drive, follow Little River Road west from the Sugarlands Visitor Center for 17.2 miles; there it will turn into Laurel Creek Road and lead you into Cades Cove in another 7.4 miles. You can also access Cades Cove by entering the park at Townsend on TN-73, then turning right on Laurel Creek Road, following it for 16 miles to the entrance to the cove. Cades Cove is **closed to vehicle** traffic every Saturday and Wednesday morning from May until late September. On those days, the loop is **open exclusively to bicycle and foot traffic** until 10am. The rest of the year the road is open to motor vehicles from sunrise to sunset daily, weather permitting.

Sights

According to some historians, long before European settlers pushed west through the Smokies the Cherokee Indians had hunting camps and possibly even a small settlement established in Cades Cove. In fact, the name Cades Cove is believed to have come from Chief Kade, a little-known Cherokee leader. By the early 1820s, the first Europeans were here, building cabins and barns and carving homesteads out of the forest. More settlers arrived having heard of the rich, fertile bottomland in Cades Cove, and by 1850 nearly 700 people called the valley home. As the collection of cabins and homesteads grew into a community, buildings like churches and schools were constructed. Families lived here even after the National Park Service began purchasing land. The last remaining school in Cades Cove closed in 1944 and the post office closed in 1947.

Today a number of historic structures remain standing along the valley floor. Among them is the most photographed structure in the park, the **Methodist Church.** From time to time a wedding is held here, though it's more common for visitors to leave handwritten prayers on scraps of paper at the altar.

The **Cable Mill Area** is the busiest section of the loop. Here you can see an actual mill in operation, and even buy cornmeal or flour ground on-site. In addition to the mill and Methodist Church, the area contains two

deer graze in a field at Cades Cove

other churches, a few barns and log houses, and a number of smaller structures.

Halfway around the loop, you'll find the **Cades Cove Visitor Center** (Cades Cove Loop Rd., Townsend, TN, 865/448-2472, 9am-4:30pm daily Dec.-Jan., except Christmas Day, 9am-5:30pm daily Feb. and Nov., 9am-6:30pm daily Mar. and Sept.-Oct., 9am-7pm daily Apr. and Aug., 9am-7:30pm daily May-June), which has a good bookstore and gift shop, and, most importantly, the only public restroom you'll find on the tour.

Hiking
ABRAMS FALLS TRAIL
Distance: 5 miles out and back
Duration: 3 hours
Elevation gain: 350 feet
Difficulty: moderate
Trailhead: Turn right onto a gravel road 4.9 miles from the start of the Cades Cove Loop; at 0.4 mile in is a parking area and the trailhead.

Several trails lead off into the woods from this parking area, but it's obvious which route to take—the most well-worn trail you see. If you're in doubt, follow the group in front of you, as Abrams Falls is the destination for most hikers who set off from this lot. Only a few steps from the trailhead is a kiosk that will set you on the right path.

The trail is pretty straightforward—it follows Abrams Creek all the way to the waterfall. The only real elevation gains come when you thrice leave the creek to climb up and around a ridge, crossing a feeder stream in the process. The first stream is Arbutus Branch, then Stony Branch, then Wilson Branch, which is very close to the falls.

After you cross Wilson Branch on a log bridge, you'll follow the trail downstream, cross Wilson Branch once again, and arrive at the falls.

Abrams Falls is pretty, and in wet weather can be downright thunderous. Slick, mossy rocks make up the wall where the 20-foot waterfall, which has the largest volume of water of any waterfall in the park, tumbles into the pool below. Tempted as you may be to take a dip after a sweaty hike, don't do it; the currents are strong and a few folks have drowned here.

ROCKY TOP AND THUNDERHEAD MOUNTAINS TRAIL
Distance: 13.9 miles out and back
Duration: 7-8 hours
Elevation gain: 3,665 feet
Difficulty: strenuous
Trailhead: Anthony Creek Trailhead at the Cades Cove picnic area

Hiking to the famed Rocky Top is borderline brutal—you gain more than 3,500 feet in elevation, and on the trail's first few miles you share the path with horses, so it can get quite muddy and slippery. However, this exceptional hike is worth it. Time your hike for mid-June to see the rhododendron and mountain laurel in full bloom.

Shortly after starting the Anthony Creek Trail, you'll reach Crib Trail Junction, then Anthony Creek Horse Camp. Follow Anthony Creek Trail 3.5 miles to the Bote Mountain Trail, where hikers will turn right.

Climbing Bote Mountain Trail, you'll enter a long series of rhododendron "tunnels" and at 5.1 miles in, you'll reach Spence Field and the Appalachian Trail. Turn left and you'll get some stunning views of North Carolina and equally stunning views of hillsides and meadows covered in mountain laurel. Continue east along the Appalachian Trail to reach Rocky Top and Thunderhead Mountain.

Thunderhead Mountain is made up of three distinct summits. The first summit is Rocky Top, 1.2 miles from the Bote Mountain/Appalachian Trail junction and arguably the best view in the park. Next is the middle peak, sometimes called Rocky Top Two, just 0.3 miles beyond Rocky Top. Finally, another 0.3 miles on, is the unremarkable summit of Thunderhead. Many hikers turn around at Rocky Top, never summiting Thunderhead.

★ RICH MOUNTAIN LOOP
Distance: 8.5-mile loop
Duration: 4-4.5 hours
Elevation gain: 1,740 feet

Difficulty: moderate

Trailhead: Park at the entrance gate to Cades Cove; the trail begins in the opposite parking lot.

The first part of this hike passes one of the meadows that makes Cades Cove such a fabulous place. For 1.4 miles you'll walk through the woods and along the edge of the meadow until you reach the John Oliver Cabin.

The trail continues behind the cabin and soon meets up with Martha's Branch and begins to climb. As you climb, you'll cross the branch a number of times. At mile 3, you'll find a place where you have a tight view of Cades Cove; don't sweat it, better views are coming.

Continue 0.3 miles to Indian Grave Gap Trail and turn right. In 0.8 miles is Campsite 5 (for backpackers) and the junction with Rich Mountain Trail. The saddle here has nice views.

Avoid the junction and follow Indian Grave Gap Trail 0.3 miles to a side trail. This path is only about 100 yards long and takes you to the highest point on Rich Mountain, Cerulean Knob, and the foundation of the former fire tower. Views are okay, but not fantastic. Get back to the main trail and continue east where you'll find a much better view than on the top.

When you reach a power-line clearance, you're almost at Scott Mountain Trail and Campsite 4. From the junction of these trails, continue straight ahead on Crooked Arm Ridge Trail (it's what Indian Grave Gap Trail turns into). This trail is steep and rutted and littered with the evidence of horses, so watch your step—that horse evidence can be slippery.

This trail leads back to Rich Mountain Loop Trail 0.5 mile from the parking area.

Biking

The **Cades Cove Camp Store** (near Cades Cove Campground, 865/448-9034, 9am-5pm daily, hours change seasonally) rents bicycles in summer and fall (adult bikes $7.50/hour, kids' bikes $4.50/hour). From the second week in May to the second-to-last Saturday in September, the park closes off the loop road through Caves Cove on Wednesday and Saturday mornings, sunrise-10am, so that cyclists and hikers can enjoy the cove without having to worry about automobile traffic.

Camping

The **Cades Cove Campground** (10042 Campground Dr., Townsend, TN, 877/444-6777, www.recreation.gov, $17-20) is a popular spot where you'll definitely want to reserve a campsite. This campground is open year-round, and though the occupancy is a little lower in the dead of winter, you'll still find a few intrepid visitors taking refuge from the cold in one of the 159 campsites here. Hikers, take note: There are several backcountry campsites off the trails in Cades Cove, making it a good base for overnight trips.

At the **Cades Cove Camp Store** (865/448-9034, www.cadescovetrading.com, 9am-5pm daily Mar.-May, 9am-9pm daily June-Aug. 15, 9am-5pm daily Aug. 16-Nov.) you can grab breakfast, a sandwich or wrap, pizza, and other snack bar items as well as a very limited selection of groceries and camping supplies.

Parsons Branch Road
10 MILES, 1 HOUR

Parsons Branch Road (closed in winter) is a great drive. Take a right turn just beyond the Cades Cove Visitor Center parking area and you'll find yourself on a 10-mile long, one-way gravel road leading to US-129 and Deals Gap on the extreme southwestern edge of the park. At times pothole riddled and crossing 18 or so small streams along the way, the road is a slow one, taking around an hour to drive. If you're careful, the drive is doable in a sedan, but you may feel more comfortable in a vehicle with a little more clearance.

The road passes **Henry Whitehead Place,** an odd-looking pair of conjoined cabins with an interesting backstory. Henry Whitehead, a widower with three daughters, remarried Matilda Shields Gregory after she and her small child had been abandoned by her husband. During the crisis, the community rallied and built her the small cabin,

Black Bears

Biologists estimate there are more than 1,500 black bears living in Great Smoky Mountains National Park, and if you know where and when to look, your chances of seeing one in the wild are quite good.

Though I've seen bears in a number of spots throughout the park, one of the most reliable places to see them is Cades Cove. Here, in the early morning and as dusk settles, the bears are more active, prowling the forest's edge and even eating apples that have fallen from the trees.

As awesome as it is to see a bear, they can present a problem to park visitors, and we can present a problem to them. With the great number of visitors to GSMNP, many bears have grown accustomed to seeing people and have therefore lost their natural fear of humans, automobiles, and horses. As they grow more used to people, we decide to give them "treats" and lure them closer to our cars and our campsites with food. Bears that are too accustomed to people, especially bears that have been fed a few times, can grow bold, even borderline aggressive, searching campsites and open cars for food or even approaching open car windows or picnic tables.

Fortunately, serious incidents with black bears are rare, but they do happen. In 2000, a mother bear and her cub attacked and killed a camper near the Elkmont Campground. Every year, campsites and trails are closed due to bear activity and the potential for interaction between bears and visitors.

Park staff and volunteers do their best to educate visitors on proper human-bear interaction. Throughout the park you'll see signs and placards advising you on how to properly store and dispose of food and reminding you not to approach bears. Remember that bears are wild animals and unpredictable, and keep these tips in mind:

- **Do not approach** within 50 yards or any distance that disturbs a bear, and do not allow a bear to approach you. For a good view, invest in a pair of binoculars.

- **Never feed bears.** It only gets them used to humans and causes them to think of us as a source of food.

- **Store food** in appropriate containers and in the proper places when camping. If you're not sure of the proper procedure, ask a ranger.

- **Dispose of garbage** in bear-proof receptacles.

- **Report** nuisance bear behavior or visitors breaking these rules to park officials.

In the unlikely event that **a bear approaches you,** stand tall, wave your arms, and make as much noise as possible. If you need to, throw sticks or rocks at the bear. In most cases, this will intimidate the bear and deter it from coming any closer. If the bear charges, don't run—they can sprint 30 miles per hour, so you don't stand a chance. Instead, keep making noise and back away slowly, never turning your back to the bear. Often, bears will make bluff charges, so this is likely what you're seeing. If a black bear actually makes contact, fight back with anything and everything available to you; with a loud-enough and fierce-enough fight, the bear may see you as too much to deal with and leave you alone.

which is in back of the main structure that Whitehead built after they married.

You'll cross the same stream several times before climbing to the crest of the drive. Here you'll find the trailheads for the Hannah Mountain and Gregory Bald Trails. This is the halfway mark of the road and it is, as they say, all downhill from here.

DEEP CREEK

Just south of Cherokee and just north of Bryson City, Deep Creek is a spot more popular with locals than tourists, but it's worth a stop. Deep Creek is relatively placid, aside from a couple of waterfalls a ways upstream. If you're not into wading or tubing, don't worry—this is a lovely place to picnic and hike or even camp away from the crowds found in some of the more popular spots in the park.

Hiking

There are two nice waterfalls to see here. Juney Whank Falls (what a name, right?) is less than a half mile from the Deep Creek Campground and cuts an impressive figure as it drops a total of 90 feet in two stages. Indian Creek Falls is a stunning, 60-foot-high set of falls and cascades located a mile from the campground.

JUNEY WHANK FALLS TRAIL

Distance: 0.6-mile loop
Duration: 30 minutes
Elevation gain: 120 feet
Difficulty: moderate
Trailhead: parking area at the end of Deep Creek Road across from the campground

Juney Whank Falls supposedly got its name from Junaluska "Juney" Whank, a Cherokee Indian said to have been buried near the falls. The path here is pretty straightforward: it's short, at times steep, and at the end, a little slick. You'll walk across a log bridge to get a look at the tall, skinny falls, which actually descend in two stages. The first stage drops 40 feet to a stone outcropping, then flows beneath the log bridge to fall and cascade another 50 feet.

INDIAN CREEK FALLS TRAIL

Distance: 2 miles round-trip
Duration: 1 hour
Elevation gain: 160 feet
Difficulty: easy to moderate
Trailhead: parking area at the end of Deep Creek Road across from the campground

This easier but longer hike takes you past a smaller waterfall, Tom's Branch Falls, on your way to Indian Creek Falls. For about a mile, you'll follow a gently graded roadbed, and soon you'll arrive at the falls. Really, Indian Creek Falls is more of a steep, long, slick cascade of water than an actual waterfall, but it's quite serene.

Camping

At the end of Deep Creek Road are the trailheads leading to the waterfalls. You'll also find the **Deep Creek Campground** (877/444-6777, www.recreation.gov, Apr.-Oct., $17). There are nearly 100 campsites here, many of which fill up with locals. If you want to camp here, arrive early or reserve well in advance.

Outside the park, there's also the **Deep Creek Tube Center and Campground** (1090 W. Deep Creek Rd., Bryson City, NC, 828/488-6055, www.deepcreekcamping.com, camping $23-50, cabins $69-195), a charming collection of tent and RV campsites and cabins for rent. As the name implies, they rent tubes for use on Deep Creek. Rentals ($5 for all-day use of your tube) are cheap, so you can play in the water as long as you like.

Road to Nowhere

An odd place to visit is the so-called **Road to Nowhere.** Just south of the Deep Creek entrance outside Bryson City is a short stretch of highway leading north into GSMNP. Lonely, even spooky, the road is all that remains of a parkway planned to trace a path through the Smokies along Fontana Lake. Construction was started on the parkway before being abandoned. Today, the road stops quite abruptly about six miles inside the park, at a stone tunnel. Though hard feelings over the failed parkway have softened, many families still hold a grudge against government officials who vowed to build a road along the lake to provide access to old family cemeteries there.

Cars are prohibited from using the tunnel at the end of the Road to Nowhere, but visitors on foot are welcome to stroll right through. After you pass through the tunnel, there's a marathon-length hike—seriously, it's 26 miles—weaving along the northern bank of Fontana Lake.

FONTANA LAKE AREA

At the southern edge of GSMNP lies Fontana Lake, a 10,230-acre reservoir created in the 1940s as part of the Tennessee Valley Authority's (TVA) efforts to supply electricity

Cades Cove and Fontana Lake Area

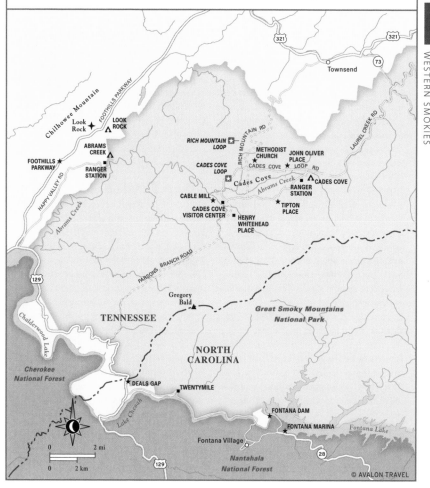

to the various communities and government and industrial facilities in the region.

Fontana Dam

The 480-foot-tall, 2,365-foot-wide **Fontana Dam,** complete with three hydroelectric generators, was completed in 1944. It provided much-needed electricity to the factories churning out materials for World War II, including Oak Ridge, Tennessee, where research leading to the atomic bomb was conducted.

To build Fontana Dam, the Tennessee Valley Authority (TVA) purchased more than 1,000 tracts of land and relocated roughly 600 families comprising five communities. Those folks left behind homes, schools, churches, and barns, all of which were covered by the lake. This displacement of so many families and elimination of these small communities was part of the tradeoff that resulted in the modernization of the region via cheap, readily available electric power, and the great number of jobs required to complete the project. The dam also provides much-needed flood control to a region that receives between 55 and 82 inches of rainfall each year. The TVA can regulate the depth of the lake by releasing water in anticipation of flood events, and the water level of Fontana Lake can vary by as much as 50 feet.

Fontana Dam is the highest concrete dam east of the Mississippi, and its impoundment provides great recreational opportunities. The Appalachian Trail crosses the dam itself, and thousands of boaters and anglers take to the lake each year. There are more than 238 miles of shoreline along Fontana Lake, and over 10,000 acres of water surface. If you have your own boat you can launch it from the **Fontana Marina** (40 Fontana Dam Rd., 828/498-2129, www.fontanavillage.com), or you can rent a kayak, canoe, or paddleboard (from $20/hour to $100/day) or a pontoon or fishing pontoon boat (from $50/hour to $330/day). Fishing guide services and seasonal tours of the lake are also available.

The exhibits at the **Fontana Dam Visitor Center** (Fontana Dam Rd., off NC-28 near the state line, www.tva.com/sites/fontana. htm, 9am-6pm daily May-Oct., free) tell the story of the region and the construction of the dam. There's also a small gift shop, and a viewing platform overlooking the dam. Hikers take note: They also sell backcountry camping permits and have showers in the back.

Accommodations and Food

Just outside the park, **Fontana Village** (300 Woods Rd., Fontana Dam, 828/498-2211 or 800/849-2258, www.fontanavillage.com, lodge $109-219, cabins $109-459, camping $15-40) offers a place to lay your head in your choice of accommodations: tent or RV camping, one- to three-bedroom cabins, and lodge rooms. There are 100 lodge rooms, 110 cabins, and 20 campsites. At the lodge you'll find complimentary wireless Internet in the public areas; other amenities include an outdoor pool and lazy river, as well as a fitness center and small day spa.

The complex contains two restaurants, a snack bar, an ice cream shop, and a general store. **Mountainview Restaurant** (828/498-2211, 7:30am-2:30pm and 5:30pm-8pm daily, breakfast $4-9, lunch $8-14, dinner $14-28) serves steaks, chicken, and a nice selection of seafood that includes several preparations of trout. Reservations are recommended during weekends and in peak season. **Wildwood Grill** (828/498-2211, 11:30am-9pm daily Apr.-Oct., $8-19) serves pizza, burgers, and an array of fried appetizers. In the summer, concerts on the deck give visitors a little listening enjoyment to go with dinner.

TWENTYMILE

One of the most remote sections of the park, Twentymile is on the southern end, just past Fontana Lake and Dam and alongside the smaller Cheoah Lake. Despite the name, Twentymile Trail only goes five miles into GSMNP, but you can make it into a 20-mile journey by combining it with other trails, or you can keep it to a manageable day hike of around eight miles by doing a smaller loop. Though this part of the park is out of the way, Twentymile is a popular hike, so expect to see some fellow hikers, especially on weekends and through the week on beautiful days in summer and autumn. There is a trio of **backcountry campsites** (reserve at www. smokiespermits.nps.gov) at Twentymile Trail: campsites 13, 92, and 93.

Hiking

TWENTYMILE LOOP TRAIL

Distance: 7.6-mile loop
Duration: 3.5-4 hours
Elevation gain: 1,200 feet
Difficulty: easy
Trailhead: Twentymile Ranger Station
Directions: Twentymile Ranger Station is six miles west from Fontana Dam on NC-28. Turn at the sign for Twentymile.

This hike is very easy, following a roadbed and a well-maintained trail along Twentymile Trail, Twentymile Loop Trail, and Wolf Ridge Trail. There are a number of stream crossings along this route, and though there are log bridges spanning Moore Springs Branch and Twentymile Creek, floods may wash them away, and if you're there before repair crews can fix the bridges you may have to wade across.

From the trailhead, go a half mile to where Wolf Ridge Trail branches off to the left. Follow Wolf Ridge Trail for 1.1 miles to Twentymile Loop Trail. Along Wolf Ridge, you'll cross Moore Springs Branch five times as you climb. Along the way, there are abundant wildflowers, including bloodroot, fire pink, and trilliums, and the opportunity to see bears, deer, and other wildlife.

After following Wolf Ridge just over a mile, you'll see Twentymile Loop Trail branching off to the right. Cross Moore Springs Branch and follow the trail 2.9 miles along an easy grade before descending to a crossing of Twentymile Creek and the junction with Twentymile Trail.

Turn right on Twentymile Trail to descend back along the creek and to the trailhead. From here, it's just over three miles back to your car.

GREGORY BALD VIA TWENTYMILE TRAIL

Distance: 15.7-mile loop
Duration: 9 hours—strenuous day hike or overnighter
Elevation gain: 3,650 feet
Difficulty: strenuous
Trailhead: Twentymile Ranger Station
Directions: Twentymile Ranger Station is six miles west from Fontana Dam on NC-28. Turn at the sign for Twentymile.

This hike makes Twentymile live up to its name, even though it's a mere 15.7 miles. It's doable in a day, but it's a long, hard day, so camping for a night in the backcountry is recommended.

From the trailhead, follow Twentymile Trail for 0.5 mile until it intersects with Wolf Ridge Trail. Turn here and follow Wolf Ridge Trail 6.3 miles to Gregory Bald Trail. The grade of Wolf Ridge Trail is somewhat steep, but more than that, it's a relentless uphill climb all the way to where you crest the ridge before reaching Parson Bald. As you approach the ridge and Parson Bald, you'll find copious amounts of blueberry bushes, and, if they're in season, a fair number of bears enjoying blueberries. The same holds true at Parson Bald, just over the ridge. If you're on the trail in August, when the blueberries tend to ripen, be cautious.

When you reach Parson Bald, it's a short, easy walk to Sheep Pen Gap, where you'll find **Campsite 13** (reservations and information 865/436-1297, www.smokiespermits.nps.gov) and the end of Wolf Ridge Trail. Turn right on Gregory Bald Trail and climb just under a half mile to Gregory Bald. There are azaleas in great abundance and during midsummer the bald is a riot of blooms. But even if you come when there's not a bloom to be found, the views make the hike worth it.

From here, keep heading east to Rich Gap, where you'll come upon a four-way trail junction. Follow Long Hungry Ridge Trail to the right, heading south. This trail is pretty flat for the first mile, then it begins to descend, and the descent becomes increasingly noticeable as you move down the trail. You'll find Campsite 92 3.4 miles from Rich Gap. Once you've reached the campsite, you've left the steepest part of the hike behind you.

Continue down Long Hungry Ridge Trail to the place where it meets Twentymile Trail, following Twentymile Creek 2.6 miles back to the junction with Wolf Ridge Trail. At this point, you're only 0.5 mile from the trailhead.

Transportation and Services

CAR

The 33-mile-long Newfound Gap Road (US-441) bisects the park from north to south. It's the most heavily traveled route in the park and provides a good introduction for first-time visitors. Newfound Gap Road starts at the southern terminus of the Blue Ridge Parkway, just outside of Cherokee, North Carolina, and ends in Knoxville, Tennessee, 70 miles to the northwest through Great Smoky Mountains National Park.

From Cherokee, you can head straight to the eastern entrance of GSMNP via Newfound Gap Road. Take US-441/TN-71 north through GSMNP and into Gatlinburg, Tennessee. It's easy to make the trip from one end to the other in an afternoon, though it may take a little longer in peak seasons. Knoxville, Tennessee, is 36 miles to the northwest of Great Smoky Mountains National Park along US-441 and TN-71.

There are **no gas stations** along Newfound Gap Road. You'll need to fuel up and buy snacks in Cherokee.

AIR

Asheville Regional Airport (61 Terminal Dr., Asheville, NC, 828/684-2226, www.flyavl.com) is about one hour east of Cherokee. **McGhee Tyson Airport** (2055 Alcoa Hwy., Alcoa, TN, 865/342-3000, www.tys.org) is about one hour west of Gatlinburg.

SERVICES

Groceries and camping supplies are quite limited in GSMNP. Food is virtually nonexistent, so bring snacks. The Sugarlands and Oconaluftee Visitor Centers have a small selection of vending machine beverages and a few convenience items (batteries, memory cards), but little else. The nearest hospital is **Swain County Hospital** (45 Plateau St., Bryson City, NC, 828/488-2155, www.westcarehealth.org), a little less than 30 minutes from the eastern park entrance in Cherokee.

Knoxville and the Tennessee Foothills

Look for ★ to find recommended
sights, activities, dining, and lodging.

Highlights

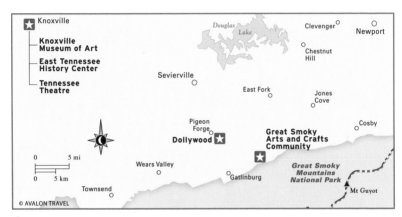

© AVALON TRAVEL

★ **Great Smoky Arts and Crafts Community:** Interact with more than 120 artists, artisans, and craftspeople as they practice traditional Appalachian arts (page 224).

★ **Dollywood:** Roller coasters go hand in hand with Appalachian music, culture, and history at this theme park owned by a country music legend (page 229).

★ **East Tennessee History Center:** This landmark tells the story of the Tennessee foothills through surprising exhibits (page 237).

★ **Knoxville Museum of Art:** This marble building houses an impressive collection of contemporary pieces, including works by artists native to the city and region (page 237).

★ **Tennessee Theatre:** The official state theater of Tennessee is an architectural marvel and glimpse of Gilded Age opulence (page 238).

There was a time when this was the frontier, when the Smoky Mountains stood too high and too rough to pass.

But settlers made their way across this a huge green wall with what few supplies they could carry to carve out an existence in the virgin wilderness, not to mention the threat—or perceived threat—of hostile natives. They found coves of rich bottomland around which to settle outposts. Eventually these outposts turned into communities, which turned into towns and cities, and something like what we see today was carved out of the wild—Gatlinburg at the foot of the Smokies, Pigeon Forge on the river just a few miles distant, and Knoxville growing large on the bluffs of the deep, wide Tennessee River.

Today the setup is the same, but the inherent risks of frontier life are gone. In their place, Gatlinburg and Pigeon Forge are tourist hot spots, or even tourist traps. (I mean that in the most flattering, fun, kitsch-filled sense of the term.) Gatlinburg is, proudly, the gateway to the Smokies, and Great Smoky Mountains National Park rubs shoulders with the town limits. Not to be outdone, Pigeon Forge is the home of Dollywood—an amusement park that's part rides, part Appalachian culture, and part homage to Dolly Parton's childhood.

The two towns are bright dots of light connected by a glittering ribbon—a sharp contrast to their next-door neighbor, the most-visited national park in the United States. Some 30 miles west of the park, Knoxville is the nearest city of any size, and it's as pretty and proper a Southern city as there ever has been. It offers a cosmopolitan respite from the wildness of the Smokies and the country kitsch of Gatlinburg and Pigeon Forge, all while maintaining its own identity as an intellectual and creative urban center that's grown up but has never forgotten its roots.

PLANNING YOUR TIME

To get a true sense of this complex place and a real taste of the cultures at work here, plan to spend at least **four days.** Split your time evenly between Gatlinburg and Pigeon Forge, with two days in each. (The in-your-face faux-hillbilly attractions are so silly you can't help but embrace them.) Pay

---

Previous: path near the Smoky Mountains; downtown Knoxville. **Above:** mural in Knoxville.

Knoxville and the Tennessee Foothills

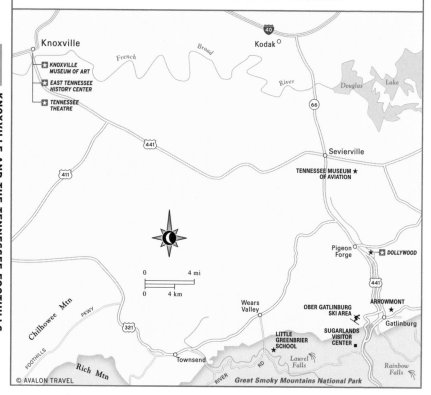

a visit to the Great Smoky Arts and Crafts Community, where more than 120 artists, artisans, and craftspeople practice traditional Appalachian arts. Head to Dollywood for a sense of the area's history while waiting in line for a roller coaster. Taste some traditional food—from barbecue to country-kitchen standards—and clear the slate for an evening of moonshine tasting, as most distilleries use versions of old family recipes likely made in the nearby hills.

After that, head to Knoxville for **two days** and soak in the contemporary, creative vibe of the city. You'll likely hear some traditional or bluegrass musicians, but listen close and you'll find the ways they're making these old styles current. At the Knoxville Museum of Art, and throughout downtown,

the art here is certainly of the place, and seeing how it blends old with new gives you an idea of how these worlds come together. Visit the Ijams Nature Center, one of the premier urban wilderness areas in the nation, and see why several magazines have called this city one of the top outdoor towns in the South. If you're here on a weekend, Market Square is a happening spot with outdoor concerts, plenty of al fresco dining options, and a lovely farmers market.

When to Go

Winter is the slowest time here. Great Smoky Mountains National Park, a major draw for Gatlinburg, sees fewer visitors; Dollywood, the major draw for Pigeon Forge, shuts down for the season. Knoxville is also slower, but it's still a city, so there's plenty to do.

Spring gets busy; it also gets rainy. Those rains bring out wildflowers and gardens in full, glorious bloom, and visitors flock in earnest as soon as the first buds show themselves.

Summer can get warm and a little humid, but brings loads of visitors. Dollywood opens, and the number of visitors grows as the temperatures climb. The cool hollows of the Smokies offer a respite from the heat, while Dollywood's Splash Country waterpark lets you cool off in a different way.

Autumn is prime time in this region. Visitors come to Knoxville to watch autumn leaves turn…and to watch University of Tennessee football. On game weekends, you may have a hard time finding parking, a hotel, a dinner reservation, or a Knoxville resident not wearing a bright Tennessee-orange shirt. Gatlinburg and Pigeon Forge are packed as well, with visitors driving through Great Smoky Mountains National Park to take thousands of photos of the awesome autumnal color. Traffic is heavy and rooms should be booked well ahead of time. It's worth the minor hassle of the crowds, though. The Smokies are stunning when the leaves change, and Knoxville on game day—especially if you score a ticket—is absolutely boiling with energy.

Gatlinburg

On a typical Saturday night, when 40,000 people pack the restaurants and sidewalks of Gatlinburg, you would never know that only about 4,000 people live here. As the unofficial capital of the Smokies and gateway to the national park, Gatlinburg benefits greatly from the 10 million visitors drawn here for the views, the wildlife, the hikes, and the kitsch. And if there's anything Gatlinburg has in abundance, it's kitsch.

Gatlinburg is unabashedly a tourist town, and owning up to that fact makes it all the more charming. On Parkway, the cheekily named main drag, there are T-shirt shops, candy stores and fudgeries, taffy pullers, more than one Ripley's attraction, novelties both racy (in that family-friendly, double-entendre way) and tame, knife shops, mini golf, ice cream parlors, restaurants, and more odd little art, craft, and gift shops than you can count. Don't let that deter you from staying (and even enjoying yourself) here. The Ripley's Aquarium is quite nice, and at Great Smoky Arts and Crafts Community and the Arrowcraft Shop, you'll find modern interpretations of traditional mountain arts that were handmade nearby.

SIGHTS
Space Needle

All of downtown Gatlinburg is a sight to behold. The mountains surround you, that namesake Smoky mist rising from them, and the street glitters and twinkles like a sort of vacationland Milky Way. One of the best ways to take it all in is from the **Space Needle** (115 Historic Nature Trail, 865-436-4629, www.gatlinburgspaceneedle.com, 9am-midnight Sun.-Thurs., 9am-1am Fri.-Sat., adults $9.50, seniors and military $6, children 4-11 $5, free under 3). I know what you're thinking, "But the Space Needle is in Seattle." Yeah, it is; this is the other one. From the observation deck 407 feet above Gatlinburg, you have truly stellar views. For the best views, get to the top shortly before sundown and watch as the mountains darken and the strip of downtown comes alive with lights. At the foot of the tower, there's a two-level, 25,000-square-foot arcade with games galore, laser tag, a gift shop, snack bar, and restrooms.

Gatlinburg Sky Lift

The **Gatlinburg Sky Lift** (765 Parkway, 865-436-4307, www.gatlinburgskylift.com,

Gatlinburg

© AVALON TRAVEL

To Ober Gatlinburg And Mountain Laurel Chalets

LODGE AT BUCKBERRY CREEK

CAMPBELL LEAD RD

GATLINBURG BYPASS

PARKWAY BYPASS

PARKWAY

441
71

Great Smoky Mountains

National Park

SKI MOUNTAIN RD

LONG BRANCH RD

SUNSET DR

COTTAGE DR

THE PEDDLER
SKI MOUNTAIN RD
RIVER RD

BIG DADDY'S PIZZERIA

LONG BRANCH RD

MAIN ST

ROUTE ST

ECON

SUGARLANDS DISTILLING

SAVAGE GARDEN RD

NANTAHALA OUTDOOR CENTER

BENNETT'S PIT BAR-B-QUE

HILTON GARDEN INN

PARKWAY

SPACE NEEDLE

MAPLE LN

GATLINBURG SKY LIFT

REAGAN RD

AIRPORT RD

HISTORIC NATURE TRAIL

BELLEAIRE LN

REAGAN DR

HILLVALE LN

441
71

REAGAN LN

RIVER RD

THE VILLAGE

RIPLEY'S AQUARIUM OF THE SMOKIES

PANCAKE PANTRY

CHEROKEE DR

ASBURY RD

E HOLLY RIDGE RD

CHEROKEE ORCHARD RD

CIRCLE DR

TURKEY NEST RD

NEWTON LN

WOLISS LN

BISHOP LN

ARROWMONT SCHOOL OF ARTS AND CRAFTS

NO WAY JOSE'S CANTINA

GREYSTONE HEIGHTS RD

321
441

PARKWAY

321
73

BASKINS CREEK BYPASS

BASKINS CREEK RD

SPRUCE LN

EAST PKWY

GREAT SMOKY ARTS AND CRAFTS COMMUNITY

To Roaring Fork Motor Nature Trail

CHEROKEE ORCHARD RD

0   300 yds
0   300 m

Mon.-Sat., noon-7pm Sun., tours free). Sugarlands' distillery puts their whole distilling process on display. Watch from screened windows open to the distilling floor or show up for a free tour. There's a gift shop where you can buy all sorts of logo-emblazoned clothing and drinking gear and, of course, moonshine. Before you buy a quart or two (or a case—it's that good and it makes a fun gift), stop by the Sippin' Posts where, with valid ID, you can sample all of the moonshine flavors Sugarlands sells. Sugarlands also has a great performance space called The Back Porch where all sorts of musicians and storytellers come to play songs and spin yarns.

At the other end of downtown from Sugarlands is **Doc Collier Moonshine** (519 Parkway, 800/398-5132, www.doccollier.co, 10am-7pm Mon.-Thurs., 10am-7pm Fri.-Sat., noon-7pm Sun.). Using the recipe of famed (he was famous locally anyway) Doc Collier, his ancestors continue the tradition of making some of the finest 'shine in Tennessee and selling it to the thirsty public at their Gatlinburg storefront. According to the family, Doc's moonshine was in such high demand that he needed a better way to distribute it, so he bought a mercantile, selling provisions to some customers and jars of white lightning to those in the know. In the store, you can see some great photos and even pieces of Doc's equipment while you sample some moonshine before grabbing a bottle and going on your way.

Ripley's Aquarium of the Smokies

Ripley's Aquarium of the Smokies (traffic light #5, 88 River Rd., 865/430-8808, www. ripleyaquariums.com/gatlinburg, 9am-8pm Mon.-Thurs., 9am-10pm Fri.-Sun. Jan.-Feb.; 9am-9pm Mon.-Thurs., 9am-10pm Fri.-Sun. Mar.-Memorial Day; 9am-10pm Mon.-Thurs., 9am-11pm Fri.-Sun. Memorial Day-Labor Day; 9am-9pm Mon.-Thurs., 9am-10pm Fri.-Sun. Labor Day-New Year's Day; adults $28, children 6-11 $16, children 2-5 $8) is one of countless Ripley's attractions in Gatlinburg

Sugarlands Distilling Company

9am-9pm daily Apr.-May, 9am-11pm daily June-Aug., 9am-10pm daily Sept.-Oct., as posted Nov.-Mar., adults $15.50, children 3-11 $12) is a ski lift that carries you 1,800 feet up the side of Crockett Mountain to a gift shop and snack bar. You have pretty views of Gatlinburg on the way up and back down, and even better views from the top; nighttime tends to be the best time to ride the Sky Lift. The Sky Lift was built in the early 1950s and was the first chair lift in the region, seeing more than 100,000 visitors by its third season in operation. You'll find it in the heart of downtown; it's impossible to miss.

Moonshine Distilleries

Moonshine is a high-octane corn liquor made in the hills, hollows, and coves all throughout and around GSMNP, especially in Gatlinburg. Today, moonshine is brewed legally and there are a few distilleries right in Gatlinburg, the best of which is **Sugarlands Distilling Company** (805 Parkway, 865/325-1355, www.sugarlandsdistilling.com, 10am-11pm

Wedding Fever

To say that Gatlinburg is a popular place to get married is a gross understatement. This tiny town is second in the nation only to Las Vegas in the number of weddings held each year. On average, around 20,000 couples tie the knot here (that's 55 ceremonies a day) and the number of witnesses and guests they bring push the number of people in town for weddings north of 600,000. Guess that explains why Gatlinburg is called the "wedding capital of the South."

What makes Gatlinburg such a hot spot for weddings, even celebrity weddings (Billy Ray Cyrus, Patty Loveless, and a few other names of note were married here)? It could be that Tennessee makes it easy. No blood tests or waiting periods are required before getting married. It could be the abundance of wedding venues both natural and man-made. It could be the fact that there are plenty of romantic spots where one can retreat with their betrothed.

If being here has you in the mood for marriage, it's easy to find a place. In Gatlinburg alone there are more than a dozen chapels and more officiants than you can count. You can find all the information you'll ever need for planning a Smoky Mountain wedding at the website of the **Smoky Mountain Wedding Association** (www.somkymountainweddingassociation.com).

and Pigeon Forge. The other attractions are skippable unless you have kids in tow, but the aquarium is another story. Ripley's Aquarium is the largest aquarium in the state, with more than 1.4 million gallons of water. Exhibits include the Touch a Ray Bay, where you can touch a stingray; the Penguin Playhouse, where tunnels lead you through the exhibit, putting you eye to eye with penguins as they do their thing; and Shark Lagoon, where a 340-foot-long glide path takes you under the lagoon where sand tiger and nurse sharks swim with sea turtles and moray eels. There are two on-site restaurants and a monstrous gift shop.

Arrowmont School of Arts and Crafts

Gatlinburg has a surprising artistic side, and the artists and craftspeople here take their work very seriously. Many of them are carrying on mountain traditions, while others are finding new modes and mediums to express the inspiration they draw from the landscape. Artists go to the **Arrowmont School of Arts and Crafts** (556 Parkway, 865/436-5860, www.arrowmont.org, 8:30am-5pm Mon.-Fri., 8:30am-4pm Sat., workshops $325-1,100) to hone their techniques. Founded in 1912 as a philanthropic project by the Pi Beta Phi women's fraternity, the

Phi Beta Phi Settlement School sought to deliver basic education and health services to the children of the area. The schoolchildren brought the school staff homemade gifts—baskets, weavings, woodcarvings—made by their parents. Recognizing the talent here, the school brought in a weaving teacher and began some vocational education. Then in 1926, the school opened the Arrowcraft Shop, a market selling crafts and wares made by the people of the region. As this gained popularity, the idea of summer craft workshops came about. In 1945, 50 students attended the first of many summer workshops. Today the school holds weekend and one- and two-week workshops for adults every spring, summer, and fall. Classes include traditional and contemporary takes on weaving and fiber arts, pottery, metal and jewelry, painting, and drawing. Three galleries in the school include rotating and permanent exhibitions and are open year-round.

ENTERTAINMENT AND EVENTS
Nightlife

One spot to grab a drink other than moonshine is **Smoky Mountain Brewery** (1004 Parkway, 865/436-4200, www.smoky-mtn-brewery.com, 11:30am-1am daily, food $5-25, drinks $3-12), a microbrewery with close to a dozen handcrafted beers brewed here or at one of the three nearby sister breweries. Mainstay beers include a light beer, red ale, pilsner, porter, and pale ale; they also brew seasonal and specialty beers, like the creamy Winter Warmer Ale and the Brown Trout Stout. Stop in and grab a hot pretzel (or some wings or a pizza) and a sampler flight of beers.

Performing Arts

There are a number of stage shows going on nightly throughout Gatlinburg. The Iris Theater (115 Historic Nature Trail, 888/482-3330, www.iristheater.com, showtimes vary, tickets adults $25, military and seniors $18, children 5-12 $8) is the home stage to several performers. Head Case Starring Mentalist Bill Gladwell (7pm Tues. and Fri.-Sat.) uses Bill's mastery of suggestion, skills as a hypnotist, and untold mental powers to create a thought-provoking, family-friendly show where he'll demonstrate everything from mindreading to psychokinesis. A Brit of Magic! (check schedule and buy tickets well in advance, they sell out) is a comedy and magic show with Keith Fields, a Briton living here in the Smokies. Comedy Hypnosis with Guy Michaels (usually 7pm Wed. and 9pm Thurs.-Sat.) is just that, family-friendly hypnosis where the hypnotist Guy Michaels gets willing audience members to become the stars of the show.

Then there's the Sweet Fanny Adams Theatre (461 Parkway, 877/388-5784, www. sweetfannyadams.com, box office open 10am-10pm on show days, shows vary, tickets adults $25, seniors, military, and AAA $23, children under 12 $9), home to a musical comedy revue and "outrageous humor and hilarious fun" since 1977. Shows vary by the theater season, but typically include an improv showcase, a vaudeville-type revue, a holiday show, and other original musical comedies.

Festivals and Events

Throughout the year there are several events that draw attention to the things that make Gatlinburg the place it is. The Spring Wildflower Pilgrimage (865/974-0280, www.springwildflowerpilgrimage.org, adults $25-75, students $15, children under 12 free), usually during mid-April, is a five-day event with around 150 guided walks and presentations that celebrate the spring blooms, a photography contest, and more. From the end of September to early November, celebrate Oktoberfest at Ober Gatlinburg (865/436-5423, www.obergatlinburg.com) with a beer hall, sing-alongs, yodeling, and authentic German food. Gatlinburg Winter Magic (800/588-1817) is a 120-day celebration of all things winter and holiday. From early November through February, the city is a riot of millions of LED bulbs strung up in trees and forming elaborate displays. There's a chili cook-off, carolers, a Christmas parade, and more.

SHOPPING

Gatlinburg's touristy side has a big personality, and there are plenty of shops selling T-shirts and the expected souvenirs, but for something that truly speaks to the heritage of this place, you'll need to do a little looking around.

For a unique shop/museum (there is only one other place in the world like this and it's in Spain), stop in at The Salt and Pepper Shaker Museum (461 Brookside Village Way, 865/430-5515, www.thesaltandpeppershakermuseum.com, 10am-4pm daily in summer; 10am-2pm Mon.-Sat., noon-4pm Sun. in winter; $3 adults, ages 12 and under free). The name tells you what you'll find here, but it doesn't prepare you for the more than 20,000 salt and pepper shakers from around the world and the growing collection of pepper mills. The collection began on a lark, growing from one pepper mill into this massive assembly of the most banal of kitchen accessories. It's weird, so it's worth the cost of admission, especially when you can apply your admission fee to any gift shop purchase—and who doesn't want a salt and pepper set shaped like outhouses?

★ Great Smoky Arts and Crafts Community

Your first stop should be the **Great Smoky Arts and Crafts Community** (turn right at traffic light #3 and go three miles to Glades Rd., www.gatlinburgcrafts.com). Founded in 1937, it is among the largest (if not *the* largest) group of independent artisans in the United States. There are more than 120 artisans and craftspeople running shops, studios, and galleries along this eight-mile loop consisting of Glades Road, Buckhorn Road, and US-321. Look for the logo denoting membership in the community so you know that the goods you're seeing and buying are from genuine local and regional artisans. One thing that sets this community apart is the fact that you can interact with the artists in their studios and galleries. You can watch them work, ask questions, maybe even lend a hand (if asked). With so many galleries and studios to visit, you can easily spend a day or two if you want to take a peek into each and every gallery, shop, and studio.

The shop artisans range from candlemakers to watercolor artists to photographers to leatherworkers to the creators of traditional mountain crafts. **Ogle's Broom Shop** (670 Glades Rd., 865/430-4402, 10am-5pm Mon.-Sat.) is one such traditional crafts shop, with third-generation broom makers. The shop was opened by the grandfather of current owner David Ogle. He carries on the tradition today, making brooms from broomstraw and hand carving canes and walking sticks.

Otto Preske, Artist in Wood (535 Buckhorn Rd., 865/436-5339, www.ottopreskeartistinwood.com) is a superb woodcarver. He carves and turns Christmas ornaments, hiking staffs, fireplace mantels, religious carvings, and highly detailed figures and relief carvings. The work is stunning, and to watch him carve is simply amazing.

Throughout the community there are several basket weavers, but none like those you'll find at **Licklog Hollow Baskets** (1360 E. Parkway, 865/436-3823). Not only do they have the strangest name, the work here is

superb. Whether you're buying for form or function, you'll find a basket that fits your style and probably your budget.

One of my favorite stops is **Woodland Tiles** (220 Buckhorn Rd., 865/640-0989, www.woodlandtilesbyvmarie.com). Here they make tiles and functional pottery pieces inspired by the leaves on the trees surrounding Gatlinburg. Custom glazes capture the jewel green of summer and the blazing colors of fall, and the sizes and shapes are spot-on—the tiles mirror the leaves that inspired them.

The Village

In downtown Gatlinburg you'll find **The Village** (634 Parkway, 865/436-3995, www.thevillageshops.com, 10am-5pm daily Jan.-Feb., 10am-6pm daily Mar., 10am-8pm Sun.-Fri. and 10am-10pm Sat. Apr.-May and Nov., 10am-10pm June-Oct., hours vary Dec.), a collection of 27 shops centered on a courtyard and housed in a Bavarian-style structure. Among the shops here are **The Sock Shop** (865/325-6000, www.sockshoptn.com), where you'll find comfy, crazy, cool, and quirky socks. They also sell wool socks, dress socks, and more, as long as it goes on your feet. **The Day Hiker** (865/430-0970, www.thedayhiker.com) provides the basic gear you need to take day and short overnight hikes in GSMNP. **The Silver Tree** (865/430-3573) is a silver lover's paradise with plenty of silver jewelry and accessories to peruse. Last but not least is **The Donut Friar** (865/436-7306, www.the-donut-friar.com, from 5am daily), an amazing bakery making donuts, cinnamon bread, and other pastries. They sell coffee to go with your morning donut.

RECREATION

There is no end to the outdoor recreation opportunities near Gatlinburg. At **Nantahala Outdoor Center Gatlinburg** (1138 Parkway, 865/277-8209, www.noc.com, 10am-9pm daily), you'll find a huge retail store selling everything you'd ever need to gear up for an outdoor adventure. NOC is the region's leader in outdoor guide services, providing white-water rafting, float trips, and kayaking on several rivers across the region; guided hikes and fly-fishing trips; and more. Their trips vary by season, so check the website or ask someone at the store about current trips and activities.

Rafting in the Smokies (813 E. Parkway, 800/776-7238, www.raftinginthesmokies. com, Tues.-Thurs. and Sat. Memorial Day–Labor Day, $42, but they often run specials) is another white-water rafting outfitter. Trips depend on the weather and water levels, so it's a good idea to call ahead or check online for current trips and reservations. Once you've gotten it nailed down, check in at the rafting outpost in Hartford and I-40 Exit 447. Rafting in the Smokies has a number of other outdoor offerings on deck, such as a zip line canopy tour ($39), ropes course ($33), and family adventure packages that roll all this (and geocaching, horseback riding, and more) into one day ($65-116).

Zip Gatlinburg (125 Historic Nature Trail, 865/430-9475, www.thegatlinburg-zipline.com, zip line $59, ropes course $50, trapeze net $10) has a 9-element zip course, a 27-element ropes course, and a trapeze net on the hillside overlooking town. Between the zips, the swinging platforms, and a pair of sky bridges, you'll get your fill of high-flying thrills. The trapeze net was originally intended for aerial adrenaline enthusiasts too young or light for the zip line (read: the kids), but it's plenty of fun for anyone with the gumption to jump on.

Ober Gatlinburg

Ober Gatlinburg (1001 Parkway, 865/436-5423, www.obergatlinburg.com, hours vary by activity, but generally 9:30am-9pm daily in spring, summer, and fall, 10am-7pm in winter, individual activities $4-12, activity passes $22-33 adults, $19-28 children 5-11), the mountaintop resort that looks out over Gatlinburg, is a ski resort in the winter and a mountain playground the rest of the year. There are eight ski and snowboard trails and Ober Gatlinburg is equipped with plenty of snowmaking equipment to make up for what Mother Nature doesn't supply. Warm-weather activities include the awesome Alpine Slide, a sort of luge that follows one of the ski slopes down the hill; a pair of raft-based waterslides; a maze; and year-round indoor ice skating. There's also the Wildlife Encounter, where you can see many of the native species found in the area. If you're hungry, there are several places to grab a bite ranging from a slice of pizza to a steak.

The resort is a little dated and leans toward the cheesy end of the spectrum, and many people skip it if it's not ski season. Others think it's worth the little bit of time and money to take the tram to the top of the hill and ride the Alpine Slide.

ACCOMMODATIONS

Something about being in Gatlinburg makes me want to stay in a cabin. Fortunately, there are plenty of options whether you're traveling solo, as a pair, or with even the largest of groups. ★ **Mountain Laurel Chalets** (440 Ski Mountain Rd., 800/626-3431, www.mtn-laurelchalets.com, $99-899/night) has several lodges and large houses sleeping anywhere from 10-20 people if you're traveling with your extended family, or smaller cabins that sleep a couple or small group on a getaway. The cabins are spread out over a huge property, so they're private in addition to being cozy. Some of the cabins, the last ones in line for a refresh, are dated, but others are quite nice inside, so it's worth checking cabin descriptions online.

Located between Gatlinburg and Pigeon Forge, **Autumn Ridge** (505 Crest Rd., 865/436-4111 or 800/397-4343, www.autumnridgerentals.com, Jan.-Mar. from $105, Apr.-Dec. from $115, Oct. and holidays from $125) has five cabins, each with a two-night minimum and a view you'll come back for. King-size beds are the norm here, as are whirlpool tubs or hot tubs and wood-burning fireplaces (firewood provided). This is a romantic spot and a popular one for honeymooners, so make your reservation sooner rather than later.

Laurel Springs Lodge Bed and Breakfast (204 Hill St., 865/430-9211 or 888/430-9211, www.laurelspringslodge.com, $135-169) is lovely, comfortable, and highly regarded. There are five rooms, all well decorated and comfortable, and a gourmet breakfast is served every morning. Downtown is a short walk away, but even though you're close, you're away from the buzz of Gatlinburg's main drag and can relax when you come back to your room.

The Foxtrot Bed and Breakfast (1520 Garrett Lane, 865/436-3033, www.thefoxtrot.com, $190-230) is a little different than most B&Bs in that an actual chef prepares breakfast. That's just one thing that sets it apart. The Foxtrot is high on a hill well above the noise, traffic, and bustle of downtown Gatlinburg, making it a true retreat. There are several packages you can add to your room, like spa packages, honeymoon and anniversary packages, cooking schools, and more.

One of the finest places to stay in Gatlinburg is ★ **The Lodge at Buckberry Creek** (961 Campbell Lead Rd., 865/430-8030, www.buckberrylodge.com, $205-460). Though it calls itself "The Great Camp of the Smokies," the rooms here are anything but camp-like. Sure, the walls are wood paneled and elements of the decor say rustic, but the finishes speak to luxury. Situated on 26 acres, The Lodge is surrounded by hiking trails, a trout stream, and romantic pavilions along the banks of Buckberry Creek. With the best fine-dining restaurant in Gatlinburg located in the complex, this is the kind of place you could come for the weekend and never leave the property.

Throughout Gatlinburg there are a number of chain hotels with prices ranging from budget to mid-range. Three of the more reliable hotels are The Park Vista, Hampton Inn Gatlinburg, and Hilton Garden Inn. **The Park Vista** (705 Cherokee Orchard Rd., 865/436-9211, www.parkvista.com, $135-190), a Doubletree by Hilton hotel, has excellent views from each room's private balcony. The rooms are spacious and comfortable, and the hotel is adjacent to the Roaring Fork Motor Nature Trail. The **Hampton Inn Gatlinburg** (967 Parkway, 865/436-4878, www.hamptoninn3.hilton.com, $150-199) has private balconies and is within walking distance of most of Gatlinburg's attractions. Finally, the **Hilton Garden Inn** (635 River Rd., 865/436-0048, www.hiltongardeninn3.hilton.com, $140-249) is also walkable to downtown and has free parking.

FOOD

Dining in Gatlinburg, especially for foodies, can be tricky. In a town where literally millions of people pass through, you get a lot of restaurants that have stopped caring about repeat customers and seek only to provide a heaping plate of food and mediocre service at premium prices, knowing their diners will be in for one, maybe two meals during their visit. And there are plenty of major chains ready to take your dining dollars. That said, it is possible to find a good, even great, meal here.

The **Smoky Mountain Trout House** (410 Parkway, 865/436-5416, from 5pm nightly, around $20) has a mesmerizing aquarium window teeming with rainbow trout. (It mesmerized me as a kid when, after walking past it a dozen times, I finally convinced my parents to eat there.) The menu is trout-heavy: rainbow trout grilled, broiled, pan fried, or seasoned with dill or parmesan; trout almandine; and smoked trout. There are a few menu items—prime rib, a rib eye steak, country ham, chicken, catfish, and shrimp—that aren't trout. The food tastes better than the dining room would have you believe, and this is a pretty good meal, especially if you like trout.

A longtime Gatlinburg eatery, **The Peddler** (820 River Rd., 865/436-5794, www.peddlergatlinburg.com, from 5pm Sun.-Fri., from 4:30pm Sat., $23-37) is still a solid choice for a steak. The dining room overlooks the river, making it a nice spot to eat. The menu is steak-heavy, but they also have shrimp, chicken, and trout, and every entrée comes with a pretty robust salad bar.

Bennett's Pit Bar-B-Que (714 River Rd., 865/436-2400, www.bennetts-bbq.com, breakfast from 8am daily, lunch from 11am daily, dinner from 3pm daily, breakfast buffet $9.99 adults, $4.99 kids, lunch $9-15, dinner $10-36) serves hickory-smoked barbecue in many forms: pork ribs, pulled pork, chicken, beef brisket, hot smoked sausage, and burnt ends (a brisket treat that's not to be missed). The platters of food are, as they are in most barbecue joints, obscenely big, so don't feel bad if you can't finish your meal.

For the last several years, **Alamo Steakhouse and Saloon** (705 E. Parkway, 865/436-9998, www.alamosteakhouse.com, lunch 11am-3pm daily, dinner from 3pm daily, $14-31) has been widely lauded as having the best steak, so sit down and order one—they have plenty of options to choose from. If you're not in the mood for steak, there are a number of pork, chicken, and seafood dishes. The service is generally very good, but, like all restaurants in a busy vacation town, can get bogged down in the high season.

★ **Big Daddy's Pizzeria** (714 River Rd., 865/436-5455, www.bigdaddyspizzeria. net, from 11am daily, $9-23) has locations in Gatlinburg, Pigeon Forge, and Sevierville. Their claim to fame is a wood-fired brick oven and a creative flair in the creation of their pies. Get the tried-and-true pepperoni and cheese, or go wild with the Smoky Mounty Cheese Steak (with shaved prime rib, caramelized onions, gorgonzola cheese, and potato slices), the Herbivore (a veggie-packed delight), or one of their other signature pizzas. They also have sandwiches prepared on house-made focaccia, fresh salads, and meatballs.

Across the street from the aquarium is **No Way Jose's Cantina** (555 Parkway, 865/436-5673, www.nowayjosescantina.com, 11:30am-10pm daily, $5-15). Grab a riverside seat and order a basket of chips and killer homemade salsa before you even glance at the menu. The rest of the menu is pretty standard Tex-Mex fare, but tastes fresh.

Gatlinburg has pancake houses in spades. The oldest pancake house in town opened in 1960 and it also happens to be the first of its kind in Tennessee. **Pancake Pantry** (628 Parkway, 865/436-4724, 7am-4pm daily June-Oct., 7am-3pm daily Nov.-May, $6-10) still puts out a great spread of flapjacks. There are 24 varieties of pancakes and crepes, as well as a half-dozen waffles and omelets and French toast. Breakfast is served all day, but if you feel like a burger or sandwich for lunch, they have a few of those too.

Wild Plum (555 Buckhorn Rd., 865/436-3808, www.wildplumtearoom.com, 11am-3pm Mon.-Sat., closed mid-Dec.-Mar. 1, $10-16) is a lunch-only restaurant inspired by Austrian teahouses. They serve the Southern classic, tomato pie, but the real stars of the menu are the chef's specials. The specials vary daily, but in the past have included lobster pie, a salmon burger, smoked salmon sandwiches, and yellowfin tuna.

Hands down the best fine-dining experience in Gatlinburg, ★ **The Restaurant at Buckberry Creek** (961 Campbell Lead Rd., 865/430-8030, www.buckberrylodge.com, breakfast from 8am daily, dinner 5:30pm-9pm Thurs.-Sat. Jan.-Feb., Tues.-Sat. Mar.-Sept. and Nov.-Dec., daily in Oct., $20-45) serves a small, ever-changing menu. During tomato season, expect to see fried green tomatoes as a first bite and tomatoes on and in most of the salads and entrées; wild mushrooms and ramps may appear in spring, and other ingredients will take the stage as they ripen throughout the season. Entrées commonly include pan-seared duck, beef tenderloin, and tuna, sea bass, or another flavorful fish. Don't skip dessert: The crème brûlée and the fresh sorbet are quite nice.

TRANSPORTATION AND SERVICES

Car

Most visitors arrive in Gatlinburg via Newfound Gap Road (US-441) heading west from Cherokee, North Carolina, through Great Smoky Mountains National Park. From Cherokee it's an approximately 45-minute drive through the park. Gatlinburg is easy to find: one minute you're in the park, the next minute you're in Gatlinburg.

For those driving from the north or west, I-40 is the most convenient road into town. From I-40, take Exit 407 and hop on US-66 south; this road feeds into US-441 and leads past Sevierville and Pigeon Forge to Gatlinburg. This is the easiest and most heavily traveled route into town from I-40. You can avoid the peak-season crowds by taking Exit 435 near Knoxville (an hour away) and following US-321 south into Gatlinburg.

Coming in from the east on I-40, the best bet is to take Exit 443 and drive along the beautiful Foothills Parkway to US-321 south, from which you cruise right into town.

PARKING

Finding parking in Gatlinburg can be quite tough. There are a number of public and private parking lots and garages where you can park your car if you're not staying at a hotel nearby. Parking rates vary depending on public or private ownership, so for affordability, it's often best to stick to the public parking garages at **Ripley's Aquarium of the Smokies** (88 River Rd., $1.75 first hour, $1 each hour after, or $6/day) and the **McMahan Parking Garage** (520 Parkway, at traffic light #3, $1.75 first hour, $1 each hour after, or $6/day).

Air

The **McGhee-Tyson Airport** outside of Knoxville is 42 miles from Gatlinburg. Head south to Maryville on US-129. Once you're in Maryville, take US-321 north to Pigeon Forge, then turn right and take US-441 into Gatlinburg.

Public Transit

Gatlinburg has a great trolley system that can get you to and from every attraction in Gatlinburg and nearby Pigeon Forge, including Dollywood. The **Gatlinburg Trolley** (88 River Rd., Suite 101, 865/436-3897, www.gatlinburgtrolley.org, 10am-10pm daily Mar.-Apr., 8am-midnight daily May-Oct., 10am-6pm Sun.-Thurs and 10am-10pm Fri.-Sat. Nov.-Feb., extended hours on select holiday and event dates) has more than 100 stops in Gatlinburg alone. It's cheap, with most rides only $0.50, but your best bet is to pick up an All Day Trolley Pass ($2) from the **Gatlinburg Welcome Center** (1011 Banner Rd., 865/277-8957, www.gatlinburg.com, 8:30am-7pm daily), the **Parkway Visitor Center** (520 Parkway, 10am-6pm daily) at traffic light #3, or the **Aquarium Welcome Center** (88 River Rd., 9am-9pm daily).

Services

There are three visitors centers in Gatlinburg: the **Gatlinburg Welcome Center** (1011 Banner Rd., 865/277-8957, www.gatlinburg.com, 8:30am-7pm daily), the **Parkway Visitor Center** (520 Parkway, 10am-6pm daily) at traffic light #3, and the **Aquarium Welcome Center** (88 River Rd., 9am-9pm daily).

On the radio, **WWST** (93.7 FM) plays the Top 40. **WSEV** (105.5 FM) is an adult contemporary station.

LeConte Medical Center (742 Middle Creek Rd., Sevierville, 865/446-7000, www.lecontemedicalcenter.com) is the nearest hospital, just over 20 minutes away. The **Gatlinburg Police** (1230 E. Parkway, 865/436-5181) are available if the need arises.

Pigeon Forge and Sevierville

The dominating presence in Pigeon Forge and Sevierville is that of Dolly Parton. Her namesake amusement park is in Pigeon Forge and she was born and raised in Sevierville, where a statue of Dolly stands in front of the courthouse. You'll see her face, hear her music, and maybe even meet one of her many cousins everywhere across these two towns.

These towns have grown a lot since Dolly was born, thanks largely to the popularity of Great Smoky Mountains National Park. More growth came when the amusement park that would become Dollywood opened its doors, and again when nearby Knoxville hosted the World's Fair. But to keep more than 10 million annual visitors coming back year after year, Pigeon Forge and Sevierville had to become destinations unto themselves, and, for the most part, they've succeeded. Pigeon Forge has become one of the biggest "tourist traps" (which I say not with disdain, but astonishment—the place is a wonderland of vacation delights) on the East Coast. Want to ride go-karts and go bungee jumping at 9pm on a Wednesday? No problem. Midnight mini golf? Got it. Roller coasters, neon signs, and fudge shops? Pigeon Forge has got you covered. But don't be fooled by all the neon, hotels, and attractions: Pigeon Forge remains a small town, with fewer than 7,000 year-round residents.

In the midst of this swirl of touristy flotsam is a surprising center for engaging with the community's culture: Dollywood. This amusement park has been around in some form or another since the 1960s, though in the early days it was kitsch over culture. As the park matured and expanded, so did its attention to the culture of mountain living. Today the park is home to some great bluegrass and country shows and a good deal of shops and exhibits where Appalachian crafters showcase their skills and their wares.

SIGHTS
★ Dollywood

At **Dollywood** (2700 Dollywood Parks Blvd., Pigeon Forge, 800/365-5996, www.dollywood.com, Apr.-Dec., $52-65, parking $11), you might just catch a glimpse of Dolly Parton walking through the park or performing for the crowds at the park's opening day. Even if you don't see the country music icon, the park has plenty of rides, cultural stops, shows, and nature experiences to keep you busy.

Dollywood started in 1961, when Rebel Railroad, a small attraction with a steam train, general store, blacksmith shop, and saloon, opened. By 1977, the park had grown and changed hands more than once. Renamed Silver Dollar City, the park eventually caught the attention of Dolly Parton. In 1986, Dolly became a partner and lent the park her name. Since then it's become Tennessee's most-visited tourist attraction (outside GSMNP) and is consistently named among the top theme parks in the world.

Dollywood has a great look: one-part Appalachian village, one-part small Southern town. There are tree-lined streets and paths, and several streams follow their courses through the park. You don't see the rides until you're right up on them because they're tucked away in the woods.

One of the best-known spots in the park is **Showstreet,** where stages and theaters are always busy with musicians, square dances, and storytellers. There's also a bevy of master craftspeople practicing their Appalachian arts for all to see: blacksmiths, basket-makers, candlemakers, and woodworkers. On Showstreet, you may see some of Dolly's relatives playing and singing in shows throughout the year. Seasonal shows include a half-dozen Christmas concerts, Harvest Celebration Southern Gospel, and more.

Pigeon Forge

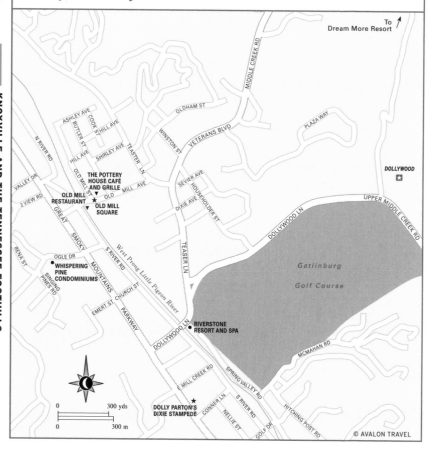

To
Dream More Resort

MIDDLE CREEK RD

PLAZA WAY

DOLLYWOOD

UPPER MIDDLE CREEK RD

OLDHAM ST

WINSTON ST

VETERANS BLVD

SEVIER AVE

HOUSEHOLDER ST

DIXIE AVE

DOLLYWOOD LN

ASHLEY AVE

BUTLER ST

COOK ST

HILL AVE

SHIRLEY AVE

TEASTER LN

N RIVER RD

HILL AVE

OLD MILL AVE

OLD MILL AVE

THE POTTERY
HOUSE CAFÉ
AND GRILLE

OLD MILL
RESTAURANT

OLD MILL
SQUARE

VALLEY DR

2 VIEW RD

GREAT

SMOKY

MOUNTAINS

PARKWAY

S RIVER RD

OGLE DR

WHISPERING
PINE
CONDOMINIUMS

SINGING PINES RD

RENA ST

West Prong Little Pigeon River

CHURCH ST

EMERT ST

TEASTER LN

Gatlinburg
Golf Course

DOLLYWOOD LN

RIVERSTONE
RESORT AND SPA

MCMAHAN RD

E MILL CREEK RD

SPRING VALLEY RD

DOLLY PARTON'S
DIXIE STAMPEDE

CONNER LN

NELLIE ST

S RIVER RD

GOLF DR

HITCHING POST RD

0   300 yds

0   300 m

© AVALON TRAVEL

Also on Showstreet is a carriage, sled, and wagon shop called **Valley Carriage Works.** The Carriage Works takes orders from clients from around the world and builds beautiful, fully functional, historically accurate carriages. At the Museum of the Cherokee Indian in Cherokee, North Carolina, you can see a replica Cherokee wagon that they built to commemorate the 165th anniversary of the Trail of Tears.

It's easy to find a souvenir in the park, whether you want a Dollywood keepsake or a handcrafted gift from one of the shops in Craftsman's Valley, where you'll find handcrafted goods like leather belts, blown glass, and baskets.

Given that the park allows nature to be such a prominent feature in its design, it's no surprise to learn that Dollywood has partnered with the American Eagle Foundation and is authorized by U.S. Fish and Wildlife Services and the Tennessee Wildlife Resources Agency to possess eagles and other birds for education, exhibition, rehabilitation, and breeding. The 30,000-square-foot **aviary** is home to the nation's largest group of non-releasable bald eagles (many of these birds have been injured and wouldn't survive if released into nature).

Daily shows put visitors in proximity to these incredible birds.

Dollywood has more than 40 rides and attractions that range from kid-friendly to thrilling. My favorites were the Blazing Fury, an indoor roller coaster where you're trying to outrun an out-of-control fire; Thunderhead, a great wooden coaster; and Daredevil Falls, an updated version of the log-flume ride.

Plenty of snack stands and restaurants are located throughout the park. I remember loving the berries and cream and having my first plate of whole-hog barbecue here. The memories are good, but those meals aren't cheap. But, it's an amusement park and you'll be there all day, so what are you going to do?

Dollywood's Splash Country

Waterparks abound in Pigeon Forge and Sevierville, but the best is **Dollywood's Splash Country** (2700 Dollywood Parks Blvd., Pigeon Forge, 800/365-5996, www. dollywood.com, May-Sept., $43-48, parking $11). This water park has 29 waterslides, a lazy river, three water-play areas for kids, a 7,500-square-foot leisure pool, and 25,000-square-foot wave pool. There are also concessions and a gift shop, stroller rentals, and lockers to rent.

Dolly Parton Statue

Local artist Jim Gray sculpted a **statue** (125 Court Ave.) that shows Dolly with a wide smile and her guitar, as if she's ready to write a song at any moment. Stop by downtown Sevierville to take a picture with the statue, located on the courthouse lawn.

Tennessee Museum of Aviation

Head to the Gatlinburg-Pigeon Forge Airport in Sevierville to brush up on your aviation history at the **Tennessee Museum of Aviation** (135 Air Museum Way, Sevierville, 866/286-8738, www.tnairmuseum.com, 10am-6pm Mon.-Sat. and 1pm-6pm Sun. Mar.-Dec., 10am-5pm Mon.-Sat. and 1pm-5pm Sun. Jan.-Feb., adults $12.75, seniors $9.75, children

6-12 $6.75). Housed in a 35,000-square-foot hangar, the museum has a number of exhibits and a dozen historic aircraft, including two airworthy P-47 Thunderbolts (that sometimes take to the air), a MiG-21, and F-86 Saberjet. But the best treat is when you visit the museum and one of the historic World War II aircraft is taking flight.

Titanic Pigeon Forge

One somewhat odd attraction is the **Titanic Pigeon Forge** (2134 Parkway, Pigeon Forge, 800/381-7670, www.titanicpigeonforge. com, 9am-close daily, closed Jan. 12-15 and Christmas Day, adults $27, children 5-12 $11.25). This massive museum includes three decks and 20 galleries spread over 30,000 square feet. The galleries feature artifacts salvaged from the sunken luxury ship. There's a reproduction of the Marconi wireless room, a first-class suite and third-class cabin, as well as a full-scale reproduction of the grand staircase. Touring the ship takes about two hours.

WonderWorks

From the outside, the building that houses **WonderWorks** (100 Music Rd., Pigeon Forge, 865/868-1800, www.wonderworksonline.com, 9am-10pm daily, adults $25, seniors and children 4-12 $17) appears to be upside down. Inside this science-inspired amusement center are more than 100 interactive exhibits; some, like the Tesla Coil and the Earthquake Café, are strange and seem dangerous, while others challenge you to use your imagination to solve puzzles or test your willpower. While it's definitely geared toward kids in the tween range, adults will find plenty to marvel at.

ENTERTAINMENT

If you want to wet your whistle in Pigeon Forge, your options are exclusively bars in restaurants. The two best of these are at the Island in Pigeon Forge. **Smoky Mountain Brewery** (2530 Parkway, Suite 15, Pigeon Forge, 865/868-1400, www.smoky-mtn-brewery.com, 11am-midnight daily, food $5-25, drinks $3-12) brews every drop of their draft beer in-house or at one of their three sister restaurants, and they serve up some good grub if you want something to munch on or are hungry enough for a full meal. **Mellow Mushroom** (131 Island Dr., #3101, Pigeon Forge, www.mellowmushroom.com, 10am-midnight daily, $9-20) specializes in the best national and regional craft beer and some very tasty pizza, subs, and salads.

Dolly Parton's Dixie Stampede (3849 Parkway, Pigeon Forge, 865/453-9473, www.dixiestampede.com, daily, call for showtimes, adults from $50, children from $25) is one-part dinner, one-part show. The dinner's a four-course country feast and the show is jam-packed with horseback stunts, comedy, pyrotechnics, and some genuinely surreal sights to take in while you're eating in what is essentially a small arena.

The Smoky Mountain Opry (2046 Parkway, Pigeon Forge, 865/428-7469, www.smokymtnopry.com, daily, showtimes vary, adults $50, children $20) is a variety show filled with singers and dancers, jugglers and aerial acrobats, magicians, comedians, and musicians; they even have a white lion for some reason. They also have a Christmas show that draws quite the crowd.

SHOPPING

There's no shortage of touristy shopping around here, but you can find specialty shops, galleries, and decent shopping if you know where to look.

Pigeon Forge earned part of its name from a forge set up in 1820 by Isaac Love. (The other part of its name came from the incredible number of passenger pigeons the early settlers found living along the banks of the Little Pigeon River.) A decade later Love's son established a mill, which is now on the National Register of Historic Places. **The Old Mill Square** (175 Old Mill Ave., Pigeon Forge, 865/428-0771, www.old-mill.com, hours vary by store) is a collection of shops and restaurants in a cute restored and re-created historic area. **The Old Mill General Store** (865/453-4628, 8:30am-9pm Mon.-Sat., 9am-8pm Sun., hours vary off-season) has all sorts of country provisions, including fresh-ground grains milled next door at the Old Mill. **The Old Mill Farmhouse Kitchen** (865/428-2044, 9:30am-8pm Sun.-Thurs., 9am-9pm Fri.-Sat., hours vary off-season) also sells a variety of provisions and ingredients that you need to cook your own country meal at home. They also have a nice pottery shop and gift baskets.

WonderWorks

You can get your fill of candy at **The Old Mill Candy Kitchen** (865/453-7516, 9am-8:30pm Mon.-Thurs., 9am-9pm Fri.-Sat., 9am-8pm Sun., hours vary off-season), and kids will love visiting **The Old Mill Toy Bin** (865/774-2258, 9:30am-8pm Sun.-Thurs., 9am-9pm Fri.-Sat., hours vary off-season), where they'll find all sorts of wooden toys and old-fashioned playthings.

The **Incredible Christmas Place** (2470 Parkway, Pigeon Forge, 865/453-0145, 9am-9pm daily Memorial Day-July 4, 9am-10pm daily July 4-Dec., call for hours Jan.-May) is just that, an incredible store that's all Christmas, all the time. Get bows, ornaments, decorations, trees, lights, and any number of collectibles from Boyds Bears, Department 56, and Snow Buddies.

At **The Apple Barn Cider Mill and General Store** (230 Apple Valley Rd., Sevierville, 865/453-9319, www.applebarn-cidermill.com, 9am-7pm Mon.-Thurs., 9am-9pm Fri.-Sat., 9am-5:30pm Sun.), you can buy fresh cider, a bushel of just-picked apples, a pie hot from the oven, and more. At this great stop, you'll be in a working orchard with more than 4,000 trees, and you can watch the cider presses at work while you munch on an apple donut.

Tanger Outlets (1645 Parkway, Sevierville, 865/453-1053, www.tangeroutlet.com, 9am-9pm Mon.-Sat., 10am-7pm Sun.) in Sevierville has dozens of shops including brand-name outlets like Coach, Levi's, Michael Kors, Polo Ralph Lauren, Samsonite, Vera Bradley, and Banana Republic.

If you're looking for a home decor souvenir, look no further than **Aunt Debbie's Country Store** (1753 Wears Valley Rd., Sevierville, 865/366-7359, www.auntdebbiescountrystore.com, 8am-5pm Mon.-Sat.). Barnwood signs, cedar swings, primitive decor, and rustic elements that would bring a touch of the Smokies into your home are on display here. There's a lot to see, so when you stop by, be sure you budget a bit of time to this store.

RECREATION

There is plenty to get into when you're in Pigeon Forge and Sevierville. Of course you can hike in the national park, but you can also go white-water rafting, ride a crazy alpine coaster, or even skydive—with a twist.

You can try indoor skydiving at **Flyaway Indoor Skydiving** (3106 Parkway, Pigeon Forge, 877/293-0639, www.flyawayindoorskydiving.com, 10am-8pm daily, $34 first flight, $22 additional flight). Indoor skydiving is done in a vertical wind tunnel—think a silo with some giant fans in the base—with an experienced skydiving instructor. After a brief ground school where you'll familiarize yourself with the proper body positions, basics of maneuvering yourself, and hand signals used to communicate with your instructor, you'll get dressed and be ready to fly. In the wind tunnel, it's disorienting the first time you leave your feet and assume the skydiving position because you're floating a few feet off the net where you were just standing. Relax, follow your instructor's directions, and enjoy the experience. If you're lucky, before or after your session, you'll get to see some experienced indoor skydivers perform amazing acrobatic tricks that look like something out of *The Matrix* as they whirl around the tunnel with precise control.

One of the newest, and most interesting, outdoor activities is the **Smoky Mountain Alpine Coaster** (867 Wears Valley Rd., Pigeon Forge, 865/365-5000, www.smokymountainalpinecoaster.com, 9am-9pm daily weather permitting, adults $15, children 7-12 $12, children 3-6 $5). This odd little quasi-roller coaster puts you in a track-mounted sled complete with an automatic speed control and manual brakes and sends you down a one-mile track, spiraling through tight turns and down a few steep(ish) drops.

Get a view of the Smokies that few others see with **Scenic Helicopter Tours** (tickets at 1965 Parkway, Sevierville, heliport at 1949 Winfield Dunn Parkway, Sevierville, 865/453-6342, www.scenichelicoptertours.

com, flight times vary, $28-1,230). Choose from a dozen tours flying over different parts of the region. Short tours like the 8-mile flight along the French Broad River are fun and affordable, while the huge, 100-mile Smoky Mountains Spectacular will set you back more than a thousand bucks, but it's worth it because this tour circles much of the national park.

Smoky Mountain Ziplines (509 Mill Creek Rd., Pigeon Forge, 865/429-9004, www.smokymountainziplines.com, daily, times vary, call for availability, $70-125) has a 9-line and 14-line canopy tour as well as two super zip lines that are 800 feet long and 100 feet high. This is fun and family-friendly. Note that for kids to zip solo, they must be at least 8 years old and 60 pounds; children 5-7 or under 60 pounds may be able to ride tandem with the guide.

Though most of the golf you've seen has been of the mini variety, the **Gatlinburg Golf Course** (520 Dollywood Lane, Pigeon Forge, 800/231-4128, www.golf.gatlinburg. com, daily, call for hours and tee times, $30-60) offers you a full-sized round on a beautiful course. Designed by William Langford and renovated twice by Bob Cupp & Associates, this 18-hole course has some dramatic holes. The signature 12th hole, nicknamed "Sky Hi," is 194 yards long and has a 200-foot drop from the tee to the green, making it a puzzling hole for many golfers and a fun one for all. The pro shop here has everything you'll need to play a round, including a full-service restaurant so you can grab a bite and a beer after you're finished.

The Island In Pigeon Forge (131 Island Dr., 865/286-0119, www.islandpigeonforge. com, 10am-11pm Mon.-Thurs., 10am-midnight Fri.-Sat., 10am-10pm Sun.) is a tourist extravaganza. You'll find a half-dozen restaurants and as many snack shops, 20 or so stores selling everything from jerky to puzzles to gems, and rides galore. Rides and entertainment options include the 200-foot-tall Great Smoky Mountain Wheel, a mirror maze, and a huge arcade.

ACCOMMODATIONS

There are several chain hotels in Pigeon Forge and Sevierville, and for the most part they're all the same. However, the **Clarion Inn** (124 Waldens Main St., Pigeon Forge, 865/868-5300, www.pigeonforgeclarion.com, $55-180) is convenient to anything you'll want to do in Pigeon Forge, and it has a pool, lazy river, and slide for the kids. Plus, they have a pretty good breakfast.

Whispering Pines Condominiums (205 Ogle Dr., Pigeon Forge, 800/429-4361, www. whisperingpinescondos.com, $100-300) has a great location if you want a front-row seat for the action of Pigeon Forge, or you can opt for mountain views and unwind a little. The condos here are large, so they're ideal for families or small groups traveling together, especially if you don't want to break the bank.

The Inn at Christmas Place (119 Christmas Tree Lane, Pigeon Forge, 888/465-9644, www.innatchristmasplace.com, $150-349) is an outstanding place to stay. Given that the place is permanently festooned with Christmas decorations (they are somewhat subdued from January to October) and they play Christmas music on a constant loop, I was surprised at how great this property is. Impeccable landscaping; a beautiful, turreted building; a robust breakfast; an indoor and outdoor pool, complete with a 95-foot waterslide; and a game room are only a few of the reasons this inn is such a find.

RiverStone Resort and Spa (212 Dollywood Lane, Pigeon Forge, 877/703-3220, www.riverstoneresort.com, $145-460) has condos and cabins that are luxurious through and through. Add to that an on-site full-service spa, and you have a truly relaxing place to stay. A playground and a lazy river keep the youngest guests occupied outdoors. There is a game room indoors. This is a great hotel for golfers, as it's adjacent to the Gatlinburg Golf Course.

★ **Dollywood's DreamMore Resort** (2525 DreamMore Way, Pigeon Forge, 800/365-5996, www.dollywoodsdreammoreresort.dollywood.com, from $190) was inspired by Dolly's own family-filled front porch. Though it's just a little bigger than the tiny cabin where she grew up, DreamMore promises that same family focus in its 307 rooms, indoor and outdoor pools, storytelling stations, restaurant, and Smoky Mountain views. It's the first hotel on Dollywood property, and as such, staying here has its privileges, like a complimentary shuttle to the park.

FOOD

At the Old Mill there's a quaint collection of shops and a pair of restaurants. **The Old Mill Restaurant** (160 Old Mill Ave., Pigeon Forge, 865/429-3463, www.old-mill.com, 8am-8pm daily, off-season hours vary, breakfast $7-11, lunch $9-11, dinner $13-28, kids $6-9 at each meal) is family-friendly and has a small selection for kids. The Pigeon River flows by right outside the dining room, and this is a bigger draw than the food, which is traditional country fare (though breakfast is pretty good).

The Pottery House Café and Grill (175 Old Mill Ave., Pigeon Forge, 865/453-6002, www.old-mill.com, lunch 11am-4pm daily, dinner 4pm-late Sun.-Thurs., 4pm-8pm Fri.-Sat., lunch $8.50-12, dinner $8-19) is known for its delicious quiche and outstanding dessert. They serve everything from steaks to fried chicken livers (served with buffalo sauce and blue cheese dressing) and sandwiches. Rather than trout, which is served by many area eateries, they serve catfish here, which is just as good. If you like what you get for dessert, it's likely you can get a whole cake or pie to take home with you.

★ **Poynor's Pommes Frites** (131 The Island Dr., Suite 3107, Pigeon Forge, 865/774-7744, 11am-10pm daily, $5-10) may not look like much from the outside, but the food is great. The specialty is the pommes frites (french fries). Done in a Belgian style (fried, cooled, then fried again), they're crispy on the outside and fluffy inside, and served either plain, with your choice of sauce, or even topped with cheese, bacon, onions, and jalapenos. You can't make a meal of french fries,

so Poynor's serves a short menu of bratwurst served on a German hard roll.

★ **Mel's Diner** (119 Wears Valley Rd., Pigeon Forge, 865/429-2184, www.melsdinerpf.com, 7am-1am daily, breakfast $3-10, lunch and dinner $6-10) serves up classic diner food with a side of 1950s flair. With tasty, relatively inexpensive dishes served at breakfast, lunch, and dinner (and even rare late-night dining), you can't go wrong here. The breakfast plates are quite hearty, and the burgers and sandwiches piled high with toppings, but save room for dessert and order a whopping six-scoop banana split or a more reasonable shake or malt.

If you're prepared for a feast, head to **Huck Finn's Catfish** (3330 Parkway, Pigeon Forge, 865/429-3353, www.huckfinnsrestaurant.com, from 11:30am daily, lunch $8, dinner $12-19). Their all-you-can-eat catfish and chicken dinners are their claim to fame. They serve a limited lunch menu of catfish and chicken done up several ways and "all 'u' can eat vittles"; vittles include hush puppies, mashed potatoes, fries, coleslaw, pickles, and baked beans. If you like your meal, buy a T-shirt to commemorate it, because if you buy a shirt, your next meal is free.

All throughout the Smokies, pancake houses rule the breakfast world. Though it looks nothing like a log cabin, one of the best in Pigeon Forge is **Log Cabin Pancake House** (4235 Parkway, Pigeon Forge, 865/453-5748, www.logcabinpancakehouse.com, 7am-2pm daily). The silver-dollar pancakes are good, and there are 20 pancake choices plus waffles and the expected breakfast dishes. They have a lunch buffet if you're starving when it's time for your midday meal, otherwise, it's hard to beat their patty melt.

The wings at **Blue Moose Burgers and Wings** (2430 Teaster Lane #108, Pigeon Forge, 865/286-0364, www.bluemooseburgersandwings.com, 11am-midnight daily, $8-24) are the best in town. There are around two dozen wing sauces, plus a menu that includes wraps, sandwiches, burgers, salads, and a couple of platters. If you're a wing nut, they have a

25-wing sampler comprising five flavors, five wings each. Unfortunately, their beer selection is bottom-shelf.

Mama's Farmhouse (208 Pickel St., Pigeon Forge, 865/908-4646, www.mamas-farmhouse.com, 11am-9pm Sun.-Thurs., 11am-10pm Fri.-Sat., closed an hour earlier in winter) is the place for a family-style Southern meal. Every meal is all you can eat (adults $13 breakfast, $16 lunch, $20 dinner; kids 5-12 $6 breakfast, $8 lunch, $9 dinner). Once you put in your drink order, the food will arrive, and there's a whole lot of it. For dinner, you'll get three meats—fried chicken with meatloaf, turkey and stuffing, ham, country-fried steak, or turkey pot pie—and your choice of five sides, plus soup or salad, biscuits, and dessert. Try the peach butter on your biscuits; you can thank me later.

TRANSPORTATION AND SERVICES
Car
The most-traveled route to Pigeon Forge and Sevierville is I-40, carrying visitors in from the east and west. Exit 407 puts you on US-66 southeast, which leads into Sevierville and then feeds into US-441, taking you to Pigeon Forge. Most travelers will be going north on US-441, following Newfound Gap Road from Great Smoky Mountains National Park and Gatlinburg.

Public Transit
It's surprising to see a well-organized public transit system in a town the size of Pigeon Forge, but the **Fun Time Trolley** (186 Old Mill Ave., 865/453-6444, www.

pigeonforgetrolley.org, 8am-midnight daily Mar.-Oct., 10am-10pm daily Nov.-Dec., $0.50-0.75 or an all-day pass for $2.50) has more than 100 regular stops in Pigeon Forge, Sevierville, and Gatlinburg. Routes run on a regular schedule (as traffic allows), and stops include all of the high points in the area. Passes are available at the address listed.

Services
The **Pigeon Forge Welcome Center** (1950 Parkway, 800/251-9100, www.mypigeon-forge.com, 8:30am-5pm Mon.-Sat., 1pm-5pm Sun.) is located at traffic light #0 on Parkway. Here, and at the **Pigeon Forge Information Center** (3107 Parkway, 8:30am-5pm Mon.-Fri.), you can find information on the area and volunteers ready to help you plan your time here.

The folks at the **Sevierville Chamber of Commerce Visitors Center** (3099 Winfield Dunn Parkway, 888/738-4378, www.visitse-vierville.com, 8:30am-5:30pm Mon.-Sat., 9am-6pm Sun.) are ready to help with trip planning, or they can simply point you in the right direction and help you enjoy your vacation.

If you need a hospital, **LeConte Medical Center** (742 Middle Creek Rd., Sevierville, 865/446-7000, www.lecontemedicalcenter. com) is your best bet.

There are three police departments here: the **Sevier County Sheriff's Office** (106 W. Bruce St., 865/453-4668), the **Pigeon Forge Police Department** (225 Pine Mountain Rd., 865/453-9063), and the **Sevier County Police Department** (300 Gary Wade Blvd., 865/453-5506).

Knoxville

Perhaps best known among college football fans, Knoxville is the biggest city in East Tennessee and a major travel hub granting access to Great Smoky Mountains National Park and, beyond that, the Blue Ridge Parkway. Unlike Nashville and Memphis, which have national reputations as music towns, Knoxville's fame comes from University of Tennessee Volunteers athletics, but that's a bit unfair because the city is also home to the historic Tennessee Theatre and the Bijou Theatre, and has a very lively music scene of its own.

In the last decade or so, downtown Knoxville has undergone a significant revitalization. Knoxville's downtown had suffered as businesses and residents left in favor of suburbs, office parks, and strip malls. Then, in 1982, the World's Fair came along and reignited Knoxville's hometown pride. Throughout the preparation for the fair, for the six months it was here, and for the year afterward, the city rode this wave of positive energy. When that wave lifted many residents and business owners saw what Knoxville could become. Historic restoration projects, downtown revitalization initiatives, and awareness campaigns began to roll out, and slowly, Knoxville began to turn. By the early 2000s, downtown Knoxville resonated with businesses. Restaurants and shops began to open in spruced-up buildings from yesteryear. Bars followed, and boutiques began to flourish. Soon, downtown had turned into what it is today—a fun cultural center for the city and a place to visit rather than flee.

SIGHTS
★ East Tennessee History Center

In the heart of downtown, there's a great little museum telling the story of more than 200 years of East Tennessee's history. The **East Tennessee History Center** (601 S. Gay St., 865/215-8830, www.easttnhistory.org, 9am-4pm Mon.-Fri., 10am-4pm Sat., 1pm-5pm Sun., adults $5, seniors $4, children 16 and under free, free admission on Sun.) has exhibits on the Cherokee, the local involvement in skirmishes and battles of the Civil War, notable slaves and former slaves from the region, the origins of country music, and many displays and scenes showing Knoxville throughout the years. There are also exhibits on logging and mining, two vocations important to the region, as well as Oak Ridge National Laboratory, where important work in World War II's Manhattan Project was conducted.

The museum itself is great, but also take note of the wonderful neoclassical Italianate architecture of the building as you walk in. It's Knoxville's old Customs House, built in 1874. Since then, it has served several purposes—a courthouse, post office, TVA offices. Like many buildings around town, it's built from Tennessee marble.

★ Knoxville Museum of Art

The **Knoxville Museum of Art** (1050 World's Fair Park Dr., 865/525-6101, www.knoxart.org, 10am-5pm Tues.-Sat., 1pm-5pm Sun., free, donations accepted) is a three-story showcase of art and artists of East Tennessee. A huge exhibition, *Cycle of Life: Within the Power of Dreams and the Wonder of Infinity,* from renowned glass artist Richard Jolley, hangs on the walls and ceiling of the ground floor, and a colorful, impressive element of it—a nebula of colored glass orbs—can be seen as you walk through the museum doors. On the top level, two galleries show historic and contemporary works created by artists from or inspired by East Tennessee. The main level has another pair of galleries with rotating exhibits where they display national, international, and regional works, single-artist shows, and themed

Downtown Knoxville

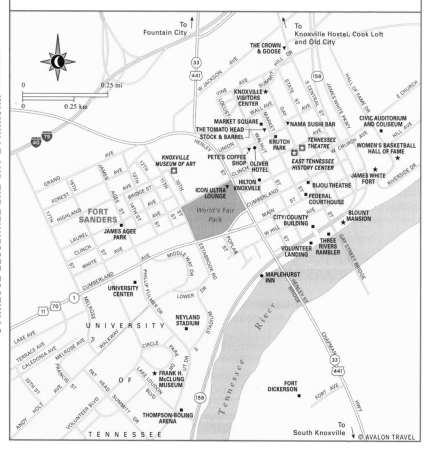

collections, like the assembly of more than a dozen pieces of amazing blown and cast glass sculptures.

★ Tennessee Theatre

The **Tennessee Theatre** (604 S. Gay St., 865/684-1200, www.tennesseetheatre.com, box office 10am-5pm Mon.-Fri., showtimes and ticket prices vary) is magnificent. In October 1928, this fabulous space opened its doors to rave reviews. The exterior features that classic marquee we just don't make today, and the inside puts any contemporary movie theater or music hall to shame. The Spanish-Moorish-style interior was painstakingly restored to its original grandeur in 2003 with a price tag north of $25 million, funded through public expenditures and private donations. Today, when you walk into the lobby, huge chandeliers twinkle high above. You follow the lines of the ceiling and the patterns on the wall to the marble floor. Twin staircases lead to the balcony upstairs, and once in the theater, there's more ornate wood- and plasterwork. On stage, there's a gorgeous Wurlitzer organ from the same era as the theater. The best part is the theater actually has someone who knows how to play the organ, and play it well. Shows here vary from national and international musicians to plays and stage shows to a handful of films.

Sunsphere

When the World's Fair came in 1982, the city was transformed. The most dramatic change is one that has permanently transformed the skyline and become an easily recognizable symbol of the city. The **Sunsphere** (810 Clinch Ave., Fl. 5, 865/251-8161, www.worldsfairpark.org, 9am-10pm daily Apr.-Oct., 11am-6pm daily Nov.-Mar., free) is a 266-foot-tall tower topped by a huge golden ball. Inside the ball are private offices, a lounge, and a great observation deck that gives you a 360-degree view of Knoxville. It's a shame that the Sunsphere sat mostly unused from the end of the fair until 1999, when it was reopened briefly, then closed again just as suddenly. In 2005, Knoxville's mayor announced that the Sunsphere and the adjacent Tennessee Amphitheater (6am-midnight, showtimes vary), another World's Fair attraction, would be renovated and returned to public use. This is a great structure that symbolizes many things for this city, so it's good to see it in use again.

Knoxville Zoo

The **Knoxville Zoo** (3500 Knoxville Zoo Dr., 865/637-5331, www.knoxville-zoo.org, 10am-4:30pm daily, closed Christmas Day, adults $20, seniors and children 4-12 $17, parking $5) has more than 900 animals from all over the world including the expected zoo animals and some surprises. There are a number of red pandas here (the zoo is a breeding facility for them), a giraffe you can feed, and Budgie Landing, an enclosed aviary in the Clayton Family Kids Cove that's filled with what seems like a million budgies (a type of small parrot) flying around.

Women's Basketball Hall of Fame

Given the basketball prowess of the University of Tennessee Lady Vols and famed former coach Pat Summitt, Knoxville is a fitting place for the **Women's Basketball Hall of Fame** (700 Hall of Fame Dr., 865/633-9000, www.wbhof.com, 11am-5pm Tues.-Fri., 10am-5pm Sat. Labor Day-Apr., 10am-5pm Mon.-Sat. May-Labor Day, adults $8, seniors and children 6-15 $6). This facility, the only one devoted entirely to women's basketball achievements at all levels, opened in 1999 and celebrates the rich history of women's

the Sunsphere in World's Fair Park

KNOXVILLE AND THE TENNESSEE FOOTHILLS
KNOXVILLE

basketball. The exhibits here are more than just a plaque and write-up on Hall of Fame members; there are interactive areas like the court where you can practice passing and dribbling skills or shoot a few balls at baskets both contemporary and from the earliest days of the game. Other exhibits include displays honoring current NCAA national champions and a set of mannequins dressed in uniforms from over the years. There's also a gift shop where you can pick up basketballs autographed by Hall of Fame members. Oh, and the building is hard to miss—one end has the world's largest basketball, which appears to be dropping into a net.

Circle G Ranch

The **Circle G Ranch** (831 Thorngrove Pike, Strawberry Plains, 865/932-0070, www.ridecamels.com, 10am-5pm daily, adults $9, children 2-13 $7, safari truck tours $15 per person) is a drive-through zoo with more than 500 animals including camels, zebras, ostriches, and emus, to name a few. It's weird and it's fun, but it's even better if you take a guided tour with Matt, one of the owners of the ranch. His knowledge of these animals and anecdotes about working with them makes the drive very entertaining indeed. No matter how you choose to tour, buy a few buckets of food (three buckets for $10 or $4 for a single bucket): The animals know it's coming and they'll beat a path to your car, making for some entertaining photos. Even more than the variety of animals at Circle G, the thing that sets them apart from other drive-through animal parks is the Camel Safari ($60), a one-hour trek through the park atop a camel. You'll need to make a reservation at least 48 hours in advance, but it's worth the effort.

Haunted Knoxville Ghost Tours

Haunted Knoxville Ghost Tours (301 S. Gay St., 865/377-9677, www.hauntedknoxville.net, adults $40, children 9-12 $35, tour dates and times vary, reserve online) is more than just a person walking around telling

craft beer at Hops & Hollers

some "scary" stories filled with local color—these guides offer one of the leading historical and investigation-based ghost tours. They've dug up some juicy, and creepy, stories that reveal a hidden side of this friendly city. And they continue to carry out investigations, bringing with them on every tour a host of tools used to gather information on the paranormal.

ENTERTAINMENT AND EVENTS
Nightlife

Hops & Hollers (937 N. Central St., 865/312-5733, www.hopsandhollers.com, noon-midnight Mon.-Thurs., 2pm-late Fri., noon-late Sat., 11am-10pm Sun.) is a fun little craft beer bar with 100 beers in bottles and cans and 32 more on draft. Of those taps, 20 are dedicated to Tennessee brews, which will give craft beer connoisseurs a taste of some of the best beer the state has to offer. The bartenders know their brews and can make reliable recommendations (when in doubt, ask for a tasting

Tennessee's Unsung Music Town

Knoxville gets short shrift when folks talk about Tennessee music. Ever eclipsed by Nashville and overlooked by bluegrass and mountain string band lovers for spots like Gatlinburg and Pigeon Forge, Knoxville is often forgotten. But no more. The music scene in this hip Southern town is lively and growing livelier by the minute. Bands like The Black Lillies, with their mountain-influenced indie rock, and The Black Cadillacs, who take a more bluesy spin, have made a name for themselves nationally in recent years, playing at Bonnaroo and the Grand Ole Opry.

All across town you'll find buskers playing on the street, bands tucked into restaurants and bars, and free concerts on Market Square during the summer. Jam sessions pop up and musicians flow freely from one impromptu band to another until they find the perfect fit. Two historic venues—The **Tennessee Theatre** (the state's official theater, and a stunning place to see a band) and the **Bijou Theatre**—host concerts with clockwork regularity.

Music festivals, like **Big Ears Festival** (www.bigearsfestival.com), **Smoky Mountain Music Fest** (www.smmfestival.com), and **Rhythm N Blooms Fest** (www.rhythmnblooms-fest.com), celebrate the sounds of the city and bring in visiting bands and music fans from all over.

Make it a point while you're in town to take in one of the daily free shows at **WDVX-FM**, where their noontime Blue Plate Special concert series brings in local and regional acts to play for a live radio broadcast in front of a studio audience.

pour). Musicians play here on a regular basis and food trucks stop by just about every night of the week.

Casual Pint (421 Union St., 865/951-2160, www.thecasualpint.com, 3pm-11pm Mon.-Thurs., 3pm-2am Fri., 11am-2am. Sat., noon-11pm Sun.) brews several beers in-house and always has a deep lineup on draft. Grab a sampler flight or the pint of your choice, or fill up a growler to take your brew home with you.

Club XYZ (1215 N. Central St., 865/637-4999, 7pm-3am nightly) is one of the best gay bars in Knoxville. They have drag shows, karaoke nights, dance parties, and great happy hour specials.

Icon Ultra Lounge (810 Clinch Ave., on the 5th fl. of the Sunsphere, 865/249-7321, www.knoxvilleicon.com, 4pm-midnight Tues.-Thurs., 4pm-2am Fri.-Sat.) has some fantastic views, good drinks, and a dinner and late-night menu. It's a great place to visit for a drink or two before heading out for further adventures, or for stopping by for a nightcap and something to munch on before heading back to your hotel.

Performing Arts

The **Bijou Theatre** (803 S. Gay St.,

865/522-0832, www.knoxbijou.com, ticket prices vary) is one of Knoxville's most important venues for live musical performances. Everyone from The Marx Brothers and Dolly Parton to The Ramones and Dave Matthews played here, and the audience at one time included President Andrew Jackson.

The Bijou (well, the building anyway) dates to 1817 and has been a hotel and tavern, a place for social gatherings, and an object of some consternation for its myriad owners until it finally opened as a theater in 1908. A vaudeville stage for a long time (with a rare-for-the-time policy of admitting black patrons to the gallery seating), the Bijou showed films on occasion, but that stopped when the Tennessee Theatre opened up the street. (The builders of the Tennessee bought the Bijou, then sold it with one caveat: the Bijou couldn't be used as a theater for the next five years.) After various incarnations, the Bijou reopened as a fully renovated theater in 2006.

Knox Comedy Live (www.knoxcomedy.com) isn't a comedy club, but rather a group of comedians living in the region who are helping to spread the word about smaller comedy shows and open mic opportunities. Check their website for upcoming shows. **The Pilot Light** (106 E. Jackson Ave., 865/524-8188, www.thepilotlight.com, 6pm-late nightly), a nightclub in Knoxville's Old City, hosts comedy shows as well as frequent musical acts.

Festivals and Events

Knoxville has great events going on throughout the year, including the **International Biscuit Festival** (865/238-5219, www.biscuitfest.com, mid-May), an annual spring gathering of foodies, food writers, and biscuit enthusiasts. **Big Ears** (www.bigearsfestival.com, weekend passes start at $135, day passes $50) brings all sorts of odd performers, films, and musical acts to Knoxville at the end of March. At the end of April, the **Scruffy City Film & Music Festival** (865/245-0411, www.knoxvillefilms.com, ticket prices from $8) invades downtown, filling it with musical performances and film screenings. There's no telling what local and regional musical acts will show up, but it's guaranteed they'll be interesting and wide ranging in terms of genre and style. Films run the gamut from documentary shorts to music videos to full features, plus there are workshops designed to help filmmakers and musicians push their art to the limits. The very popular 24 Hour Film Festival is part of this six-day creative extravaganza.

Film is big in Knoxville and the **Knoxville Film Festival** (www.knoxvillefilmfestival.com, festival pass $50, film blocks from $10) takes place in mid-September. In addition to excellent film screenings, there's a student filmmaking competition and a high-stakes seven-minute film competition. The 7-Day Shootout happens in August, when teams of filmmakers gather in Knoxville to develop their scripts and shoot them. The completed films are shown at the festival; the grand prize winner takes home $20,000 to turn their seven-minute film into a full feature.

SHOPPING

Market Square (865/524-2224) provides a center square (actually, a rectangle) around which people can gather. Just one block off Gay Street, this excellent little shopping and dining district is always busy. There are summer concerts, buskers, and a small fountain for the kids to play in, and the variety of people walking by and stores to peruse makes it easy to kill time while waiting for your table to be ready. There are a half-dozen restaurants on the square, and close to a dozen

Knoxville's Market Square

shops, including the **Mast General Store** (865/546-1336, www.maststoreknoxville, 10am-6pm Mon.-Wed., 10am-9pm Thurs.-Sat., noon-6pm Sun.), where you can buy everything from camping gear to home goods to penny candy; **Earth to Old City** (865/522-8270, www.earthtooldcity.com, 10am-9pm Mon.-Sat., noon-6pm Sun.) carries all sorts of odd and funky home decor (some of it may be more at home in a dorm room than your house); and twin shops **Bliss** (865/329-8868, www.shopinbliss.com, 10am-9pm Mon.-Thurs., 10am-10pm Fri.-Sat., 11am-8pm Sun.) and **Bliss Home** (865/673-6711, 10am-7pm Mon.-Sat., noon-5pm Sun.), selling home goods and lifestyle accessories. **Nothing Too Fancy** (435 Union Ave., 865/951-2916, www.nothingtoofancy.com, 10am-9pm Mon.-Fri., 9am-9pm Sat., 11am-6pm Sun.) has some very cool T-shirts and other silk-screened goods designed by local artists. Reflecting the culture, in-jokes, and vibe of Knoxville in their work, the shirts are fun, even for those not in the know.

The **Market Square Farmers Market** (www.marketsquarefarmersmarket.org, 11am-2pm Wed. and 9am-2pm Sat., May-Nov.) shows up in late spring, bringing with it dozens of farmers and craftspeople selling their wares, edible or not.

RECREATION

The unquestioned star of Knoxville's recreational scene is **Ijams Nature Center** (2915 Island Home Ave., 865/577-4717, www.ijams.org, 9am-5pm Mon.-Sat., 11am-5pm Sun.). This 300-acre urban wilderness is laced with hiking and single-track mountain biking trails, former quarries to explore on foot or even paddle around, and it's dog-friendly. This vast, wild space is a strange thing so close to the city, but people love it. At any time of any day there are walkers, hikers, trail runners, bikers, families, couples, and singles on the trails here. From Ijams Nature Center, you can connect with a larger, nearly contiguous loop of some 40 miles. Grab a map when you come in or download one and plan your route

ahead of time, or you could just bring some water and your camera and wander.

World's Fair Park (www.worldsfairpark.org) is the best city park in Knoxville. This 10-acre park has walking paths, a small lake, open grassy spaces, soccer fields, fountains, and a gorgeous stream running right down the middle of it. It's the home of the Sunsphere and Tennessee Amphitheatre, and at the north end of the park, past a fantastically large fountain, is a 4,200-square-foot playground. The playground and fountain get pretty crowded with kids, but there are other places you can go if you're traveling without a few of your own.

ACCOMMODATIONS

★ **The Oliver Hotel** (407 Union Ave., 865/521-0050, www.theoliverhotel.com, $160-265) is an outstanding boutique hotel. The service is impeccable and the rooms amazing—everything is done to a luxurious, but not ostentatious, level. When you first find it, you'll likely walk right past it—it blends in with the rest of the block almost seamlessly. Built in 1876 as a bakery, it was converted into a hotel for the World's Fair. There are 24 guest rooms with wet bars, coffee service, and fabulous bedding.

Maplehurst Inn (800 West Hill Ave., 865/851-8383, www.maplehurstinn.com, $125-175) is dated, but worth considering because of the friendly service and a pretty good breakfast. Your hosts make you feel at home and you can tell they care about your experience. Plus, it's a mansion in a truly lovely part of town.

Maple Grove Inn (8800 Westland Dr., 865/951-2315, www.maplegroveinn.com, $150-300) has seven rooms in one of the oldest residences in Knoxville. A popular spot for weddings, this full-service bed-and-breakfast sits on 15 acres of gardens, giving you the opportunity to truly check out of day-to-day life and relax in the moment.

Hilton Knoxville (501 W. Church Ave., 865/523-2300, www.hilton.com, $192-200) is only two blocks off Gay Street and has fantastic rooms. With on-site dining, a Starbucks right in the lobby, and parking next door, it's the best of the name-brand hotels you'll find.

There are a number of other chain hotels in town, including the **Hampton Inn Knoxville North** (5411 Pratt Rd., 855/271-3622, www.hamptoninn3.hilton.com, $120-170) and the **Country Inn & Suites Knoxville at Cedar Bluff** (9137 Cross Park Dr., 800/596-2375, www.countryinns.com, $120-185).

FOOD

Knoxville Food Tours (865/201-7270, www.knoxvillefoodtours.com, $99) shows off some of the best spots to drink and dine in downtown Knoxville. Tour dates are Friday and Saturday afternoons and evenings, but custom tours are available any day. The walk's not far—generally less than a mile—and you get to find a place to have dinner, all while under the tutelage of a local foodie.

The tiny shop **Just Ripe** (513 Union Ave., 865/851-9327, 8am-2pm Mon.-Sat., $1.50-10) sells coffee, a few baked goods, a pair of burritos, healthy grab-and-go lunch items, and these incredible biscuits and biscuit sandwiches. They're just the right mix of dense and fluffy, and with a little bacon or smoky tomato jam (or both) they are out of this world.

When a former rock musician opens a restaurant, you expect it to have a lot of personality, and ★ **Sweet P's Barbecue & Soul House** (3725 Maryville Pike, 865/247-7748, www.sweetpbbq.com, 11am-8pm Tues.-Thurs., 11am-9pm Fri.-Sat., noon-7pm Sun., $4-22) delivers. Owner and Pitmaster Chris Ford ate in every barbecue joint he could find while on tour with his band and began developing recipes long before he had the idea for a restaurant. When the time came to open Sweet P's, he was ready. This is some fine barbecue, whether it's the ribs, the brisket, or the sides. The potato salad is good and the mac and cheese done just right, but the coleslaw is out of this world. Good news if you're going to stick to downtown Knoxville: **Sweet P's Downtown Dive** (410 W. Jackson Ave.,

865/281-1738, www.sweetpbbq.com, 11am-9pm Tues.-Thurs., 11am-10pm Fri.-Sat., noon-9pm Sun., $5-20) lets you get your fix of 'cue without venturing far from the city's heart.

★ **Dead End BBQ** (3621 Sutherland Ave., 865/212-5655, www.deadendbbq.com, 11am-9pm Sun.-Thurs., 11am-10pm Fri.-Sat., $8-23) was started by a group of guys who would get together and make barbecue. Turns out they were onto something good. After their neighbors and wives praised them enough, they decided to enter a barbecue competition. They did well, very well, and entered another—and it wasn't long before they had accumulated a wall of trophies. Naturally, this little obsession turned into a restaurant, and a damn good one at that. Everything they do here is top-notch, so unless the brisket or ribs or some other dish catches your eye, get the sampler plate. They have one dish you don't see very often—beef brisket burnt ends. Far from being burnt, these succulent little morsels are trimmings off the brisket, and they go down easy. The sauce here is fantastic, and the sides outstanding. Save room for dessert; their banana pudding is so rich and thick that it's more like cheesecake.

Pete's Coffee Shop (540 Union Ave., 865/523-2860, www.petescoffeeshop.com, 6:30am-2:30pm Mon.-Fri., 7am-2pm Sat., $2-8) is a diner that's dirt cheap and super tasty. Their French toast is exceptional, as are their pancakes, and for lunch, Pete's Supreme (ham and melted Swiss on a hoagie) is excellent, as is the patty melt.

At **The Tomato Head** (12 Market Square, 865/637-4067, www.thetomatohead.com, 11am-9:30pm Mon.-Thurs., 11am-10:30pm Fri., 10am-10:30pm Sat., 10am-9pm Sun., brunch 10am-3pm Sat.-Sun., $3-28) you can sit outside, weather permitting, and watch the crowds on Market Square while you eat your pizza. The menu here features pizzas, sandwiches, burritos, and salads, but stick to the pizza—not because the other stuff is bad, but because the pizza is so good. You can build your own or choose one of their topping combinations. Odd combos like fresh spinach and black bean, lamb sausage and sundried tomato, and smoked salmon and pesto actually go down quite easily.

Stock & Barrel (35 Market Square, 865/766-2075, www.thestockandbarrel.com, 11am-late daily, $7-16) has an unparalleled bourbon selection, a list of burgers that are as tasty as they are creative, and a line out the door. Even if you make a reservation, you'll wait for a seat, but it's worth it because once you get in, you won't want to leave. Get a flight of bourbon and whatever burger pushes your buttons, and enjoy.

Nama Sushi Bar (506 S. Gay St., 865/633-8539, www.namasushibar.com, 11am-midnight Mon.-Thurs., 11am-2am Fri.-Sat., noon-midnight Sun., $4-24) is the best option for sushi in Knoxville. Their fish is always fresh and they serve both traditional rolls and rolls that are a little more inventive. The Moon Special Roll and the Orange Crush go pretty far afield from your basic roll and make for a delicious bite. This place gets crowded, especially on weekends or when Knoxville is hopping, so get there early or make a reservation.

The Crown & Goose (123 S. Central St., 865/524-2100, www.thecrownandgoose.com, 11am-11pm Mon.-Wed., 11am-midnight Thurs., 11am-1am Fri.-Sat., 11am-3pm Sun., $8-26) is a gastropub serving a fusion of traditional British and contemporary European dishes and techniques. Nothing here pushes the boundaries too far, but they do use some great ingredients in their interpretations of fish-and-chips and shepherd's pie, as well as in their small plates.

TRANSPORTATION AND SERVICES
Car
Driving to Knoxville is easy. If you've followed the Blue Ridge Parkway through Great Smoky Mountains National Park, just stay on US-441, which runs right into downtown. Coming from the east or west via I-40, take Exit 388 for Gay Street.

From Asheville, take I-40 West 116 miles (2 hours) to Knoxville. From Charlotte, where

you'll find a major airport, take US-74 West to I-40 West into Knoxville, a four-hour drive. Alternatively, take the same route, but leave I-40 for US-19 into Cherokee, then take US-441/TN-71 through GSMNP and into Knoxville.

From the south, I-75 offers a direct route into Knoxville from Chattanooga, Tennessee (1 hour 45 minutes), and Atlanta, Georgia (3 hours). I-40 is likewise a direct route from Nashville to Knoxville (2 hours 45 minutes). From the north, Knoxville is accessible via I-81.

Air
McGhee Tyson Airport (2055 Alcoa Highway, Alcoa, 865/342-3000, www.flyknoxville.com) is located 20 minutes south of Knoxville in Alcoa, Tennessee. You can get there on US-129. From I-40, take Exit 386-B to US-129 south; it's 12 miles to the airport. Airlines serving McGhee Tyson include **Allegiant** (702/505-8888, www.allegiantair.com), **American Airlines** (800/433-7300, www.aa.com), **Delta** (800/221-1212, www.delta.com), **Frontier** (800/432-1359, www.flyfrontier.com), and **United** (800/525-0208, www.ual.com).

If you need taxi service between the airport and Knoxville, **A&B Ground Transportation** (865/389-0312), **Discount Taxi** (865/755-5143), **Odyssey Airport Taxi** (865/577-6767), and **Knoxville Taxi** (865/691-1900) are just a few of the car services you can call.

Public Transit
Once you're in town, there is plenty to walk to. **Knoxville Trolley Lines** (301 Church Ave., 865/637-3000, free), operated by Knoxville Area Transit, also runs throughout downtown. Check online or call for current schedules and routes.

Services
The **Knoxville Visitors Center** (301 S. Gay St., 800/727-8045, www.visitknoxville.com, 8:30am-5pm Mon.-Fri., 9am-5pm

Sat., noon-4pm Sun.) is what visitors centers should be. They have the expected rack of maps and helpful volunteers on hand to answer questions, but what sets them apart is the gift shop filled with locally made art and foodstuffs, a kids' corner, coffee, and a radio station. This is the only visitors center I know of where you can watch a free concert every day at lunch or listen to it as a live radio broadcast.

The local public radio station, **WDVX-FM** (301 S. Gay St., 865/544-1029, www.wdvx.com) at 89.9 FM, is also the host of the Blue Plate Special concert series held on the stage in the Knoxville Visitors Center during lunch hour on weekdays. Listen to classic rock at **WIMZ** (103.5 FM). **WUTK** (90.3 FM) is a college station from the University of Tennessee. Tune in to public radio from UT at **WUOT** (91.9).

If you need medical care, there are more than a half-dozen clinics and hospitals in Knoxville. The **University of Tennessee Medical Center** (1924 Alcoa Highway, 865/305-9000, www.utmedicalcenter.org) is a 581-bed teaching hospital, and **Fort Sanders Regional Medical Center** (1901 Clinch Ave., 865/541-1111, www.fsregional.com) is conveniently located downtown.

Background

The Land

GEOGRAPHY

North Carolina is made up of three distinct regions: the coast and coastal plain, the Piedmont, and the mountains. Divided roughly by interstate highways, the state looks like this—east of I-95 is the coastal plain and 300 miles of shoreline; west of I-77 is the mountains; between, the Piedmont and Sandhills. The state's tobacco farms and former mill towns—the onetime economic drivers of North Carolina—are found in the Piedmont, as are the state's largest cities. Along the coast are the state's oldest towns. In the mountains are a few cities, a number of small towns, and one of the oldest mountain chains in the world.

The Mountain Region forms the western border of the state. The ridges of the Blue Ridge and Great Smoky Mountains, both subranges of the Appalachian Mountain chain, undulate like the folds of a great quilt, running northeast-to-southwest from Virginia along the border with Tennessee and into the southwestern corner where the inland tip of North Carolina meets Georgia. This is a land of waterfalls, rivers, and fast-flowing creeks, and rugged, beautiful peaks of smaller mountain configurations. Hemmed in among the peaks and hollows of the Blue Ridge and the Smokies are the Black Mountains, the Pisgah Range, and the Unka Range. The Black Mountains are only about 15 miles wide and are confined mostly to Yancey County, but they're the highest in the state, and six of the ten highest peaks in the eastern United States are here, including Mount Mitchell, the highest at 6,684 feet.

This is a region rich in resources, with coal seams, limestone and marble quarries, natural gas deposits, and, surprisingly, pockets and veins of precious and semiprecious gems. The rivers here are old, with the ironically named New River, one of the oldest in the world, flowing northward from North Carolina's Blue Ridge through Virginia and into West Virginia.

CLIMATE

Generalizing about North Carolina's climate is difficult. It's not as hot as at the equator and not as cold as at the poles, but beyond that, each region has its own range of variables and has to be examined separately.

The mountains are much cooler than either the Piedmont or the coast, and winter lasts longer. Towns like Asheville and Boone can be blanketed in snow while less than 100 miles away the trees in Piedmont towns aren't even showing their fall colors. The coldest temperature ever recorded in North Carolina, -34°F, was recorded in 1985 on Mount Mitchell. Spring and fall can bring cool to temperate days and chilly nights, while summer days can hit the 80s, and the evenings bring a welcome relief. The Piedmont, on the other hand, can be brutally hot during the summer and quite warm on spring and fall days, though winter is milder. The coast sees long, hot summers and cool—not cold—winters with rare snowfall.

The Blue Ridge and Smoky Mountains experience four distinct seasons, with temperatures and microclimates that can vary wildly depending on elevation and sun exposure. Temperatures can swing drastically with those elevation shifts, changing as much as 15 or 20 degrees as you go from the lowest elevations to the highest. That means on warm summer days, when cities like Asheville might see temperatures in the 80s, Mount Mitchell,

The weather changes in an instant at high elevations.

6,000 feet above sea level, will be in the low 50s and possibly cooler, depending on wind.

During spring, temperatures in this region range from the low 40s to the mid- or upper 60s, and rain or even an early-spring snowfall is common. Summer sees higher temperatures, reaching 80 degrees with some regularity, higher on rare occasions; summer lows can dip down into the 60s and may be even lower at high elevations along the Blue Ridge Parkway. In fall, temperatures are similar to spring, with daytime temperatures in the 40s to 60s, and nights plunging to 30 degrees on occasion. Winter is cold, with ranges from the low 30s to the high 40s; nighttime temperatures, and temperatures in the deepest hollows, can fall into the teens and single digits. Temperatures that low are possible across the region during the coldest periods of winter, even lower at elevations where it's not uncommon to experience a few freezing days.

This is a wet place, with regular snowfall from late fall through early spring, and rains common any time of year. Winter storms can dump a few inches of wet snow on the mountains here, or they can dust it with some fine, powdery snow. Thunderstorms in spring, summer, and fall can be heavy, though the worst of the weather is only occasional; regular rain showers contribute to the 50-80 inches of precipitation falling annually.

Tornadoes, most common in the spring, can cause trouble any time of year. A rare November twister touched down in 2006, smashing the Columbus County community of Riegelwood, killing eight people and leaving a seven-mile swath of destruction. Even plain old **thunderstorms** can be dangerous, bringing lightning, flash flooding, difficult driving conditions, and even hail. **Snowstorms** are rare, and usually occur in the mountains. The Piedmont sees more snow than the coast, which sees flurries once or twice each winter and the occasional dusting of snow. Outside the mountains, most North Carolinians are woefully inexperienced snow drivers, and the state Department of Transportation doesn't have the equipment in coastal counties to handle much more than a little snow.

ENVIRONMENTAL CONCERNS

The parklands and forests along the routes through the Blue Ridge and Smoky Mountains are preserved so future generations can enjoy nature in as pristine a state as possible. That's why there's no gas available on the Blue Ridge Parkway. It also explains the constant reminders to adhere to **Leave No Trace** (www.LNT. org) principles. Leave No Trace principles are similar to the Boy Scouts of America teachings: plan ahead and prepare, travel and camp on durable surfaces, dispose of waste properly, leave what you find, minimize campfire impacts, respect wildlife, be considerate of other visitors. These easy rules can improve the outdoor experience for everyone.

If you pack something in, pack it out, and consider carrying a **trash bag** on trails to pick up after less responsible hikers. If each of us would make this a habit, we could clean

Geographical Vocabulary

North Carolina has some unusual landscapes and environments, and some unusual vocabulary to describe them. As you explore the state, you may encounter the following terms.

HOLLER

Here's a term that's really more of a regional pronunciation than a unique word. A holler is what is on paper termed a "hollow"—a mountain cove. It's just that in the South we aren't much for rounding words that end in "ow." If you don't believe me, just beller out the winda to that feller wallering in yonder meada.

BALD

An ecological mystery, the Appalachian bald is a mountaintop area on which there are no trees, even though surrounding areas of the same elevation may be forested. Typically, a bald is either grassy or a heath. Heaths are more easily explained, as they are caused by soil conditions that don't support forest. Grassy balds, though, occur on land where logically trees should be found. Some theories hold that grassy balds were caused by generations of livestock grazing, but soil studies show that they were grassy meadows before the first cattle or sheep arrived. Grazing may still be the answer, though: The balds may originally have been chomped and trampled down by prehistoric megafauna—ancient bison, mastodons, and mammoths. Today, in the absence of mammoths or free-ranging cattle, some balds are gradually becoming woodland, except where deliberately maintained.

SANDHILLS

If you're in Wilmington or Southport, or somewhere else along the state's southeastern coast, take note of what the soil beneath your feet looks like. Now, turn your back to the ocean and head inland. Travel 100 miles west and then look down again. What you'll see is very similar—sandy, light-colored ground, wiry vegetation (and a few carnivorous plants), maybe even some scattered shells. About 20 million years ago, during the Miocene Epoch, the areas of present-day Fayetteville, Southern Pines, and Sanford were sand dunes on the shores of an ocean that covered what is now North Carolina's coastal plain. Imagine the landscape millions of years ago, when the Uwharrie Mountains, just west of the Sandhills, towered 20,000 feet over an ocean that swirled at their feet.

POCOSIN

Pronounced "puh-COH-sin," the word is said to come from the Algonquin for "swamp on a hill." A pocosin is a moist peat bog of a sort unique to the Southeast and particularly associated with eastern North Carolina. The peat layer is thinnest around the edges and usually supports communities of pine trees. Moving toward the center of the bog, the ground becomes slightly higher, and the peat thicker, more acidic, and less welcoming to plant species. Because the soil is so poor and leeched of nutrients, carnivorous plants, which have their meals delivered rather than depending on the soil's bounty, are particularly well suited to life in pocosins.

CAROLINA BAY

The word *bay* here refers not to an inlet on the coast but to another kind of upland swamp. The bays' origins are mysterious, and their regularity of form and commonness in this region is uncanny. If you look down at eastern North and South Carolina from an airplane, or in a satellite image, the bays are unmistakable. They're oval-shaped depressions, varying in size from Lake Waccamaw to mere puddles, and are always aligned in a northeast-to-southwest configuration. Unlike ponds and regular swamps, Carolina bays are usually unconnected to any groundwater source but are fed solely by rainwater. Like pocosins, bays attract colonies of carnivorous plants, which love to establish their dens of iniquity in such unwholesome soil.

up a lot of litter that clutters up our view and is detrimental to the environment.

Dogs are allowed on some trails throughout this route, though they must be on leash or under physical control at all times. If you have Fido out on the trail or let him use the grassy facilities at an overlook or wayside, be sure to pick up what he's putting down.

You'll pass several ponds and lakes as you travel this region, but unless there's a designated **swimming** area, going for a dip isn't cool. There are exceptions, but those exceptions are noted near the potential swimming hole. When in doubt, ask before you dive in.

You'll spot lots of **wildlife** on your trip. Common animals include white-tailed deer, raccoons, opossums, turtles, bobcats, and even black bears. Coyotes are becoming a more frequent sight along the way, and in certain areas of the Smoky Mountains, you can even see the occasional elk. Many times, a herd of deer will be in a pasture off the Parkway. If you see deer (or any other animal), and you want to get a photograph, keep a safe distance from the animal and don't offer them any food; this makes them grow accustomed to people and can have negative impacts on their health.

Plants

In the early 1700s, John Lawson, an English explorer who would soon be one of the first victims of the Tuscarora War, wrote of a magnificent tree house somewhere in the very young colony of North Carolina. "I have been informed of a Tulip-Tree," he wrote, "that was ten Foot Diameter; and another, wherein a lusty Man had his Bed and Household Furniture, and liv'd in it, till his Labour got him a more fashionable Mansion. He afterwards became a noted Man, in his Country, for Wealth and Conduct." Whether or not there was ever a tulip poplar large enough to serve as a furnished bachelor pad, colonial North Carolina's forests must have seemed miraculous to the first Europeans to see them.

FORESTS

Today, after generations of logging and farming across the state, few old-growth forests exist. In the Smoky Mountains, stands of old-growth timber, like the Joyce Kilmer Memorial Forest, are a sight to behold, and some of the trees almost validate Lawson's anecdote. Across the state, scores of specialized ecosystems support a marvelous diversity of plant and animal life. In the east, cypress swamps and a few patches of maritime forest still stand; across the Sandhills are longleaf

pine forests; in the mountains are fragrant balsam forests and stands of hardwoods.

Because the state is so geographically and climatically varied, there's a greater diversity in tree species than anywhere in the eastern United States. More than half of the land in the Piedmont and eastern North Carolina is forested. Coastal forests are dominated by hardwoods—**oaks** of many varieties, **gum,** **cypress,** and **cedar**—and the barrier islands have a few remaining patches of maritime forest where the branches of **live oak** trees intertwine to shed storm wind and their roots sink deep to keep islands stable. The best and largest remaining example of a pristine maritime forest is on Bald Head Island, where the Bald Head Island Conservancy provides education and studies the form, function, and future of barrier islands, including these important maritime forest ecosystems. In the Piedmont, oak and **hickory** dominate the hardwoods alongside bands of piney woods. In the mountains oak and hickory are also the rule, but a number of conifers, including **pine** and **balsam,** appear.

The science and profession of forestry were born in North Carolina: In the 1880s and 1890s, George W. Vanderbilt, lord of the manner at Biltmore, engaged Fredrick

Law Olmsted, who designed New York City's Central Park, to plan a managed forest of the finest, healthiest, and hardiest trees. Vanderbilt hired Gifford Pinchot and later Carl Schenck to be the stewards of the thousands of wooded acres he owned in the Pisgah Forest south of Asheville. The contributions these men made to the nascent field are still felt today and are commemorated at the Cradle of Forestry Museum near Brevard.

Longleaf Pine

Arguably, the most important plant in North Carolina's history is the longleaf pine, sometimes called the pitch pine. This beautiful tree is something of a rare sight today, as the vast stands of longleaf pines that formerly blanketed the eastern part of the state were used extensively in the naval stores industry in the 18th and 19th centuries, providing valuable turpentine, pitch, tar, and lumber. The overharvesting of this tree has a lot to do with the disappearance of North Carolina's once-legendary pine barrens, but an unanticipated ancillary cause is the efficiency of modern firefighting. Longleaf pines depend on periodic forest fires to clear out competition from the underbrush and provide layers of nutrient-rich singed earth. In the 20th century the rule was to put out forest fires, cutting down on smoke but disturbing the natural growth cycles of these trees. In some longleaf-harboring nature preserves today, controlled burns keep the woods alive and healthy as crucial habitats for several endangered species, including the red-cockaded woodpecker and the Pine Barrens treefrog.

FLOWERS

Some of North Carolina's flora puts on great annual shows, drawing flocks of admirers—the gaudy **azaleas** of springtime in Wilmington, the **wildflowers** of the first warm weather in the hills, the **rhododendrons** and **mountain laurel** of the Appalachian summer. The Ericaceae family, a race of great woody bushes with star-shaped blossoms that includes azaleas, rhododendrons, and laurel, is the headliner in North Carolina's floral fashion show. Spring comes earliest to the southeastern corner of the state, and the Wilmington area is explosively beautiful when the azaleas are in bloom. The **Azalea Festival,** held annually for more than 50 years, draws hundreds of thousands of people to the city in early to mid-April, around the time that public gardens and private yards are spangled with azaleas.

rhododendron blooms

Horticultural Havens

North Carolina's natural scenery provides inspiration for landscapes of almost equal beauty. Asheville is the home of the **North Carolina Arboretum,** a garden of more than 400 acres that borders the Pisgah National Forest and the Blue Ridge Parkway. Special collections include the National Native Azalea Repository and more than 200 bonsai. You can tour the arboretum on foot, by Segway, or on your bike, and you can even bring your dog on some of the trails.

At the **Biltmore Estate,** Frederick Law Olmsted created formal gardens of beauty to match the opulent mansion, and architect Richard Morris Hunt designed the conservatory where young plants are still raised for the gardens. Self-guided tours of the conservatory—and the walled, shrub, Italian, vernal, and azalea gardens—are all included in admission to the estate.

Asheville is also an excellent home base for excursions to other garden spots in the mountains. Don't miss the **Rivercane Walk** at the John C. Campbell Folk School in Brasstown, where modern Cherokee sculpture lines a path along Little Brasstown Creek. The **Mountain Farm Museum** at the edge of Great Smoky Mountains National Park demonstrates gardening methods used on the early mountain homesteads. The **Cradle of Forestry** in Pisgah National Forest explains how the science of modern forestry was born here in western North Carolina.

The flame azalea makes a late-spring appearance on the mountainsides of the Blue Ridge and Great Smokies, joined by its cousins the mountain laurel and Catawba rhododendron in May and June. The ways of the rhododendron are a little mysterious; not every plant blooms every year, and there's no surefire way of predicting when they'll put on big shows. The area's widely varying elevation also figures into bloom times. If you're interested in timing your trip to coincide with some of these flowering seasons, your best bet is to call ahead and speak with a ranger from Great Smoky Mountains National Park or the Blue Ridge Parkway to find out how the season is coming along.

Around the end of April and into May, when spring finally arrives in the mountains but the forest floor is not yet sequestered in leafy shade, a profusion of delicate flowers emerges. **Violets** and **chickweed** emerge early on, as do the white **trillium** and the wake-robin, a trillium that looks something like a small poinsettia. Every year since 1950, around the end of April, Great Smoky Mountains National Park has hosted the **Spring Wildflower Pilgrimage,** a weeklong festival featuring scores of nature walks that also reveal salamanders, birds, and wild hogs, along with workshops and art exhibits.

Visit www.springwildflowerpilgrimage.org for a schedule of events.

Surprisingly, one of the best places in North Carolina to view displays of wildflowers is along the major highways. For more than 20 years the state Department of Transportation has carried out a highway beautification project that involves planting large banks of wildflowers along highways and in wide medians. The displays are not landscaped but are allowed to grow up in unkempt profusion, often planted in inspired combinations of wildly contrasting colors that make the flowerbeds a genuinely beautiful addition to the environment. The website of the state's **Department of Transportation** (www.ncdot.org) offers a guide to the locations and seasons of the wildflower beds.

FALL FOLIAGE

Arriving as early as mid-September at the highest elevations and gradually sliding down the mountains through late October, autumn colors bring a late-season wave of visitors to western North Carolina. Dropping temperatures change trees' sugar production, resulting in a palette of colors, while simple fatigue causes the green to fade in others, exposing underlying hues. Countless climatic factors can alter the onset and progress of leaf season, so the mountains blush at slightly different times every year. The latter weeks of October tend to be the peak; during those weeks it can be difficult to find lodging in the mountains, so be sure to plan ahead. Some of the best places for leaf peeping are along the Blue Ridge Parkway and in Great Smoky Mountains National Park.

CARNIVOROUS PLANTS

There are many species of **pitcher plants,** a familiar predator of the plant world. Shaped like tubular vases with a graceful elfin flap shading the mouth, pitcher plants attract insects with an irresistible brew. Unsuspecting bugs pile in, thinking they've found a keg party, but instead find themselves paddling in a sticky mess from which they're unable to escape, pinned down by spiny hairs that line the inside of the pitcher. Enterprising frogs and spiders that are either strong or clever enough to come and go safely from inside the pitcher will often set up shop inside a plant and help themselves to stragglers. Another local character is the **sundew,** perhaps the creepiest of the carnivorous plants. Sundews extend their paddle-shaped leaf-hands up into the air, hairy palms baited with a sticky mess that bugs can't resist. When a fly lands among the hairs, the sundew closes on it like a fist and gorges on it until it's ready for more.

Animals

Among the familiar wildlife most commonly seen in the state, **white-tailed deer** are out in force in the countryside and in the woods; they populate suburban areas in large numbers as well. **Raccoons** and **opossums** prowl at night, happy to scavenge from trash cans and the forest floor. **Skunks** are common, particularly in the mountains, and are often smelled rather than seen. They leave an odor something like a cross between grape soda and Sharpie markers. There are also a fair number of **black bears,** not only in the mountains but in swamps and deep woods across the state.

In woods and yards alike, **gray squirrels** and a host of familiar **songbirds** are a daily

a young doe along the Blue Ridge Parkway

presence. Different species of **tree frogs** produce beautiful choruses on spring and summer nights, while **fireflies** mount sparkly shows in the trees and grass in the upper Piedmont and mountains.

The town of Brevard, in the Blue Ridge south of Asheville, is famous for its population of ghostly **white squirrels**. They're the same regular old gray squirrels that live all over North America, but their fur ranges from speckled gray and white to pure bone white. They're not albinos; it's thought that Brevard's white squirrels are cousins of a clan that lives in Florida and that their ancestors may have found their way to the Blue Ridge in a circus or with a dealer of exotic pets in the early 20th century.

The Carolina woods harbor colonies of **Southern flying squirrels**. It's very unlikely that you'll see one unless it's at a nature center or wildlife rehabilitation clinic because flying squirrels are both nocturnal and shy. They're also almost unspeakably cute. Fully extended, they're about nine inches long snout to tail, weigh about four ounces, and have super-silky fur and pink noses, and like many nocturnal animals have comically long whiskers and huge, wide-set eyes that suggest amphetamine use. When they're flying—gliding, really—they spread their limbs to extend the patagium, a membrane that stretches between their front and hind legs, and glide along like little magic carpets.

Also deep in the Smokies are some herds of **wild hogs,** game boar brought to the area about 100 years ago and allowed to go feral. The official line among wildlife officials is that **mountain lions**—in this region called panthers—have been extinct in North Carolina for some time. But mountain dwellers claim there are still panthers in the Blue Ridge and Smokies, and most people here have seen or heard one—their cry sounds like a terror-filled scream. There are even tales of a panther in the inland woods of Brunswick and Columbus Counties on the southeast coast.

REINTRODUCED SPECIES

In the 1990s and early 2000s a federal program to reestablish **red wolf** colonies in the Southeast focused its efforts on parkland in North Carolina. Red wolves, thought to have existed in North Carolina in past centuries, were first reintroduced to Great Smoky Mountains National Park. They did not thrive, and the colony was moved to the Alligator River National Wildlife Refuge on the northeast coast. The packs have fared better in this corner of the state and now roam several wilderness areas in the sound country.

The Smokies proved a more hospitable place for the reintroduction of **elk.** Now the largest animals in Great Smoky Mountains National Park, elk, which can grow up to 700 pounds, are most often observed in the Cataloochee section of the park, grazing happily and lounging in the mist in the early morning and at twilight.

BIRDS

Bird-watchers flock to North Carolina because of the great diversity of songbirds, raptors, and even hummingbirds across the state—a 2013 count put the number of species at 473—but the state is best known for waterfowl. In the sounds of eastern North Carolina, waterfowl descend en masse as they migrate. Hundreds of thousands of birds crowd the lakes, ponds, trees, marshes, and waterways as they move to and from their winter homes. Many hunters take birds during hunting season, but they're outnumbered by bird-watchers.

There are many books and websites about birding in North Carolina. One of the most helpful is the North Carolina Birding Trail, both a website (www.ncbirdingtrail.org) and a series of print guidebooks. Organized by region (mountains, Piedmont, and coast), these resources list dozens of top sites for bird-watching and favorite bird-watching events throughout the state. Another good resource is the **Carolina Bird Club** (www.carolina-birdclub.org).

AMPHIBIANS

Dozens of species of **salamanders** and their close kin, including **mudpuppies, sirens,** and **amphiumas,** call North Carolina home, and Great Smoky Mountains National Park harbors so many of them that it's known as the Salamander Capital of the World. Throughout the state, **frogs** and **toads** are numerous and vociferous, especially the many species of dainty **tree frogs.** Two species, the gray tree frog and the spring peeper, are found in every part of North Carolina, and beginning in late winter they create the impression that the trees are filled with ringing cell phones.

Hellbenders are quite possibly the strangest animal in North Carolina. They are enormous salamanders—not the slick little pencil-thin five-inch salamanders easily spotted along creeks, but hulking brutes that grow to more than two feet long and can weigh five pounds. Rare and hermetic, they live in rocky mountain streams, venturing out from under rocks at night to gobble up crayfish and minnows. They're hard to see even if they do emerge in the daytime because they're lumpy and mud-colored, camouflaged against streambeds. Aggressive with each other, the males often sport battle scars on their stumpy legs. They've been known to bite humans, but as rare as it is to spot a hellbender, it's an exponentially rarer occurrence to be bitten by one.

REPTILES

Turtles and **snakes** are the state's most common reptiles. **Box turtles,** found everywhere, and **bog turtles,** found in the Smokies, are the only land terrapins. A great many freshwater turtles inhabit the swamps and ponds, and on a sunny day every log or branch sticking out of fresh water will become a sunbathing terrace for as many turtles as it can hold. Common water turtles include **cooters, sliders,** and **painted turtles. Snapping turtles** can be found in fresh water throughout the state, so mind your toes. They grow up to a couple of feet long and can weigh more than 50 pounds. Not only will they bite—hard!—if provoked, they will actually initiate hostilities, lunging for you if they so much as disapprove of the fashion of your shoes. Even the tiny hatchlings are vicious, so give them a wide berth.

There are plenty of real **snakes** in North Carolina. The vast majority are shy, gentle, and totally harmless to anything larger than a rat. There are a few species of venomous snakes that are very dangerous. These include three kinds of **rattlesnake:** the huge diamondback, whose diet of rabbits testifies to its size and strength; the pigmy; and the timber or canebrake rattler. Other venomous species are the beautiful mottled **copperhead** and the **cottonmouth or water moccasin,** famous for flinging its mouth open in hostility and flashing its brilliant white palate. The **coral snake** is a fantastically beautiful and venomous species.

Most Carolina snakes are entirely benign to humans, including old familiars such as **black racers** and **king snakes** as well as **milk, corn,** and **rat snakes.** One particularly endearing character is the **hognose snake,** which can be found throughout North Carolina but is most common in the east. Colloquially known as a spreading adder, the hognose snake compensates for its total harmlessness with amazing displays of histrionics. If you startle one, it will first flatten and greatly widen its head and neck and hiss most passionately. If it sees that you're not frightened by plan A, it will panic and go straight to plan B: playing dead. The hognose snake won't simply lie inert until you go away, though; it goes to the dramatic lengths of flipping onto its back, exposing its pitiably vulnerable belly, opening its mouth, throwing its head back limply, and sticking out its tongue as if it had just been poisoned. It is such a devoted method actor that should you call its bluff and poke it back onto its belly, it will fling itself energetically back into the mortuary pose and resume being deceased.

History

ANCIENT CIVILIZATION

By the time the first colonists arrived and called this place Carolina, the land had already sustained some 20,000 years of human history. We know that Paleo-Indians hunted these lands during the last ice age, when there were probably more mammoths and saber-toothed tigers in North Carolina than people. Civilization came around 4,000 BC, when the first inhabitants settled down to farm, make art, and trade goods. By the first century, Southern Woodland and Mississippian Indians were also living in advanced societies with complex religious systems, economic interaction among communities, advanced farming methods, and the creation of art and architecture.

When the Europeans arrived, there were more than a dozen major Native American groups within what is now North Carolina. The Cherokee people ruled the mountains while the Catawba, Pee Dees, Tutelo, and Saura, among others, were their neighbors in the Piedmont. In the east, the Cheraw, Waccamaw, and Tuscarora were some of the larger communities, while many bands occupied land along the Outer Banks and sounds.

CONQUEST

The first Europeans to land here were Spanish. We know conquistador Hernando de Soto and his troops marched around western North Carolina in 1539, but they were just passing through. In 1566, another band of Spanish explorers, led by conquistador Juan Pardo, came for a longer visit. They were making a circuitous trek in the general direction of Mexico, and along the way they established several forts in what are now the Carolinas and Tennessee. One of these forts, called San Juan, has been identified by archaeologists outside present-day Morganton in a community called Worry Crossroads. Although the

troops who were garrisoned for a year and a half at Fort San Juan eventually disappeared into the woods or were killed, it's theorized that they may have had a profound impact on the course of history, possibly spreading European diseases among the Native Americans and weakening them so much that, a couple of decades later, the indigenous people would be unable to repel the invasion of English colonists.

The next episode in the European settlement of North Carolina is one of the strangest mysteries in American history, the Lost Colonists of Roanoke. After two previous failed attempts to establish an English stronghold on the island of Roanoke, fraught by poor planning and disastrous diplomacy, a third group of English colonists tried their luck. Sometime between being dropped off in the New World in 1587 and one of their leaders returning three years later to resupply them, all of the colonists—including Virginia Dare, the first English person born in the Americas—had vanished into the woods. To this day, their fate is unknown, although a host of fascinating theories are still debated and probably always will be.

The disappearance of the Roanoke colonists did little to slow the process of the European conquest of North America. After the establishment of the Virginia colony in 1607, new English settlers began to trickle southward into Carolina, while Barbadians and Europeans from Charles Town (present-day Charleston, South Carolina) gradually began to populate the area around Wilmington. The town of Bath was established in 1706, and New Bern was settled shortly thereafter. The bloody Tuscarora War followed, and after a crushing defeat near present-day Snow Hill, in which hundreds were killed, the Tuscarora people retreated, opening the land along the Neuse River to European colonization.

COLONIALISM

The conflict between Europeans and Native Americans wasn't the only world-changing cultural encounter going on in the Southern colonies. By the middle of the 18th century, nearly 100,000 enslaved people had been brought to North Carolina from West Africa. By the end of the 18th century, many areas, especially those around Wilmington, had populations where enslaved African Americans outnumbered whites. Although North Carolina did not experience slavery on as vast a scale as South Carolina, there were a handful of plantations with more than 100 slaves, and many smaller plantations and town homes of wealthy planters, merchants, and politicians with smaller numbers of slaves. Africans and African Americans were an early and potent cultural force in the South, influencing the economy, politics, language, religion, music, architecture, and cuisine in ways still seen today.

In the 1730s the Great Wagon Road connected Pennsylvania with Georgia by cutting through the Mid-Atlantic and Southern backcountry of Virginia and North Carolina. Many travelers migrated south from Pennsylvania, among them a good number of German and Scots-Irish settlers who found the mountains and Piedmont of North Carolina to their liking. Meanwhile, the port of Wilmington, growing into one of the most important in the state, saw a number of Gaelic-speaking Scots move through, following the river north and putting down roots around what is now Fayetteville. Shortly before the American Revolution, a group of German-speaking religious settlers known as the Moravians constructed a beautiful and industrious town, Salem, in the heart of the Piedmont, later to become Winston-Salem. Their pacifist beliefs, Germanic heritage, and artistry set them apart from other communities in colonial North Carolina, and they left an indelible mark on the state's history.

The 18th century brought one conflict after another to the colony, from fights over the Vestry Act in the early 1700s, which attempted to establish the Anglican Church as the one official faith of the colony, through various regional conflicts with Native Americans, and events that played out at a global level during the French and Indian War. At mid-century the population and economic importance of the Piedmont was growing exponentially, but colonial representation continued to be focused along the coast. Protesting local corruption and lack of governmental concern for the western region, a group of backcountry farmers organized themselves into an armed posse in resistance to colonial corruption. Calling themselves the Regulators, they eventually numbered more than 6,000. Mounting frustrations led to an attack by the Regulators on the Orange County courthouse in Hillsborough. Finally, a colonial militia was dispatched to crush the movement, which it did at the Battle of Alamance in 1771. Six Regulators were captured and hanged at Hillsborough.

REVOLUTION AND STATEHOOD

Many believe the seeds of the American Revolution were sown, tended, and reaped in New England, but the southern colonies, particularly North Carolina, played important roles before and during the rebellion. In 1765, as the War of the Regulation was heating up, the residents of Brunswick Town, the colonial capital and the only deepwater port in the southern half of the colony, revolted in protest of the Stamp Act. They placed the royal governor under house arrest and put an end to taxation in the Cape Fear region, sending a strong message to the crown and to fellow patriots hungry to shake off the yoke of British rule. In the ensuing years, well-documented events like the Boston Tea Party, the battles of Lexington and Concord, and the signing of the Declaration of Independence occurred, but North Carolina's role in leading the rebellion was far from over.

After the battles of Lexington and Concord, the colonies were aflame with patriotic fervor, and Mecklenburg County (around Charlotte) passed the first colonial declaration rejecting the crown's authority. By this time, North Carolina, like the other colonies, had formed a provincial government, and it was busy in the tavern at Halifax writing the Halifax Resolves, the first official action in the colonies calling for independence from Britain. On April 12, 1776, the resolves were ratified and delegates carried them to the Second Continental Congress in Philadelphia. Delegates elsewhere were so inspired that more such resolves appeared in Philadelphia; ultimately the Declaration of Independence was written and ratified, and the revolution was on in earnest.

Although North Carolina may have been the first to call for independence, the state was divided in its loyalties. Among the most noteworthy Loyalists was the community of Highland Scots living in and around modern-day Fayetteville. Men from this community were marching to join General Cornwallis near Brunswick Town and Southport (then Smithville) when patriots ambushed them at the bloody battle of Moore's Creek, killing 30 Scots and routing the Loyalist force.

North Carolinians fought all over the eastern seaboard during the Revolution, including about 1,000 who were with Washington at Valley Forge. The year 1780 brought fighting back home, particularly in the area around Charlotte, which a daunted General Cornwallis referred to as "the hornets' nest." The battle of Kings Mountain, west of Charlotte, was a pivotal moment in the war, and one that was particularly costly to the Loyalist forces. Cornwallis received another blow at the battle of Guilford Courthouse; although technically a British victory, it weakened his forces considerably. By the time the war ended, thousands of North Carolinians were dead and the treasury was far in debt. But North Carolina was now a state with the business of statehood to attend to. The capital was moved inland to Raleigh, and 20 miles away at Chapel Hill, ground was broken for the establishment of the University of North Carolina, the first state university in the country.

THE FEDERAL ERA

The early 19th century in North Carolina was a good deal more peaceful than the previous hundred years had been. The first decade of the 1800s saw a religious awakening in which thousands of North Carolinians became devout Christians. At the same time, the introduction of the cotton gin and bright-leaf tobacco were economic boons in the state, particularly the eastern counties. Railroads and plank roads made trade immeasurably more efficient, bringing new prosperity to the Piedmont.

Despite the relative peace, there was also conflict. Andrew Jackson's administration presided over the passage of the Indian Removal Act in 1830, which assigned reservations in the Indian Territory of present-day Oklahoma to the "Five Civilized Tribes" of the southeastern United States—the Cherokee, Choctaw, Creek, Chickasaw, and Seminole. Thousands of Cherokee people were forced out of western North Carolina, northern Georgia, eastern Tennessee, and Alabama and marched west on the Trail of Tears. About 4,000 died along the way. Another 1,000 or so Cherokee people, through hiding, fighting, and negotiation, managed to win the right to stay in North Carolina—an act of resistance that was the birth of the modern Eastern Band of the Cherokee, still centered on the town of Cherokee on the Qualla Boundary in North Carolina's Great Smoky Mountains. The Eastern Band of the Cherokee tell the story of their relocation in the enlightening outdoor drama *Unto These Hills.*

THE CIVIL WAR

Compared to South Carolina and a few other Southern states, North Carolina was considered politically moderate in the mid-19th century because it was less invested economically and politically in slavery. As some states voted to remove themselves from the Union, North Carolina's voters rejected a ballot measure authorizing a secession convention. As grand a gesture as that victory may have been, when fighting erupted at Fort Sumter in South Carolina's Charleston Harbor, North Carolina's hand was forced and its secession was a reality. Secessionist governor John Ellis rejected Lincoln's call to federalize state militias, instead seizing control of the state and all federal military installations within its boundaries as well as the Charlotte Mint. North Carolina officially seceded on May 20, 1861, and a few weeks later Union ships began to blockade the coast. Roanoke Island in the Outer Banks fell, and a freedmen's colony (a home for enslaved people who had been freed or escaped) sprung up. New Bern, which fell in the spring of 1862, became a major focal point of Union military strategy and a thriving political base for freed and escaped African Americans. To the south, Fort Fisher, on the Cape Fear River just south of Wilmington, guarded the river's inlet and was crucial to the success of the blockade runners—smugglers whose speedy boats eluded the Union blockade. Fort Fisher kept Wilmington in Confederate hands until nearly the end of the war. When it finally did fall to Union forces in February 1865, it required what would be the largest amphibious assault in American military history until World War II. Wilmington was the last major port on the Confederacy's eastern seaboard, and its fall severed supply lines and crippled what remained of the Confederate army in the area.

The varying opinions felt by Southerners about the Civil War (also called the War between the States in the South) were particularly strong in North Carolina, where today you'll still hear whites refer to it as the War of Northern Aggression or the War of Yankee Aggression. More than 5,000 African Americans from North Carolina joined and fought in the Union Army, and there were pockets of strong Union sentiment and support among white North Carolinians, especially in the mountains. Some 10,000 North Carolinians fought for the Union. Zebulon Vance, who won the 1862 gubernatorial election and served as governor through the duration of the war, was a native of Weaverville, near Asheville, and felt acutely the state's ambivalence toward the Confederacy. Much to the consternation of Richmond (the Confederate capital), Governor Vance was adamant in his refusal to put the interests of the Confederacy over those of his own state. Mountain communities suffered tremendously during the war from acts of terrorism by deserters and rogues from both armies.

The latter years of the Civil War were particularly difficult for North Carolina and the rest of the South. Approximately 4,000 North Carolina men died at the battle of Gettysburg alone. After laying waste to Georgia and South Carolina, General William T. Sherman's army entered North Carolina in the spring of 1865, destroying homes and farms. His march of fire and pillage spared Wilmington, which is one reason the town contains such an incredible collection of federal architecture. The last major battle of the war was fought in North Carolina, when General Sherman and Confederate General Joseph Johnston engaged at Bentonville. Johnston surrendered to Sherman in Durham in April 1865.

By the end of the war more than 40,000 North Carolina soldiers were dead—a number equivalent to the entire present-day population of Hickory, Apex, or Kannapolis.

RECONSTRUCTION AND THE NEW SOUTH

The years immediately after the war were painful as well, as a vast population of newly free African Americans tried to make new lives for themselves economically and politically in the face of tremendous opposition and violence from whites. The Ku Klux Klan was set up during this time, inaugurating an era of horror for African Americans throughout the country. Federal occupation and domination of the Southern states' political and legal systems also exacerbated resentment toward the North. The state's ratification of the 14th Amendment on July 4, 1868, brought North Carolina back into the Union.

The late 1800s saw large-scale investment in North Carolina's railroad system, launching the industrial boom of the New South. Agriculture changed in this era as the rise of tenancy created a new form of enslavement for many farmers—black, white, and Native American. R. J. Reynolds, Washington Duke, and other entrepreneurs built a massively lucrative empire of tobacco production from field to factory. Textile and furniture mills sprouted throughout the Piedmont, creating a new cultural landscape as rural Southerners migrated to mill towns.

THE 20TH CENTURY AND TODAY

The early decades of the 1900s brought an expanded global perspective to North Carolina, not only through the expanded economy and the coming of radio, but as natives of the state scattered across the globe. About 80,000 North Carolinians served in World War I, many of them young men who had never before left the state or perhaps even their home counties. Hundreds of thousands of African Americans migrated north during what became known as the Great Migration. The communities created by black North Carolinians in the Mid-Atlantic and the Northeast are still closely connected by culture and kinship to their cousins whose ancestors remained in the South. The invasion of the boll weevil, an insect that devastated the cotton industry, hastened the departure of Southerners of all races who had farmed cotton. The Great Depression hit hard across all economic sectors of the state in the 1930s, but New Deal employment programs were a boon to North Carolina's infrastructure, with the construction of hydroelectric dams, the Blue Ridge Parkway, and other public works.

North Carolina's modern-day military importance largely dates to the World War II era. Installations at Fort Bragg, Camp Lejeune, and other still-vital bases were constructed or expanded. About 350,000 North Carolinians fought in World War II, and 7,000 of them died.

A few old-timers remember World War II quite vividly because they witnessed it firsthand: German U-boats prowled the waters off the coast, torpedoing ships and sinking them with frightening regularity. These German submarines were often visible from the beach, but more often the evidence of their mission of terror and supply-chain disruption—corpses, wounded sailors, and the flotsam of exploded ships—washed up on the shore. More than 10,000 German prisoners were interned in prisoner-of-war camps, in some parts of the state becoming forced farm laborers. In Wilmington, just a few blocks from downtown, is an apartment complex that was part of a large prisoner-of-war compound for U-boat officers.

In the 1950s and 1960s, African Americans in North Carolina and throughout the United States struggled against the monolithic system of segregation and racism enshrined in the nation's Jim Crow laws. The Ku Klux Klan stepped up its pro-segregation efforts with political and physical violence against Native Americans as well as African Americans; in the famous 1958 Battle of Maxton, 500 armed Lumbee people foiled a Klan rally and sent the Knights running for their lives. Change arrived slowly. The University of North Carolina accepted its first African American graduate student in 1951 and the first black undergraduates four years later. Sit-ins in 1960 at the Woolworth's lunch counter in Greensboro began with four African American men, students at North Carolina A&T. On the second day of their protest they were joined by 23 other demonstrators; on the third day there were 300, and by day four about 1,000. This was a pivotal moment in the national civil rights movement, sparking sit-ins across the country in which an estimated 50,000 people participated. You can see the counter today at the International Civil Rights Center and Museum in Greensboro. Even as victories were won at the level of Congress and in the federal courts, as in *Brown v. the Board of Education* and the 1964 Civil Rights Act, actual change on the ground was inexorably slow and hard-won. North Carolina's contribution to the civil rights movement continues to be invaluable for the whole nation.

North Carolina continues to adapt and contribute to the global community. It is now a place of ethnic diversity, growing especially in Latino residents. There are also significant communities of Dega and Hmong people from Southeast Asia as well as Eastern Europeans, among many others.

Government and Economy

POLITICAL LIFE
Liberal Enclaves

Although historically a red state, North Carolina's large population of college students, professors, and artists has created several boisterous enclaves of progressive politics. The outspoken archconservative U.S. Senator Jesse Helms supposedly questioned the need to spend public money on a state zoo in North Carolina "when we can just put up a fence around Chapel Hill." The Chapel Hill area is indeed the epicenter of North Carolina's liberalism, with its smaller neighboring town of Carrboro at its heart. Would-be Democratic presidential candidates and politicians on the campaign trail regularly stop here to bolster support in the state. Helms might well have said the same thing about Asheville.

Although you'll find a mixture of political views statewide, the Triangle is not the only famously liberal community. In Asheville, lefty politics are part of the community's devotion to all things organic and DIY. Significant pockets of liberalism also exist in Boone, the cities of the Triad, and Wilmington.

Famous Figures

Several major players in modern American politics are from North Carolina. The best-known politician in recent years is former U.S. senator John Edwards, who made two runs for the White House, the first leading to a vice presidential spot on the Democratic ticket. Edwards was born in South Carolina but grew up here in the Sandhills. At the other end of the political spectrum, Monroe native Jesse Helms spent 30 years in the U.S. Senate, becoming one of the most prominent and outspoken conservative Republicans of our times. Upon his retirement, Helms was succeeded in the Senate by Salisbury-born Duke University graduate Elizabeth Dole, who had previously served in Ronald Reagan's cabinet and George H. W. Bush's cabinet. She was also president of the American Red Cross and had a close brush with the White House when her husband, Kansas senator Bob Dole, ran for president in 1996.

MAJOR INDUSTRIES

Over the last 20 years, North Carolina has experienced tremendous shifts in its economy as the industries that once dominated the landscape and brought wealth and development declined. The **tobacco** industry ruled the state's economy for generations, employing innumerable North Carolinians from field to factory and funding a colossal portion of the state's physical and cultural infrastructure. The slow decline of the tobacco industry worldwide beginning in the 1980s changed the state dramatically, especially the rural east, where tobacco fields once went from green to gold every fall. Other agricultural industries, especially **livestock**—chickens and hogs—are still important in the east. The **textile** industry, a giant for most of the 20th century, suffered the same decline as manufacturers sought cheaper labor overseas. Likewise, the **furniture** industry slipped into obscurity. Today, the once-thriving **fishing** industry is in steep decline, largely due to globalization and overfishing.

In the mountains, the main industries have been mining and logging, agriculture, and tourism. As the way we care for our

skiing Beech Mountain

quilt and craft trails across rural counties, and more and more come for classes and workshops at the **Penland School** and **John C. Campbell Folk School**. This is helping grow interest in lesser-known cities and small towns throughout the mountains. **Skiing** in Boone, Blowing Rock, and Beech Mountain was, before a few years ago, a local secret, but now visitors from across the Southeast come for a few days on the slopes. The state's Department of Commerce estimates nearly 46 million people visit North Carolina annually, and those visitors bring in more than $19 billion in spending, employing 200,000 state residents in industries directly related to tourism.

DISTRIBUTION OF WEALTH

For the most part, North Carolina is basically working-class. Pockets of significant wealth exist in urban areas, and as more and more retirees relocate to North Carolina, there are moneyed people in the mountains and coastal counties. Extensive white-collar job availability makes the Triangle a comparatively prosperous region, with average household incomes in 2010 exceeding $60,000, much higher than the state's average of just over $40,000.

The state also experiences significant poverty. The proportion of people living in poverty has been rising since 2000, partly due to the ongoing worldwide economic slowdown but also due to the derailment of many of North Carolina's backbone industries. As recently as 15 years ago, a high school graduate in small-town North Carolina could count on making a living wage in a mill or factory; nowadays those opportunities have dried up, and the poverty rate in 2011 was just over 16 percent. Even more distressing, the number of children living in poverty is just over 24 percent, and for children under age 6 climbing to 28 percent.

The northeastern quadrant of North Carolina is the most critically impoverished, but throughout the mountains you can see evidence of an unbalanced economy, one that's

environment has evolved, mining and logging have largely fallen by the wayside and been replaced by small pockets of manufacturing from national and international companies or larger local companies. Through this, the importance of tourism has increased, especially in the western part of the state.

Tourism

North Carolina has always drawn visitors to its mountains, waters, beaches, and cities, and as the economy evolves, the tourism sector has become vital to the state's well-being. In the mountains, the **Blue Ridge Parkway** and **Great Smoky Mountain National Park** are recognizable, even marquee, names for visitors, and **Asheville**, with its superb dining and much-lauded craft beer scene, is atop many visitors' lists. **North Carolina wine** is also coming back on the radar of many visitors, with the wineries and tasting rooms in the **Yadkin Valley Viticultural Area** reporting more visitors every year. Heritage tourism is helping small towns as visitors follow

How Can You Tell a Tar Heel?

What manner of man is a North Carolinian? How can you tell a Tar Heel? What ingredients went into his making? Is he different, and if so, how and why? There is no slide-rule answer to these questions, but it may be interesting to explore them. The Tar Heel is not a distinct species, but he may have some distinguishing marks. [We are] independent, courageous, resourceful, democratic, gregarious and individualistic, although we would use plainer words than these Latin terms to describe ourselves.... There is a progressive strain in this Tar Heel, a realistic and resourceful determination to get ahead with the work for a better way of life for himself and his fellows.... There is often a kindness in the voice which covers a lot of humanity in its acceptance of all sorts and conditions of men.... But there is no pouring Tar Heels into a mold. The point is that we are by preference and habit individualists, or what we call "characters."

So much for our good side. Generally, we are liable to be pretty good folks, but we have a bad side too, and the truth is that we can be, when we take a notion or for no reason at all, as violent, ornery, cantankerous, stubborn, narrow and lazy as any people anywhere on earth, civilized or uncivilized. We cut and shoot one another at a rate not even equaled in the centers of urban civilization. True, we consider our violence too valuable to waste on outsiders and so confine it to ourselves.... Tar Heels hardly ever kill or maim anybody unless he is either an old friend or a close relative.

Blackwell P. Robinson, ed., *The North Carolina Guide*, UNC Press, 1955.

forgotten the rural portion of the state. Small businesses are alive though, with many mom-and-pop shops, restaurants, and hotels serving the local population and visitors alike.

Several hardworking organizations and activists are trying to alleviate the economic hardship found in North Carolina. National organizations like Habitat for Humanity (www.habitat.org) and regional groups like the Southern Coalition for Social Justice (http://southerncoalition.org) and the Institute for Southern Studies (www.southernstudies.org) bring community activism and research to the state. There are also excellent North Carolina-based advocates in groups such as the North Carolina Rural Economic Development Center (www.ncruralcenter.org), the North Carolina Justice Center (www.ncjustice.org), the Black Family Land Trust (www.bflt.org), and Student Action with Farmworkers (http://saf-unite.org).

Local Culture

The 10th-most populous state in the union, North Carolina's population of 9.75 million residents is slightly larger than New Jersey and slightly smaller than Georgia. More than two-thirds of North Carolinians are white, primarily of German and Scots-Irish descent, and not quite one-quarter are African American. The state's population is about 8.6 percent Latino, and has the 7th-largest Native American population of any state after California, Arizona, Oklahoma, New Mexico, Washington, and Alaska.

More than 40 percent of North Carolinians are between the ages of 25 and 59, but the older population is steadily rising, due in large part to the state's popularity with retirees. The majority—about 70 percent—of North Carolinians live in family groups, with married couples constituting about half of those, and married couples with children (not mutually exclusive data sets) making up almost one-quarter of households. Of the remaining one-third of the state's population who live in "nonfamily households"—that is, not with blood relatives or a legally recognized spouse—the vast majority are individuals living on their own.

Unmarried couples, both straight and gay, have a much lower rate of cohabitation here than in more urban parts of the United States. Such households are common and accepted in the Triangle, Asheville, Charlotte, and other urban areas.

North Carolina has one of the fastest-growing Latino populations in the United States. The community has swelled since the 1990s as hundreds of thousands of Mexican and Central American laborers came to work in the agricultural, industrial, and formerly booming construction trades.

INDIGENOUS CULTURES

In the Great Smoky Mountains, the town of Cherokee on the Qualla Boundary, which is Cherokee-administered land, is the governmental seat of the Eastern Band of the Cherokee. The Eastern Band are largely descended from those Cherokee people who escaped arrest during the deportation of the Southeast's Native Americans on the Trail of Tears in the 19th century, or who made the forced march to Oklahoma but survived and walked home to the North Carolina mountains.

RELIGION

As early as the 17th century, North Carolina's religious landscape foreshadowed the diversity we enjoy today. The first Christians in North Carolina were Quakers, soon followed by Anglicans, Presbyterians, Baptists, Moravians, Methodists, and Roman Catholics. Native American and African religions, present in the early colonial days, were never totally quashed by European influence, and Barbadian Sephardic Jews were here early on as well. All of these religions remain today, with enrichment by the presence of Muslims, Buddhists, and an amazing mosaic of other Christian groups.

North Carolina claims as its own one of the world's most influential modern religious figures, Billy Graham, who was raised on a dairy farm outside Charlotte and experienced his Christian religious awakening in 1934. After preaching in person to more people around the world than anyone in human history, and being involved with every U.S. president since Harry Truman, Billy Graham is now home in his native state, where he divides his time between Charlotte and Montreat, outside Asheville.

LANGUAGE

North Carolina has quite the linguistic diversity both in terms of language and accent. While much of the linguistic diversity is represented in the cities of Charlotte, Raleigh,

Understanding Local Lingo

North Carolina speech features delightful and sometimes perplexing regional vocabulary and grammar. Following are some of the common Carolinianisms most likely to stump travelers.

- **Bless your/his/her heart:** A complex declaration with infinitely varied intentions, interpreted depending on context or tone. In its most basic use, "Bless your heart," is a sincere thank-you for a favor or a kindness paid. It's also an exclamation of affection, usually applied to children and the elderly, as in, "You're *not* 92 years old! You are? Well, bless your heart." Frequently, though, hearts are blessed to frame criticism in a charitable light, as in, "Bless his heart; that man from New York don't know not to shout."

- **buggy:** a shopping cart, as at a grocery store.

- **carry:** convey, escort, give a ride to. "I carried my mother up to the mountains for her birthday."

- **cattywampus:** topsy-turvy, mixed up. Used especially in the Piedmont and farther west.

- **Coke:** any soft drink; may be called "pop" in the mountains.

- **come back:** often uttered by shopkeepers as a customer leaves, not to ask them to return immediately, but simply an invitation to patronize the establishment again someday.

- **dinner:** the midday meal.

- **evening:** not just the twilight hours, but all the hours between about 3pm and nightfall.

- **ever-how:** however; similarly, "ever-when," "ever-what," and "ever-who."

- **fair to middling:** so-so, in response to "How you?"; a holdover term from North Carolina's moonshining days, the term originally applied to grading 'shine by examining bubbles in a shaken mason jar.

- **fixing:** about to or preparing to do something. "She's fixing to have a baby any day now."

- **holler:** hollow, a mountain cove.

- **mash:** press, as a button. "I keep mashing the button, but the elevator won't come."

Durham, and other college towns, there's a range of dialects present in rural areas along the coast, throughout the Piedmont, and in the mountains. These variations have to do with historical patterns of settlement in a given area, and in the mountains the blend of Scottish brogue, Irish lilt, and guttural German have, over time, formed a unique dialect that once you hear it will be in your ear forever.

In the mountains you'll encounter English as the standard written and spoken language. That's not to say there aren't exceptions. Across North Carolina Spanish is more and more commonly heard, spoken, and written, but in the far west of the state, on the edge of the Smoky Mountains, there's one language

you'll hear and see in a couple of tiny pockets: Cherokee.

Throughout the town of Cherokee you'll see many street and commercial signs written in English and a set of pretty, twisty symbols that look like a cross between Khmer or Sanskrit and Cyrillic. This is Cherokee, written in the alphabet famously devised by Sequoyah in the early 19th century. Cherokee also survives as a spoken language, though typically among the elders in traditional communities. To combat the slow death of the language, Eastern Band of Cherokee leadership has started a program to teach tribal youth to speak and write the language, though the pool of fluent speakers is very small.

- **mess:** discombobulated, in a rut, not living right. "I was a mess until I joined the church."

- **might could/should/would:** could/should/would perhaps. "Looks like it's fixing to rain. You might should go roll up your car windows."

- **piece:** a vague measure of distance, as in, "down the road a piece" (a little ways down the road) or "a fair piece" (a long way).

- **poke:** a bag, such as a paper shopping bag. Used especially in the mountains.

- **reckon:** believe, think. Often used in interrogative statements that end in a falling tone, as in, "Reckon what we're having for dinner." (That is, "What do you suppose is for lunch?")

- **right:** quite, very. Variations include "right quick" (soon, hurriedly), "right much" (often), and "a right many" or "a right smart of" (a great quantity).

- **sorry:** worthless, lame, shoddy. "I wanted to play basketball in college, but I was too sorry of an athlete."

- **speck so:** "I expect so," or, "Yes, I guess that's correct."

- **supper:** the evening meal (as opposed to "dinner," the midday meal).

- **sy-goggling:** see *cattywampus*. Used especially in the mountains.

- **ugly:** mean or unfriendly, spiteful. Sometimes referred to as "acting ugly." "Hateful" is a common synonym. The favorite Southern injunction that "God don't like ugly" does not mean that God wants us to be pretty, but rather that we should be nice.

- **wait on:** to wait for.

- **y'all:** pronoun used to address any group of two or more people.

- **yonder:** over there.

- **y'uns:** mountain variation of *y'all*.

LITERATURE

Storytelling seems to come naturally to Southerners. From the master storytellers of Jack Tales in the Blue Ridge to the distinguished journalists we see every night on television, North Carolinians have a singular gift for communication. Thomas Wolfe was an Asheville native, and O. Henry, whose real name was William Sidney Porter, was born and raised in Greensboro. Tom Robbins (*Even Cowgirls Get the Blues*) was born in Blowing Rock. Charles Frazier (*Cold Mountain*) is from Asheville. Sarah Dessen (*Just Listen*) is from Chapel Hill. Kaye Gibbons, Lee Smith, Fred Chappell, Randall Kenan, and Clyde Edgerton, leading lights in Southern fiction, are all natives or residents of North Carolina. Also closely associated with the state are David Sedaris, Armistead Maupin, and Betsy Byars, who have all lived here at some point in their lives. New writers like Taylor Brown, who's spent time in Asheville and Wilmington, and Jason Mott, a North Carolina native, have novels set in the Blue Ridge and note that the place has a special influence on their work. Arts programs focused on creative writing have sprung up across the state, imbuing the literary scenes in towns like Wilmington, Greensboro, Asheville, and Chapel Hill with talented undergraduate and graduate students and their professors. Notable writers teaching creative writing programs include poet A. Van Jordan, essayist

David Gessner, and novelist and short story writer Jill McCorkle.

North Carolina has also given the world some of the giants of 20th-century journalism. Edward R. Murrow, Charles Kuralt, David Brinkley, and Howard Cosell were all sons of Carolina, and Charlie Rose carries their torch today.

MUSIC

It's hard to know where to begin in describing the importance of music to North Carolinians. With fiddlers' conventions, renowned symphony orchestras, busy indie-rock scenes, and a thriving gospel-music industry, there is no escaping good music here. Since the earliest days of recorded country music, North Carolinians have shared their songs with the world. Charlie Poole and Wade Mainer were among the first to record, and became influential artists in the 1930s. By 1945 a banjo player named Earl Scruggs was helping create what would become the quintessential sound of **bluegrass** music, particularly his three-fingered picking style. Bluegrass greats like Del McCoury helped further define the sound. Today, bluegrass is alive and well in North Carolina; Steve Martin's collaboration with the Steep Canyon Rangers sells out venues around the world and garners awards at every turn, and the late Doc Watson's annual **MerleFest** is still going strong. **Country** musicians like Ronnie Milsap, Donna Fargo, Charlie Daniels, and Randy Travis made big names for themselves from the 1970s to the 1990s; more recently, Kellie Pickler and Scottie McCreery (of *American Idol* fame) and Eric Church have made waves on the country charts. In Asheville, the **Warren Haynes Christmas Jam** has become a holiday staple for fans of improvisational rock, but a weekly **drum circle** in a downtown park and music venues like **Orange Peel** and **Grey Eagle** bring in acts of all genres and are nationally known for excellent shows.

Along the coastal plains and across the Piedmont, **jazz**, **funk**, and **soul** artists of note—John Coltrane, Thelonious Monk, Nina Simone, George Clinton, and Maceo and Melvin Parker—grew up or developed their sound here. Their influence is evident in contemporary acts, whether they be bluegrass, old-time, or straight up rock and roll.

In North Carolina, you're never far from some good **gospel** music. In the mountains, you're more likely to find gospel quartets and old-time gospel music, which is more inspired by bluegrass and traditional music, at camp meetings and gospel sings on weekend nights. The state's Native American communities also have thriving gospel traditions of their own.

THEATER

Regional theater companies such as the venerable Flat Rock Playhouse near Hendersonville make great theater accessible in small towns and rural areas. The North Carolina School for the Arts in Winston-Salem mints great actors and filmmakers, among other artists. The film and television industries have long recognized North Carolina as a hotbed of talent as well as a place with amazing locations for filming.

For some reason, **outdoor historical dramas** have long flourished in North Carolina. The most famous is North Carolina playwright Paul Green's *Lost Colony,* which has been performed every summer since 1937 on Roanoke Island, except during World War II when German U-boats lurked nearby, but it's not all focused on the coast. The Cherokee people depict emblematic episodes in their history in the outdoor drama *Unto These Hills,* in production since 1950. The community of Boone has presented *Horn in the West* since 1952, and it is joined by Valdese and several other communities in North Carolina in turning to performance tableaux to commemorate their heritage. It's especially important to note that among the characteristics of outdoor drama in North Carolina is the fact that the cast, crew, and often the producers and playwrights are members of the communities whose stories the plays tell.

ARTS AND CRAFTS

Folk art and studio craft show vitality in North Carolina. Several communities are known worldwide for their local traditions, and countless individual artists, studios, and galleries can be found across the state.

Cherokee craft is an important aesthetic school comprising a wide range of techniques and media such as wood and stone carving, fiber arts, traditional weaponry, and avant-garde sculpture and painting. **Qualla Arts and Crafts Mutual,** located in the town of Cherokee, has a wonderful sales gallery that will dazzle lovers of fine craft.

Asheville is an epicenter of the arts, the heart of a vast community of artists that stretches throughout western North Carolina and includes such major folk schools as **John C. Campbell** in Brasstown, near the Georgia state line, and **Penland,** close to Tennessee in the northeastern mountains. In Asheville you can see and purchase an infinite variety of crafts that include handmade baskets, quilts, furniture, clothing, jewelry, and iron architectural elements. The **Southern Highland Craft Guild** (www.southernhighlandguild. org), an old and accomplished organization, deserves a lot of the credit for the thriving craft movement in western North Carolina.

Its website has a great deal of information about contemporary master crafters and their work.

As people become more accustomed to a world where almost every object we see and use was mass-produced far away, we develop an ever-deeper appreciation for the depth of skill and aesthetic complexity that went into the production of everyday objects in past generations. North Carolinians have always been great crafters of utilitarian and occupational necessities. As you travel through the state, keep an eye out for objects that you might not immediately recognize as art—barns, fishing nets, woven chair bottoms—but that were made with the skill and artistry of generations-old traditions. In North Carolina, art is everywhere.

FOOD

For many, North Carolina is synonymous with **barbecue,** but just ordering a plate of barbecue or a sandwich or some ribs isn't that easy because of the three distinct regional styles. In the east, barbecue is a whole hog cooked over wood coals, then chopped or shredded and doused with a tart vinegar-pepper sauce. In the Piedmont, the meat is all shoulders and butts and the sauce is slightly

Dogwood Crafters in Dillsboro features traditional mountain crafts.

sweeter. In the mountains, **western-style barbecue** uses butts and shoulders, occasionally adding in ribs and even brisket, but the sauce is the real difference. Thicker and sweeter than other North Carolina sauces, it's more familiar to many diners than the other styles.

Up in the Great Smoky Mountains, the early spring is the season for **ramps,** sometimes called skunk cabbage—very pungent wild onions that grow along creek beds in the deep mountains. They're another of those foods passionately defended by those who grew up eating them but are greeted with trepidation by outsiders. The reason they're feared by the uninitiated is their atomically powerful taste, which will emanate from every part of your body for days if the ramps are too strong or not prepared correctly. Ramps taste like a cross between regular onions, garlic, leeks, shallots, and kryptonite. When they're young, they're perfectly pungent—not too overwhelming, but still powerful enough to let you know they're in the dish. Folks skillet-cook them, fry them up in grease, boil them with fatback, or just chomp on them raw. For a special treat and a gentle introduction to ramps, stop in at the Stecoah Valley Center near Robbinsville and pick up a bag of the Smoky Mountain Native Plants Association's special cornmeal mix with dried ramps, and make yourself a skillet of deliciously tangy cornbread. You can also try them at the local ramps festivals held in Robbinsville and Cherokee in spring. A growing number of restaurants from Asheville to Wilmington are buying ramps and **morel mushrooms** from mountain foragers and preparing them every way from skillet fried to pickled, so ramp lovers can get a taste of this springtime mountain delicacy even on the coast.

You can read all about these and other acquired tastes at **NCFOOD** (www.ncfolk.org) or **Our State Eats** by *Our State* magazine (www.ourstate.com), two food blogs devoted to Carolina cooking, or on the **Southern Foodways Alliance** (www.southernfoodways.com) and **Dixie Dining** (www.dixiedining.com) websites.

Vegetarians and devotees of organic food, fear not; North Carolina is an unusually progressive state when it comes to healthy and homegrown grub. Nevertheless, if you want to avoid meat, you have to be cautious when ordering at a restaurant: Make sure the beans are made with vegetable oil rather than lard, ask if the salad dressing contains anchovies, and beware of hidden fish and oyster sauce. Traditional Southern cooking makes liberal use of fatback (cured pork fat) and other animal products; greens are often boiled with a strip of fatback or a hambone, as are most soups and stews. Even pie crusts are still made with lard in many old-time kitchens.

You'll find organic grocery stores in the major cities. Earth Fare and Whole Foods are the most common chains, but there are also plenty of small independent markets. Farmers markets and roadside stands are so plentiful that they almost have to fight for space. Visit the state Department of Agriculture's **North Carolina Farm Fresh** site (www.ncfarmfresh.com) for directories of farmers markets and pick-your-own farms and orchards.

Essentials

Transportation

AIR

Most visitors to the Blue Ridge Mountains, Smoky Mountains, and Great Smoky Mountains National Park will arrive by car, but for those flying in, several airports offer reasonably convenient access to the surrounding regions.

North Carolina

Asheville Regional Airport (61 Terminal Dr., 828/684-2226, www.flyavl.com) is located south of the city in Fletcher. The next-closest airport in North Carolina is **Charlotte-Douglas International Airport** (5501 Josh Birmingham Pkwy., 704/359-4910, www. charmeck.org), two hours away. Charlotte-Douglas is the 10th-largest hub in the United States, with nonstop flights to and from more than 125 destinations worldwide.

The **Piedmont Triad International Airport** (1000 A. Ted Johnson Pkwy., Greensboro, 336/665-5600, www.flyfrompti. com) is less than 90 minutes from Boone and the Blue Ridge Parkway and is served by Allegiant, American Airlines/American Eagle, Delta, Frontier, and United.

Farther east, the **Raleigh-Durham International Airport** (RDU, 2400 John Brantley Blvd., Morrisville, 919/840-2123, www.rdu.com) sits between the cities of Durham and Raleigh. Nine airlines serve RDU, providing close to 400 nonstop flights to approximately 40 destinations daily: Alaska Airlines, Allegiant, Air Canada, American Airlines, Delta, Frontier, Jet Blue, Southwest, and United. The airport is close to two hours from the Boone and Blue Ridge Parkway, and about 3.5 hours to Asheville, but the volume of air traffic and the ease of reaching the Parkway make this a good choice when pricing flights.

South Carolina

The **Greenville-Spartanburg International Airport** (2000 GSP Dr., Greer, SC, 864/848-6254, www.gspairport.com) is 80 minutes south of Asheville. Airlines serving Greenville-Spartanburg include Allegiant, American Airlines, Delta, Southwest, and United. It's a drive of a little over an hour from Greenville-Spartanburg to Asheville.

Tennessee

The **McGhee-Tyson Airport** (2055 Alcoa Hwy., Alcoa, TN, 865/342-3000, www.tys. org) in Alcoa, Tennessee, is about two hours from Cherokee and about 20 minutes south of Knoxville. Airlines serving McGhee-Tyson include Allegiant, American Airlines/American Eagle, Delta, Frontier, and United. Gatlinburg and the western entrance to Great Smoky Mountains National Park is just over 1 hour away; Knoxville is closer, a drive of 20 minutes without traffic.

Virginia

The largest airport in southwest Virginia is the **Roanoke-Blacksburg Regional Airport** (5202 Aviation Dr. NW, Roanoke, VA, 540/362-1999, www.flyroa.com). Airlines serving this airport include Allegiant, American Airlines, Delta, and United. From Roanoke it's about a 2.5-hour drive southwest along I-81 and I-77 to Fancy Gap, where you can pick up the Blue Ridge Parkway just a few miles away. It's another 90 minutes south along the Blue Ridge Parkway to Boone, North Carolina.

TRAIN

Amtrak (800/872-7245, www.amtrak.com) service is limited in North Carolina in general, with only a few stops; the nearest to the Blue Ridge is in Charlotte (1914 N. Tryon St.). Trains also stop in High Point (100 W. High Ave.), Greensboro (236 E. Washington St.), Durham (601 W. Main St.), and Raleigh (320 W. Cabarrus St.).

BUS

You can take a **Greyhound bus** (800/231-2222, www.greyhound.com) to Knoxville and Asheville, but other than those two cities, service is limited. Once you arrive, you'll need a rental car because meaningful public transportation in this region is virtually nonexistent. The **Knoxville Greyhound station** (100 E. Magnolia Ave., 865/525-9483) is not far from downtown, and some public transit options (taxis, Uber, other rideshare services) make it easy to get from the bus station to your accommodations. To get to the national park or North Carolina's Smoky Mountains, you'll need a rental car. The **Asheville Greyhound station** (2 Tunnel Rd., 828/253-8451) is also far from the real heart of downtown, and again, you'll need transportation once you arrive.

CAR

Four major interstates—**I-77, I-40, I-75, and I-81**—serve this region, making it easy to reach and traverse by car. Running north-south through Charlotte, I-77 makes up the eastern boundary of the region; its proximity to Charlotte, Winston-Salem, and Mount Airy, as well as the fact that it intersects with I-40 and the Blue Ridge Parkway, make it a natural choice for many drivers. I-81 and I-75 are the other north-south interstates that go through the region; they meet in Knoxville, Tennessee, just 30 miles outside the western entrance to Great Smoky Mountains National Park. Coming up from the south, I-75 is a natural feeder from Chattanooga, Tennessee, and Atlanta, Georgia; I-81 cuts a south-southwest diagonal through Virginia along the Shenandoah Valley, passing by or through Winchester, Lexington, Roanoke, Blacksburg, and Radford, Virginia, before hitting Bristol and Johnson City, Tennessee, and finally Knoxville. Running east-west, I-40 carries westbound visitors right by Asheville, across the Tennessee border just north of the national park, and to Knoxville; eastbound drivers will find Little Rock, Arkansas, and Memphis and Nashville, Tennessee, on the route.

Driving the Blue Ridge Parkway is a great way to experience the wildness of the mountains.

Car Rental

Rental cars are available at every airport, and if you take a train to your departure point, you'll find rental agencies in or near the station. Since many bus and train stations share a facility or are near one another, the same is true if you bus in. The major rental players—Hertz, National, and Enterprise, among others—will be readily available with their standard fleet of cars, but if you are looking for a specific vehicle (like a 4x4 or convertible), check availability with the agencies and reserve your vehicle. Most of these vehicles will be available for one-way rental, allowing you to rent a car at one end and drive it to another, returning it there before boarding a plane, or hopping a bus or train back home. Before you embark on a long, one-way trip with a rental vehicle, be sure you can return it at the other end. Check with your car rental agency about additional fees for one-way rentals, as some charge hefty fees for this type of rental.

Driving the Blue Ridge Parkway

The Blue Ridge Parkway was a huge road-building project, requiring engineers to be sensitive to preserving the natural experience along the drive. There are several **viaducts, 168 bridges,** and **26 tunnels** along the route, and they are some of the most distinctive architectural elements you'll find along the Blue Ridge Parkway. The bridges make extensive use of native stone as a decorative and functional element (the stonework was used as the form for the concrete frames on each bridge). The same goes for the tunnels: their faces are both decorative and structural and make the same use of native materials.

While the bridges are regular features for the length of the Parkway, the tunnels and the most striking of the viaducts (the Linn Cove Viaduct at Milepost 304.4) are a North Carolina thing. In North Carolina, the mountains grow sharper and steeper, and at times it's easier to go through rather than around them. That's why of the 26 tunnels, only one,

the Bluff Mountain Tunnel at Milepost 53.1, is found in Virginia; the other 25 are contained within a 130-mile stretch of the Parkway's southern section in North Carolina.

For those traveling in cars or on motorcycles, the tunnels are little more than another pretty aspect of the roadway. But if you're hauling a **trailer** or driving an **RV,** you'll be more concerned with the tunnels' height and length. Visit http://www.nps.gov/blri/planyourvisit/tunnel-heights.htm for a list of the 26 tunnels, complete with mileposts and length and height restrictions.

SEASONAL CONSIDERATIONS

From where the Blue Ridge Parkway crosses the North Carolina line through to Gatlinburg, Tennessee, the weather can slow and stop traffic or even shut down sections of the route. Generally, though, the weather is quite pleasant and **winter** is the only time when there are widespread closures of the Blue Ridge Parkway. This route is high and exposed, making it vulnerable to ice and snow; that, combined with the expense of the equipment necessary for proper snow and ice removal make wintertime closures an inevitability. Newfound Gap Road through Great Smoky Mountains National Park is a public highway and is maintained throughout the year. It may still close if heavy snowfall is expected or is more than road crews can cope with, but closure is rare. More often you'll be delayed as crews clear the road. Road conditions are available by contacting the **National Park Service** (828/298-0398, www.nps.gov/maps/blri/road-closures).

Spring generally brings a good amount of rain to the Blue Ridge Mountains. During the earliest months, and even toward the first part of April in the highest elevations, you can experience road closures if a spring snowstorm visits the high passes. The rest of the season, it may rain, but it doesn't impede traffic.

In **summer,** there is a chance of thunderstorms, and on rare occasions hail, along the route. Most likely, you'll encounter a rain shower or fog. The fog can be quite dense, so slowing down or even pulling off at a socked-in overlook is advisable.

In **autumn,** there are occasional rainstorms, and in the latest part of the season, the rare high-altitude snowstorm that dusts the tops of the mountains white. Traffic is generally not a consideration on the Blue Ridge Parkway or elsewhere along the route, but autumn sees the highest number of visitors to the Parkway and GSMNP, and leaf-lookers often slow down well below the speed limit, causing some **congestion on the roadway.** Autumn color seekers also fill overlooks and line the sides of the road to snap pictures and take in the views, slowing traffic in these busy areas.

MILEPOSTS

Along the Blue Ridge Parkway, **mileposts** mark the way. Starting at the southern end of Shenandoah National Park with Milepost 0 at Rockfish Gap all the way through Milepost 469 in Cherokee, North Carolina, you'll pass stone markers along the side of the road. Overlooks, hikes, historic sites, and spots to stop and explore are referenced both by name and milepost. Keep an eye out for the markers, as they're handy references not only for sights, hikes, and stops, but also for emergencies, should one arise.

GAPS

You'll encounter more **gaps** in the Blue Ridge Parkway than you can count, and if you're not from the mountains, this may be an unfamiliar term. Gaps, sometimes called passes, are simply low spots in the mountain chain. If you needed to get across the mountain, you'd look for these low spots for your crossing, as opposed to going up and over the high, steep, rocky places. Rockfish Gap, at Blue Ridge Parkway Milepost 0, is one such low spot. At only 1,909 feet high, it offered wildlife, then Native Americans, then colonists and settlers, and now endless interstate traffic an easy place to pass through these mountains.

SPEED LIMIT

On the Blue Ridge Parkway and on Newfound Gap Road in Great Smoky Mountains National Park, the speed limit is **45 miles per hour,** though it does slow in areas. Please observe the posted speed limit. Maintaining the speed limit allows you time to stop or avoid wildlife, debris, or other hazards on the road surface as well as pedestrians or other vehicles. Since long sections of the Blue Ridge Parkway are unprotected—read: no guardrails to break up the view—obeying the speed limit has the added benefit of keeping you and your passengers safe from leaving the roadway on an unexpected downhill trip. And if you think you can speed on the Parkway or in the national park because rangers can't pull you over, think again: they can, and they will, delivering hefty fines to reckless drivers.

One reason for the low speed limits along this scenic drive is to keep **wildlife** free from harm. You'll see a number of woodland creatures on your drive, and as your route cuts through the forests where they live, you'll see many animals on or near the roadway. Be extra-vigilant at dawn and dusk, when wildlife is most active. If you must stop in the road to allow an animal to cross, use your hazard flashers to alert other drivers, and try not to stop in blind curves or just over the crest of a hill where you'll be difficult to see.

PARKING

All along the Blue Ridge Parkway, and in Great Smoky Mountains National Park, parking is usually limited to designated parking areas at overlooks and trailheads; parking is permitted along the road shoulder, provided all four wheels are off the road surface and your vehicle doesn't impede traffic. On interstates and other highways, stop only when necessary, and when you do, be sure to pull fully off the road so you're not a danger to passing motorists and so you don't put yourself in harm's way.

FUEL

Fuel is not readily available on the Blue Ridge Parkway, a slightly inconvenient by-product of efforts to protect the Parkway from unintentional spills or leaks, but it is available in every town mentioned in this guide. The **Blue Ridge Parkway Association** (www.blueridgeparkway.org) provides an index of fuel availability by milepost. At major highway intersections and any place you meet a town or city, you'll find fuel close at hand.

You won't find any fuel inside Great Smoky Mountains National Park either, but you will find it in Cherokee and the other towns on the North Carolina side. Gas stations are plentiful on the Tennessee side once you leave the national park.

BIKING

The Blue Ridge Parkway is popular with cyclists. This 469-mile ride amid picturesque peaks provides challenges and thrills to cyclists in spring, summer, and fall. Elevations range from 600 feet to more than 6,000, so there's the challenge of long climbs and the reward of lazy downhills. The Parkway was originally intended for automobile traffic, so there are **no bike lanes** along the route. It's best to adopt a defensive mindset and assume that most drivers have no experience around cyclists. Always wear your helmet, be sure lights and reflectors are in good condition, and ride in single file.

The route is spread out, and there is almost nothing by way of bicycle-specific facilities, so prepare for the worst, bringing your tool

Cyclists tour the Blue Ridge Parkway.

kit, spare tubes, and anything else you'll need to perform a quick repair. The facilities that exist—campgrounds, visitors centers, and the like—do have potable water, though it isn't advisable to drink from streams without purification first.

Keep in mind that **mountain bikes** aren't permitted on Blue Ridge Parkway trails, but they are permitted in national forests, of which the Parkway abuts a number. Check for specific trails within each national forest.

Travel Tips

VISAS AND OFFICIALDOM

Visitors from other countries must present a valid **passport** and **visa** issued by a U.S. consular official in order to enter the United States; visas are not necessary for citizens of countries eligible for the Visa Waiver Program (such as Canada). For more information on traveling to the United States from a foreign country, visit www.usa.gov.

Foreign visitors who wish to drive should obtain an **International Driving Permit,** which is available from the nation that issued your driver's license. Driver's licensing rules vary from state to state. It's a good idea to familiarize yourself with the driving rules in the states that you'll be visiting (you can do this at www.usa.gov). Throughout the United States, drivers drive on the right side of the road, and distance and speed is measured in miles. Speedometers display both miles and kilometers; road signs display only miles.

If you're traveling to the United States from a foreign country, you'll need to exchange your currency at the airport or at a bank or currency exchange in your destination city; every attraction, restaurant, and lodging on the route accepts U.S. dollars only. Credit cards are widely accepted, but for moments when you need cash, there are plenty of ATMs along the route. Though ATMs are limited in Great Smoky Mountains National Park and along the Blue Ridge Parkway, you will find them at some visitors centers.

TOURIST INFORMATION
What to Bring

Depending on the season, you'll need slightly different clothing, and your supplies will depend on the activities you plan to include as part of your trip. No matter what, you'll want sunscreen and bug spray if you're travelling in spring, summer, or fall, and sunscreen if you're visiting in winter (especially for skiers).

Bring your binoculars and a camera with a zoom lens so you can enjoy the wildlife up close without disturbing it, keeping all parties involved safe and sound.

If you plan to hike, dress in layers so you can easily regulate your temperature, and have a sturdy pair of hiking boots on hand; trekking poles or a hiking staff isn't a bad idea either. Throw in some rain gear and a day pack with your first-aid kit, extra water, and some snacks and you're good to go.

Many visitors enjoy water activities here, whether it's white-water rafting, wading in the streams, or going for a float on the river, and so you'll want a bathing suit. Since the white-water rivers can be cold even in summer, you'll want something warm, preferably a lightweight wool shirt; wool dries quickly and keeps you quite warm.

Other than these basics, you'll want any specialty gear that caters to your wants, needs, and plans—golf clubs, disc golf gear, skis, maps, rock-climbing gear, whatever it may be.

Internet Access

Nearly every hotel, B&B, inn, or lodge will have Wi-Fi, often for free. You won't find Wi-Fi at most of the campgrounds along the Blue Ridge Parkway, but you will find that every hotel and just about every B&B has Internet access. With the exception of campgrounds, in most places where Wi-Fi is not available you'll find a computer or business center you can use at your lodging. When you have cell service, you will likely have a 3G or 4G connection, affording you Internet access on your phone.

Cell Phones

Around all of the cities and most of the towns, cell reception should be fine and free Wi-Fi abundant. Expect pockets of dead air for different providers as you get deeper into the mountains and away from larger towns and cities. Along the Blue Ridge Parkway, service can be spotty, but my service (AT&T) has been reliable in every town mentioned in this guide, with only a couple of dead spots.

Maps

One of the best resources for exploring a new region is a good map. DeLorme's atlas and gazetteers are indispensable. The detail provided is enough to plan short day hikes or longer expeditions, and they point out everything from trailheads and boat launches to campgrounds, hunting and fishing spots, and back roads of all types. Look for the *North Carolina Atlas & Gazetteer* (Yarmouth, ME: DeLorme, 2012) and the *Tennessee Atlas & Gazetteer* (Yarmouth, ME: DeLorme, 2014). If you're doing any backcountry camping, these will give you a good overview, but you may want to get quadrant maps for greater detail. Excellent guides are available from any good outdoor retailer, and since Great Smoky Mountains National Park is the most visited national park, quality guidebooks are always on hand.

Accommodations and Camping

The great thing about chain hotels is this: they're everywhere and you always know what you're getting. They make it easy to travel on a budget and also to travel without reservations, as they typically have a large number of rooms and, when full, can refer you to a sister hotel in the area. I prefer inns, cottages, and B&Bs, but those may require advance reservations. Chain hotels come in a variety of budgets and amenity levels. All along the route you'll find chain hotels and motels including Marriott, Holiday Inn, Hilton (in larger cities), Hampton Inn, Sleep Inn, and La Quinta.

Along the Blue Ridge Parkway and in Great Smoky Mountains National Park, no unauthorized backcountry camping is allowed. Reserve a spot at a backcountry shelter or campground, or get a spot at a front-country campground. In the Pisgah National Forest, you can camp in the backcountry so long as you do so responsibly. This means adhering to Leave No Trace principles and absolutely no campfires. Due to the hazard of fire, campfires are generally only permitted in front-country campsites. If you are front-country camping, be aware that you can't bring in your own firewood; you'll need to purchase or gather it on site. This is to prevent the spread of insect infestations, parasites, and disease that may harm local plants.

For much of the year, you should be able to

the Blowing Rock Inn in Blowing Rock

travel without reservations, though even in the off-season you may not be able to get into your first choice of campgrounds, lodges, hotels, or B&Bs. During peak seasons, namely October and late summer, you'll need reservations because visitors flood the area to see the autumn color show or squeeze in one more summer getaway. For some of the most popular campgrounds and lodging along the route, you will want to book months in advance.

ACCESS FOR TRAVELERS WITH DISABILITIES

The overwhelming majority of hikes in Shenandoah National Park, the Blue Ridge Parkway, and Great Smoky Mountains National Park are not accessible for travelers with disabilities, particularly those that impede mobility. Luckily, a huge number of attractions, accommodations, and restaurants are accessible.

TRAVELING WITH CHILDREN

There's no shortage of kid-friendly activities along the Blue Ridge Parkway and in Great Smoky Mountains National Park. Along the route, there are kid-friendly hikes, Junior Ranger programs, animals galore, and visitors centers and gift shops where you can pick up a little something to keep the youngest traveler occupied while in transit. In the cities, you'll find children's museums, parks, zoos, and playgrounds.

SENIOR TRAVELERS

Aside from stubble-faced and bearded bikers cruising the Parkway, one of the most common sights is the gray-haired couple tooling about in their Subaru, RV, or truck towing an RV. Many attractions, accommodations, and dining options have senior discounts, so flash that AARP card and save a few bucks. Overall, the route described in this guide is a safe and leisurely one for seniors and solo travelers.

GAY AND LESBIAN TRAVELERS

While the Blue Ridge Mountains doesn't have the same kind of atmosphere as San Francisco or Key West, LGBTQ travelers may be pleasantly surprised at how tolerant the region is, despite being rural and, in some areas, part of the Bible Belt. In Asheville and Knoxville, you'll find open and active gay cultures, and in most spots along the way the culture is open and accepting. This isn't to say everyone you meet is open to every lifestyle choice made, but it is to say that those closed-off individuals are fewer and farther between with each passing year.

Health and Safety

For the most part, your trip should be unremarkable as far as health and safety are concerned, provided you're attentive to your situation and surroundings, but there are a few things you should know. Those going on long hikes would also be wise to familiarize themselves with the **10 essentials** (www.rei.com/learn/expert-advice/ten-essentials.html).

EMERGENCIES

For emergencies anywhere in the United States, dial **911** on your phone for immediate assistance. In North Carolina, dialing ***77** connects you to state police and ***67** puts you in contact with the highway patrol. In Tennessee, dial ***847** for police assistance. If you have to call, try to note your mile marker or a nearby exit or landmark as a reference point for any assistance that's headed your way.

WILDERNESS SAFETY

Hikers should beware of **ticks,** some of which can transmit Lyme disease. An insect repellant and some thorough body checks (use a partner for more fun) should keep you tick-free after a jaunt through the woods. If you do get a bite or if you notice a red circular rash that's similar to a bull's-eye, consult a physician; Lyme disease can be life-threatening in the worst cases.

You'll encounter woodland animals including bees, wasps, yellow jackets, and hornets, so if you're allergic, be sure to have an **EpiPen** on hand. A number of **snakes,** including rattlesnakes and copperheads, live in these woods. Be alert and keep an ear open for that warning rattle, and if you unexpectedly smell cucumbers in the woods, you may be near a copperhead; in either case, back away slowly and detour around. **Spiders** can be a concern in places, namely woodpiles and some backcountry shelters. Most are harmless, though the brown recluse is seen from time to time, and the more commonly seen black widow spider is easily identifiable by the red hourglass on the female's abdomen.

Along the trails and roadsides you'll likely encounter **poison ivy, poison oak,** and **poison sumac,** all of which deliver an itchy blister when you come in contact with the oils they secrete. These oils are active for several months, so if you walk through a field of poison ivy, be sure to wash your pants, socks, and boots well lest you inadvertently get poison ivy a month later. You may also come upon **stinging nettles,** which leave itchy welts akin to mosquito bites; these are harmless and generally go away quickly.

Resources

Suggested Reading

TRAVEL

Daniels, Diane. *Farm Fresh North Carolina.* Chapel Hill: UNC Press, 2011. This guidebook will help you find the perfect place to pick apples, cut Christmas trees, visit a pumpkin patch, or pick a bushel of blueberries, and it lists every farmers market across the state. You'll find recipes from chefs and farmers as well.

Duncan, Barbara, and Brett Riggs. *Cherokee Heritage Trails.* Chapel Hill: UNC Press, 2003; online companion at www.cherokeeheritage.org. A fascinating guide to both the historical and present-day home of the Eastern Band of the Cherokee in North Carolina, Tennessee, and Georgia, from ancient mounds and petroglyphs to modern-day arts co-ops and sporting events.

Eubanks, Georgann. *Literary Trails of the North Carolina Mountains: A Guidebook.* Chapel Hill: UNC Press, 2007. This book and its companion books, *Literary Trails of the North Carolina Piedmont: A Guidebook* (2010) and *Literary Trails of Eastern North Carolina: A Guidebook* (2013), introduce fans of Southern literature to the places that produced and inspired various scribes. Also included are descriptions of the best bookstores and book events across the state.

Fussell, Fred, and Steve Kruger. *Blue Ridge Music Trails of North Carolina: A Guide to Music Sites, Artists, and Traditions of the Mountains and Foothills.* Chapel Hill: UNC Press, 2013. A guide to destinations—festivals, restaurants, oprys, church singings—in North Carolina, where authentic bluegrass, old-time, and sacred music rings through the hills and hollers. An accompanying CD gives you a chance to hear some tunes rather than just read about them.

North Carolina Atlas and Gazetteer. Yarmouth, ME: DeLorme, 2012. Since I was in Boy Scouts, I have always been partial to DeLorme's state atlases. This series represents in great detail the topography and other natural features of an area, providing users with far more useful and comprehensive information than the standard highway map.

Our State. www.ourstate.com. For a lively and informative look at North Carolina destinations and the cultural quirks and treasures you may find in your travels, *Our State* magazine is one of the best resources around. The magazine is easy to find, sold at most bookstores and even on grocery store and drugstore magazine racks. It covers arts, nature, folklore, history, scenery, sports, and lots of food, all from a traveler's perspective.

Simmons, Nye. *Best of the Blue Ridge Parkway: The Ultimate Guide to the Parkway's Best Attractions.* Johnson City, TN: Mountain Trail Press, 2008. Beautiful photography of some of the most iconic and picturesque spots along the Parkway is accompanied by write-ups of some of the highlights.

HIKING

Adams, Kevin. *Hiking Great Smoky Mountains National Park*. Guilford, CT: Globe Pequot Press, 2013. An excellent hiking-only guide to trails and on-foot sights in Great Smoky Mountains National Park, from Falcon Guides.

Johnson, Randy. *Hiking the Blue Ridge Parkway: The Ultimate Travel Guide to America's Most Popular Scenic Roadway*. Guilford, CT: Globe Pequot Press, 2010. A thorough trail guide to the Blue Ridge Parkway, from Falcon Guides.

HISTORY AND CULTURE

Cecelski, David. *The Waterman's Song: Slavery and Freedom in Maritime North Carolina*. Chapel Hill: UNC Press, 2001. A marvelous treatment of the African American heritage of resistance in eastern North Carolina, and how the region's rivers and sounds were passages to freedom for many enslaved people.

Hall, Karen J. *Building the Blue Ridge Parkway*. Charleston, SC: Arcadia Publishing, 2007. Narrative and archival photos combine to tell the story of the early days of the Blue Ridge Parkway including construction, folkways, and cultural tidbits.

Pegram, Tim. *The Blue Ridge Parkway by Foot: A Park Ranger's Memoir*. Jefferson, NC: McFarland & Company, 2007. A fascinating story of a former park ranger who decided to hike the Parkway—not the trails along the Parkway, but along the roadside, experiencing the 469-mile drive on foot.

Powell, William S. *North Carolina: A History*. Chapel Hill: UNC Press, 1988. A readable, concise account of our fascinating and varied past.

Powell, William S., and Jay Mazzocchi, editors. *Encyclopedia of North Carolina*. Chapel Hill: UNC Press, 2006. A fantastic compendium of all sorts of North Carolina history, letters, and politics. If you can lift this mammoth book, you'll learn about everything from Carolina basketball to presidential elections to ghosts.

Setzer, Lynn. *Tar Heel History on Foot: Great Walks through 400 Years of North Carolina's Fascinating Past*. Chapel Hill: UNC Press, 2013. This book sends you on a series of short walks in all parts of the state—coastal and mountain, city and country, historic sites and state parks—to discover the history of the state. The walks are arranged by theme and location, making it simple to find one near you.

SPORTS

Blythe, Will. *To Hate Like This Is to Be Happy Forever: A Thoroughly Obsessive, Intermittently Uplifting, and Occasionally Unbiased Account of the Duke-North Carolina Basketball Rivalry*. New York: Harper, 2007. A highly entertaining book about the hatred that exists between partisans of UNC and Duke, and how the famous basketball rivalry brings out the best and worst in the fans.

Thompson, Neal. *Driving with the Devil: Southern Moonshine, Detroit Wheels, and the Birth of NASCAR*. New York: Broadway Books, 2008. The creation story of a great sport, the rise of stock-car racing from moonshiners' getaway wheels to a multibillion-dollar industry.

Internet Resources

GENERAL TOURIST INFORMATION
North Carolina
North Carolina Division of Tourism
www.visitnc.com
This comprehensive guide contains trip itineraries in each region, including a dedicated section on the Blue Ridge Parkway. The site is rich with photos and videos, and it contains a wide-ranging index of accommodations, attractions, and more.

Tennessee
Tennessee Department of Tourist Development
www.tnvacation.com
The official site of Tennessee's state tourism office is user-friendly, allowing you to narrow your focus on one region with just a couple of clicks. Resources for the Smokies and East Tennessee include interactive maps that provide a great overview of the region's offerings from natural sights to man-made attractions.

NATIONAL PARK INFORMATION
Blue Ridge Parkway
Blue Ridge Parkway
www.nps.gov/blri
Details the history of the park and provides real-time road maps that show detours, delays, and closures; has downloadable maps that make hiking and planning a trip section-by-section easy; and contains write-ups on the flora, fauna, and geographical features of the Parkway.

Virtual Blue Ridge
www.virtualblueridge.com
Information on the Blue Ridge Parkway including wildflower and fall color reports, road conditions and closures, and weather along the route. You'll also find a store with maps, books, and mementos.

Blue Ridge National Heritage Area
www.blueridgeheritage.com
Created in 2003 to recognize the unique character, culture, landscape, and beauty of the Blue Ridge, this organization promotes the history, folkways, arts and crafts, and exploration of the region.

Blue Ridge Parkway Association
www.blueridgeparkway.org
A nonprofit association of businesses and individuals promoting tourism along the Blue Ridge Parkway, from Virginia to Tennessee. Their website includes interactive maps; indexes to activities, sights, restaurants, hikes, and more along the Parkway; highlights of the route; real-time road reports; regional breakdowns; and other resources to help you plan a trip.

Great Smoky Mountains National Park
Great Smoky Mountains National Park
www.nps.gov/grsm
An extensive history of the park, with details on flora, fauna, and natural features and downloadable maps and contact information for rangers and park offices.

Friends of the Smokies
www.friendsofthesmokies.org
Friends of the Smokies works to raise funds for park initiatives, trail maintenance and improvement, and a variety of other needs. They accept donations of time and money, so if you had a good time in the Smokies, consider lending them a hand or a few bucks.

Great Smoky Mountains Association
www.smokiesinformation.org
A nonprofit partner of Great Smoky Mountains National Park, the group operates retail stores in and benefiting the park; provides guidebooks, maps, logo-emblazoned clothing and

gear, and other gifts; and helps with expenses associated in promoting the park.

NEWSPAPERS

North Carolina newspapers have unusually rich online content, and are great resources for travel planning.

Asheville Citizen-Times
www.citizen-times.com
A good online edition for this Asheville-based paper.

Charlotte Observer
www.charlotteobserver.com
This website is packed with information about the arts, food, newcomer issues, and more.

Mountain Xpress
www.mountainx.com
Also covering the Asheville area, with a politically progressive and artistically countercultural bent—much like Asheville itself.

Mountain Times
http://mountaintimes.com
Weekly newspaper covering Boone and the High Country.

ARTS AND CULTURE

North Carolina's arts and history have an ever-growing online dimension, telling the story of the state in ways that paper and ink simply can't.

North Carolina Folklife Institute
www.ncfolk.org
The website will fill you in on the many organizations across the state that promote traditional music, crafts, and folkways. You'll also find a calendar of folk life-related events in North Carolina, and travel itineraries for weekends exploring Core Sound, the Seagrove potteries, and Cherokee heritage in the Smokies.

NCFOOD
www.ncfolk.org/category/food
This wonderful food blog, maintained by the Folklife Institute, features articles about the culinary back roads of the state.

North Carolina Arts Council
www.ncarts.org
The Arts Council provides information about performing arts, literature, cultural trails, galleries, and fun happenings.

North Carolina ECHO
www.ncecho.org
ECHO stands for "Exploring Cultural Heritage Online," and this great site has links to hundreds of online exhibits and brick-and-mortar museums.

Carolina Music Ways
www.carolinamusicways.org
A lively guide to the extremely varied musical traditions of the North Carolina Piedmont.

Blue Ridge Heritage Area
www.blueridgeheritage.com
This resource has a huge amount of mountain-area travel information and an ever-growing directory of traditional artists of all kinds in the Carolina mountains.

Southern Highland Craft Guild
www.southernhighlandguild.org
An Asheville-based regional arts giant with an extensive online guide to craftspeople throughout the region.

Our State
www.ourstate.com
The online companion to this print publication provides expanded coverage of the history, people, food, and arts across North Carolina. An extensive archive of stories lets you look back several years for the best the state has to offer.

OUTDOORS

Great online resources exist for planning outdoor adventures in North Carolina, where rich arts and blockbuster sports are matched by natural resources.

Appalachian Trail Conservancy
www.appalachiantrail.org

The Appalachian Trail Conservancy provides support to the Appalachian Trail, which parallels and even crosses the Blue Ridge Parkway in many places.

Friends of the Mountains-to-Sea Trail
www.ncmst.org

Find details, hike-planning tools, and resources for a day or longer on the 1,000-mile-long Mountains-to-Sea Trail that crosses North Carolina.

North Carolina Sierra Club
http://nc2.sierraclub.org

Find information about upcoming hikes and excursions as well as an overview of the state's natural areas and environmental issues.

North Carolina Birding Trail
www.ncbirdingtrail.org

Covering bird-watching across the state, this site contains information about dozens of pristine locations and active flyways along the coast, in the Piedmont, and in the mountains.

North Carolina Sportsman
www.northcarolinasportsman.com

Covering hunting and fishing news, destinations, and seasonal trends across the state.

North Carolina State Parks
www.ncparks.gov

A number of state parks brush against the Blue Ridge Parkway in North Carolina, and many travelers use the parks' campgrounds and facilities as resources and waypoints along their journey. Learn more about the facilities and amenities of Parkway-adjacent parks at the website of the North Carolina State Parks system.

NC Hikes
www.nchikes.com

All things hiking-related, including trails in every corner of the state, books, and trip recommendations.

North Carolina Wildlife Resources Commission
www.ncwildlife.org

Information on hunting, fishing, and boating in North Carolina, including easy-to-understand hunting and fishing regulations and online license procurement.

Tennessee Wildlife Resources Agency
www.tn.gov/twra

Need-to-know information regarding hunting and fishing regulations and licenses.

Index

List of Maps

Photo Credits

MOON BLUE RIDGE & SMOKY MOUNTAINS

Avalon Travel
An imprint of Perseus Books
A Hachette Book Group company
1700 Fourth Street
Berkeley, CA 94710, USA
www.moon.com

Editor: Sabrina Young
Series Manager: Kathryn Ettinger
Copy Editor: Brett Keener
Production and Graphics Coordinator: Rue Flaherty
Cover Design: Faceout Studios, Charles Brock
Interior Design: Domini Dragoone
Moon Logo: Tim McGrath
Map Editor: Albert Angulo
Cartographers: Austin Ehrhardt, Brian Shotwell
Proofreader: Alissa Cyphers
Indexer: Greg Jewett

ISBN-13: 978-1-63121-391-5
ISSN: 2154-2309

Printing History
1st Edition — 2010
2nd Edition — October 2016
5 4 3 2 1

Front cover photo: Blue Ridge Parkway at sunset, Great Smoky Mountains National Park © 500px / Aurora Photos

Printed in Canada by Friesens